Modernism and the European Unconscious

Edited by
Peter Collier and Judy Davies

St. Martin's Press,
New York.

All rights reserved. For information, write:
Scholarly and Reference Division,
St. Martin's Press, Inc., 175 Fifth Avenue,
New York, N.Y. 10010

First published in the United States of America in 1990

Printed in Great Britain

ISBN 0-312-04223-X

Library of Congress Cataloging-in-Publication Data
A CIP catalog record for this book is available from the Library of Congress

Modernism and the European Unconscious

Contents

List of Illustrations

List of Contributors

Elza Adamowicz, Lecturer in French, Goldsmith's College, London.

Malcolm Bowie, Professor of French, Queen Mary College, London, author of *Mallarmé and the Art of Being Difficult* (Cambridge University Press, 1978) and *Freud, Proust and Lacan: Theory as Fiction* (Cambridge University Press, 1987).

Ann Caesar, Fellow of Corpus Christi College and University Lecturer in Italian, Cambridge.

Peter Collier, Fellow of Sidney Sussex College and University Lecturer in French, Cambridge, author of *Proust and Venice* (Cambridge University Press, 1989), and co-editor of *Visions and Blueprints* (Manchester University Press, 1988).

Tim Cribb, Fellow and Lecturer in English, Churchill College, Cambridge.

Judy Davies, formerly Fellow of Girton College and University Lecturer in Italian, Cambridge, now working in analytic psychotherapy.

Anne Fernihough, Fellow and Lecturer in English, Girton College, Cambridge.

David Kelley, Fellow of Trinity College, and University Lecturer in French, Cambridge, author of *Baudelaire, 'Le salon de 1846'* (Clarendon Press, 1975), and co-editor of *Unreal City* (Manchester University Press, 1985).

Sorley Macdonald, graduate of Edinburgh University and House Manager of the Arts Cinema, Cambridge.

Robin Mackenzie, Lecturer in French, University of St. Andrew's.

David Midgley, Fellow of St John's College and University Lecturer in German, Cambridge, author of *Arnold Zweig: Zu Werk und Wandlung* (Athenäum, 1980).

Ritchie Robertson, Fellow and Lecturer in German, St John's College, Oxford and author of *Kafka: Judaism, Politics, and Literature* (Clarendon Press, 1985)›

Naomi Segal, Fellow and Lecturer in French, St John's College, Cambridge, and author of *The Banal Object* (Institute of Germanic Studies, 1981) and *Narcissus and Echo: Women in the French récit* (Manchester University Press, 1988).

Alison Sinclair, Fellow of Clare College and University Lecturer in Spanish, Cambridge, and author of *Valle-Inclán's 'Rhedo Ibérico': A Popular View of Revolution* (Támesis, 1977).

Edward Timms, Fellow of Gonville and Caius College and University Lecturer in German, Cambridge, author of *Karl Kraus, Apocalyptic Satirist* (Yale University Press, 1986), and co-editor of *Unreal City* (Manchester University Press, 1985) and *Visions and Blueprints* (Manchester University Press, 1988).

Elizabeth Wright, Fellow and Lecturer in German, Girton College, Cambridge, and author of *Psychoanalytic Criticism: Theory in Practice* (Methuen, 1984) and *Postmodern Brecht: A Re-Presentation* (Routledge, 1989).

Note on Sources and Abbreviations

Sigmund Freud

References are to *The Standard Edition of the Complete Psychological Works of Sigmund Freud*, general editor James Strachey (24 vols, Hogarth Press, London, 1953–73). They are designated, in both text and notes, *SE*, followed by volume number, and page number where appropriate.

In 1973 Penguin Books began the republication, under the editorship of Angela Richards and based on the *Standard Edition*, of a generous selection of Freud's works, and the paperback 'Pelican Freud Library' currently numbers fifteen volumes. For ease of consultation the reader may be referred to this publication (Pelican, followed by volume number) as well as to the *Standard Edition*. Readers may, for example, find it convenient to consult Pelican 14 (*Art and Literature*) where they will find such papers as 'Delusions and Dreams in Jensen's *Gradiva*', 'Creative Writers and Day-Dreaming' and 'The Uncanny' (see especially chapters 2 and 15), as well as Pelican 1 (*Introductory Lectures on Psycho-Analysis*) which provides a survey of Freud's thinking to the year 1917.

Carl Jung

All the volumes of *The Collected Works of C. G. Jung*, general editor William McGuire, translated by R. F. C. Hull (20 vols, Routledge & Kegan Paul, London, 1953–79), have seen republication, some volumes being re-edited and an extra volume being added. Since some work remains excluded, and in view of the fact that Jung frequently made substantial revision to his original texts at the time of their republication, contributors have not confined their references to the *Collected Works*, but have also referred to the original texts (and their early English translations) where this was necessary or appropriate.

The reader may find it useful to know that Routledge in particular, under the imprint of Ark Paperbacks, have made easily available a wide selection of Jungian writing. Among their paperback titles are *The Psychology of the Transference* (1983); *Modern Man in Search of a Soul* (1984, 1985 and 1989); *Four Archetypes* (1986 and 1988); *Dreams* (1985 and 1986); *Aspects of the Feminine* (1986); *Analytical Psychology* (1986); *Psychological Reflections* (1986); *Psychology and the Occult* (1987); *On the Nature of the Psyche* (1988).

Preface

It was a defining characteristic of the Modernist movement to scrutinize and question its own forms of expression. Modernism rejected all established notions of art, and in consequence also the institutions that enshrined artistic tradition. It was also marked, as its name implies, by a fascination for novelty and especially for the rapidly evolving life-style of urban man — that creature of technological progress and new modes of communication. A sense of rupture with the culture and thinking of the past pervaded Modernist work, and imparted energy to its violent repudiation of bourgeois values, including those aesthetic values that kept life separate from art.

Underlying and uniting these characteristic attitudes, however, was a revulsion against the limits set by the rationalism and scientism of the last half of the nineteenth century, and a desire to open up uninvestigated areas of the mind — the whole mind, in its unconscious and irrational aspects, as disclosed by the new forms of depth psychology at the turn of the century. So it was that Modernists came to feel the appeal of the unconscious, and it is their paradoxical search for the deepest, often mythical sources of the modern psyche that our book examines, for we believe that this provides the richest insight into the epistemological configurations and historical origins of our own age.

There have been studies of the impact of Freud and psychoanalysis on modern literature and art, studies of individual authors and artists in a Freudian light, and ambitious theories of writing that take into account the relation of language to the unconscious. But there has not yet been a single study that examines the impact of psychoanalytic, and allied, theories of the unconscious on European literature and art as a whole, with regard to the historical detail of that interaction, its theoretical diversity, and the multiplicity of stylistic solutions which it generated during the first half of the twentieth century.

The central aim of our book is to remedy this lack, through a study of the convergence of two forces, the Modernist revolution in form, and the emergence of new models of mind. Our approach is both comparative and interdisciplinary, for we include painting, music and cinema. We have taken into account not only the classic canon of great Modernist writers, like Kafka or Virginia Woolf, who evolved careful narrative strategies exploiting the labyrinths of the unconscious, but also avant-garde movements like Surrealism which paraded the irrational more aggressively.

Recent theorists have made important distinctions between 'Modernism' and the 'avant-garde'. In respecting these distinctions, we share the position taken by Raymond Williams in his contributions to *Unreal City* and *Visions and Blueprints*. But the present book, like those two earlier ones, also reflects our belief that the definition of a cultural complex should arise out of the detailed comparison and collation of individual case studies, rather than be theorized in advance. Thus the grouping of the book into sections is not intended to imply judgement about whether, let us say, Joyce should be seen in predominantly Modernist terms and Pirandello viewed in avantgardist ones. Nor does any special emphasis in its contents aim to suggest, for example, that Freud is a better aesthetician than Pound. Rather what we have adopted is a working division, one that seeks to provoke questions and re-readings, and to throw open again the whole issue of Modernism. If we have highlighted the impact of the new theorists of the unconscious, we have done so not only in recognition of the actual spread and depth of their influence, but also because their theories offer illuminating approaches to the creative minds of Modernism which were so often turned towards intense self-scrutiny.

There are those who claim that we now live in a 'postmodern' era. This perhaps remains to be proved: the term, in any event, begs many political and cultural questions. If and when we ever arrive at the totally technologized history-free world imagined by Lyotard in *The Postmodern Condition*, such a book as this, working to define the conditions of creation and reception of a modern culture, trying to open the way to fresh perceptions of familiar horizons, will have no place. Until then we shall continue to ask the questions that still seem to matter, about the relation of artistic form and expression to the mind's structure, about the historical and cultural determinants of ideological movements like psychoanalysis and Surrealism, about the models of mind which find their vehicles in theatre and cinema, about the rationality and reasonableness of art, about the provenance and destination of Romantic aesthetics and post-Enlightenment philosophy.

In re-opening the question of Modernism we have looked critically at some of the assumptions and commonplaces which, sometimes unconsciously, underlie our modern culture. We look at Freud in the context of Nietzsche and the English Romantics, we note the difficulties of translating ideas into the visual or gestural media of painting and cinema, we face the forces of the primitive and the Dionysiac as well as the difficulties of attaining psychic liberation through new modes of linguistic expression. We look afresh at various cases of specific influence – Jung on Hesse, Freud on Breton. We also trace some alternative trajectories, ones which start from Nietzsche, or Coleridge, or Flaubert. The issue of derivation is never an easy matter, and we are as much on guard against the temptation to over-simplify when dealing with a case of Freudian propaganda in the cinema, as we are in the case of Lawrence's anti-Freudian stance. Working whenever necessary against the grain, we study traditional aesthetic strategies in Joyce or Freudian overtones in Pound.

Many of the ideas developed here have been aired and debated in student seminars or lectures in Cambridge. The book is the result of collaboration and discussion. At the same time, contributors have been encouraged to allow a variety of expertise to colour their writing – that expertise includes experience in sculpture, in women's action, psychotherapy, cinema management, adult education, music criticism, translation and creative writing, as well as the shared experience of teaching and writing within an academic context. The diversity of our critical responses mirrors, we trust, the diversity of responses made by Modernist writers and artists to the new psychologies of our modern age.

Peter Collier and Judy Davies

PART I

Towards a Freudian Aesthetic?

1

A Message from Kakania: Freud, Music, Criticism

MALCOLM BOWIE

For admirers of Freud's achievement as a psychologist, there is likely to be something piquantly absurd about the idea of a 'European unconscious'. The phrase will seem to enshrine a category mistake of the kind that Macaulay ridiculed when he spoke of 'Protestant cookery' and 'Christian horsemanship'. For, as a modeller of the 'psychical apparatus', Freud attended to its transhistorical and supracontinental characteristics, to those mechanisms of mind which came into operation wherever sexuality held sway and wherever the human individual grew towards adulthood under pressure from the family group or from one of its surrogates. As a clinician, observing individual minds in action and piecing together individual case-histories, Freud attended to each patient's report on his or her family and sexual relationships. Such larger collectivities as class, profession, municipality, nation, religion or political party could well be sketched in as background or ambience, but they explained very little and were granted no determining power in the production of neurotic symptoms. 'Europe' was thus doubly irrelevant to Freud's two-level investigation of the mind: if the general principles of mental functioning were at issue, Europe was too small to be worth studying; if, on the other hand, a suffering individual presented himself or herself, Europe was an unfocusable vastness. For the purposes of the new psychoanalytic science, the unconscious could no more be European than it could be Melanesian, or Romanesque, or anarcho-syndicalist.

Yet from the viewpoint of cultural history, the modern idea of the unconscious is of course profoundly – incurably, one might say – European. Whether we examine psychoanalysis in the historical perspective outlined by Lancelot Law Whyte in *The Unconscious before Freud* (1962)[1] or resituate it among the alternative theories of mind with which it competed in its formative years, it is clear that Freud's dramatic reformulation of the idea depended for its impact upon a variety of time-honoured European theoretical issues and procedures. And the Freudian unconscious has become an object of fascinated pursuit for a whole new generation of Freud scholars precisely because it is so variously reconnectable to a given cultural epoch and its ingrained intellectual habits.

The history of the unconscious in late nineteenth- and early twentieth-century Europe is a ramifying tale of scientific originality lost and found, of intellectual legitimacy claimed and disputed. 'How original was Freud?' is still a question of seemingly inexhaustible historical interest. A characteristic sequence of answers and counter-answers to it might go like this: (1) he was not original, other than as a publicist, because the unconscious had come and gone in European thinking since antiquity and become positively fashionable during the period of Freud's early maturity; (2) but Freud differed crucially from his predecessors in that he was a thoroughgoing systematist, and promoted the unconscious only in so far as the psycho-dynamic system of which it was part could explain mental facts; (3) but the very notion of 'system' that Freud resorted to was a commonplace of the new and topical evolutionary biology that he grew up with, and even when he repudiated biological science in favour of a supposedly 'pure' psychology he was still adhering to a biologically inspired theoretical mode; (4) but in doing this he was exploiting biology for his own purposes, not remaining subservient to it: all spectacular paradigm-shifts in the history of science begin with a switching or a mixing of metaphors; (5) but this is exactly the problem with Freud: he metaphorized science; (6) but . . . At each stage in this argumentative game as it is nowadays played, Freud's abstract mental models are re-immersed in their native sea of particulars, and his family history, education and social background — together with his professional relationships, reading habits and pastimes — are relentlessly trawled and dredged. Can any self-proclaimed universalist ever have been returned with such self-righteousness on the part of his commentators to the local habitat in which he and his ideas were born?

For Freud's 'unconscious' is European, alas. And it belongs not to the continent at large, but to the Austro-Hungarian empire in its declining years. And not just to the empire at large, but to the imperial capital during the combined best and worst of times that preceded the First World War. Freud's Vienna, we are often reminded, was the home also of Mahler, Schoenberg, Berg, Webern, Klimt, Kokoschka, Schiele, Loos, Kraus, Schnitzler, Musil and Wittgenstein. If the mere roll-call of names is insufficiently eloquent, we can easily remind ourselves of what this astonishing array of artists, musicians, writers and thinkers had in common: a sense of impending cataclysm permeated by an equally powerful sense of creative opportunity. An old order was crumbling away and a bright morning light was flooding into the artistic, scientific and philosophical laboratories of the city. But late-Hapsburg Vienna placed a special burden upon these brilliant individuals as they worked: it kept darkness and decay alive even in their most fervently optimistic imaginings, made savage irony into their daily bread and shadowed their new-found meanings with panic and despair.

Freud's theory of the human mind contained a moral fable for the fallen times in which it first appeared. For psychoanalysis, the mind was a scene of interminable conflict. It was a realm of competing drives, incompatible systems, irreconcilable agencies or dispositions, adjacent territories between which no reliable channels of communication could exist. Freud tirelessly re-imagined this discord and redramatized its consequences for civilization. Sometimes his descriptions have a light quotidian touch. 'The ego is not master in its own house', he wrote in 'A Difficulty in the Path of Psycho-Analysis' (1917),[2] espousing with some relish the voice of a paterfamilias who has begun to hear murmurings from below stairs. But at other times the voice is epic and self-heroizing: from its Virgilian epigraph onwards, *The Interpretation of Dreams* is the autobiography of one who has dared to enter Hell and subject his intellectual and moral authority to a series of truly infernal indignities. The evidence of dreams and of neurotic disorders made it necessary to grant the unconscious a mode of action, a logic and an entelechy of its own and these threatened to disrupt even the most straightforward-seeming cognitive operations. For the mind, pictured in this way, not only desires more than one thing at a time, not only drives the individual in separate directions at once: it is the realm of the incommensurable, a mechanism installed within the human creature for the production of endless dissonances and discrepancies. Freud's multi-systemic 'psychical apparatus' was to some extent the psychological model that Viennese high culture needed in order to understand its own predilection for irony, but there is a sense of extremity about the first main phase of Freud's theorizing, and especially about the books on dreams, slips and jokes that he wrote between 1899 and 1905, that belongs not just to Vienna but to Kakania, Musil's hyper-ironical dream Austria. If the conscious mind had ambitions to be *kaiserlich und königlich* in its handling of experience, the unconscious exerted upon it a continuous downward suction – towards the low-life world of the human drives, the genital, excremental and homicidal urges that high-toned 'mind' none the less also harboured. The very first dream to be discussed psychoanalytically in *The Interpretation of Dreams*[3] – the celebrated dream of 'Irma's injection' – dramatizes the clash between high professional calling and abject unconscious desire and is an allegorical anticipation of much that is to follow later in the work. In this dream, one of Freud's real-life female patients presents bizarre organic symptoms, which are discussed, diagnosed and treated by a group of four medical men, including Freud himself. Their behaviour brings together incompetence, spurious theorizing and demented clinical practice. Simple contact with the clinical material turns the good sense and good intentions of the practitioners involved into a black comedy of self-promotion and obfuscation. It is scarcely surprising that this dream should reappear as a leitmotif later in Freud's book, for here was a potent image of the worst that could befall the public-spirited instigator of a new mental science.

This is not the place to re-examine in detail those features of psychoanalysis that are specific to the Viennese *fin-de-siècle*. What I shall do briefly, in the pages that follow, is look again at one kind of relationship – between Freud and the musicians who were his contemporaries – and suggest two distinct ways in which the Freudian idea of the unconscious, 'European' or not, may illuminate early twentieth-century art. 'Freud and modern music' is not a new subject, of course: Theodor Adorno, Hans Keller and Carl Schorske, among others, have written penetratingly on various aspects of the relationship. But it has lagged far behind comparative discussions of Freud and literature or painting, and figures only sketchily in general accounts of Freud and the Austrian intelligentsia of his time. Music, I shall suggest, can help us to perceive clearly the scope and the limitations of 'the unconscious' as a critical idea and to check its recent slide into imprecise and indulgent usage.

I shall begin with one of the very few moments of contact between music and psychoanalysis to have been recognized as 'official' and instructive by historians of both disciplines: the meeting between Freud and Mahler that took place in Leyden in August 1910. In such standard accounts of this meeting as those given by Ernest Jones and Donald Mitchell, the relationship between the two great men is self-evidently an asymmetrical one. Mahler had requested an interview with Freud for the purposes of discussing a marital difficulty, and Mahler was the only obvious beneficiary of the occasion: the informal psychoanalysis conducted during a four-hour perambulation through Leyden produced, we are told, positive therapeutic effects. Similarly, it is Mahler's work rather than Freud's that is immediately illuminated by the traumatic childhood memory that reappeared during their discussion. Jones summarizes the composer's new access of artistic self-knowledge in these terms:

> In the course of the talk Mahler suddenly said that now he understood why his music had always been prevented from achieving the highest rank through the noblest passages, those inspired by the most profound emotions, being spoilt by the intrusion of some commonplace melody. His father, apparently a brutal person, treated his wife very badly, and when Mahler was a young boy there was a specially painful scene between them. It became quite unbearable to the boy, who rushed away from the house. At that moment, however, a hurdy-gurdy in the street was grinding out the popular Viennese air 'Ach, du lieber Augustin'. In Mahler's opinion the conjunction of high tragedy and light amusement was from then on inextricably fixed in his mind, and one mood inevitably brought the other with it.[4]

And Mitchell describes persuasively the various Mahlerian routes by which 'the vivid contrast between high tragedy and low farce, sublimated, disguised and transfigured though it often was, emerged as a leading artistic principle of his music, a principle almost always ironic in intent and execution'.[5]

Yet what is striking about the Freud–Mahler encounter, once Freud has been freed from the role of benevolent counsellor and sage, is the parallelism between the two participants, and the predicament they share. At one level, of course, Mahler tells Freud what he already knows, and confirms him in the leading psychoanalytic principle which holds that repressed memories of painful childhood experiences, if they are reactivated in the controlled conditions of the analytic dialogue, can relieve or remove neurotic symptoms. But Mahler is at the same time addressing a fellow victim of baseness and banality, one whose theoretical work no less than his case-histories is marked by a syncopated rhythm of 'high tragedy and low farce'. Freud's science has its own intrusive hurdy-gurdy music; his clinical practice involved 'grubbing about in human dirt'. The unconscious was at one and the same time the 'true psychical reality', the main source of certainty for the new psychology, and an agency that disturbed and contaminated its explanatory procedures; it provided psychology with its essential subject-matter, yet was never fully circumscribable and available for inspection. 'Knowing' the unconscious was a matter of espousing a rhythm of appearance and disappearance in the quest for meaning, of accommodating oneself to an intermittence seemingly inherent in the structure of the human mind.

Let us examine a precise case of 'contamination' in Mahler's music: in the sixth symphony (1905), the cowbells which announce an interlude of pastoral rapture amid the trampling march-rhythms of the first movement. The 'low'–'high' antithesis serves, as we have just seen, a multitude of expressive purposes for the student of modern Viennese culture. It sets plebeian music against serious music, primitive libidinal impulse against the 'spiritual' striving of the artist, the brutish unconscious against the artful indirections of socialized desire. But in the case of Mahler's suddenly intruding cowbells the distinction works only by refusing to work. They are 'low' in that they are pieces of dairy-farming equipment, 'high' in that they suggest the uplands and uplift; they are gatecrashers in the modern orchestra, yet offer a privileged glimpse of bliss and resolution; the sound they make is inarticulate and monotone, yet it frames a partial reprise of the movement's tenderly soaring second subject. What is still shocking about Mahler's bells – even to a musical age that has heard far stranger special effects from the percussion section of the orchestra – is not their bovine lowness but their seeming irrelevance to the advancing symphonic argument. They interrupt. They interject another zone of experience – low in one way, high in another – which, for all the delicate allusions to the main thematic material of the movement that this pastoral episode contains, in acoustic terms refuses to blend and merge. They herald a premature bliss, a higher state that has not been attained in musical argument but dumped gratuitously upon a still emerging symphonic structure.

Faced with a disruptive blatancy of this kind, we could find ourselves tempted to speculate on the unconscious mental processes involved. Commentators have suggested that a fragment of word-play could have been at work: Mahler associated the second subject with his wife *Alma*, and in the intrusive interlude summons the reader to the green landscape of an *Alm* (Alpine pasture). But, although name-magic of this kind figures in the Mahler–Freud interview as reported by Jones, such connections cast only a feeble Freudian half-light upon the movement and understate by far its drama. The crucial connection with Freud lies in the suddenness and the unaccountability of the musical event. In the Mahler symphony, one structure intrudes upon another, seeming to come from another – obscure, irrelevant, disconnected – mental region. In due course, this hiatus is to be overcome and the emotional hesitation that accompanies it is to be further exploited and integrated within the four-movement span of the symphony, but early on the gap is unbridgeable. For Freud in one of his theoretical moods, the surest sign of the unconscious at work was to be found exactly in the unforeseeable grinding of one structural order against another. In the continuous fabric of experience, a sudden snag appeared. The reasonable-seeming individual, equipped with comprehensible motives and creditable goals, gave evidence – in a symptom, a slip of the tongue, a word-association or a metaphor – of other desires that were not reasonable at all. He or she seemed suddenly to be speaking or behaving from an alien region. And although that region could be expected in due course to reveal its continuities and regularities, its first emergence upon the scene was a scandal. One of Freud's extraordinary achievements as a writer was to preserve this sense of outrage in defiance of his own proficiency as a psychoanalytic explainer: rather than allow an all-purpose discourse of otherness and unknowability to inform his accounts of mind in action, he constantly rediscovered otherness in his own surprise, and wrote of it surprisingly. At the end of *The Interpretation of Dreams*, Freud reminds his reader that the ancients had already displayed in their superstitious respect for dreams an awareness of 'the uncontrolled and indestructible forces in the human mind', and that it was the task of the psychoanalyst to retain this awareness for scientific purposes. The proliferating catalogue of instantaneous unconscious effects that fills the pages of his early psychoanalytic works is his homage to this power, which he himself called 'daemonic'.

The discontinuity between musical worlds that Mahler introduces into the first movement of his sixth symphony speaks of a dangerous openness to fluctuating and multiform desire. Desire has rushed ahead of the opportunities for expression that the composer's chosen structure affords. Re-using a grammatical image of which Freud was particularly fond, we could say of the wish-fulfilment taking place in these bars that 'a thought expressed in the optative has been replaced by a representation in the present tense'. 'Oh, if only . . . ' has been replaced by 'It is.' 'If only I could experience my mountain rapture *now*' has been answered by an irresponsible internal voice saying 'You can.' Yet although the Mahlerian wish that finds outlet here cannot be cancelled or withdrawn once it has made its disruptive entry, the musical language to which Mahler still adheres has of course its own controlling tonal conventions, and these keep a tight rein on the extravagance and precociousness of the desiring imagination. Things would be very different if the musical language itself were pressing towards a new openness and a new willingness to collude in the fulfilment of wishes.

The years 1900 to 1911 were the exuberant period not only of Freud's pioneering studies of the unconscious mind and of Mahler's last symphonies and song-cycles, but of Schoenberg's atonalism and the emergence of what came to be know as the Second Viennese School. And it is in the early work of Freud's younger contemporary Schoenberg that the intellectual disarray provoked by psychoanalysis finds an altogether sharper echo and analogue. Where the kinship between Freud and Mahler is based on a common experience of discontinuity in the human passions, Schoenberg's musical practice at this time throws into relief an antithetical quality of the mental life: the unthinkable continuum of human thought and the unrelenting propulsive force that passion gives it. Schoenberg's new music, like Freud's new psychology, brought into view a world of unstoppable transformational process. Such process seemed to be a specific character of the human mind, yet the time-honoured anthropocentric or theocentric devices by which it could be humanly organized, explained and controlled now seemed only fortuitously capable of achieving purchase upon it. In Schoenberg's case, the encouragingly named 'emancipation of the dissonance' contained a threat of servitude for the artistic imagination: an interminable sprawl of acoustic relationships. In Freud's case, the seemingly autonomous systemic power of the unconscious sometimes turned the scientific, clinical or literary practitioner into a powerless bystander at a savage and scarcely human scene.

Schoenberg wrote of his own role in the development first of atonalism and then of serialism as that of an artist who was singularly attuned not just to recent developments in the history of Western music but to the gradual unfolding of a grand natural design. But however willing he was to become the compliant instrument of History or Nature – to do in his compositions what someone had to do – his situation in the years 1908–12 had major elements of anxiety and nightmare. The slow dethronement of tonality that could be observed in the works of Wagner, Richard Strauss and Debussy reached its culmination in a musical sphere where dissonances were merely 'more remote consonances' and no longer had the effect of interrupting or delaying musical sense: 'The term *emancipation of the dissonance* refers to its comprehensibility, which is considered equivalent to the consonance's comprehensibility. A style based on this premise treats dissonances like consonances and renounces a tonal centre.'[6] This prospect was gratifying in that it placed a superabundance of musical sense before any suitably audacious composer, but discouraging also: works which were at once long and powerfully integrated now became difficult to envisage. The price to be paid for length was a sense of overall structural slackness; the price to be paid for integration was extreme formulaic brevity. The solution that Schoenberg found to this problem must have seemed disappointing to one who thought of himself as an intrepid explorer of the intrinsic laws of musical thought. For his quest for principles on which to build extended musical structures took him beyond music altogether, and into the much less strictly law-bound realm of literature.

His recourse to poetic texts in, say, *Erwartung (Expectation)* (1909) and *Pierrot Lunaire* (1912) was not in itself a new venture. Indeed the power of literature as a compositional aid had already been forcibly proclaimed in 1905, at an extraordinary double premiere of late-tonal works by Zemlinsky and Schoenberg. The concert featured *Die Seejungfrau (The Mermaid)* and *Pelleas und Melisande*, and in each of these opulent works an imaginative writer had been given a major formal or form-inspiring role. Andersen in Zemlinsky's case and Maeterlinck in Schoenberg's were called upon to supply both an overall dramatic shape for a forty-minute span of musical invention and a series of clearly differentiated episodes or tableaux. Moreover the warring passions and triangular love-drama that each work sets forth could be thought of as a non-musical expedient for achieving a musical end: thanks to these argumentative literary plots, certain of the contrastive and resolution-seeking components of sonata form could be conserved and remotivated by composers whose harmonic explorations proper were taking them in quite different directions. The classical sonata tradition was able to enjoy a shadowy, intermittent afterlife in these tales of long-deferred amorous expiration.

In *Erwartung*, however, the relationship between music and text is altogether more intimate and complex. In this work, which is often spoken of as the supreme masterpiece of atonal and athematic musical thinking, Schoenberg tirelessly pursues the 'more remote consonances'. It is a continuous weave of non-repeating and seemingly limitless contrapuntal argument which nevertheless culminates, in the final bars, in a closural passage of astonishing power. Charles Rosen has described the passage in these terms:

> This massed chromatic movement at different speeds, both up and down and accelerating, is a saturation of the musical space in a few short seconds; and in a movement that gets ever faster, every note in the range of the orchestra is played in a kind of *glissando*. The saturation of musical space is Schoenberg's substitute for the tonic chord of the traditional musical language. The absolute consonance is a state of chromatic plenitude.[7]

Yet the pressure within the music towards this final moment of plenitude and saturation does not tell us how, as hearers, to proceed in an acoustic landscape that has no landmarks. The text, with its micro-dynamics of fear and desire, performs this role. In setting the words of Marie Pappenheim's monodrama, Schoenberg invented a language of hyper-expressive vocal gesture whose sharply delineated contours provide a constant stimulus to the discriminating perception of the work's instrumental counterpoint: textual motifs are transposed into vocal motifs, and these in their turn alert us to motivic interconnections in the instrumental writing. It is to some extent surprising that the Pappenheim text should act as a selective and perspectival device of this kind, for it is in itself rough and repetitious, and expressive only in a gasping, expostulatory vein. And its tapestry of psychopathic effects – hallucination, prurient jealousy, homicidal rage – is woven not from a set of original dramatic or psychological ideas but from the sexual small-talk that psychoanalysis had helped to make fashionable in 'advanced' sections of the Viennese bourgeoisie. Yet precisely the low level of the text, its unashamed closeness to hysterical case-material, seems to have acted as a catalyst upon Schoenberg during the inspired fortnight in which *Erwartung* was composed. For here was a text which belonged, or affected to belong, so completely to the primitive libidinal substratum that it had to be resculpted and refocused from moment to moment: its impoverished verbal gestures demanded to be vocally re-apparelled. *Erwartung* may have been constructed, in Adorno's words, as an instrument for 'the seismographic registration of traumatic shock', but it was crucial for each new shock to sound different from the one before. The work of musical composition is going on in terrifying self-imposed proximity to the indifferent, undifferentiated flux of desire and impulse, and proceeds under perpetual threat of dissolution. In the face of this threat, the composer had to find ways of securing articulateness and longevity for his ideas. 'In *Erwartung*', Schoenberg wrote in a retrospective essay of around 1930, 'the aim is to represent in *slow motion* everything that occurs during a single second of maximum spiritual excitement, stretching it out to half an hour.'[8] This sounds like the language of rapture, but the lesson of such remarks is invariably one of artistic prudence. The 'single second' of spiritual excitement, like Rosen's moment of chromatic saturation and plenitude, may promise a single apocalyptic swing of the seismographic needle but it makes sense only in stretched-out, time-bound terms. The continuous 'now' of human desire is a fine thing, a treasure trove, but it does not make music.

Erwartung is a response to the problem of creating a long atonal work of high expressive intensity and to this end it uses its literary text in a perfectly ambiguous fashion: Pappenheim's words provide both an enlivening contact with a savage underworld of feeling and a stimulus to the invention of vocal lines that will serenely and abstractly float upon the tumult; they are at once a threat and an inspiration, a zero point of expressivity and a call to unimaginable intensities of musical utterance. This knife edge is the familiar terrain of psychoanalysis. For Freud, unconscious desire, the daemonic primary stuff of experience, lay just beneath the text both of the consulting-room narrative and of the clinical meta-narrative that extended and embellished it, and his hermeneutic performances have an air of delicious Houdinery about them: the chasm above which this master interpreter performed his feats of eleventh-hour calculation was that of mute, blind, intractable and unsubduable natural force. It was the world of Schopenhauer's 'Will', as Freud himself proclaimed in the later stages of his career, but, he was at pains to assure his reader, discovered by means of cautious clinical observation and articulated with slow sobriety in theoretical models. The unconscious exerted upon its scientist a fascination so dangerous that it was repeatedly necessary for him to refortify his scientific resolve. This could be done on the one hand by identifying the primary drives and the fundamental modes of mental functioning – by separating out within the restless, swarming, encompassing world-energy the specific attributes and propensities of human mentality. But on the other hand it could be done by the application of practical analytic skill to those productions of the unconscious that tantalizingly half-revealed themselves in discourse. The analyst constructed sequential narratives and firm explanatory schemes from the plastic raw materials of the patient's speech; he drew lines where none had previously existed; and the countless local choices that he made as he worked were all motivated by an implacable drive towards intelligibility: such error-inducing mechanisms as condensation, displacement and overdetermination were the defining features of unconscious mental process, and had to be held in check by a strong interpretative hand. Yet in neither case could knowledge of the mind be had from the disinterested pursuit of speculative thought alone. The imprudent unconscious had to be frequented, fraternized with, and its seductive power had to be experienced at first hand if this threatening source of our humanity was to be properly – 'scientifically' – known.

Living on the knife edge, suspended over the abyss of desire, Schoenberg invented a new music and Freud a new hermeneutic style. Both of them seemed reprehensible to the quieter spirits of the age, and recklessly drawn to their own intellectual ruin. However, what still seems strange about both cases is not their willingness to heed the call of primitive instinctual life, nor yet their half-willingness to collude with the babble and blur that seemed to characterize the unconscious, but their trusting belief that the passage from the brutish to the exalted, from disorderly passion to a higher intimation of sensible and intelligible structure, could and should be rapid and untroubled. Time and again during this 'advanced' age of sexual self-awareness, the unconscious became Woman, just as it had during the heyday of Romantic agony. But whichever woman it now became – the deranged heroine of *Erwartung*, Breuer's Anna O., Freud's Emmy von N., the Salome of Richard Strauss, the Lulu of Berg and Pabst, Klimt's Judith or any one of the lesser hysterics, houris and earth spirits who crowd the annals of European culture at this time – it was wondrously removed from the complicating life of the social group. An enchanted access-route to the instincts had been discovered, and the path which led from their terrifying domain back to artistic form and epistemic certainty was now short and straight. Desire no longer needed to be individualized in order to be manipulable by scientist or artist, and the desire that individuals unmistakably possessed, or were possessed by, no longer seemed to acquire its distinctive features – its case-historical specificity – under pressure from the desire of others. At moments, Schopenhauerian 'Will' could be seen surging upwards from the biosphere to the noosphere and nowhere colliding with such awkward angularities as money, work, class, the family or the nation state.

Schoenberg and Freud both saw themselves as deriving a unique advantage from their decision to remain close to the turmoil of primitive mental life. Despite the risks of confusion or of grandiose mythical simplification that this frequentation brought with it, the unconscious was the fountain-head of all creative thinking. Indeed 'genius', for each of them, lay in an ability to preserve the elemental pulse of human desire in the higher inventions of the mind and to create a sense of structure large enough to overarch the small-scale daily inventiveness that all minds seemed to possess in abundance and to excess. The unconscious was an essential ally in any such quest for a higher pattern nourished, propelled and made rhythmic by the ordinary passions of mankind. For not only was it incurably desirous, it was the archive where fundamental human experiences, those of the young child, were stored – not as an inert residue but as a series of indefinitely re-usable templates on the basis of which the overall system of things could be modelled.

Neither Schoenberg nor Freud had any reason to be modest about his creative powers and it is clear that for each of them the attempt to sketch out a psychology of 'the genius' was in part a practical exercise in self-understanding. Where Schoenberg's account differs most sharply from Freud's is in its passionate and uncompromising espousal of theological language. Ingenious musical structure can be the product of hard cerebral work, but 'it can also be a subconsciously received gift from the Supreme Commander'. There is nothing light-hearted or whimsical about these self-indentifications with the divinity, which occur frequently in his theoretical writings and musical projects. His fascination with Balzac's *Séraphita*, for example, which was never to find full expression in his musical works, although strong traces of it are to be found in *Die Jakobsleiter* (1917–22), reached a culmination of sorts in his essay on 'Composition with Twelve Tones', where Swedenborg's heaven as mediated by Balzac's novel is employed as a metaphor for the unity of musical space. Genius works on the grandest imaginable scale: it has its origins in the depths of the human mind, but the realm that it compels the artist to inhabit in his creative strivings is none other than the mind of God. In comparison with this, Freud's claims for genius are quiet and self-apologetic: there was something 'incomprehensible and irresponsible about it', and it was not one of the subjects on which Freud's otherwise loquacious new science could be expected to have much of note to say. He identified himself with Michelangelo, Leonardo, the pre-Socratics and the 'divine Plato', but the psychoanalytic critique of religion as the fulfilment of infantile wishes gave him powerful reasons for going no further.

Freud and Schoenberg in their talk of genius were addressing a problem which was ancient and famous but which nevertheless had a modern, up-to-the-minute force: after the moment of intellectual emancipation, when a new source of structure and meaning had come with sudden clarity into view, how could its bounties be regulated? Geniuses were those who could see connections where others could not, but more especially they were those who could triumph over what to others was an ungovernable superfluity of connections. But the task could never be easy, even for these sovereign figures. For Freud the unconscious was 'inside' the human being, the essential component of each individual's psychical apparatus, but it could as easily be thought of as something external to him or her, for it seemed also to possess an intractable, self-fertilizing quality upon which the conscious wishes and designs of the individual left no imprint. For Schoenberg the emancipated dissonance was a natural resource that echoed upon the inner ear and seemed miraculously attuned to the connection-seeking human mind, yet even the most vigilant and cunning artist could easily be defeated by it. Both men had discovered a force that was at once a friend and an enemy of form and that belonged, in an unsettled and enigmatic way, not only to the human person but to the suprapersonal world of nature. There was no position of safety from which this power-source could be surveyed and exploited. The best that could be hoped for was a creative technique which allowed the theoretical or musical intelligence to construct for itself an ever-changing inside-outside zone from within which the quest for form could perpetually rebegin.

Mahler and Schoenberg reveal, then, two different but complementary kinds of affinity with Freud. During the heroic early years of the century, when the unconscious was being rediscovered by Freud and launched by him on the most eventful phase of its European career, it could be viewed either as an alternative mental order that occasionally broke through into everyday perception and behaviour, and mattered to human beings only when it broke through, or as the underlying condition of all mental acts, operating uninterruptedly and without regard to the individual's declared goals. These two views of the unconscious – the 'instantaneous' and the 'continuous' – are each amply illustrated in Freud's own writings, and each of them holds out a promise to criticism.

I shall take a simple pair of examples from modern painting, and focus for a moment longer upon Woman as the custodian of unconscious desire. If the unconscious is to be thought of as an interruptive energy, producing momentary snags or isolated structural dissonances within the work of art, numerous Surrealist canvases may be called in evidence. In Magritte's *Collective Invention* (1934) or in Ernst's *The Robing of the Bride* (1939), the erotic power of the work, its 'uncanny' affective charge, may be localized upon the picture surface. Magritte's mermaid comprises the upper body of a fish grafted upon the lower body of a woman; Ernst's bride dons a robe that is as alive as she herself is and threatens to turn her into a monstrous bird of prey. The transformations enacted by these artists – from warm into cold, skin into scales, mouth into beak and so forth – produce their *frissons* economically, by the mere inversion of a received erotic idea. The desires and fears of the spectator are urgently intensified by those sections of the painting where the transformation is articulated and tranquillized again by other sections – by, say, a featureless stretch of sea or sky.

In Matisse's extended sequence of domestic nudes, on the other hand, the female body is perceived as a repository of linear and coloristic motifs which overspill the confines of the central figure itself: the line of breast or buttock, the colour of hair or belly, may be freely borrowed by, or derived from, other elements of the scene. Window, sofa, rug or vase recapitulate and inflect the sensual life of the human body in such a way that the entire picture surface is eroticized. Desire flows across the variegations of the scene and is continuously moulded, fragmented and reconstituted as it travels.

The idea of the unconscious is productive in cases like these in that it invites the critic to make connections between the finite array of structural elements spread out upon the canvas and the indefinite array of drives and impulses that those elements activate in the spectator. Instantaneously or continuously, desire emerges and achieves form as we look, and the 'unconscious' is a useful quasi-topographical term for those who wish to recapture some of the drama of this process: it designates the mental place, the overflowing reservoir within the individual, from which the affective states and libidinal motions kindled by works of art ultimately derive. And it reminds us again of what, in the wake of Freud, we can scarcely forget: that desire is not a uniform flow or force or pressure; that it is shaped by repression, fixation and taboo; and that whatever 'place' desire may occupy within the mind, it has structure. The unconscious in this account is one dramaturgical device among others for the critic wishing to describe the passage from relatively undifferentiated mental process to expressive artistic form, from an already-structured 'mind' to the more elaborated structures characteristic of art.

At the level of critical diction, however, matters are less clear. Freud's own technical language, as is now well known, was the product of a daring syncretistic verbal imagination, and it was a triumph of rhetorical ingenuity. Similarly, the underlying mechanisms that he sought to delineate as a basis for his explanations of both normal and pathological mental processes were assembled from a variety of conceptual components; they were schematic and parsimonious despite these varied origins; and they always needed to be made malleable again if they were to handle successfully the shifting complexity of actual clinical cases. Freud as clinician brought a new rhetoric into play, one that spoke not of systems, mechanisms, apparatus or modes of functioning but of autobiographical human speech seized on the wing and in the density of its affective life.

But there is a paradox here, and one that has been given less attention than it deserves by those who import technical psychoanalytic notions into the vernacular of criticism. For there is no compelling reason why those who wish to adopt a 'Freudian' approach to modern art should employ Freudian terminology at all, nor why their explorations of desire at work and at play in texts, pictures and musical compositions should be expected to vindicate any one psychoanalytic paradigm. Simplifying matters a good deal, we could say that just as psychoanalysis, considered as a practical science working with the material of speech, needs to stay in touch with the specificity of its subject-matter, so the psychoanalytic or *psychanalysant* critic needs to speak resourcefully, specifyingly, the language of the art-forms on which he or she chooses to dwell. If the critic has the ambition to be a dramatist of desire as manifest in art, or a seismographer of the subterranean mental forces that shape our culture, let him or her employ, in speaking of the structuring medium in which desire flows, the most *nuancé* and discriminating of the formal languages available. In the case of *Erwartung* this will mean in the first instance the language of harmony and counterpoint; in the case of Magritte, Ernst or Matisse, it will mean that of line, volume, colour and ornament. And in all cases, the additional pressures exerted by linguistic and textual structure upon the production and reception of art-works will also need to be characterised in their appropriate terms. In the course of such critical activity, the language of psychoanalysis offers clues but not solutions, calls to action for the interpreter but not interpretations.

Freud's account of the unconscious in its instantaneous intrusions contains a lesson at once inspiring and cautionary for criticism. His account of the inscrutable continuum of unconscious mental process contains a further lesson of the same sort. Throughout his writings, he constructs theoretical models and describes their possible uses. He talks of 'regions' and 'territories' within the mind, but his topography – like his hydraulics, his archaeology and his economics – is a conjectural one, mobile and open to revision. There is no place within the individual mind from which all artistic meanings come and to which, under guidance from criticism, they can be expected to return. Psychoanalysis is not that sort of discipline, and criticism cannot expect that sort of anchorage from it.

If the 'European unconscious' still has an urgent message for criticism today, this message stems perhaps above all from its early twentieth-century Kakanian phase. For if criticism is to make productive use of psychoanalytic notions, it must remember – however little it can expect to emulate them – the passion, gaiety and transformational power of Freud's theoretical imagination, and the cataclysmic conditions in which it went to work. And remember too that for Freud the construction of a persuasive new theory of the human mind brought with it, as a more than incidental benefit, a whole new sense of opportunity for the cultural critic: an empire was falling into brutal disarray, the European monarchies were preparing themselves for their war to end wars, civilization itself was in peril . . . and psychoanalysis was ready armed with a vision of the human psyche that could make a desperate kind of sense out of this discouraging public spectacle. Freud's tales of the unconscious, seen in the company of Robert Musil's *The Man without Qualities* and Italo Svevo's *The Confessions of Zeno*, belong to a moment of extraordinary richness and exigency in the still-to-be written history of European irony. These works all chronicle the survival of the fleet-footed ironist amid the collapsing empires, epistemologies and value-systems of Europe. Svevo's novel, it will be remembered, has an impressionistic and heterodox version of psychoanalysis among its themes, but that is not of course the remarkable thing about Svevo. The remarkable thing about him, and about his fellow Austro-Hungarians Freud and Musil, is an ability to navigate dextrously in conditions of extreme intellectual and moral uncertainty and to write with a critical intelligence that is at once volatile and firm. Modern critics of the European unconscious facing their own *fin-de-siècle* have every reason to heed these lessons from Kakania, especially as the destruction of the planet foreseen by Zeno at the end of his confessions is now advancing at speed.

Notes

1   L. L. Whyte, *The Unconscious before Freud* (Tavistock Publications, London, 1962).
2   S. Freud, 'A Difficulty in the Path of Psycho-Analysis' (1917) *SE*, XVII, p. 143.
3   S. Freud, *The Interpretation of Dreams* (1900), *SE*, IV, pp. 106–20; Pelican 4.
4   E. Jones, *Sigmund Freud: Life and Work*, vol. II (Hogarth Press, London, 1958), p. 89.
5   D. Mitchell, *Gustav Mahler: The Wunderhorn Years* (Faber, London, 1974), p. 74.
6   A. Schoenberg, *Style and Idea* (Faber, London, 1975), p. 217.
7   C. Rosen, *Schoenberg* (Collins-Fontana, Glasgow, 1976), p. 66.
8   Schoenberg, *Style and Idea*, p. 105.

SUGGESTED READING

Dahlhaus, C., *Schoenberg and the New Music,* Cambridge University Press, Cambridge, 1987.
Del Mar, N., *Mahler's Sixth Symphony: A Study,* Eulenberg Books, London, 1980.
Gay, P., *Freud, Jews and Other Germans: Masters and Victims in Modernist Culture*, Oxford University Press, New York, 1978.
Janik, A. and Toulmin, S., *Wittgenstein's Vienna*, Simon & Schuster, New York, 1973.
Rosen, C., *Schoenberg*, Collins-Fontana, Glasgow, 1976.
Schorske, C. E., *Fin de Siècle Vienna: Politics and Culture*, Vintage Books, New York, and Cambridge University Press, Cambridge, 1981.

2

The Unconscious Image

PETER COLLIER

'It is better to present one Image in a lifetime than to produce voluminous works.'

Ezra Pound, *'A few don'ts for Imagistes'*[1]

Imagination Unconscious Imagine[2]

Frank Kermode argues that the 'Romantic Image' and the Modernist image are both 'organic': that is, intuitive rather than discursive, an organism rather than a machine. The form of this organism supposes a complete act of the imagination, rather than a limited operation of the intelligence.[3] Yet it seems to me that there is a moment when the aesthetic of the 'organic' image in Romantic and Symbolist literature tends to give way to a Modernist image, which is 'organic' in some respects, but which differs in two key ways. Firstly, it accommodates the idea that the mind is split against itself. Secondly, it regards and expresses itself as process. One might for instance look at two late Symbolist novels, Henry James's *The Golden Bowl* (1904) and Marcel Proust's *A la recherche du temps perdu* (1913–22). Suddenly the image of the golden bowl, or that of the madeleine cake dipped in tea, fails to be interpretable by the characters and narrators. Different readings of these images are offered. They are not simply anti-discursive in Kermode's sense. They are self-scrutinizing, and, if they seem to resist construal, it is not merely because they suggest a whole experience irreducible to paraphrase, it is rather that they offer layers of sense rooted in the unconscious which are incompatible with other levels of interpretation offered in the novels concerned. In short, I would argue that, although Proust's novel, for instance, seems Modernist in its construction of a fiction around the hypothesis of an unstable, self-constructing narrative presence, its Modernism is even more crucially to be found in its bold distillation of awkwardly intermeshing modes of experience into an unresolved, conflicting nexus of imagery figuring that self.

Similar 'epiphanies' in Joyce or 'moments of being' in Woolf are traced by Tim Cribb and Naomi Segal to rich cultural constellations – that of the English Romantics, that of a feminist sensibility and consciousness. My own purpose is to look more closely at the limited paradigm of the privileged moment formed by the Modernist image in poetry – to study its isolated, fragmentary nature, to explore the understanding that the Modernists had of the relation of such privileged images to the process of artistic creativity, and to trace as circumstantially as possible the relation of such a creative image to the notion of the unconscious.

In Modernist poetry, as opposed to the Symbolist novel, it often seems that the image is less a locus of symbolic meaning, serving an overarching structure powered by the imagination, than some kind of residue of imaginative activity, a self-questioning trace of its passage rather than a substantive event. A programmatic Imagist poem by Ezra Pound's friend William Carlos Williams spells out this particular extreme of Modernist form. The poem highlights a single image, it scrutinizes that image for significance, and it self-consciously foregrounds its own process of image-production:

> Rather notice, mon cher,
> that the moon is
> tilted above
> the point of the steeple
> than that its colour
> is shell-pink.[4]

Williams's text sketches the contours of the image to be ignored, as well as those of the perceptual vector to be followed. However, if we look at a contemporary piece of Surrealist 'automatic writing' by André Breton, we seem to find an almost total contrast to Williams's palimpsest of the allegedly occulted image. Breton's Surrealist poem appears to stand almost as an equivalent of brute experience: it looks chaotically unwritten, hypnotically unself-aware, as if bathing in a pre-conscious flow of language – yet it, too, offers essentially a confrontation of single images, as ambiguously overlapping as Williams's are mutually refractive:

> Colourless gases are suspended
> Two thousand three hundred scruples
> Snow from sources
> Smiles are permitted
> Make no sailors promises
> Polar lions
> The sea the sea the natural sand
> The poor relations grey parrot.[5]

Thus very different writing strategies may be served by the single, isolated image that becomes the most characteristic feature of Modernist poetry. Its relation to the unconscious is enhanced as other more hierarchized structures of art fall away. The demise of unproblematic 'representation' and 'the dissociation of sensibility'[6] tend to leave the wild stream or the brute collage. The founding image is left more clearly exposed to our view, its status more vulnerable, its import more urgent – whether as pure vision, as perception of nature, as act of consciousness, as transcription of the preverbal, or as theory of a new aesthetic.

For the Modernist movement of the early twentieth century did not only produce art that claimed to be radically new. It also generated new theories of artistic production and consumption to accompany such works, since their break with tradition made existing theories of creation and reception seem inadequate to explain their genesis or guide their interpretation. The imagination as posited by Coleridge[7] and variously adapted by Shelley, Poe or Baudelaire, was a holistic, inclusive faculty, whereas the Modernist image promoted by Benjamin or Woolf, Proust or Joyce, implies by definition a conflict between different parts of the mind.

It seemed axiomatic to the early Romantics that the condition of 'inspiration' gives priority to the faculty of imagination, and that creative insight arises partly beyond the control of the conscious mind. Coleridge, for instance, argues that the poet draws not upon a single inspirational faculty but a complex mental faculty, the imagination, yet he is keen to separate this from what he calls 'fancy', which is what many would vulgarly suppose imagination to be. In thus supposing a mind operating between two poles, those of fancy and imagination (which opposition cuts across rather than repeats more familiar oppositions as between reason and passion), Coleridge schematizes fancy as passive, mechanical and imitative, while the imagination itself is active, creative and living. Nonetheless, the visions that presented themselves to the imagination had then to be analysed and organized. It was in the conjunction of vision and analysis that the organic work arose. And perhaps the most surprising feature of the Coleridgean imagination for us now, informed as we all are by a sensibility permeated with Modernist fragmentation and the Freudian unconscious, is that it supposes an ingredient of intelligent, conscious structuring, and excludes raw, hallucinatory vision, such as occurs in dreaming. Even the dreams or visions of 'Kubla Khan' or 'Intimations of Immortality' are consistently integrated into a moral and intellectual narrative structure. There is really very little place for the isolated, hallucinatory single image in Romantic theory or practice.

The modern French philosopher Gabriel Marcel points out that Coleridge criticized the associationism of Locke, whose theory tended to deduce the activities of the mind from the senses alone, because Coleridge rejected the determinism and mental fragmentation implied by such a theory. Coleridge, on the contrary, must necessarily posit an organic mind, with a higher unity, able to override the chaos of individual sense-data. It seems certain that Coleridge's 'imagination' implies the supposition of pre-existing essences, or forms, in the Platonic sense.[8] It is this hidden realm of mental meaning that we find taking on the role of the unconscious towards the end of the nineteenth century. Yet, simultaneously, it anticipates that demise of the organic work, that fracturing of the whole faculty of the imagination, out of which the Modernist image springs.

To a certain extent the demystification of aesthetic values had already started with the French Romantics. Hugo wished to reinstate the grotesque, and to avoid investing only the beautiful with meaning; Stendhal insisted on the relativity of beauty; Baudelaire on its amorality and assymmetry. Yet even for these first modern (post-Kantian, post-Lapsarian) aestheticians there was no idea or temptation that poetry and painting should or could be reduced to the single image. The Modernist insistence on the single, unconscious, reflexive image has its roots perhaps less in the subjectivity of Romanticism than in the self-consciousness of the works of the Symbolists. Mallarmé's Symbolism at first inherits from Coleridge the supposition of a hidden plane of meaning, roughly corresponding to the world of Platonic forms, but Mallarmé's attitude is rendered problematic by what he identifies as a crisis of language in the modern world. Since language cannot directly describe things, it should abandon the attempt altogether. For Mallarmé, language is as inadequate a representation of things as for Plato appearances are an inadequate representation of essences. Once referential language is distrusted, once it is admitted that language only ever operates obliquely, hinting at a transcendental world which it can never describe, nor even directly symbolize, then its only possible functions are to suggest what it cannot grasp, and to question its own sublunary procedures.[9]

This linguistic self-consciousness signals a major break. The Modernists seem to call into question the central faculty of imagination itself, even though both Pound's 'Imagistes' and Breton's 'Surréalistes' concentrate their theory and practice on the 'image' itself. I shall concentrate my demonstration on a few key figures, and look at the conflicting views of the unconscious image held by Freud and Breton, the self-consciously non-representational imagery of Mallarmé and Apollinaire, and the implications of the variously fragmented imagery of Eliot and Pound.

The Text of the Unconscious

Just as the Imagist and Surrealist practices of a poetry based on the single image seem diametrically opposed, so the two major theorists of the imagery of the unconscious and its relation to art, Sigmund Freud and André Breton, are strongly divergent. All Freud's early, major works on normal psychology[10] reveal that the dynamics of the mind rely on unconscious forces rather than intelligence; they show the thoughts, imagery and even vocabulary of the mind to be driven by a process of (visual and/or linguistic) association, rather than one of logical analysis or deduction. Much that had been considered conscious became unconscious, but much of what was now a newly expanded category of the unconscious took on a new purposefulness. The unconscious – whether expressed in terms of madness, desire, infantile wishes, humour or dream – ceased to be trivial, meaningless, dominated by consciousness and absorbed into its interpretative modes.

This theory of the mind has implications for the process of artistic creation. The mind is conflictual, and has no overarching homogenizing faculty like Coleridge's 'imagination'. Indeed, for Freud, the unconscious itself *totally lacks* imagination, it harbours only desire and destruction – where imagination intervenes it is as a subsidiary process, transforming unacceptable unconscious drives into symbolic forms that the ego can cope with. In stark contrast to Coleridge, Freud argues that the imagination is driven by desire, not by vision. Yet ultimately Freud's revolutionary theories of the mind share with Symbolism a bias towards an oblique view of mental sense. There is a hidden plane of meaning (the unconscious for Freud; the imagination, perhaps the divine, in Symbolism). The transcendental plane in Freud is internal, but has Platonic overtones.[11] Its true forms are hidden emotional forces which we can never know directly. These forces can be known and expressed only indirectly, through the condensations and displacements of dream imagery. The censorious ego uses these narrative paths, based on association, to bestow acceptable formulation on the basically unknowable and unformulable latent dream thoughts. Thus it is not the primal desire which is formulated; the manifest content produced by the dream work is a recombination of the (visual or linguistic) residue associated with the desire. Thus, as with Mallarmé's Symbolism, we have not a one-to-one system of symbolism, but an enigmatic, conflictual model of signification, where the text overtly delivered is a trace of the struggle towards meaning. Powerfully, however, Freud appears to remove the privilege of meaningful fantasy and narrative skill from the sovereign domain of the poet. Each dreamer poeticizes his/her own self-sufficient truth.

Yet coexisting with this indirect and private system, there is in Freud's dream theory an entailment that dream images of erotic desire (however enigmatic and circumstantial the narrative which embeds them) partake of a universal symbolism, just as there is a concomitant entailment of their readability: the dream becomes a text to renarrate, to revise, to listen to, to read, to analyse. It becomes a medium of psychic exchange and cultural significance, like the literary text, or the joke. In fact, communicability of experience in narrative form, and the transformation of experience through that very narrative (re)structuring, is vital to Freud's project. Freud's most explicit theory of artistic creativity is that it is a kind of disguised wish-fulfilment (just as he argues of dreams). He supposes in 'Creative Writers and Day Dreaming' (*SE*, IX; Pelican 14) that the artist and the neurotic are essentially similar, that unhappiness leads to 'phantasy'; and that art is a kind of 'aesthetic forepleasure'. The model is based on the premise that instinctual urges are blocked by our rational minds, that the frustrated energy has to be released through acceptable channels in 'sublimated' form, and that sublimation is in fact a creative, as it were artistic, process. The work of art, then, is motivated and structured just like the dream; its import is resumed in a leading image; that image bears an unconscious structure beneath its superficial plastic significance and effect. In chapter 15 below, Elizabeth Wright has drawn attention to the aesthetic implications of the theory of the uncanny in Freud's essay on E.T.A. Hoffmann's tale *The Sandman*, where irrational images loom up from forgotten childhood and inform mature art-works.[12] But it is Wilhelm Jensen's *Gradiva*, structured – like Hoffmann's story – around an obsession with an erotically exciting but radically displaced female image (a violent female automaton in *The Sandman*, a delicate female sculpture in *Gradiva*), which provided Freud with his most detailed reconstruction of the artistic process of the representation of desire.

In Freud's major essay on creativity, *Delusions and Dreams in Jensen's 'Gradiva'*,[13] repressed desire for a woman (Zoe Bertgang) surreptitiously motivates the hero's interest in an artistic female image (the look-alike sculpture which he names Gradiva). The hero, Norbert Hanold, is a dessicated archaeologist, who suddenly fixates upon the image of the oddly-poised foot of an attractive girl in an antique bas-relief. He finds himself driven to observe girls' legs in the street, and his attempt to fit the image into his scientific practice is disturbed by strange inner feelings, and then by a dramatic dream, where he and Gradiva are being buried by the eruption of Vesuvius at Pompeii, and she lies down to sleep on a marble slab. Once awakened from this dream, he seems to recognize the girl outside in the street, and rushes out clad only in his dressing gown. He pursues his scientific quest by travelling to Rome to study the original sculpture, but he is disturbed by honeymoon couples and by a second dream, where Apollo carries off Venus and lays her down on a ramshackle cart. He finally arrives in Pompeii, having forgotten his dream of Vesuvius, and when he apparently meets there the living original of Gradiva, he feels that he is dreaming, and invites her to lie down again as she had done in his previous vision. Hanold's scientific study gives way to a frankly obsessive search for his mysteriously revived vision. He finds himself buying a dubious souvenir brooch of a pair of lovers mummified *in flagrante* at Pompeii, stumbling into an antique house decorated with lubricious frescoes, offering Gradiva flowers, and dreaming of a lizard, snared by Gradiva, gobbled up by a bird. All the while he is dogged by occasional apparitions of the attractive but demure Zoe, whom he takes to be a Greek statue reincarnated, until he finally yields, both to the mood of the neighbouring honeymooners and to the evidence that the real Gradiva is his long-forgotten childhood playmate Zoe who has chased him to Pompeii in the wake of her father, a naturalist, and that he loves her.

Jensen's charming, witty, richly suggestive story, written in 1903, has many features which suggest the active presence of a specifically Freudian unconscious. There are *actes manqués*: Hanold loses his way and finds by accident an unsuspected hotel at Pompeii, where Gradiva is staying; he stumbles into a culturally unedifying building at Pompeii whose rude frescoes he had not intended to study, and interrupts the embrace of a pair of honeymooners who turn out to be friends of Gradiva's. There are slips of the tongue: Hanold asks Gradiva to lie down for him when he intends only to see if she matches the shape of the girl on the marble slab. There is repression and sublimation: Hanold represses his nascent desire for the figure of his childhood girlfriend by forgetting her existence, by burying himself in aesthetic and mathematical study of the disturbing image of the attractive girl in the bas-relief, by talking to her in ancient Greek.

Above all, there are dreams, where real events from Hanold's life become significantly transformed, in an overtly erotic symbolism. In one the girl lies down to be buried alive among the stones and lava of Pompeii, as if buried beneath the rubble of Hanold's antiquarian studies, but she lies down as if in bed; in another Apollo abducts Venus and prostrates her, although the sleeping Hanold has tried to avoid noticing the sound of a honeymoon couple in the adjoining hotel bedroom. The real lizards chased by Zoe's father and the real canary from the cage at her bedroom window merge into a third dream the source of whose anxiety could as easily be fear of sexuality as fear of marriage: Gradiva lassoes a hapless lizard and allows it to be snapped up by a passing bird. This anxiety dream is the more striking for not being transformed by the dreamer into an erudite classical model, as the first two dreams were.

Freud has been much praised for his reading of this story. Yet he makes rather heavy weather of it. He worries unduly over whether Hanold's hallucinations are realistic. He glosses over the parapraxes and slips of the tongue (although he had recently written a considerable tome on these phenomena, showing how they revealed the unconscious). He doesn't seem interested in the fact that Hanold forgets his first, archaeological, dream until he finds himself in the Pompeii he had dreamed of. On the other hand, Freud's analysis of the three dreams embedded in the story is masterly. More persuasively than with many of his own one-line dreams in *The Interpretation of Dreams*, Freud shows the process of condensation and displacement of Hanold's desire, as the 'latent meaning' is transposed into the 'manifest content' using the residue of the previous day. He lays bare the mechanisms that construct a narrative whose secondary revisions are attempts to deny the very desire which it expresses, a desire which is nonetheless readable by the analyst who knows how to unscramble the code of the dream unconscious, where persons are interchangeable, the time is always the present, where positives may signify negatives and vice versa.

Freud wants to avoid the suggestion, that Jensen, his contemporary, was consciously using his ideas. He wants the artist's insights to confirm his, the scientist's, independently. Hence no doubt Freud's repression of his own vocabulary of the parapraxis, the slip of the tongue; hence, even more importantly, his avoidance of any mention of over-obviously 'Freudian' symbolism: yet the image of Gradiva lassoing the lizard with a blade of grass and then offering it up to the beak of a passing bird is potentially as good a symbol of castration anxiety as that of the eyes which are threatened by the Sandman in the Hoffmann tale analysed in *The Uncanny*. In this attempt to find an artistic confirmation and hence consecration of his science, Freud avoids as far as possible the erotic overtones of the recumbent Gradiva, the half-dressed Hanold, Venus's creaky bedsprings, and so on. One curious result of this is that what is repressed appears to be no more than a sage, sweet, nuptial love, rather than erotic desire; and, as such, it seems hardly worth repressing. If this repression lies behind Hanold's obsessions and hallucinations, the modern reader, armed with the later Freud, would want to know what lay behind that repression. And indeed, if Freud is able to found his reading of *Gradiva* on the overlap between two limpid and graceful female images, the bas-relief and the girl that it echoes, it is no doubt because this is a piece of early Freud, written at a time when his ideas on the Oedipus complex and infantile desire were still quite fluid. In fact, this article furnishes one of the stages in Freud's developing theories, with his discussion of Hanold's forgetting of his aggressively physical childhood games with Zoe. Freud also entirely ignores the death wish in Hanold's first and third dream[14] whilst he is enchanted with the metaphor of archaeology for memory unevenly buried in an unstable mental terrain (a metaphor which was to become one of his most creative models of the mind); he ignores the potential violence of Jensen's images of burial, flattening, cutting, measuring. Some of Jensen's *non*-dream images – the mummified lovers, the lewd frescoes – seem now to the post-Freudian reader of this late Symbolist fiction to reveal Jensen's own precocious ability to symbolize the destructive frenzy of the repressed libido.

Freud acknowledges in passing the wit and ingenuity of Jensen, but he denies Jensen as artist any analytical knowledge of the psyche, allowing him only artistic intuition and observation. Thus he has no qualms in treating Jensen's *whole* novella as a dream text: in his postscript to the second edition he talks of the 'manifest content' and the 'latent meaning', in a massive *glissando* which suggests inevitably that artistic composition creates its narrative in the way that the dream is structured. Indeed, in his reading of *Gradiva* Freud symptomatically finds a concentration of desire and signification in a series of single symbolic dream images, tendentiously underestimating Jensen's various narrative ploys and non-dream images, which already show symbolism working in Hanold's conscious mind as an elaborate dialectic between different psychic strategies. Hanold applies historical, mythical, literary, stylistic, mathematical, racial, aesthetic and linguistic grids to his interpretation of Gradiva, and Jensen organizes all sorts of ambiguities, double entendres, coincidences, misunderstandings and ironies – but Freud concentrates on the three embedded dream narratives as if they were the controlling structure. One has to object that the whole text can hardly be a dream, since Jensen embeds in the text dreams which clearly transform parts of the surrounding story. Moreover, Jensen's narrative is carefully designed to refute the obsessively literal interpretations of dreams which Hanold uses to fuel his hallucinations – for Hanold himself offers a fantastical narrative version of events, designed to disguise the dangerously clear insight offered by the two-dimensional, monochrome image of his desired but misconstrued object. Most interestingly of all, Jensen's novella – like that of Hoffmann – invokes the quasi-erotic power of the work of art. The alluring automaton of *The Sandman*, Olympia, is a more beautiful object than a living girl; in *Gradiva*, no girl on the streets has a gait that can match the sublime poise of the ankle of a scantily clad girl in a Greek bas-relief. Jensen, cleverly, allows Hanold to create the flat, ashen, immobile sculpture of Gradiva out of the threateningly nubile Zoe, until life gradually overruns his cultural structures. In Jensen's story Hanold's wish-fulfilment operates through a work of art at first *studied*, then *recreated*; Hanold indulges in creative play, manipulating his desired image through various scientific, artistic and cultural grids, which lead Jensen's reader into some exhilarating mental gymnastics. We enjoy guessing at the conscious but secret pursuit undertaken by Zoe Bertgang, and we enjoy double-guessing the constant misreading of her activities as Gradiva by Hanold, who believes that she must be interpreted in terms of cultural history rather than private desire. The aesthetic and erotic pleasure afforded by speculative and creative play upon the image and the text seems to have been underestimated by Freud, who reads the text as if Jensen himself were unwittingly revealing mental forces beyond his ken. And yet Freud's own concentration on the complex, devious structuring of the image, his own elaborate and pleasureable decoding of the unconscious drive beneath the aesthetic image, seem to suggest that we can read into his dream aesthetic an implicit argument that the work of art should offer sublimation and wish-fulfilment to the consumer as well as to the creator. The implication is that reading itself may be a process of therapy, if we accept that reading is a dialogic process, where the writer sets up imagic structures which draw us into a playful but therapeutic realization of our desires, through a process of imaginative creativity by proxy. Freud's brilliant decoding of the embedded dream image itself seems to have held him back from didactic formulation of this insight.

Nonetheless, Freud's essay is a landmark in literary theory, with its patient investigation of the way in which a narrative may manipulate symbolic structures in a form impenetrable to its narrator. As a reader, Freud was hardly a Modernist. He appreciated Sophocles, Goethe, Shakespeare. Yet his location of a nub of hermeneutic significance in a single conflictual image places him unwittingly in the mainstream of Modernism. On the other hand, André Breton quite explicitly referred to psychoanalysis as the basis of Surrealist writing and painting. His *First Surrealist Manifesto* (1924) promotes an uncritical application of Freud's *Interpretation of Dreams*. Breton seems to suggest that the irrational image, as provided by the dream and driven by the sexual impulse, is sufficient to create art, or rather, to create public images which will supersede the specifically aesthetic category of art. Breton argues that even the traditional metaphorical trope is to be rejected, since its basis in comparison is too rationalistic: 'The image cannot be created through comparison but from the confrontation of two more or less unrelated realities. The more the relation between the realities confronted is distant but apt, the stronger the image will be – the more emotional power and poetic reality it will have.'[15] Breton upsets the conventions of literary criticism, where even a Modernist critic like I. A. Richards can describe metaphor in terms of 'tenor' and 'vehicle' (one would now tend to say 'focus' and 'frame', using Max Black's terminology).[16] For Breton, there is no reality that is not image, and all images are distillations of a complex psychic reality. Both Breton and Freud see the image as a primary psychic form, pre-existing the study of nature, a view of imagery which recalls the search of Coleridge or Baudelaire or Rimbaud for total visionary enlightenment, but ignores their belief in a process of imaginative elaboration. (One even wonders if Breton's exploration of the minds of shell-shocked soldiers, like Freud's experience with cocaine, may have left some lasting impression of the power of the psychic vision dominating external reality).

Yet Freud insists on the significance of structure in the formation of the image, as various concerns of Hanold's are condensed into the charged figure of Gradiva. This obsessive image is a magnet which beneath the screen of rational consciousness attracts a cluster of secretly libidinous wishes, disguised and informed by erudite displacement. In Breton's practice of automatic writing, the surrealist text is *nothing but* the string of images which it generates. Their very expression denotes the *liberation* of desire. There is no privileged, cryptic single image, invested with a meaning to be unravelled, but a series of equivalent images, which are themselves the very substance of the secret self; they are a form of self-expression superior to hermeneutic meaning. But the function of the image for the Surrealists is not to encode the text of desire, as Freud argued that it did in the dream, or in the dream narratives of *Gradiva*. Where Freud argues that Jensen articulates images of desire in misconstrued form, Breton's poetry claims to be action, able to liberate from *any* rationalizing narrative all otherwise repressed desires in the writer.

The key to the discrepancy lies probably in Breton's assumption of the position of the writer, for whom writing is therapy, whereas the Freudian approach develops a posture of closer identification with the reader, and the task of interpreting an initially misconstrued imagic formation. In his key theoretical text of 1932, *Les Vases communicants*, Breton subscribes to Freud's theory that art is sublimated wish-fulfilment expressing personal preoccupations in oblique form. Yet in exemplification he uses an extremely primitive kind of universal Freudian symbolism to interpret Lautréamont's aggressively irrational anti-simile 'as beautiful as the chance encounter of an umbrella and a sewing machine on a dissecting table', saying that the umbrella can *only* represent woman; and the dissecting table *only* a bed.[17] Whereas Freud himself, despite his use in the *Interpretation of Dreams* of a symbolic lexicon classified in terms of the male or female genitalia, had not in his analysis of *Gradiva* pursued, for instance, the potentially over-obvious symbolism of Hanold's third and final dream, where the lizard lassoed by Gradiva is snapped up in a bird's beak, nor Hanold's glimpse of a lizard disappearing into a crack as Zoe walks by.

But although Breton talks of the creative act as if it were equivalent to dreaming 'out loud', he also seems to assume in *Les Vases communicants* that the joke provides a model of the matrix of creativity. For Freud and the Surrealists, humour, like madness, involved an attempt to elude rationalist censorship. Freud's theory of humour – like his theory of the dream – is a narrative theory. Where the dream condensed and displaced experience, constructing strings of images so that they form acceptable stories, jokes liberate disguised forms of desire, anxiety and aggression through the felicity of verbal play (most typically through the unstoppable, unstable interplay between two incompatible but treacherously similar terms, as in the pun). Freud himself thus seems to provide an alternative theory of creativity. The joke offers a model of instantaneous deflagration of alien meanings, with the hidden meaning erupting obliquely through the surface coincidence in a single verbal image of two incongrous levels of meaning. It is a one-word or one-image theory perhaps rather suited to poetry, as the structured dream-story was to prose fiction. Yet Breton himself fails to develop the implications of this theory. Even when he uses an example of his own creativity, where he seems to have exploited the procedure of the pun, he interprets the process in terms of the dream work rather than in terms of the pun. Breton had transposed the word 'silence' into a drawing of eyelashes ('cils') and a handle ('l'anse'). Then he realized that he had created the image of a chamber-pot. But he insists that this must be interpreted in terms of 'condensation' and 'displacement'. The implication is that Breton's scatological libido breaks out into the imagery of the chamber-pot, even when he tries to represent a serious, meditative project, silence.

Thus the one-word art-work resulting is, like Picasso's 'taureau' or Duchamp's 'fontaine', an instantaneous aesthetic experience for the consumer – although the Surrealist automatic drawing and the Surrealist 'ready-made', like the pun (or Freud's pun-like one-line dreams), will not bear much repetition. It is instructive to compare Breton's insight into his moment of scatological creativity with the imagery which Proust uses to describe Marcel's vision of his chamber-pot, its watery contents consciously transformed in the narrator's mind into a fantastic asparagus-tinted rainbow. Proust actually seems closer than Breton to the spirit of Freud's 'joke-theory' of creativity, for Freud supposes in the joke-teller a conscious procedure of associative construction and artful disguise, just as he supposes in the listener a desire to appreciate playful disguise, and knowingly to glimpse for a moment, when acceptably veiled, the naked desire beneath the meretricious surface image.

In fact, although Breton constantly pays lip-service to procedures of condensation and displacement, he more often seems to assume that the text is equivalent to the dream, which is equivalent to the unconscious, which is equivalent to the image. And whereas for Freud, the joke and the dream both have to use artistic patterning (word play in the pun, narrative structuring and rationalization of imagery in the dream), in order to violate the refusal of the self to represent its desiring, for Breton the transition between desire and image is smooth and uncomplicated: 'desire, which remains essentially unchanged grasps indiscriminately at whatever may serve to satisfy it . . . everything becomes an *image* and . . . the least object which doesn't have a specific symbolic role assigned to it, is liable to figure absolutely anything.'[18] This symbiotic theory suits Breton's militant belief, adopted from Lautréamont, that 'poetry should be written by everyone, for everyone.' The only technique needed in order to attain universal expression seems to be the knack of unlearning knowledge and rhetoric, which collude with the repressive ego. But there is a difficulty which Breton glosses over, as he develops his view of the random and unconscious production of art. Breton seems in *Les Vases communicants* to envisage a cognitive and interventionist role, but by the reader as analyst rather than by the writer as joker:

> the manifest content of a poetic improvisation, just like that of a dream, should not deceive us as to its latent content, for some innocent dream . . . may need quite an array of unattractive interpretations in order to be analysed, whereas some apparently 'shocking' dream . . . may be interpretable in not inelegant terms.[19]

Ultimately Breton poses, without analysing all its implications, the question of the readability and accessibility of the Surrealist image. In Breton's view the poet acts like a dreamer, unable to control his associations. But we then wonder why in transcribing his dream images he does not claim to use the process of secondary revision which Freud shows at work in the construction of a dream narrative. Should we see the artist as joker, *consciously* allowing his readers unrepeatable moments of libidinous liberation? Or should we see him as a neurotic patient, allowing the reader as analyst to interpret his desire, which is best transmitted by a deliberate *loss* of conscious narrative control? Above all, there is the problem of how the reader, whether invited to rehearse in the mind the imagery offered by the poet, or to undertake a quasi-psychoanalytic interpretation, can in any real sense re-enact the unconscious position of the writer, can genuinely preserve the power to regenerate a set of new, free associations.

'We are the words, we are the music . . . '

If the lesson I have tried to draw from my reading of Freud's and Breton's aesthetic positions is that the Modernist reader is bound to be transported into a participatory posture, becoming the self-analysing reader and writer of her/his own imagery, it is with no very different intention that I now wish to turn to an alternative strand of the Modernist image, that of Symbolism.

I argued earlier that Symbolism had a largely Platonic premise. Yet it was Mallarmé himself at the end of his life who produced an extraordinary experimental text which seemed to jettison transcendence. The poem, *Un Coup de dés* (1897)[20] is a cumulative single image, a single vast sentence, but so protracted as to become an area within which to hunt, invent or create meaning, rather than a statement, even of a symbolic kind. This poem seems to be the datable moment when the organic image is superseded by the negative, self-reflexive implosion of the Modernist image. In his preface Mallarmé declares that the blank paper will 'intrude every time that an image, spontaneously, ceases or recurs, accepting succession by others', and that the regular metric or phonetic structure of verse will yield to 'prismatic subdivisions of the Idea, their momentary appearance and momentary contribution, their accurate mental dramatisation'. The text will prevail intermittently, 'sometimes near, sometimes far from the latent main thread, according to a principle of verisimilitude'.[21] The verisimilitude is not that of external reality but that of the fluctuating drama of the mind; the images are no longer overarching symbols, but fragments of the struggle of the mind to represent its own activity to itself in an attempt to create meaning. In this key statement of Modernism, Mallarmé evokes the fragmentation of ideas as well as vision; he reduces the intellectual to the status of image-component, albeit one as fraught and forceful as the visual and emotional ones. And indeed, although there is an overall symbolic vision in the poem, referring to a foundering ship and its master, this area of symbolism is intersected with the philosophical image of the dice-throw standing for chance, which appears to be enacted textually in the random scatter of the words over the page rather than conventionally argued or symbolized. These leading symbols are disturbingly, irrationally merged on occasions; on other occasions the debris of shipwreck turns back into the self-induced wreckage of the writing of imagery:

Choit
        la plume
                rythmique suspens du sinistre
[*Falls / the quill / rhythmic suspense of disaster left pending*].

However, the powerful spatialization of syntax, of thinking, of imagining is further fragmented by the agglutination of what seem to be self-magnetizing images which overrun the contours of rational thought and realistic description, just as the pagination, in pursuit of its own emotional, visual or linguistic logic, strives to replace syntactic logic. Even the performative vector implodes: the text in straining to catch its own formulation throws up individual words as suddenly absurd concrete items, seemingly unavailable to the controlling intellect, insubordinate even to the rationalizing manipulation of typography (which has taken on the role of vestigial sign-system, the only one left in control of any systematic sense, after the demise of punctuation and prosody); the text ultimately becomes a prey to brutal eruptions of blankness which destroy its efforts towards linear expression:

soucieux
     expiatoire et pubère
           muet
             rire
              que
              SI

[*worried / (in) adolescent atonement / mute(ly) / (to) laugh / that / IF*].

Mallarmé in this extraordinary poem, immediately perceived as revolutionary by his first reader, Valéry, seems to spurn in advance the elaborate stages of Freud's symbolic transformation of desire into concentrated imagery, as he does Breton's facility in generating serial imagery. The poem lacks pattern to such an extent that even its external guise of consecutive and performative utterance fails to attain significant realization. It makes gestures towards statement, but it formulates itself only inchoately, negatively, hypothetically, and *in medias res*: ('UN COUP DE DES / JAMAIS /QUAND BIEN MEME ... [*A DICE THROW / NEVER / EVEN IF ...*].'). It has no message but that it has happened, leaving no substance ('RIEN N'AURA EU LIEU QUE LE LIEU' [*NOTHING WILL HAVE TAKEN PLACE BUT THE PLACE*]). Language has become spectacle, the image has become event. The poem dramatizes the unspoken aporia of the unconscious mind, in the guise of disruptive blanks and non sequiturs, always available to consciousness in the moment of their disappearance, instead of recording the mind's rational, descriptive, analytic or narrative projects, or painting an organic imaginative picture of its visions. In his preface, Mallarmé evokes symphonic form, but if the poem is the score that he says it is, it is one that has to be played according to the reader's mental arrangement, and one which foregrounds the 'interruptive' form of the unconscious posited by Malcolm Bowie in the previous essay.

This dynamic enactment of the irrational intellectual and emotional drama underlying language lay undeveloped for two decades, until Apollinaire in his turn saw how spatialization of linguistic form could be decisively innovative. Apollinaire referred to a notion of the unconscious, and to its link with creativity, in *Calligrammes* (1918). He evokes the hidden depths of the mind, notably in 'Les Collines':

> Tomorrow we shall explore
> The depths of the mind
> And who knows what live creatures
> We may draw from the abyss
> Bringing with them new worlds[22]

and in 'La Jolie Rousse':

> We want to present you with strange and enormous dominions
> Where mystery blooms and invites you to pluck it
> Where new lights blaze, and unseen colours,
> And a thousand unimaginable fantasies
> Which need us to give them reality.[23]

Yet, rather than this somewhat Romantic vision of mental depths and the fantastic, what is typically Modernist in the poems themselves is the refusal to elaborate a structured network of argument or symbolism; the tendency to present a series of irrational images which express mental activity in contingent visual and sensory form, above all in terms of desire. This invasion by the unconscious is most apparent in the less didactic poems, where the images enact the fragmentation and the free association of perception and of unstructured mental activity. There is more than a relaxed style of 'vers libre' in the most associative poems of *Calligrammes*, such as 'Liens' and 'Les Fenêtres'. They appear to be structured along a vector of semantic or phonetic suggestion, or visual reminiscence. 'Liens'[24] develops linear associations linking ropes, telegraph wires, railway lines, rain, smoke, rays of light – but there is a driving force, that of anxiety and desire, as motifs of strangling and screaming and weeping break through the geometric surface imagery. 'Les Fenêtres'[25] opens with an explosion of colourful violence, albeit almost abstract, like the Delaunay painting it orignally accompanied: 'From red to green all the yellow dies away'. The realistic reference to the urban windows dissolves into wild and unrelated arabesques:

> Le pauvre jeune homme se mouchait dans sa cravate blanche
> Tu souleveras le rideau
> Et maintenant voilà que s'ouvre la fenêtre
> Araignées quand les mains tissaient la lumière.

[*The poor young man blew his nose on his white tie*
You will raise the curtain
And now the window opens
Spiders when hands wove the light.]

Here it is perhaps the irrelevant and absent fly ('mouche') accidentally evoked by the nose-blowing ('se mouchait') which spins the hand into the figure of a spider weaving light. Elsewhere the text acts out visually the tense rhythms of the city – which I try to capture in a deliberately loose translation:

> Tours
> Les Tours ce sont les rues
> Puits
> Puits ce sont des places
> Puits,

> [*Tower blocks*
> *Block the streets*
> *Well then*
> *The walled squares make square*
> *Wells*].

In a dizzying mixture of visual association (buildings resemble vertical streets, gaps between buildings plunge like wells), of performance (the lines themselves take on the shape of buildings and the gaps between them), and verbal punning ('puits' = 'wells', 'puis' = 'then'), the poem proceeds almost at random, with different irrational forces driving it from one image to the next. The logical outcome of this technique, which Apollinaire wrote out in 'Lundi rue Christine',[26] is the verbal equivalent of a collage. Just as in a Picasso collage only the superficial shapes, or sometimes the related colours or contexts, of divergent materials reconcile their disparity of reference, perspective, and texture, so in Apollinaire the accidental echoes of similar sounds or semantic clusters will throw together otherwise unrelated words, creating new, unplanned and even unsuspected images. On the face of it the poem becomes invaded with external objects and events – conversations overheard, the clatter of saucers on a café counter, the sight of a cat walking across the floor – but the presence of a mind casually processing the experience is also indicated ('Looks like that rhymes'). And at one point a fluid concatenation of female and feline, of rippling, flowing darkness, of hardness and softness (crimped waffles, fur coat, black cat, fountain, black dress, black-varnished finger nails, malachite ring) brings the desirous, associative mind – of reader as much as author – to the fore.

Some of the poems of *Alcools* (1914) attempt to stage the very process whereby the mental event is transposed into imagery. In a poem like 'Cortège'[27] Apollinaire makes the image enact the difficult process of its own formulation ('oiseau tranquille au vol inverse oiseau' [*bird quietly flying backward bird*]); in 'Les Fiançailles'[28] he shows his awareness of self being tentatively constructed from a series of images:

> I bravely looked behind
> The corpses of my days
> Milestones on my road I'm missing
> Rotting in Italian churches
> Unless they're stuck on lemon trees
> . . .
>
> And other days have wept in pubs and died
> Where blazing posies catherine-wheeled
> With half-caste girls inventing poesy
> Electric never-fading roses
> Still blooming in my memory.

Apollinaire's text turns inward towards the activity of the image itself, both as signal of the presence of meaningful creative activity, and as substance contributing to the construction of a self from an amalgam of imagery – a construction that seemingly ignores the usual criteria of self-imagery (intelligibility, a fixed mental viewpoint, psychological consistency). This turning inwards is allied to the creation of verse which rejects literary and moral standards of seriousness, aesthetic unity, cultural communicability, and is explicitly foregrounded in the performative aspect of the Modernist image as commented on in Apollinaire's poem 'Zone':[29]

> And the image possessing you ensures your survival in
> insomnia and anguish
> It's always close by you that passing image.

The collage of images in 'Zone', where mental events and external observation coexist indiscriminately, reveals the self not only in the plurality of its experience, but also in the mobility of its responses and perceptions. There is quite simply no neatly buried self to be discovered, only a self being constructed as it discovers images of its activity reflected in the fragmented world, whether internal or external – here an omnibus, there an amorous encounter, here a factory siren, there a childhood memory. Thus for Apollinaire the image is not a simple vision of the inner self, any more than it is of the outside world, but a difficult, exhilarating moment of confrontation, a shifting analogical formulation of the perceiving and experiencing mind.

This desire-driven drifting of the mind is only one side of the psychic collage performed by Apollinaire. The force of the desire is as often present in the fracturing of the smooth running of the verse. Thus at the beginning of 'L'Emigrant de Landor Road'[30] the reader is led by the unpunctuated verse into a scene of decapitation before being allowed to readjust the events into something more harmless:

> The merchant cut off sundry heads
> Of tailor's dummies,

but the violent fantasy of decapitation is not entirely eliminated. It festers subliminally, anticipating the generalized upswell of the irrational imagery which comes to swamp the end of the poem. It is as if the imagery has been unwittingly driven by pain of separation and fantasy of departure which have deflected it from its original descriptive project:

> Gonfle-toi vers la nuit O Mer Les yeux des squales
> Jusqu'à l'aube ont guetté de loin avidement
> Des cadavres de jours rongés par les étoiles
> Parmi le bruit des flots et les derniers serments
>
> [*Swell nightwards Sea The eyes of sharks*
> *Have dawnlong hungrily laid wait*
> *for corpsey days devoured by stars*
> *Amid last rites and crashing waves*].

As well as finding a fluid form for the expression of timeless desire, and recycling old symbols ('Bergère ô tour Eiffel . . .' [*Shepherdess, oh Eiffel Tower*], in 'Zone'), Apollinaire was an articulate spokesman for a revolutionary new art that would match the revolution in communications of the turning century. In 'L'Espirit nouveau et les poètes'[31] he argues that developments in technology and communications have made the experiences of modern life 'simultaneous', and that modern art responds to this in its form. Technology seems the opposite of the unconscious, yet Apollinaire's point is that telecommunications can reflect the dynamism of the multi-layered mind better than conventional writing.

In various domains he tries to overcome the limitations imposed by the sequential and linear nature of writing, and imitate the immediacy of modern telecommunications. In his *Calligrammes* he tries to spatialize form. This obliges the reader to re-invent the associative process which generated the poet's imagery, rather than automatically to repeat links offered by the poet in a pre-established order. The title of 'La Colombe poignardée et le jet d'eau',[32] for instance, sets up certain narrative and symbolic expectations.

The dove of love or peace, although its shape is constructed from girls' names, is stabbed with the Caesarian cry 'Et toi Marie'. The fountain, we realize, is constructed from lines lamenting lost friends, and as the semi-circular layers of the text are explored, the semantic imagery starts inflecting our reading of the surrounding visual imagery. The lament turns the curving lines into tears, into the echoes of steps, into the vaults of churches, into the arcs of tombstones, into the traces of names in memory. What appeared at first to be merely the picture of an oval pool of water collecting the falling spray of words at the bottom of the page becomes a staring eye, a screaming mouth, a sea of blood, a flower bed, as our reception of it interacts with the statements composing it. And no discursive gloss within the poem gives a metalanguage to privilege one particular reading of the image cluster. Nothing verbal relates the dove to the fountain. Meaning has to be inferred spatially. The romantic reading of the dove dying of cupid's dart beside the fountain yields, perhaps, to more sombre visions of slaughtered relationships, frozen nature, rivers of blood, fading experience. Or the spread-eagled bird composed of girls' names bayoneted (spayed?) by a spurt composed of men's names may throw up other suggestions, perhaps not formulated by Apollinaire. Apollinaire enables his reader to create new imagery. Nor is it possible to predict the moments at which the reader's reactions to the visual shape will irrationally overdetermine the semantic rationale of the text, will block, divert, develop or contradict it.

'. . . . we are the thing itself'[33]

Like those of Apollinaire, Eliot's theoretical statements of the activities of the unconscious mind might seem superficially unexciting. He has perhaps assimilated the Freudian orthodoxy of the libidinous sources of the dream, but he simplifies, suggesting, like Breton, that the dream displays untransformed pictures of desire to the beholder. The activity of the mind, reduced to a pile of discrete images, is none the less couched in self-reflexive terms:

> You dozed, and watched the night revealing
> The thousand sordid images of which your soul was constituted;
> ('Preludes', *Prufrock*, 1917).

Memory for Eliot also distorts, but seems to present perverted experience homogeneously, without obvious censorship. Yet here again the hidden libidinous premise is perhaps covertly acknowledged, as is the disjunction between the conscious mind and its deeper concerns, which are figured as a collection of multiple single objects:

> The memory throws up high and dry
> A crowd of twisted things
> ('Rhapsody on a Windy Night', *Prufrock*, 1917)

But, like that of Apollinaire again, Eliot's achievement cannot be limited to his theoretical claims or allusions. In the first place, Eliot's starting point is not the contents and workings of the individual mind, but a new appreciation of the collective mind. Although we might be tempted to see the artist as an individual, creating culture which then becomes collective property, Eliot insists on the extent to which the artist is at first also a consumer of public imagery. For him, the private image derives from an anterior image, as it does for Breton and Freud, but from the rather more Jungian collective psyche of religion, anthropology, literature, not the personal unconscious. Indeed, the crisis of Modernism, for Eliot, is a crisis in the community of shared culture and imagery. Eliot's collage of old images is a collage of literary images, that is, of second-degree representations, which have already been mediated through texts and received as pre-formed images. But where once they informed and enriched our spiritual depths, they now remind us that our collective unconscious of a unified culture has been broken. Yet as the images come in fragments, it is only those irrational fragments that can signal our lost depth and preserve it in patches. Eliot will try to use single images, wrecked fragments of a lost spiritual culture, to reconstruct at least a collage or perhaps a mosaic, building a precarious permanence out of the unconscious associations that even the fragments bring with them, particularly in their suggestively aporetic assemblage:

> You cannot say, or guess, for you know only
> A heap of broken images . . .
> These fragments I have shored against my ruins
> (*The Waste Land*, 1922).

Eliot's clearest statement of the means by which the poet could come to terms with this collapse of values and reconstruct a meaningful experience through the obliquity of imagery was in his essay on 'Hamlet' (1919), where he argues that: 'The only way of expressing emotion in the form of art is by finding an "objective correlative", in other words, a set of objects, a situation, a chain of events which shall be the formula of that *particular* emotion; such that when the external facts, which must terminate in sensory experience, are given, the emotion is immediately evoked.'[34]

Where for Freud the finished image disguises the unconscious, for Eliot it tries to retrieve and recreate what is left of it. As with many poets, the practice implies a theory more creative and exciting than any explicit statement. However much the individual images of *The Waste Land* fulfil

Eliot's brief of moving out from their objectal fragmentation into the evocation of a state of mind, the poem is much more than the sum of its individual images, and the mood which they evoke. It is their juxtaposition and collage, their quotation and enigma, the sheer opaque mystery of them, which recreates in the reader not only a vertiginous diving down into the depths of the individual soul, but also a sense of the rich, violent, shifting nature of the unconscious, an unconscious which reaches out into areas of mystical or social experience that are lost, and yet leave their nostalgic echo.

It is a sobering experience, however, to study the draft of *The Waste Land* which Pound edited, abruptly changing Eliot's witty but discursive and regular verse into an impromptu mosaic of fragmentary images with gaps in their intellectual progression.[35] Eliot must no doubt be given credit for his extraordinarily *schadenfreundlich* decision to publish as such the mutilated, unreconstructed poem, which instantly created a new fragmented style of imagistic collage, instead of rewriting it, as we (and perhaps Pound himself?) might have expected. Ezra Pound himself had of course already perfected the style and the rationale of this disjointed 'Imagisme' in his 'Imagiste' movement. The image announces itself as image; it signals the presence of poetic creativity; it constitutes itself as the essence of poetry, rejecting centuries of rhyme and rhythm. It becomes so dominant that the work of art is often reduced to the single image, rather even than a cluster or a collage.

Pound was tempted by a direct grasping of the thing itself. His 'Imagisme' was as much an attack on Symbolism as on Romanticism. Objects become images, images become objects. But his theory does not take us back to a naive, pre-Symbolist world, where a single word may designate a single concept, despite his occasional theoretical simplification: 'Use no super-fluous word, no adjective, which does not reveal something.'[36] For the 'direct treatment of the "thing", whether subjective or objective',[37] allows the referent to be a complex mental event:

> An 'image' is that which presents an intellectual and emotional complex in an instant of time. I use the term 'complex' rather in the technical sense employed by the newer psychologists, such as Hart, though we might not agree absolutely in our appreciation.
>
> It is the presentation of such a 'complex' instantaneously which gives that sense of sudden liberation; that sense of freedom from time limits and space limits; that sudden sense of growth, which we experience in the presence of the greatest works of art.[38]

As in Eliot, we find the idea of an essential internal form (at once intellectual and emotional) being traced and expressed obliquely, but instantaneously, fragmentarily. The image is not the catalytic link in an associative chain that it was in Freud, not the explosively liberating collection of separate mental fragments that it was in Breton. The reference to Hart, a popularizer of

Freud, warns us to look for a complex working below the level of consciousness, seeking transcendence only within the psyche. It is perhaps as much in its structure as in its content that the image expresses the mental event. One can see this in the concentrated poetic work of the early Pound, as in the following famous poem, best read, no doubt, as a three-line haiku where the title is also the first line:

> IN A STATION OF THE METRO
> The apparition of these faces in the crowd
> Petals on a wet, black bough.[39]

The superficial juxtaposition of the urban image and the Japanese pastoral is not as 'hard and clear' as Pound claimed that poetry should be.[40] A Christian unconscious clings to the moment of illumination of this anti-Christian poet (the 'station' [of the cross]; the 'apparition' [of Christ]; perhaps even a kind of horizontal crucifixion or a post-Baptismal decollation). But even within the more superficial connotations of the imagery used by Pound, we have a suggestion of irrational beauty formed unintentionally by an urban vision or rather, the sudden surge of both aesthetic and natural urges in the mind of the subject perceiving an urban scene. The city is reduced to the most meaningless fragment, but that fragment electrifies the grid of the analytic structures of our simultaneously rationalizing and associative minds to form a more complex image, through the mediation of Japanese painting and Christian mythology, an image which incorporates the alienation and nostalgia of the viewer. Through a coincidence of fragmentary images Pound achieves a vista of multiple mental layering. Once again, the reader has to work through his/her own associations, there is no reading imposed by the poet. Pound presents the process of image-formation, he refuses to represent the end result of the image once processed.

The renewal of European literature through the efforts of transatlantic writers is only an apparent paradox. Pound and Eliot were steeped in the traditions of European literature. Political Europe may have been an 'old bitch gone in the teeth' for Pound, and spiritual Europe 'Waste Land' peopled with 'Hollow Men' for Eliot, but the ideal literary models for these two Modernists were the Provençal troubadours and the English metaphysicals. For Pound the medieval courtly lyric had achieved a concentrated language of feeling which was preferable to Romantic and Symbolist verbiage, and for Eliot it was John Donne's 'conceit' (the complex but unified cluster of imagery) which had last expressed the reconciliation of sensibility and intelligence.

In the new idiom of Modernist English, as shorn of transcendental French Symbols as it is of English Romantic effusion, it is Pound's disciple William Carlos Williams who most acutely expresses the split consciousness and self-reflexive linguistic processes of the post-Freudian mind, and transposes these intuitions into a new imagery. Remembering 'To a Solitary Disciple', the poem which I quoted at the outset in contrast to the poetry of psycho-therapeutic release, we find that it invokes an intellectual, formal, perceptual area of imagery, in preference to a decorative and sensory imagery. Yet the poem actually produces, and notes the intrusiveness of, the opaque ornamental imagery which its perceptual imagery overtly negates:

> Rather grasp
> how the dark
> converging lines
> of the steeple
> meet at the pinnacle —
> perceive how
> its little ornament
> tries to stop them —
>
> See how it fails!

The process of production of meaningful imagery, with its tense dramatic conflict between two simultaneous mental and figurative strategies, enacts a rhetorical failure. The model of the steeple is constructed so that it echoes the operations of the conscious mind, reaching out and upwards for meaning, but there is a disjunction with the visual and sensory image of the moon, looming irrelevantly but seductively, from beyond conscious control, as if from within. Yet we have a process more complex than the enactment of a struggle between rival image-forming areas of the mind. The poem performs an experience of conceptual instability challenging any straight-forward compartmentalization of rhetoric according to diverse mental stratification. The contours of the mental faculties originally suggested are disturbed. An elusive kinetic experience is figured, a process of polymor-phous exchange. The once sensory image of the irreducible moon becomes strangely aerial, and the linear mental figure that tried to integrate it into an orderly emotional and intellectual structure becomes massively earth-bound:

> Observe
> how motionless
> the eaten moon
> lies in the protecting lines.
> It is true:
> in the light colours
> of morning

brown-stone and slate
shine orange and dark blue.

But observe
the oppressive weight
of the squat edifice!
Observe
the jasmine lightness
of the moon

In this exquisite language of self-critical image-production, intermittent intellectual insight and rhetorical failure, we have, of course, the terms of critical self-scrutiny allied to opaquely allusive process which are the keynotes of Modernism and its creative splitting of consciousness. Williams's complex image presents the world as objective correlative, it also enacts the structure of vision reaching out to relate to that mediated world and failing to grasp it, as well as the coincidence of the two within a moment of charged mental and emotional energy. Williams's work, like that of Pound, suggests an unfinished work of imagination and interpretation to be undertaken within the range of his/her own mental associations by every new reader. The intellectual and emotional 'complex' liberates from conscious time and space and leads us back into our own unconscious, by exploring simultaneously our vision and our process. As we explore these enigmatic images on the fringes of consciousness, we may experience that fugitive moment of self-coincidence sought by Pound, the 'precise instant when a thing outward and objective transforms itself, or darts into a thing inward and subjective',[41] we may experience that sudden sense of growth: then the Modernist text will have turned its readers into writers.

Notes

1   E. Pound 'A few don'ts for Imagistes' (*Poetry*, March 1923), quoted in P. Jones (ed.), *Imagist Poetry* (Penguin, Harmondsworth, 1972), p. 130.
2   With apologies to Beckett for not thinking the imagination as dead as he does.
3   F. Kermode, *Romantic Image* (1957; repr. Ark Paperbacks, London, 1986).
4   W. C. Williams, 'To a Solitary Disciple', in *Al Que Quiere!* (1917), *Selected Poems* (Penguin, Harmondsworth, 1976), pp. 31–2.
5   A. Breton and P. Soupault, 'Bulletins', *Les Champs magnétiques* (1919) (Gallimard (Poésie), Paris, 1971). This translation is my own, as are all other translations in this chapter.
6   T. S. Eliot, 'The Metaphysical Poets' (1921), in *Selected Essays* (Faber, London, 1964), p. 247.
7   cf. S. T. Coleridge, *Biographia Literaria*, ed. G. Watson (Dent, London, 1975), and J. Beer, *Coleridge's Poetic Intelligence* (Macmillan, London 1977; repr. 1986).

8   G. Marcel, *Coleridge et Schelling* (Aubier Montaigne, Paris, 1971). There is no, need to follow Marcel's neo-Platonic erudition. The original formulation of the theory of forms in the *Phaedo* is sufficient. (Marcel, p. 60, referring to Coleridge's note of 14 April 1805.) Coleridge's argument is that symbolic language recalls something already existing, but he insists on the need for *intellectual* intuition in order to attain rational knowledge of this ideal reality (letter to Wordsworth of 30 May 1815).

9   S. Mallarmé: 'Peindre non la chose, mais l'effet qu'elle produit', *Correspondance*, vol. I, 1862–1871 (Gallimard, Paris, 1957), p. 137.

10   S. Freud, *The Interpretation of Dreams* (1900), *SE*, IV and V; Pelican 4; *Jokes and their Relation to the Unconscious* (1905), *SE*, VIII; Pelican 6; *The Psychopathology of Everyday Life* (1901), *SE*, VI; Pelican 5.

11   S. Schwarz in *The Matrix of Modernism: Pound, Eliot and Early Twentieth-Century Thought* (Princeton University Press, Princeton, 1985), argues that late nineteenth-century philosophy (Bergson, James) operates an 'inverse Platonism' (finding meaning in the flux of appearances as opposed to positing meaningful structures within), which then influences the Modernist writing of Eliot and Pound. Schwarz's book is persuasive, but I think that this argument does not apply well to Freud.

12   S. Freud, *The Uncanny* (1919), *SE*, XVII; Pelican 14. See also S. Kofman, *Quatre Romans analytiques* (Galilée, Paris, 1974), and M. V. Jones, '*Der Sandmann* and "The Uncanny"'; a sketch for an alternative approach', *Paragraph*, 7 (March 1986), pp. 77–101.

13   S. Freud, *Delusions and Dreams in Jensen's 'Gradiva'* (1907), *SE* IX; Pelican 14. See also S. Kofman, *The Childhood of Art* (Columbia University Press, New York, 1988), and L. Russo, *La nascita dell'estetica di Freud* (Il Mulino, Bologna, 1983).

14   (As, at a later stage, having developed his ideas on the Oedipus complex and castration anxiety more fully, he was to see castration everywhere in *The Sandman,* and underplay the death wish, in the interest of showing the uncanny to be a return of repressed childhood fears and fantasies.)

15   A. Breton, *Manifestes du Surréalisme* (Gallimard (Idées), Paris, 1966).

16   M. Black, *Models and Metaphors* (Cornell University Press, Ithaca, 1962).

17   A. Breton, *Les Vases communicants* (1932; repr. Gallimard (Idées), Paris, 1985), p. 67.

18   ibid., p. 128.

19   ibid., p. 68.

20   S. Mallarmé, *Oeuvres Complètes*, (Gallimard (Pléiade), Paris, 1970), pp. 457–77.

21   ibid., p. 455

22   G. Apollinaire, *Oeuvres poétiques* (Gallimard (Pléiade), Paris, 1965), p. 171.

23   ibid., p. 313.

24   ibid., p. 167.

25   ibid., p. 168.

26   ibid., p. 180–1.

27   ibid., p. 74.

28   ibid., p. 131.

29   ibid., p. 39–44.

30   ibid., pp. 105–6.

31 G. Apollinaire, *L'Espirit nouveau et les poètes* (1917) (J. Haumont, Paris, 1946).
32 *Oeuvres poétiques* (Pléiade), p 213.
33 'There is no Shakespeare, there is no Beethoven; certainly and emphatically there is no God; we are the words; we are the music; we are the thing itself.' V. Woolf, 'A sketch of the past', in *Moments of Being*, ed. J. Schulkind (1976; repr. Triad Grafton, London, 1986), p. 84.
34 T. S. Eliot, 'Hamlet' (1919), in *Selected Prose* (Peregrine, Harmondsworth, 1963), p. 102.
35 T. S. Eliot, *The Waste Land*, ed. V. Eliot (Faber, London, 1971).
36 Pound, 'A few don'ts for Imagistes', in Jones, (ed.), *Imagist Poetry*, p. 131.
37 F. S. Flint, 'Imagisme' (1913), in Jones (ed.), *Imagist Poetry*, p. 129.
38 Jones (ed.), *Imagist Poetry*, p. 130.
39 E. Pound, *Selected Poems* (1975); repr. Faber, London, 1981), p. 53.
40 'Preface to *Some Imagist Poets 1915*', in Jones (ed.), *Imagist Poetry*, p. 135: 'To produce poetry that is hard and clear, never blurred nor indefinite.'
41 Quoted in ibid., p. 40.

SUGGESTED READING

Coleridge, S. T., *Biographia Literaria*, ed. G. Watson, Dent (Everyman), London, 1975.
Hulme, T. E., *Speculations*, 1924; 2nd ed, International Library of Psychology, Philosophy and Scientific Method, London, 1936.
Johnson, B.,*The Critical Difference*, Johns Hopkins University Press, Baltimore, 1980.
Jones, P. (ed.), *Imagist Poetry*, 1972; repr. Penguin, Harmondsworth, 1981.
Kermode, F., *Romantic Image*, 1957, repr. Ark Paperbacks, London, 1986.
Kofman, S., *The Childhood of Art*, Columbia University Press, New York, 1988.
Schwarz, S., *The Matrix of Modernism. Pound, Eliot and Early Twentieth-Century Thought*, Princeton University Press, Princeton, 1985.
Woolf, V., *Moments of Being*, ed. J. Schulkind, 1976; repr. Triad Grafton, London, 1986.

PART II

Fictions of the Unconscious

3

The Tyranny of the Text: Lawrence, Freud and the Modernist Aesthetic

ANNE FERNIHOUGH

In April 1918, Lawrence was reading *The Voice of Africa* (1913), Leo Frobenius's record of his attempts to 'unriddle the surface' of a continent inhabited by aboriginal peoples with 'no recorded history'. Frobenius's voyage was precipitated by what he described as the 'European thirst for investigating the unknown', and sustained by the expectation of 'wresting some relics of antiquity every now and again from the lap of the earth'.[1] During the same period, Freud had been concerning himself, in his 1915 paper *The Unconscious* (*SE*, XIV, p. 195), with the 'aboriginal population' inhabiting what he would later call, in his *New Introductory Lectures on Psycho-Analysis* (1933), the 'internal foreign territory' of the mind (*SE*, XXII, p. 57); and he likened his researches to the unearthing of the long-buried relics of Pompeii (*Notes upon a Case of Obsessional Neurosis*, *SE*, X, p. 176). In 1921, Lawrence published his bitter indictment of Freud, *Psychoanalysis and the Unconscious*, written 'to establish the smallest foothold in the swamp of vagueness which now goes by the name of the unconscious',[2] and not long afterwards came *Fantasia of the Unconscious* (1922), for which Lawrence cites Frobenius as one of his sources.

Frobenius entitles his preface to *The Voice of Africa* 'Fiat Lux': he sets out to shed light, as he tells us, over Stanley's 'dark continent' (p. xiv). Freud's parallel project is that of reclaiming land from the primordial chaos of the unconscious mind, and again the opening of Genesis provides the analogue: 'Where id was, there ego shall be. It is a work of culture – not unlike the draining of the Zuider Zee' (*New Introductory Lectures*, *SE*, XXII, p. 80). While Frobenius and his co-imperialists scar the African earth with their 'spades' and 'picks', Freud, the self-styled 'conquistador',[3] engages in his colonization of the human psyche. These geopolitical and psychic models merge in Lawrence's *Studies in Classic American Literature* (1923), one of the earliest examples of an extended work of psychoanalytic criticism, where the American texts are seen in terms of 'the development of the orthodox European ideal on American soil', an enactment of colonization. The French-American writer Crèvecoeur, for instance, 'invents from his own ego' as a European, while his 'rudimentary', 'aboriginal' vision enables him to see 'insects, birds and snakes in their own pristine being'. The hunting down of the whale in Melville's *Moby Dick* becomes the tracking down and subduing of unconscious forces, and the capture of Moby Dick himself, a gleaming white trophy, symbolizes 'the last attainment of extended consciousness', the triumph of Lawrence's 'white' consciousness, his own version of the Freudian ego.[4]

Lawrence's attack on Freud, in the opening paragraph of *Psychoanalysis and the Unconscious*, as 'the psychiatric quack who vehemently demonstrated the serpent of sex coiled round the root of all our actions' is well known. The Biblical allusion, typical of Lawrence's references to psychoanalysis, makes it clear that Freud, in seeking to 'redeem' humanity through the 'civilizing' powers of the ego, had somehow, for Lawrence, only re-inscribed the Fall. Here Nietzsche provides a clue. Nietzsche was one of the philosophers to familiarize Lawrence with the unconscious long before he had even heard of the Freudian model. Readings in Hegel, Schopenhauer, Herbart and Nietzsche are all recorded as early as 1908; but it was Nietzsche who saw the overdeveloped consciousness of the European psyche as a 'sickness', and who provided the link, in *Ecce Homo* (1908) between self-analysis or 'clarity about oneself', and uncleanliness.[5] Lawrence's study of the American classics becomes the story of the 'fallen Puritan psyche' (*The Symbolic Meaning*, p. 168), fallen in the sense that mind and body have become tragically separated, severing sex from the spirit which alone, for Lawrence, validates it. The instrument of the Fall is seen to have been, in other words, an insatiable intellectual curiosity, synonymous for Lawrence with an insatiable lust for power.

At the root, then, of Lawrence's objection to Freud is the concept of the ego as a coercive occupying force. In a parody of the Hegelian master/slave dialectic employed so frequently by Freud, the ego's mastery becomes for Lawrence a horrifying mental tyranny, a subjection of the spontaneous sources of being to the 'psychic-mechanical law' (*The Symbolic Meaning*, p. 59). In a striking reversal of Freud's equation of the 'primitive' with something 'older in time' and 'nearer to the perceptual end' in psychical topography (*The Interpretation of Dreams*, SE, V, p. 548), we witness a rampant intellectual barbarism, a taking over of 'the remnants of the once civilized world-people, who had their splendour and their being for countless centuries in the way of sensual knowledge . . . It is we from the North, starting new centres of life in ourselves, who have become young' (*The Symbolic Meaning*, p. 223). This in turn leads to a reversal of the Freudian teleology as regards the Oedipus complex.

Lawrence probably first encountered Freudian theory (in a diluted and perhaps distorted form) on meeting Frieda Weekley in 1912, and subsequently through discussions with Freudian analysts David Eder and

Barbara Low in 1914. Frieda, who was by her own account 'full of undigested theories' about Freud on meeting Lawrence,[6] undoubtedly left her mark on the final revision of *Sons and Lovers* (1913). None the less Lawrence's first novel, *The White Peacock* (1911), together with certain of the early short stories ('The Shades of Spring', 'A Modern Lover'), makes it clear that at least some of his views on 'the unconscious', and in particular his critique of the 'self-consciousness' of modern civilization, were already firmly established before any recorded knowledge of Freud. Those critics who greeted *Sons and Lovers* as a 'Freudian' novel failed to take into account the fact that Paul Morel's predicament differs from Freud's Oedipus complex in certain crucial respects.

In a 1912 paper entitled *On the Universal Tendency to Debasement in the Sphere of Love* (*SE*, XI, pp. 177–90), Freud distinguishes between two libidinal currents, the 'affectionate' and the 'sensual' currents. The 'affectionate' current goes back to the earliest years of infancy and directs itself in the first instance towards those people who minister to the child's basic needs. It does, however, carry along with it certain 'components of erotic interest', which are usually directed towards the mother or mother-surrogates and are accompanied by hostility towards and fear of the father. This fear represents itself in the child's mind as the threat of castration, and leads to the suppression of the incestuous wishes. With the onset of puberty, however, the affectionate current is joined by the 'sensual' current, cathecting the object or objects of the primary infantile choice with quotas of libido which are now far stronger, but in the meantime a barrier against incest has been erected. If the child's attachment to his infantile object-choices is too great (and this, Freud stresses, is directly connected to the amount of 'affection' shown by those caring for the child), the libido retreats into a realm of imaginative activity and becomes fixated to those first object-choices. In cases of what Freud terms 'psychical impotence', the adolescent's 'sensual' current manages to find some outlet, but in a severely restricted way, seeking only those objects which do not recall the incestuous figures forbidden to it. Freud goes on to argue that 'if someone makes an impression that might lead to a high psychical estimation of her, this impression does not find an issue in any sensual excitation but in affection which has no erotic effect. The whole sphere of love in such people remains divided in the two directions personified in art as sacred and profane (animal) love' (pp. 182–3).

Although the symptoms of Freud's hypothetical complex bear a striking resemblance to Paul Morel's situation in *Sons and Lovers* (Paul's 'spiritual' love is directed towards Miriam Lievers, who has obvious affinities with Mrs Morel, while Clara Dawes corresponds to the 'harlot' figure of Freudian fantasy), we should not lose sight of the fact that when Lawrence finally came to formulate his ideas on the *cause* of such problems, in his two treatises on the unconscious, his account differed radically from Freud's. Lawrence does not make Freud's distinction between 'affectionate' and 'sensual' currents; rather, he explains his own version of the Oedipus complex in terms which correspond more closely to the Freudian ego and id. He divides the child's responses into two main categories, the 'sympathetic' (roughly corresponding to a spiritual response, uncontaminated by sexuality), and the 'voluntary' (indicating a passional or sexual response). Where for Freud the child's libidinal impulses towards its parents exist as it were from the beginning, constituting a part of the 'cauldron of seething excitement' which is the Freudian id, for Lawrence the Oedipal situation originates in a kind of invasion of the id by the ego. More specifically, it originates in the excessive parental fostering of the child's 'sympathetic' centres, in what is a kind of *'spiritual* incest' (*Fantasia of the Unconscious*, p. 118; italics in original). This sparks off a corresponding activity in the child's 'lower', 'voluntary' centres, which, however, refuses to connect with the mother (or, one might infer, with anyone resembling the mother). We are back on a more domestic level to the excessive emphasis on the intellect, on what Lawrence terms the 'ideal', which he attributes to the psychoanalytic enterprise as a whole: 'This motivizing of the passional sphere from the ideal', Lawrence warns, 'is the final peril of human consciousness. It is the death of all spontaneous, creative life, and the substituting of the mechanical principle' (*Psychoanalysis of the Unconscious*, p. 207).

Behind the domination of the ego which Lawrence sees to be central to Freud's project lies the complicity between textuality and power or coercion. Lawrence sees a violence lurking in the very 'framing' of reality into a language-system which must take place before we can have any positive or communicable knowledge, and thus before we can embark upon the scientific endeavours which for Lawrence always lead to the domination of nature. In this sense, 'The mind is the instrument of instruments; it is not a creative reality' (*Psychoanalysis and the Unconscious*, p. 246). Freud, in attempting to 'frame' the unconscious, fails to respect what Lawrence calls its 'untranslatable otherness' (*The Symbolic Meaning*, p. 17). Long before Lacan and Derrida, Lawrence argues that, since there is no metalanguage, Freud's hermeneutic enterprise is misguided. Freud is seen by Lawrence to diminish the unconscious into concepts which can never pretend to more than a provisional status, and thus to be a product of the 'disintegration', the tragic mind/body division which is the sickness of modern society. As we shall see, the epistemology known as 'Modernism' represents, among other things, an attempt to heal this division.

For Lawrence, then, psychoanalysis is not only an epistemology of the unknowable, but it is, in medical terms, a 'symptom' of the sicknesses, the psychic imbalances, it claims to cure. For Freud, in Lawrence's view, is nothing if not 'repressive' himself, engaging in the repressive interpretation of the psychic text. Dispensing with conscious or surface intention, he becomes intentionalist in a new way; indeed, he becomes, for Lawrence, the archetypal intentionalist critic in his semantic precision, his determination to 'decipher' the elements of the text and to trace them back to a solid bedrock of psychoanalytic 'truth'. J. Hillis Miller, in his 1976 essay 'Stevens'

Rock and Criticism as Cure, II', conflates Nietzschean and Freudian terminologies by dividing critics into two groups: 'Socratic, theoretical or canny critics on the one hand, and Apollonian/Dionysian, tragic, or uncanny critics on the other'.[7] The Nietzschean categories employed here are also central to Lawrence's epistemology. In section XV of *The Birth of Tragedy* (1872), Nietzsche speaks of Socrates in connection with 'the illusion that thought, guided by the thread of causation, might plumb the farthest abysses of being and even *correct* it'.[8] Freud's obsession with causality would seem at first sight to place him in Miller's 'Socratic' category; it becomes clear, however, that Freud has admitted elements into his procedure which are subversive of the causal chain when he repudiates the notion that it is possible to predict whether a person will develop a neurosis or not. His enterprise, we come to realise, is more hermeneutical than strictly 'scientific', and his analyses can only be retrospective. Lawrence is one of the first to draw attention to this 'retrospective teleology' in Freud. The analyst, Lawrence suggests, provides a view of the patient's history which the patient projects back onto reality and then experiences. It is in this sense that, for Lawrence, 'the Freudian unconscious is the cellar in which the mind keeps its own bastard spawn' (*Psychoanalysis and the Unconscious*, p. 204).

In Lawrence's view, then, Freud's quest for the unconscious in its pristine form is a hopeless one if it is to be conducted along the signifying chains of language. Indeed Freud's descriptions of the unconscious, as if in acknowledgement of the fact that it will forever remain recalcitrant to the constraints of a 'fallen' language, are pervaded by the imagery of the *signifier*: he compares the interpretation of dreams to 'the decipherment of an ancient pictographic script such as Egyptian hieroglyphs', and informs us that 'the unconscious speaks more than one dialect'. Whether these 'dialects' are 'gesture-languages' (hysteria), 'picture-languages' (dreams), or 'thought-languages' (obsessional neuroses), there is a sense that none of them can quite penetrate to this stubbornly elusive 'signified' (*The Claims of Psycho-Analysis to Scientific Interest*, SE, XIII, pp. 177–8).

Freud seems, then, to be aware of the quixotic no man's land in which psychoanalysis resides: his essay on Leonardo is, he confesses, 'partly fiction',[9] yet at the same time he grants a paradoxical validity to the insights of literature as a supplementary form of 'scientific' evidence (*Delusions and Dreams in Jensen's* Gradiva, SE, IX, p. 8). He explains that he is obliged to operate with 'the figurative language peculiar to psychology' and points out that even if he were able to use physiological and chemical terms, they too would be figurative, not the mimetic discourse of a positivist science (*Beyond the Pleasure Principle*, SE, XVIII, p. 60). Time and again, his pursuit leads us into alogical and absurd situations; his notion of regression to some origin or bedrock, seems only to lead to infinite regress, to the point at which, in Nietzsche's words, 'logic . . . curls about itself and bites its own tail' (*The Birth of Tragedy*, p. 95).

Derrida's well-known deconstruction of Freud, in *Writing and Difference*

(1978), has shown us how in any meditation on origins (if 'origin' is to denote some kind of authenticity or essence), the object of the interpretative quest is always deferred. In a startling adumbration of Derrida's celebrated description of the unconscious text as 'a text nowhere present, consisting of archives which are *always already* transcriptions' in which 'Everything begins with reproduction,'[10] Lawrence dismisses the contents of the Freudian unconscious as 'spawn produced by secondary propagation from the mental consciousness itself' (*Psychoanalysis and the Unconscious*, p. 204). The reverse side of the coin here, as Derrida shows, is that when we supposedly 'translate' the terms of the unconscious into conscious terms, all we have, as opposed to a derived origin, is an originary secondariness. In other words, where some psychoanalysts might choose to see their discipline as a 'bridge', it can more pessimistically be seen to articulate a 'gap'.

By insisting on a teleology or history of sexuality, Freud is forced into adopting the enabling fiction of the 'primal repression' (*Repression, SE*, XIV, p. 148), in which the unconscious both initiates the repression and is constituted as repression; without it his story of the psyche could not begin. For Harold Bloom in 'Freud and the Poetic Sublime' (1978), primal repression is the model for the structure of literary reference itself (and one might extend this to all reference); the retroactive installation of a referent, which language situates, through rhetoric, outside itself.[11] Lawrence is acutely aware of such problems, and therefore anxious to separate his own 'unconscious' from Freud's implicit plotting: 'When we postulate a beginning, we only do so to fix a starting-point for our thought. There never was a beginning . . .' (*The Symbolic Meaning* p. 176). Where, according to Derrida's reading of the Freudian unconscious, we are dealing 'not with horizons of modified presents – past or future – but with a 'past' that has never been present, and which never will be, whose future to come will never be a *production* or a reproduction in the form of presence',[12] for Lawrence the unconscious *is* 'the pure present, and the pure presence, of the soul – present beyond all knowing or willing. Knowing and willing . . . are as it were the reflex or *afterwards* of being' (*The Symbolic Meaning*, p. 37; italics in original). Lawrence posits an unconscious which *is* pristine, raw, primary, uncorrupted by bias or teleology, and he does so by placing it outside and beyond any 'fallen' epistemological enterprise: 'The supreme lesson of human consciousness is to learn how *not to know*. That is, how not to *interfere*. That is, how to live dynamically, from the great source, and not statically, like machines driven by ideas and principles from the head, or automatically, from one fixed desire' (*Fantasia of the Unconscious*, p. 72; italics in orginal). This is the only escape from the circular and self-deconstructing traps which Freud lays for himself. Ideas, principles, fixed desires, all imply some kind of reification, where the Lawrentian unconscious is a mode of existence (of being and acting), not an essence.

For Lawrence, then, the unconscious operates 'beyond, where there is no speech and no terms of agreement . . . It is quite inhuman, – so there can be no calling to book, in any form whatsoever – because one is outside the pale of all that is accepted, and nothing known applies.'[13] Elsewhere, he refers to it as 'blood-consciousness, . . . the nearest thing in us to pure material consciousness' (*Fantasia of the Unconscious*, p. 171). This is, of course, a religious affirmation of the unconscious; its 'verification' through the signifying chains of logic would be of no value.

Lawrence's position in relation to 'Modernism', generally thought to be complex and problematic, is clarified considerably by his reaction to Freud. For Lawrence's aesthetic is rooted in his notion of an intractable unconscious, inaccessible to the conscious mind. When he claims, in his essay 'Morality and the Novel' (1925), that art exists in what he terms 'the fourth dimension', 'in-between everything',[14] he shows that he is involved in that challenging of disciplinary boundaries which can be seen to be central to the Modernist movement. In the essay 'Art and Morality' (1925), he praises the African fetish-statue which 'sits in the place where no kodak can snap it'.[15] Here the photographic frame becomes metaphor for any Saussurean frame or closed system; the statue is art by virtue of the fact that, like the unconscious, it knows no containment or closure; it somehow overspills all discourses or disciplines. The weakness of Victorian art was, for Lawrence, as for the Bloomsbury art critics Clive Bell and Roger Fry whose aesthetic theories were closely bound up with the Modernist movement, that it had tended towards discursivity, towards the presentation of what they termed visual 'labels'. In 'An Essay in Aesthetics' (1909), Fry explains how 'In actual life, the normal person really only reads the labels as it were on the objects around him and troubles no further. Almost all the things which are useful in any way put on . . . this cap of invisibility.'[16] Such 'invisibility' is for Fry the very antithesis of art. We see the same preoccupation in Virginia Woolf's *Flush* (1933), where the baby, each time he adds a new word to his vocabulary, is removed a stage further from Flush's world of pristine sensations, of light and colour and reflection uncontaminated by language; the child learns to 'read' appearances and thus to live life at one remove.

Pseudo-photographic, 'illusionist' art is seen by Lawrence to cheat us, like Freud's pseudo-scientific discourse, with a false perspicuity, creating the illusion of a denotative simplicity, a one-to-one correspondence with objects in the 'outside' world; it claims an omniscience, a god-like view of things, which it does not in actuality possess. 'Whenever art becomes perfect', Lawrence warns, 'it becomes a lie' (*Study of Thomas Hardy*, p. 87). Here Lawrence's affinities with Cubism become clear. Picasso's *Demoiselles d'Avignon*, begun in 1906, heralded the Cubist movement in its synthesis of numerous impressions of an image seen from different angles; it was an attempt at the 'simultaneous' vision that the camera could never achieve. Picasso, like Lawrence, was to find in African sculpture the inspiration for this subversion of the photographic vision. Of the works of his primitivist phase, Picasso claimed that each figure could easily be realized in terms of free-standing sculpture.[17] Yet, like Cézanne's still-lifes (a second important influence on both Lawrence and Cubism), Picasso's *Demoiselles*, whilst on one level attempting a more comprehensive representation than pseudo-photographic art could achieve, nonetheless remained, on another level, pre-eminently 'painted' and profoundly anti-naturalistic; in this way it could 'convey' without deceiving.

Since language is seen by Modernists to cause a disjunction between the self and the world, it follows that overly anecdotal or 'literary' paintings are the product of the same disjunction. The formal experimentation so central to Modernism can be seen to represent an attempt to 'escape' the constraints of 'language' in a broad sense. Leo Bersani, in *The Freudian Body, Psychoanalysis and Art* (1986), encapsulates the paradox inherent in this experimentation when he refers to the aesthetizing movement as both a 'coming-into-form' and a 'subversion of forms'.[18] The conscious search for the unideational, the subverting of the institutionalized forms of the Royal Academy, is a self-renewing battle with the cliché. Form is temporary resolution, acceptable on condition that it is prevented from reifying into marmoreal rigidity.

We see at the heart of this Modernist exaltation of 'form' what in the light of recent critical theory seems a somewhat naive assumption that art-forms, as opposed to other forms of discourse, can somehow enact rather than state. For Lawrence, as for other Modernists, art somehow reaches beyond itself as discourse to a deeper, non-conceptual level of apprehension. In *The Symbolic Meaning*, he defines 'art-speech' as 'a language of pure symbols. But whereas the authorized symbol stands always for a thought or an idea, some mental *concept*, the art-symbol or art-term stands for a pure experience, emotional and passional, spiritual and perceptual, all at once ... Art communicates a state of being ...' (p. 19; italics in original). Susanne Langer's distinction, in *Philosophy in a New Key* (1942), between 'discursive' and 'non-discursive' symbolism, helps to clarify this Modernist concern to separate art from the non-artistic systems attempting to embrace, categorize and explain it. It is a distinction which points not only to Lawrence's distinction between 'art-speech' and ordinary discourse, but to Clive Bell's distinction between 'significant form' and 'labels', and ultimately to the distinction between a Modernist aesthetic and Victorian illusionism. For Langer, 'discursive symbolism' is language as the term is ordinarily understood (i.e. words with relatively 'fixed' meanings arranged in sequence according to established conventions); in 'non-discursive symbolism' images derive their meaning from their relations to one another in the total pattern. Because non-discursive symbolism is not seen to have the one-to-one correspondence with things outside itself upon which the age-old concept of pictorial mimesis is based, it can be made to generate an infinite number of meanings.[19]

Unfortunately, Langer goes on to argue that what she terms 'language proper' (the written/spoken word) is always discursive, while paintings are always non-discursive. She fails to acknowledge that the written/spoken word (and this is especially true of self-consciously 'literary' language) need not be seen to be 'discursive'; it, too, can be approached holisitically, generating the meanings produced by its own rhetoric. Indeed, in the light of the numerous linguistic theories inaugurated by Saussurean linguistics, Langer's distinction is now recognized to be a misleading one, in that all discourses generate the meanings produced by their own rhetoric, and are therefore subsumed by the 'non-discursive' category. Yet the distinction, in some shape or form, is one to which even the most subtle of critical theorists (and Lawrence is no exception) seem to cling. Even Lacan, whilst boldly asserting that there is no metalanguage, nonetheless seems in practice to favour a particular *kind* of language which in its ebullient polysemy manifests a kind of 'textual distress'. Malcolm Bowie, in his study *Freud, Proust and Lacan: Theory as Fiction* (1987), raises the very relevant question, 'Why . . . is a sumptuously polyvalent language to be preferred to the one-thing-at-a-time language of logic, or conceptual analysis, or empirical description or traditional psychoanalytic theory?' 'Is it', he ventures, 'that such a language, having more goals for desire visibly on the move within it, may be thought to maintain a closer, more robust contact with the matrix of desire?'[20] Thirty years before Langer, Roger Fry had made essentially the same distinction, with the crucial difference that he had transferred the locus of the aesthetic from the symbols themselves to *us*, to audience-response, thus avoiding the trap of privileging some forms of discourse and not others. For Fry, the 'imaginative' (or non-discursive) vision is that which transforms *any* fragment of 'life' into a work of art. We generally respond to illusionist paintings, like those of Sargent, as we would respond to a family snapshot or a street-scene. But even a street-scene is potentially a work of art; it is all a question of our framing, 'imaginative' vision, which 'lifts' what would otherwise be 'labels' out of their commonplace, one-to-one context ('An Essay in Aesthetics', p. 13). Adrian Stokes, in 'Form in Art: A Psychoanalytic Interpretation' (1959), was to make use of the same analogy as Fry, that of a mirror which 'makes more comprehensive the turbulent scene reflected there', connecting the art-experience with the restoration of a lost *wholeness*.[21] For Fry, art is a question of recognizing something as a complete, self-contained entity, of approaching it holistically and not trying, literalistically, to connect its various elements with corresponding elements in the 'outside' world. Such connections are, as Lawrence was to show, the business of scientific research, not of art. This is *not* to dissociate art from life altogether, as many critics have tried to assert in connection with Fry. Rather it is to increase and enrich the art-work's connections with life by making an infinite number of 'readings' or responses possible. Taking both Fry's and Langer's theories into account, we can now see how misleading Freud's categories of 'word-presentation' and 'thing-presentation' (*The Unconscious, SE*, XIV, p. 201) actually are. Where verbalization is seen by Freud as the hallmark of 'secondary process thinking' (a view reinforced by Ernest Jones's 1916 paper, 'The Theory of Symbolism'), it can be argued that words themselves are only a special kind of symbol and that all words and symbols, all languages in short, can be used and understood discursively and non-discursively.

Just as the recognition of the art-work as a self-contained entity is the key both to Fry's 'imaginative vision' and to Langer's 'non-discursive symbolism', so for Lawrence the recognition of *wholeness* is the key to aesthetic experience in that this recognition comes about as a result of an *integrated* response, a fusion of body and mind, or 'soul' and 'spirit'. He relates the 'imaginative' response to the unconscious far more explicitly than Fry: 'The imagination', he tells us, 'is a more powerful and more comprehensive flow of consciousness than our ordinary flow. In the flow of the imagination, we know, mentally and physically at once, in a greater, kindled awareness.'[22] It is when soul and spirit are split that we lapse into the dichotomizing of form and content central, for example, to the scientific pursuit, and that we begin to believe that our symbols can actually stand for 'real' entities. As soon as we are able to grasp this, we can see that the 'formalism' of modern art-critics like Bell and Fry is, paradoxically, a return to the body. This is something Herbert Read was to stress in *The Meaning of Art* (1931):

> Form, though it can be analysed into intellectual terms like measure, balance, rhythm and harmony, is really intuitive in origin; it is not in the actual practice of artists an intellectual product. It is rather emotion directed and defined . . . When we describe art as 'the will to form', we are not imagining an exclusively intellectual activity, but rather an exclusively instinctive one . . . Frankly, I do not know how we are to judge form except by the same instinct that creates it.[23]

Cézanne's apple, that touchstone of modern art for so many critics, becomes symbolic for Lawrence of 'knowing the other side as well, the side you don't see, the hidden side of the moon'. 'The eye sees only fronts', he explains, 'and the mind, on the whole, is satisfied with fronts. But intuition needs all-aroundness, and instinct needs insideness' ('Introduction to These Paintings', p. 579). The non-aesthetic becomes the post lapsarian for Lawrence: modern civilization, in losing touch with this experience of the integrated self, has in effect lost the world as work of art. It seems that in our industrialized, commercialized society, it is only when we enter the aesthetic space offered by the art-work that we renounce the endlessly metaphoric process of abstracting from the world and allow our unconscious the free play which alone will help us to penetrate our environment. The Modernist pursuit of form can be seen as the pursuit of the conditions which will enable us to do this most easily. This brings us back to Lawrence's objection to the command of the subject which psychoanalysis seems to foster, to the dominance of what he refers to, in explicitly Freudian terms, as the 'old stable ego'. It should not, he argues, in his frequently quoted letter to Edward Garnett, be allowed to predominate in art.[24]

Freud, too, connects creativity with the attenuation of the powers of the ego. He suggests that the artist has what he calls a 'flexibility of repression', a greater freedom at his disposal owing to his ability to relax the controls of reason. He quotes Schiller: 'Where there's a creative mind, Reason . . . relaxes its watch upon the gates, and the ideas rush in pell-mell' (*The Interpretation of Dreams, SE,* IV, p. 103). He analyses Wilhelm Jensen's novella *Gradiva* in the following terms (*SE,* IX, p. 92):

> The author directs his attention to the unconscious in his own mind, he listens to its possible developments and lends them artistic expression instead of suppressing them by conscious criticism. Thus he experiences from himself what we learn from others – the laws which the activities of the unconscious must obey. But he need not state these laws, nor even be clearly aware of them; as a result of the tolerance of his intelligence, they are incorporated within his creations.

In Jensen's tale itself Norbert Hanold's world becomes a palimpsestic one in which misreading and cross-reading seem inevitable: Zoe Bertgang's name (the first part of which is the Greek for 'life') is overwritten (as a result of Hanold's repression of his desires for her) by that of the dead Gradiva (a Greek translation of the German 'Bertgang'), just as Zoe's living flesh is overlaid with antique marble. Hanold's childhood is repeatedly re-articulated in the terms of the classical past, and the repression of his desires is equated by Zoe to the burial of Pompeii by the Vesuvian ashes. Towards the end of his analysis of *Gradiva*, Freud extends his discussion of the 'burying over' and 'uncovering' activities of Jensen's plot into a more general observation of the way in which literary works themselves are many-layered: they are never the 'innocent' works their authors may take them to be (p. 91).

For Lawrence, too, literary texts are palimpsestic, for, whilst stressing the importance of an integrated response to works of art (in other words, of the reader's injection, as it were, of textual distress into a work), he would none the less hold that some texts encourage such a response more than others. The problem with the American writers, according to Lawrence's study of them, would appear to be that they are not endowed with quite enough of Freud's 'flexibility of repression'; they 'give tight mental allegiance to a morality which all their passion goes to destroy' (*Studies in Classic American Literature*, p. 162). 'What Hawthorne says in *The Scarlet Letter*', we are told, 'is on the whole a falsification of what he unconsciously says in his art-language' (*The Symbolic Meaning*, p. 18). But the 'double language' or 'perfect duplicity' of the American writers is seen to be preferable to a 'truth' which, though asserted through language with all its metaphoric limitations, claims an absolute status. Lawrence's own prose-style represents an attempt to render palpable the energies of the unconscious through the relaxation of the control of the 'old stable ego'. He does this partly through the 'continual, slightly modified repetition', the 'pulsing, frictional to-and-fro' which he defends in the 'Foreword' to *Women in Love* (p. 486) and which is inseparable from an endless semantic modification: we are never allowed to feel that a final 'signified' has been reached. In addition, supposedly 'key' words prove alarmingly polysemous, sometimes even turning themselves inside out to become their polar opposites. 'Abstraction', for example, is used in connection with the African fetishes to connote, among other things, an overdevelopment of the sensual centres at the expense of the intellect: the face of the African woman in labour is 'abstracted in utter physical stress', 'abstracted almost into meaninglessness by the weight of sensation beneath' (p. 79). Yet in the same novel 'abstraction' is repeatedly associated with Gerald Crich, who epitomizes the overdevelopment of the intellect in the white races who 'having the arctic north behind them, the vast abstraction of ice and snow', are about to 'fulfil a mystery of ice-destructive knowledge, snow-abstract annihilation' (p. 254). 'Abstraction' is both the regression to an 'uncreate' state of physical mindlessness, and the assertion of Gerald's hypertrophied, mechanizing will.

For Lawrence and Fry, then, there is no absolute 'meaning' to which a work of art points; rather, an endless number of meanings are generated by the ever-shifting relations between the elements of the art-work, its system of differences. In therapeutic practice, Freud, too, laid stress on free association, on a proportional mode of interpretation which derived the 'meaning' of symbols from the context provided by the patient: 'My procedure', he claims, 'is not so convenient as the popular decoding of dreams which translates any given piece of a dream's content by a fixed key. I, on the contrary, am prepared to find that the same piece of content may concede a different meaning when it occurs in various people in various contexts' (*The Interpretation of Dreams*, SE, IV, p. 105). It has been argued by Paul Ricoeur in this connection that the clue to Freud's aesthetic is to be found in the essay on Michelangelo's *Moses*, where the focus is on the overdetermination of the various features of the statue; far from reducing the enigma, Ricoeur suggests, Freud multiplies it.[25] On the other hand, and rather tellingly, music, which of all art-forms would most firmly be categorized as 'non-discursive', which as the most 'formalistic' of the arts paradoxically allows the unconscious freest play, had little appeal for Freud, precisely because he felt unable to explain its effect upon him (*The Moses of Michelangelo*, SE, XIII, p. 211). All too often Freud seems to wish to ground art in *legibility*. 'Only with the greatest reluctance', he confesses, could he bring himself to believe that 'intellectual bewilderment' is a necessary component of the aesthetic experience. In this emphasis on deciphering and decoding, art simply becomes a passageway, a lure, to an unconscious 'reality', and 'incentive bonus' ['*bestechende Lustprämien*'] (*Creative Writers and Day-Dreaming*, SE, IX, p. 153), which enables the viewer to enter into enjoyment of the fantasies covertly offered, such fantasies being the semantic bedrock of art. If art can be seen by many aestheticians to stretch from the figural or painterly to the discursive, Freud locates it towards the pole of pure discursivity; it consists of 'decorative' pictograms, where the meaning has been 'softened' or 'concealed' by form (*The Claims of Psycho-Analysis to Scientific Interest, SE*, XIII, p. 187). Where Freud's aesthetic revolves around a form/content dichotomy, a central tenet of Modernism is that a work of art is a piece of 'reality' whole and entire, form and content identical. Herbert Read argues in *Icon and Idea* (1955) that 'the specifically aesthetic act is to take possession of a revealed segment of the real; to establish its dimension and to define its form. Reality is thus what we articulate, and what we articulate is communicable only in virtue of its aesthetic form.'[26] Art as Freud presents it is, from Lawrence's perspective, in danger of becoming enmeshed in the whole deterministic mechanism, the cause-and-effect chain which for Lawrence is the very negation of art.

We have seen that, insofar as art both operates through language and transcends it in its tapping of unconscious sources, it elicits an 'integrated' response. In this sense, it is not regressive. Lawrence warns us in the 'Foreword' to *Women in Love* that the 'struggle for verbal consciousness should not be left out in art. It is not superimposition of a theory. *It is the passionate struggle into conscious being*' (p. 486; italics in original). We see, for example, Rupert Birkin's ambivalence towards the African fetishes in *Women in Love* with their 'impulse for knowledge all in one sort, mindless progressive knowledge through the senses . . . knowledge in dissolution and corruption' (p. 253). Loerke, the Dresden sculptor in the same novel, is described as a 'mud-child' (p. 427), both 'mud' and 'child' connoting an 'uncreate' regression. Michael Ragussis, in *The Subterfuge of Art* (1978), places Lawrence in a Romantic tradition which, though it has so often been associated with both primitivism and transcendentalism, is in fact a criticism of both: it 'refuses the myths of the child and of the god as models for the man'.[27] Freud himself is notoriously confusing on the issue of the 'regressiveness' of art. For each of his comments to the effect that art is an 'illusion', a 'substitute gratification', a 'narcotic', there are others which seem to link art with some effort of control over reality.[28] In *Beyond the Pleasure Principle* we find Freud's speculative discovery that there are dreams whose purpose is not hallucinatory but which are attempts to master a stimulus retroactively by first developing the anxiety (*SE*, XVIII, p. 32). This has been developed into a theory of creativity by, among others, Harold Bloom in his 'Freud and the Poetic Sublime'. For Paul Ricoeur, too, Freud presents art as both symptom and cure in that, where instincts as such are unreachable, inaccessible, traceable only in their 'psychical derivatives', the psychical derivative of art involves an element of production or creation, a making present and palpable: 'Leonardo's brush does not recreate the memory of the mother; it creates it as a work of art' (*Freud and Philosophy*, p. 174). Certainly Freud himself would seem to place art on a scale somewhat between complete conscious control (the assertion of Lawrence's 'old stable ego') and a complete surrender to unconscious forces, when he remarks, in connection with surrealism and other experimental art-forms, that 'the notion of art defies expansion as long as the quantitative proportion of unconscious material and preconscious treatment does not remain within definite limits.'[29] Ernst Kris, in *Psychoanalytic Explorations in Art* (1952), develops this in his designation of the artist's ability to tap unconscious sources without losing control as 'regression in the service of the ego'.[30]

The connections between Lawrence and Freud in the field of aesthetics are perhaps best articulated by the theorists of the British 'Middle School' of psychoanalysts, to some extent influenced by Melanie Klein but departing from Kleinian theory on certain important issues. They have extricated themselves from a Freudian impasse by assuming that we are not naturally unintegrated but innately whole and already adapted to our environment, and that various psychic splits occur only insofar as we have experienced frustration, separation or loss. For Charles Rycroft, for example, in his 1975 essay 'Psychoanalysis and the Literary Imagination', the primary and secondary processes co-exist in the individual psyche from the beginning and may continue to function in harmony: creative people retain into adult life something of the imaginative freedom of healthy children. For Rycroft, wish-fulfilment is seen as a product of the psychic split (just as, for Lawrence, Crèvecoeur's letters enact a conflict between 'wish-fulfilment' and 'a primal, dark veracity' [*Studies in Classic American Literature*, pp. 28–30]: 'In so far as . . . the state of primary relatedness is disrupted, dissociation occurs in such a way that wishful thinking and adaptive adjustment come to operate in different psychic realms'.[31] For D. W. Winnicott, in *Playing and Reality* (1971), health and creativity depend on the establishment of a third 'intermediate' realm (he locates art in this realm) in which objects are felt to be parts of both external and internal reality, to possess both selfhood and otherness, and in which activities are both wish-fulfilling and adaptive.[32] Similarly, for Adrian Stokes, art evokes a sense of 'entity', of a lapidary wholeness, whilst being at the same time 'a contagion that spreads and spreads' ('Form in Art', p. 193). This experience is linked by all the above writers to the earliest mother/child relationship. For Stokes, the artist recreates 'the sensation of oneness with the satisfying breast no less than an acceptance of the whole mother as a separate person' (ibid., p. 197). For Lawrence, too, 'art displays . . . the living conjunction or communion between the self and its context' (*The Symbolic Meaning*, p. 117), a conjunction which he sees to involve both the solar plexus as the centre of 'sympathy' or the impulse to merge, and the lumbar ganglion as the 'voluntary' centre of separate identity (and hence of the recognition of 'object-otherness'). For Lawrence, art and love are frequently interchangeable, and he describes love in terms of both 'the sense of union, communion, at-oneness with the beloved' and 'the complementary objective *realization* of the beloved, the realization of that which is apart, different' (*Psychoanalysis and the Unconscious*, p. 239; italics in original). Lawrence also uses the mother-child paradigm: the child both 'drinks in . . . the contiguous universe' (p. 224), and asserts its own separate identity. Art is likewise a form of 'meaning-at-oneness, the state of being at one with the object',[33] in which the sense of an *object* is as important as the sense of fusion. Van Gogh's sunflowers are 'the offspring of the sunflower itself and Van Gogh himself' ('Morality and the Novel', p. 171). It is not enough that the artist should 'sympathize' with his subject; he or she must make contact with something outside him/herself to avoid the solipsism of subjugating matter completely with the mind. Loerke is both 'creature' and 'final craftsman', a god incapable of real creation, able only to recreate himself: 'Loerke, in his innermost soul, was detached from everything, for him there was neither heaven nor earth nor hell. He admitted no allegiance, he gave no adherence anywhere' (*Women in Love*, p. 452). He produces an equally solipsistic work, 'a picture of nothing . . . It has nothing to do with anything but itself' (p. 430). This assertion of the ego in art is the psychic equivalent of Gerald Crich's solipsistic will-to-power and mechanization, which leads only to production, not creation. The connection between art and the machine is made explicit in Loerke's assertion that 'machinery and the acts of labour are extremely, maddeningly beautiful' (p. 424): the people depicted by his 'industrial' frieze exult in the mechanical motion of their own bodies, imprisoned as they are by their own egotism.

Although the aesthetics of Lawrence and Freud, then, can be seen to coincide at several important junctures, Freud remains for Lawrence a Gerald Crich of the psyche, engaged in psychic subjugation. We are back to the Lawrentian antithesis between the unconscious (and art) on the one hand, and a kind of imperialism on the other. It is an antithesis made literal in Lawrence's *Etruscan Places* (1932), where the freshness and vitality of the Etruscan tomb-paintings are played off against the art of the 'law-abiding Romans – who believed in the supreme law of conquest'; the Etruscan art escapes what Lawrence terms the 'Latin-Roman mechanism and suppression'.[34] Just as in art it is important to recognize the 'otherness' of the art-object, to concede the art-image in all its plenary self-sufficiency, and not to subject it to the external control, or imperialism, of discourse, so Freud must renounce a form of therapy in which the powers of the ego are pitted against the subversive forces of the id in 'the old struggle for dominancy'.[35] For Lawrence in *The Symbolic Meaning* (p. 229), 'the whole goal of our ambition, our education, our perfect culture' is 'to be able to live in sheer full spontaneity, because of the perfect harmony between the conscious intelligence and the unconscious, pre-conscious prompting, urging of the very life itself, the living soul centre'.

Notes

1   Leo Frobenius, *The Voice of Africa*, trans. Rudolf Blind, 2 vols (Hutchinson, London, 1913), vol I, pp. 4, xiii, 5, 2.

2   *Fantasia of the Unconscious and Psychoanalysis and the Unconscious* (Heinemann, London, 1961), p. 241.

3   Ernest Jones, *Sigmund Freud: Life and Work*, 3 vols (Hogarth Press, London, 1953–7), vol. I, p. 382.

4   *The Symbolic Meaning: The Uncollected Versions of Studies in Classic American Literature* (Centaur Press, London, 1962), pp. 19, 63, 61, 249.

5   Friedrich Nietzsche, *Ecce Homo: How One Becomes What One Is*, trans. R. J. Hollingdale (Penguin, Harmondsworth, 1979), pp. 122–3.

6   Frieda Lawrence, *Not I but the Wind* (Viking, New York, 1934), p. 3.

7   J. Hillis Miller, 'Stevens' Rock and criticism as cure, II', *Georgia Review*, 30, 2 (Summer 1976), 335–8 (p. 335). For the larger part of this article, Miller uses the term 'uncanny' in connection with the notion of intellectual uncertainty, rather than in the strictly Freudian sense of 'that class of the frightening which leads back to what is known of old and long familar' (*The Uncanny, SE*, XVII, p. 222).

8   Friedrich Nietzsche, *The Birth of Tragedy and The Genealogy of Morals*, trans. Francis Golffing (Doubleday, New York, 1956), p. 93; italics in original.

9   *Letters of Sigmund Freud, 1873–1939*, ed. Ernst L. Freud (Hogarth Press, London, 1961), p. 312 (7 November 1914).

10 Jacques Derrida, 'Freud and the scene of writing', in *Writing and Difference*, trans. Alan Bass (University of Chicago Press, Chicago, 1978), pp. 196–250 (p. 211); italics in original.

11 Harold Bloom, 'Freud and the poetic sublime', *Antaeus* (Spring 1978), pp. 355–77.

12 Jacques Derrida, 'Différance', in *Margins of Philosophy*, trans. Alan Bass (University of Chicago Press, Chicago, 1982), pp. 1–27 (p. 21).

13 *Women in Love* ed. David Farmer, Lindeth Vasey and John Worthen (Cambridge University Press, Cambridge, 1987), p. 146.

14 *Study of Thomas Hardy and Other Essays*, ed. Bruce Steele (Cambridge University Press, Cambridge, 1985), p. 171.

15 ibid., p. 168.

16 Roger Fry, *Vision and Design* (Chatto & Windus, London, 1920), p. 16.

17 *Picasso sculpteur*, ed. Julio Gonzalez (Cahiers d'Art, Paris, 1954), p. 189.

18 Leo Bersani, *The Freudian Body, Psychoanalysis and Art* (Columbia University Press, New York, 1986), p. 11.

19 Susanne Langer, *Philosophy in a New Key* (Harvard University Press, Cambridge, Mass., 1942, 3rd edn 1957), pp. 79–102.

20 Malcolm Bowie, *Freud, Proust and Lacan: Theory as Fiction* (Cambridge University Press, Cambridge, 1987), pp. 129–130.

21 Adrian Stokes, 'Form in art: a psychoanalytic interpretation', *Journal of Aesthetics and Art Criticism*, 2 (1959), pp. 193–203 (p. 195).

22 'Introduction to These Paintings' in *Phoenix, The Posthumous Papers of D. H. Lawrence*, ed. Edward D. McDonald (Heinemann, London, 1936), pp. 551–84 (p. 559).

23 Herbert Read, *The Meaning of Art* (Faber, London, 1931), p. 8.

24   *The Letters of D. H. Lawrence*, ed. James T. Boulton, 7 vols (Cambridge University Press, Cambridge, 1979), vol. II, ed. George J. Zytaruk and James T. Boulton, p. 183 (5 June 1914).

25   Paul Ricoeur, *Freud and Philosophy, An Essay on Interpretation*, trans. Denis Savage (Yale University Press, New Haven and London, 1970), p. 170.

26   Herbert Read, *Icon and Idea* (Faber, London, 1955), p. 20.

27   Michael Ragussis, *The Subterfuge of Art, Language and the Romantic Tradition* (Johns Hopkins University Press, Baltimore and London, 1978), p. 11.

28   See, for example, *SE*, XI, p. 50; XII, p. 224; XIII, p. 188; XVI, pp. 375–7; XX, p. 64.

29   *Letters of Sigmund Freud*, p. 444 (20 July 1938).

30   Ernst Kris, *Psychoanalytic Explorations in Art* (International Universities Press, New York, 1952), p. 60.

31   Cited in Peter Fuller's introduction to Charles Rycroft, *Psychoanalysis and Beyond* (Chatto & Windus, London, 1985), p. 25.

32   D. W. Winnicott, *Playing and Realtiy* (Tavistock Publications, London, 1971), pp. 1–25.

33   'Making Pictures', in *Phoenix II, Uncollected, Unpublished and Other Prose Works by D. H. Lawrence*, ed. Warren Roberts and Harry T. Moore (Heinemann, London, 1968), pp. 602–7 (p. 605).

34   *Mornings in Mexico and Etruscan Places* (Heinemann, London, 1956), pp. 21, 29.

35   Review of *The Social Basis of Consciousness*, by Trigant Burrow, in *Phoenix*, ed. McDonald pp. 377–82 (p. 379).

SUGGESTED READING

Fry, R. *Vision and Design*, Chatto & Windus, London, 1920.

Lawrence, D. H., *Fantasia of the Unconscious and Psychoanalysis and the Unconscious*, Heinemann, London, 1961.

Lawrence, D. H., *The Symbolic Meaning, The Uncollected Versions of Studies in Classic American Literature*, Centaur Press, London, 1962.

Lawrence, D. H., *Studies in Classic American Literature*, Heinemann, London, 1964.

4

James Joyce: The Unconscious and the Cognitive Epiphany

TIM CRIBB

Before the semi-autobiographical essay of 1904 and the abandoned novel that preceded *A Portrait of the Artist as a Young Man* Joyce had nurtured another project – a book of images; in *Stephen Hero* they are dubbed 'epiphanies'. Stephen Dedalus recalls them ruefully in *Ulysses*: 'Remember your epiphanies written on green oval leaves, deeply deep, copies to be sent if you died to all the great libraries of the world, including Alexandria?'[1] Joyce had been compiling it at least since the age of eighteen and it seems that most of the earlier epiphanies were in dramatic form, such as the following:

	(Dublin: in the house in Glengariff Parade: evening)
MRS JOYCE	(*crimson, trembling, appears at the parlour door*) . . . Jim!
JOYCE	(*at the piano*) . . . Yes?
MRS JOYCE	Do you know anything about the body? . . . What ought I do? . . . There's some matter coming away from the hole in Georgie's stomach . . . . Did you ever hear of that happening?
JOYCE	(*surprised*) . . . I don't know . . . .
MRS JOYCE	Ought I send for the doctor, do you think?
JOYCE	I don't know . . . What hole?
MRS JOYCE	(*impatient*) . . . . The hole we all have . . . here (*points*)
JOYCE	(*stands up*)[2]

The painfulness of this experience appears to be that of life itself, in all its confusion of feelings and poverty of expression. The bare facts are embarrassing in their nakedness. The writer, although himself concerned in the scene, refrains from coming to their aid with the decency of literary clothing and his refusal to play Good Samaritan seems scandalous, an inhumanity. If this is realism, then it is realism at some kind of terminus. Only the address and time offer some relief, for thanks to them we might say that the banality and pain are perhaps not of life itself, but of life in a house in Glengariff Parade, Dublin, at a specific date. The pain is thus not solely to do with the death of Joyce's little brother, Georgie, but is compounded from the crossing of that fact with social and physical inhibitions that surround it and constitute the impossibility of family life at that time and in that place. Hence the acute feelings of embarrassment that saturate the exchange. Yet whereas another novelist would at least spell out these conditions of experience and probably also express an attitude towards them, here they are left implicit. The incident speaks for itself and its capacity to do so is what defines it.

In his memoir of his brother's life Stanislaus Joyce says that the dramatic epiphanies began as 'observations of slips, and little errors and gestures – mere straws in the wind – by which people betrayed the very things they were most careful to conceal'. And of the later, descriptive epiphanies he says that 'the revelation and importance of the subconscious had caught his interest'.[3] If this is applied to the dramatic epiphanies then what they comprise seems to be not so much a catalogue of Freudian slips or a Flaubertian *sottisier* as a symptomology of the social unconscious. Extensive descriptions of the phenomena of society are rendered redundant if its whole pathology can be read in a few symptoms. The epistemological model involved, however, is different from that implicit in the medical metaphor. What is uttered or revealed in these moments is clearly beyond the consciousness of the participants and it is important that the participant is frequently the writer himself. He is not outside the incident in the same way as is a doctor. What is revealed is beyond his consciousness too. It can thus be said that he does not even know what he is writing when he sets it down, if 'know' means prior, abstracted knowledge which facts serve merely to illustrate; rather, he recognizes the moment as significant and records it in a spirit of fidelity – its meaning is already given from some source outside him. In all these respects – intuitive revelation to the artist and thence to the reader, concrete and concentrated form, intensity of significance – it is apparent that the epiphany, the model of knowledge we are considering, is a Romantic Image. It depends for its working on the premise that, in Frank Kermode's words, 'The human mind is so constituted as to recognize images of which it can have no perceived knowledge.'[4] The image thus reveals truth by a sort of immanent transcendance that cannot be questioned by the criteria of the empirical world, but at the same time, because it is an image, presents itself with the impersonal objectivity of perceptual experience – hence its appearance of unquestionability. Following Kermode's pioneering critique, Sandford Schwartz has recently surveyed the philosophic background to this literary tradition. Earlier, Morris Beja demonstrated an epiphanic tradition in the twentieth-century novel.[5]

What particular variety of Romantic Image, then, are we faced with in Joyce? The dramatic epiphanies, with their implications of whole social strata and mores, might well be described as Hegelian: 'Ay, even such singularities as a petty occurrence, a word, express not a subjective particularity, but an age, a nation, a civilization, in striking portraiture and brevity; and to select such trifles shows the hand of a historian of genius.'[6] Joyce's genius might be said to show not only in the selection but in applying to the social stuff of the novel a sensibility which in Britain had been identified with poetry.[7] He might then be seen as transferring into prose the method that Wordsworth first developed for social material in poetry.[8] Be that as it may, his strange essay 'A Portrait of the Artist' tells us what principle he had adopted for his practice by 1902: 'Our world . . . is, for the most part, estranged from those of its members who seek through some art, by some process of the mind as yet untabulated, to liberate from the personalised lumps of matter that which is their individuating rhythm, the first or formal relation of their parts.'[9] We are still dealing with something that operates below the threshold of consciousness, but the terminology Joyce chooses to articulate the notion is not Hegelian but Aquinan or Aristotelian.[10] It is only the terminology, for Joyce singles out rhythm as a thing in itself, not as part of a system, whether providential or metaphysical. Isolated in this way, the principle of individuation is purely formal. However dense with social implication the dramatic epiphanies and however painful the experiences they evoke, it is the fact that they detach themselves from the flow of experience by their form that makes them material for the artist. That is why Joyce can take the epiphany I have been discussing and employ it in *Stephen Hero*, further emphasizing the gape of its non-ending by using it to end a chapter. He can even alter the actual facts, so that in the novel it is Isabel who is dying, not Georgie.[11]

In Joyce's early work, then, these moments only appear to owe allegiance to realism, if realism means only fidelity to fact; their true allegiance is to reality, and that is located beyond common understanding in some realm of cognition first accessible only to the artist. To maintain that access, once detached from religion and metaphysics, Joyce's poetics can appeal for their validation only to some other source, which must remain equally inscrutable.[12] The temptation to vagueness, obscurity or cultic elitism is evident; so is the contrary temptation to endless documentation. The dilemma had been on Europe's cultural agenda since the end of the eighteenth century. One way to solve it was to abandon the claim to finality of knowledge.

We can trace Joyce's progress towards such a solution by observing what happens to another epiphany when it ends up in *A Portrait of the Artist as a Young Man*. First, the early version, well before the novel:

> The children who have stayed latest are getting on their things to go home for
> the party is over. This is the last tram. The lank brown horses know it and

shake their bells to the clear night, in admonition. The conductor talks with the driver; both nod often in the green light of the lamp. There is nobody near. We seem to listen, I on the upper step and she on the lower. She comes up to my step many times and goes down again, between our phrases, and once or twice remains beside me, forgetting to go down, and then goes down. . . . Let be; let be. . . . And now she does not urge her vanities – her fine dress and sash and long black stockings – for now (wisdom of children) we seem to know that this end will please us better than any end we have laboured for.[13]

The individuating rhythm here is easy to recognize, for it is given plastic definition in the girl's movement, stepping up, hesitating, stepping down. This reflects the incident as whole, suspended at a point of equipoise between the party and home, childhood and adolescence, action and contemplation. Sexual attraction lends its magnetic charge to the surrounding details, making them concentric to the heightened consciousness of boy and girl, but instead of taking its usual course it is absorbed in that consciousness, creating the feeling of a privileged moment. Narrative and its chain of causes is cancelled as the moment becomes an end in itself.

In *A Portrait of the Artist as a Young Man* this epiphany appears again and is the direct cause of the first of the two poems that Stephen writes during the book and, as we shall see, the latent cause of the second. The first, titled 'To E— C—', written while Stephen is a schoolboy, Joyce decides not to show us. We learn only that it is dedicated by force of habit Ad Maiorem Dei Gloriam and that in the process of writing it 'all those elements which he deemed common and insignificant fell out of the scene'. These include the horses. 'The verses told only of the night and the balmy breeze and the maiden lustre of the moon.'[14]

This first poem, together with the epiphanic incident which precedes it, lies behind the second poem, which occurs in the second section of Chapter 5.[15] This time the poem gets written in three stages. The first is when Stephen is emerging from sleep. His state of mind is evoked by a mingling of the elements of air and water, each dissolving into the other and dissolving the boundaries of consciousness and language in a delicately erotic vagueness. He feels he is awaking to a new knowledge, an instant of inspiration. His images spiritualize sexuality as the Immaculate Conception of the Virgin Imagination, fertilized by some mysterious angelic impulse from beyond itself. As his consciousness becomes distincter Stephen is reminded of his lecture to Lynch in the previous episode, where he describes the artist's moment of conception as an enchantment of the heart. Yet what we read here does not in fact correspond exactly with the aesthetic principles propounded earlier, for in the lecture Stephen had married Aquinas's *claritas* to Duns Scotus's *quidditas* to evoke the revelation of beauty in the object, whatever it may be. Yet here there is no object, no image even, only vaguely delicious feeling and diffuse sensation in Stephen himself. There is thus a discrepancy between Stephen's presentation of his theory and Joyce's presentation of Stephen that alerts us to irony. The process of creation is by no means as consciously controlled as he may wish to believe. (It is true that in the earlier disquisition he had limited his analysis to aesthetics and said that he would need different terms to account for the process of creation, but whether the terms we find here are they it is of course impossible to say.) When an object does appear it is E— C—. The gestation of the poem reproduces the sequence at the end of the previous episode – first the theory, then the lady, for at the end of his lecture he had seen her chatting with a group of friends. In the light of the epiphany the spatial arrangement is significant: 'Stephen took his place silently on the step below the group of students', echoing in reverse the position in the tram. Yet even so, E— C— is given no more substance than in the first poem, figuring only as 'her strange wilful heart', a condensation of the visionary light in which Stephen feels himself to be bathed. At this point a narrative begins to emerge in Stephen's mind. The Virgin Madonna of his imagination metamorphoses into a female temptress, causing the annunciatory angels to fall. He now composes his first verse. It turns out to be a villanelle, a poem constantly returning on the same rhymes and rhyme-words, so that while it advances in meaning it marks time in sound, creating an impression of self-sustaining endlessness. In contrast to the first poem, then, Stephen appears to proceed without reference to any epiphany. This appearance is deceptive.

After three stanzas, while Stephen is seeking to prolong the poem by conjuring with associated words, the enterprise suffers an unfortunate accident: 'Smoke went up from the whole earth, from the vapoury oceans, smoke of her praise. The earth was like a swinging smoking swaying censer, a ball of incense, an ellipsoidal ball.' He is thrown brutally back on a fellow student's joke during a lecture on (appropriately) Physics: 'What price ellipsoidal balls! Chase me, ladies, I'm in the cavalry!'[16] The rebuff is not only by verbal association, however, for the whole rhythm of the villanelle is founded on the rhythm of the epiphany, which, as we have seen, is itself founded on a moment both in and out of sex. Once this is recollected we may also recollect the other associations the incense has for Stephen: 'Pride and hope and desire like crushed herbs in his heart sent up vapours of maddening incense before the eyes of his mind.'[17] He has just come down from the school stage on which he knows E— C— has been watching him and is mortified that she has not spoken to him afterwards. Even before the unfortunate mention of balls, then, his exalted vision is inherently fragile. Once betrayed into the light of common day, Stephen can only meditate irascibly on his frustrated sexual relations and the reasons for the frustration. The lumps in his pillow remind him of the lumps in the sofa at her house and this memory includes the picture of the Sacred Heart above the sideboard, supplying a retrospective comment on the 'strange heart' that prompted the first part of the poem. E— C— is plainly as much a complex of ideas, feelings, memories and cultural conditions as a person with her own unique *quidditas*. Even the memory of another epiphany, of a young woman dancing, which evokes the same idea of a poised suspense as the first, fails to restore his creative equilibrium. However, it prepares the emotional ground, so that when he thinks of the eucharist, or rather, of himself as celebrant of the eucharist, he is suddenly able to proceed with the second phase of the poem: 'Our broken cries and mournful lays / Rise in one eucharistic hymn'. The unity of the moment of inspiration, of his own sense of his mission and identity, and of the poem are restored.

Secure in this confidence he can turn his back on the growing daylight, 'making a cowl of the blanket', and begin to relax in the warmth. The young monk of the imagination snuggles into himself. In this security his memory is carried back further than the previous day and the whole student phase of his life to the original epiphany, where it was E— C— who 'had worn a shawl about her head like a cowl' – a detail not present in the book of epiphanies but insisted on in the novel. Indeed, when Stephen knew she was watching him from the audience during the school play, two years after the children's party, all he could physically recall of her was her eyes looking at him from the cowl.[18] Now the original epiphany of ten years before at last swims up into consciousness and is repeated almost verbatim, revealing the source of the poem's suspended rhythm. Indeed, in one respect the repetition is closer to the epiphany in the collection than to the formative experience in the novel: it includes the phrase 'Let be! Let be!', which the novel does not. In the novel, these words are omitted in favour of allowing the incident to evoke and merge with an earlier one, already narrated, where Eileen had run away and left the little Stephen standing watching.[19] So when recalled in connection with the villanelle, it is as if the epiphany detaches itself from that earlier association, becoming purer, more epiphanic, and this in turn reveals how Stephen's memory accommodates his needs as a poet by silent forgettings. The reader, however, is free to remember and to reflect that the layers of memory multiply beyond the recovery of the conscious mind, even at its most inspired and receptive. The language of this last section of the composition of the poem reverts to the liquid clouds of the beginning in an intensified eroticism from which the poem rises at last complete, at once spiritualized seminal emission and goddess of beauty arising from the waves.

A Portrait of the Artist as a Young Man is thus a brilliantly successful marriage of the Romantic poetics of revelation professed by Stephen and Joyce's novelistic labour of expatiation and contextualization – with the novel as loving but dominant partner. The cognitive epiphany is lent the full credence of Stephen's sophisticated mind, and his mind is the book, even to the extent that it is possible to read the book solely through the moving lens of his consciousness. But as soon as we allow ourselves to look beyond that focus, to notice recurrent patterns in space and echoes of word and rhythm across time, then we realize that the book's memory is longer than Stephen's and that it supplies dimensions to his mind of which he is unaware. Thus the subjective intuitionism of Romantic poetics and its claim of access to an inscrutable source is supplemented and displaced by another model of the unconscious: sedimented in layers deposited by all kinds of experience, inseparable from the body, its drives, processes and sensations, continuous with a society and long-established culture with its own complexes and determining forces, and living as much in language and its procedures and usages as in any personal depth, all equally and comically liable to simple mistakings and accidents – this is as radical a secularization and materialization of the artist-priest as is easily imaginable. Without direct satiric attack, the Romantic Image is comically, tenderly divested of its sacred privilege to knowledge.

Joyce finished *A Portrait of the Artist as a Young Man* in 1915. The date signals how far he had advanced beyond his senior, Yeats, and his contemporaries, Pound and Eliot, all of whom remained partially attached to the image and its implications, as Kermode has demonstrated. Moreover, his analysis was not finished with this novel. Before proceeding with the entry into the kingdom he had prepared for himself, *Ulysses*, Joyce first wrote *Exiles*. Stephen might be a definitive examination of the constituting of the artist in a particular time and place with regard to his art; he had yet to be studied with regard to personal relations. For that, drama was the fit medium and the eternal triangle of bourgeois comedy the fit matter.

Joyce's notes for the play reveal that the epiphanic approach has relaxed into something resembling, as Ellmann suggests, the Freudian technique of free association. An example: 'ship, sunshine, garden, sadness, pinafore, buttoned boots, bread and butter, a big fire'. These are all clues to the character of Bertha in the play (though in fact drawn from Joyce's wife, Nora). Joyce subjects this string of images to analysis:

> The boots suggest their giver, her uncle, and she feels vaguely the forgotten cares and affection among [which] she grew up. She thinks of them kindly, not because they were kind to her but because they were kind to her girlself which is now gone and because they are part of it, hidden away even from herself in her memory.[20]

We are reminded of Freud, or any other psychoanalyst, by the way the analyst gains access to the analysand's unconscious by recognizing particular images and references in the analysand's discourse as symptoms, that is, as coded references to something other than themselves which provides the logic of their associations. Elsewhere in the notes Joyce also invokes the assumption of repression, when memories are disagreeable. But unlike Freud, Joyce's prime material is not the pathological but the healthy. Consequently, although the chain of images may resemble a complex, it is much looser in itself than a pathological one and hence less determined. Joyce can even add in items to do with his own concerns, such as the name of one of Nora's admirers in Trieste. Joyce was fully acquainted with sexual pathology from the works of De Sade, Sacher-Masoch and others and he was well prepared to detect perverse impulses behind the mask of conscious and respectably conventional motives.[21] There is no evidence, however, that he represents human behaviour according to any single system, whether the elaborately hypothesized sexual system of the early, nor the more mythical speculations of the later Freud.[22]

It might be argued that the crucial contribution of psychoanalysis, of whatever school, to literature is the idea of the psychopathology of everyday life, the continuity, that is, of motivation between the mad and the sane. Joyce would doubtless go along with this, but only in certain company. Pound is not so fastidious and borrows support for his doctrine of the image from those he calls 'the newer psychologists', quoting Bernard Hart's *The Psychology of Insanity* of 1912. This gives a clear popular account of the principles of psychoanalysis gathered from Jung, Janet, Krafft-Ebing and Freud. It is cast, however, in a severely rationalistic style which not only insists on the psychopathology of everyday life but scorns it as such. Hence 'the class that thrives on cheap romantic literature' is remorselessly assimilated to a patient who thinks she is Queen Elizabeth and excessive indulgence in music is reproved in the best style of Plato's *Republic*. So musical a citizen as Joyce might well feel disenfranchised under such a magistrate. Although the rationality of lunacy is conceded, indeed insisted on, given the premises from which the lunatic proceeds, this is not allowed to perturb Hart's confidence in the unimpeachability of his own logic and premises and in 'genuine knowledge, the product of a scientific deduction from observed facts'.[23] This marks a further difference between Joyce and the systematic psychoanalysts. His sense of the sheer diversity and hence unpredictability of the unacknowledged forces at play in the mind's operations is only matched by the keenness of his sense of the insistence with which the mind will nonetheless be operating. This property of the mind is not necessarily harmful, but it may become so in particular cultural conditions, one of these being the severely rational pursuit of truth. His study of this arrogance of reason and the predicament it imposes on itself is focused on the artist character in his *Exiles*, Richard Rowan.

Joyce described the play as 'a rough and tumble between the Marquis de Sade and Freiherr v. Sacher-Masoch', and Richard's behaviour towards his wife, Bertha, may at first be seen as a study in perverse psychology. Although it is his friend, Robert, who, desiring Bertha, arranges an assignation with her, it is Richard, informed by Bertha, who turns up to keep it. Robert is impressed by Bertha's loyalty:

ROBERT	(*Softly.*) Do not suffer, Richard. There is no need. She is loyal to you, body and soul. Why do you fear?
RICHARD	(*Turns towards him, almost fiercely.*) Not that fear. But that I will reproach myself then for having taken all for myself because

> I would not suffer her to give to another
> what was hers and not mine to
> give. . . . That is my fear. That I stand
> between her and any moments of life that
> should be hers, between her and you,
> between her and anyone, between her and
> anything. I will not do it. I cannot and I will
> not. I dare not. (*He leans back in his chair
> breathless, with shining eyes. ROBERT
> rises quietly, and stands behind his chair.*)[24]

His words express the loftiest, most disinterested altruism, yet the energy of utterance and the stage picture express passion; the discrepancy invites us to question his motives. This sub-text is explored in the notes, where Richard 'wishes, it seems, to feel the thrill of adultery vicariously and to possess a bound woman Bertha through the organ of his friend'.[25] On this analysis, Richard's unconscious motive is sexual power, exactly the opposite of the one he professes. This in turn reveals that the clue to his motivation is not in fact his relation with Robert, which is a secondary phenomenon, but with himself. When, much to Robert's consternation, he leaves him at liberty to keep his rendezvous with Bertha, this is not in the interests of Bertha's freedom but of Richard's own quest for what he calls 'luminous certitude'. The notes again clarify what is going on by describing Bertha as 'abandoned spiritually by Richard. . . . Her state is like that of Jesus in the garden of olives.'[26] On this analogy, Richard is her God, offering himself up as sacrifice in the person of his dearly beloved to his own design, an 'automystic' indeed. Richard's sexual psychology is thus only a derivative, a consequence of his desire for certainty of knowledge. This is his true ruling passion, and it is thus possible to describe him as suffering a crisis of Cartesianism. The relentless insistence on the purity and totality of the all-knowing subject inevitably opens an unbridgeable gulf between it and all objects. The self-inflicted torment of this is that other subjects cannot be known on such terms – save by a ruthless if effectively dominating reduction of their properties. Richard's masochism therefore derives from his self-appointed enterprise of pure knowledge, based on pure self-identity. As L. L. Whyte observes in his valuable book *The Unconscious before Freud*, only after Descartes' drastic separation of the self-aware subject from that which it is aware of did it become necessary to invent an unconscious; previously men had got by with a loosely held, holistic set of assumptions about the mind. The power and tenacity of the Cartesian division is such that Freud himself, the great underminer, can none the less be called 'the last pre-Freudian rationalist', like Richard:[27]

RICHARD   (*Still gazing at her and speaking as if to an
           absent person.*) I have wounded my soul for
           you – a deep wound of doubt which can

> never be healed. I can never know, never in
> this world. I do not wish to know or to
> believe. I do not care. It is not in the
> darkness of belief that I desire you. But in
> restless living wounding doubt. . . . But
> now I am tired for a while, Bertha. My
> wound tires me.[28]

Once again the stage direction is eloquent of the sub-text. Richard is speaking to and of himself, not to the Bertha he does not truly see. The drained, defeated tone expresses even more. Richard Rowan is Joyce's Monsieur Teste.

Once Joyce had accomplished his revolution against the imperialism of the Cartesian mind and overthrown the reactive regime of the Romantic subjectivist he was free for the world of *Ulysses*. The unconscious is now united with the conscious mind, and both with the world and the body, through a constantly interacting dynamics that makes any systematic separation between the elements impossible. Knowing the mind's insatiable appetite for systems of order, Joyce defeats it by surfeit. *Ulysses* abounds in systems. It proffers clues, correspondences, perspectives, structures and themes in a multiplicity unwitnessed since the Middle Ages. Two of its principal characters are themselves compulsive theorists, in completely contrasting styles. Once we have learned to live with such redundancy of meanings the effect is exuberantly and soberly liberating. It comes as a relief to find that truth is no single absolute but something glimpsed, lost, rediscovered in a different form, always on the move. Any moment in the book is an intersection of different kinds of perception and understanding and they are not necessarily mutually comprehensible. The unconscious, for example, may be conceived as a set of spatial relations moulding the behaviour of individuals or collectivities, or it may act through a person's biological processes, such as digestion and excretion, or it may operate through the system of language itself. What happens to it in the terms in which, since Freud, it has been conventionally conceived, that is, as repressed sexuality, escaping unawares in sleep, slips, dreams and fantasy?

The obvious place to look for answers to such a question is 'Circe' and the obvious character is Mr Bloom. One of the most flamboyant sequences in that chapter is when he is forced to change sex and submit to numerous humiliations.[29] It is tempting to construe these as revealing the 'deep' truth about his character, i.e. that he is a masochist. If we look back to the earlier chapters when his character is being established in the daylight world there are plenty of indications to support this diagnosis. When queuing at the butcher's his eyes rest on the backside of the girl next door; her arms are strong and he thinks of her whacking the carpet on the clothesline and of the way her skirt swings. A little later these ideas, previously conscious memories, have detached themselves from circumstance and float in his mind half-consciously: 'He held the page aslant patiently, bending his sense and his will, his soft subject gaze at rest. The crooked skirt swinging, whack by whack by whack.' A moment later, after she fails to notice him, his reaction is tinged with the perverse: 'The sting of disregard glowed to weak pleasure within his breast.' He shows similar feelings after reading the secret letter from Martha.[30] If these velleities are linked to the monstrous exhibitions in the brothel it is easy to conclude that Bloom is defined by a specific sexual pathology, or at any rate inclination, that makes him not only a weak but a willing cuckold. This would be to succumb to the mind's reverence for its own constructions, the besetting sin of *Ulysses* criticism. It would be equally wrong to argue oppositely that the scenes in the brothel never happen, that we cannot even tell if they happen in Bloom's mind. That does not prevent them from telling us something about him, for 'him' is not a fixed, single, self-conscious entity, but a set of potentials, a series of Blooms, some of them actualized, some not.[31] More apposite is to point out that there are other truths about Bloom, perhaps inconsistent, but co-existent rather than contradictory. For instance, it is equally true that he is extremely distressed by Molly's infidelity and that we can be moved by this. A conspicuous feature of his reaction to Martha's letter is a rather cynical common sense. His presence in the brothel is marked by enterprise and courage. Perhaps he is also there as a way to get quits with Molly. And so on.

Bloom in the brothel, then, is better taken as a site for certain extrapolations of various potentialities in him than as a set of determined symptoms. Taken this way the scene is by no means as terrible as some commentators suggest. Exaggerating passive tendencies in Bloom is surely preferable to staging a full-scale exhibition of the tendencies in Private Carr or the Citizen. If these are the extremest degradations of the womanly man, then might not a world where such men were the prevalent sexual types be a more tolerable place? The values of 'Circe' are not limited to character but take on more general scope.

The brothel itself and the whole red light quarter are as important as Bloom's character in setting the drift of the chapter and have equally important implications for the unconscious. They too are a site for the extrapolation of behaviour, an area specially reserved for licence. The policemen acknowledge as much when they allow themselves to be steered away at the end by Corny Kelleher's appeals to the privilege of youth. Under this aspect the chapter is a carnival, a saturnalia, where sexual reversals and inversions are part of the game. Critics such as Bakhtin on the novel or Barber on Shakespeare have shown us that writers can draw on a repertoire of social forms that have as powerful a capacity to compel human behaviour into deviance from the norm as any syndrome. Their literary insights have been supported by symbolic anthropologists such as Van Gennep and Victor Turner, who have revealed the compulsive narrative repetitions behind apparently spontaneous social events, and these in turn have been documented by such historians as Natalie Z. Davis.[32] It is as valid to describe 'Circe' through an anthropology of the unconscious as through character. All these perspectives combine to suggest a characteristically twentieth-century idea of the unconscious as varying in mode according to the point of view adopted by the conscious, a sort of joker partner inseparable from the act of thinking and ordering. Prominent among such jokers is sex, but it is not the only one. 'Bloom' feels as guilty about eating pork, although an unbeliever, as he does about sex.

It is also important to remember that Ulysses comes through Circe's enchantments unscathed and so does Bloom. At the end, writing and reality maintain a fluid exchange in which all things are possible. Corny Kelleher leaves Bloom standing guard over the drunken Stephen, in possession of the field:

CORNY KELLEHER	Ah well, he'll get over it. No bones broken. Well, I'll shove along. (*he laughs*) I've a rendezvous in the morning. Burying the dead. Safe home!
THE HORSE	(*neighs*) Hohohohohome.[33]

The knowing horses have got back into the poem. And indeed the party is over and 'the children who have stayed latest are getting on their things to go home'. As the turmoil of the carnival recedes into a phantasmagoria the way carnival times do, on the boundary between youth and maturity, dissipation and sobriety, coming and going, life and death, this chapter and the next, there is an epiphany:

BLOOM	(*Silent, thoughtful, alert he stands on guard, his fingers at his lips in the attitude of secret master. Against the dark wall a figure appears slowly, a fairy boy of eleven, a changeling, kidnapped, dressed in an Eton suit with glass shoes and a little bronze helmet, holding a book in his hand. He reads from right to left inaudibly, smiling, kissing the page.*)
BLOOM	(*wonderstruck, calls inaudibly*) Rudy!
RUDY	(*gazes, unseeing, into Bloom's eyes and goes on reading, kissing, smiling. He has a delicate mauve face. On his suit he has diamond and ruby buttons. In his free left hand he holds a slim ivory cane with a violet bowknot. A white lambkin peeps out of his waistcoat pocket.*)[34]

This is an epiphany far removed from the revelations of truth with which Joyce began, for what is this vision? A graceful tribute to Yeats, whose verses Stephen has been muttering in his stupor? If so, it is a Yeatsean fairy redesigned for marketing in Woolworth's or Lourdes. The gracefulness would be in the way the vision rises gratuitously, as the poem sings of poetry rising above love's bitter mystery. Stephen had sung the poem to his mother on her death bed. Joyce had sung it to his little brother Georgie on his death bed. More obviously, the vision expresses one of Bloom's dearest longings – that death, the death of his son, should be no more. It seems cruel to visit him with this phantom resurrection. The poignancy is sharpened by the intimacy of the child's gazing into Bloom's eyes but not seeing him. Yet after the pollutions, carnalities and tribulations of Nighttown the vision also seems like some cathartic recompense, perhaps an act of love from the author to a favourite character whom he has made to suffer. The child's dress is perhaps influenced by Bloom's last memory of looking down on Stephen (which was probably the only other time he called him by that name) when he was a small boy, dressed in a Little Lord Fauntleroy suit; Molly shares this memory too. (Bloom has just undone the buttons of Stephen's waistcoat). In one of the brothel fantasias Bloom had worn mother-of-pearl studs, held a prismatic champagne glass and slipped a ruby ring on Mrs Breen's finger. The woolly jacket Molly buried Rudy in has also resurrected as the lambkin in his pocket. Yet to whom does Bloom call 'Rudy'? If he calls inaudibly, can we be sure that he does call? Can this be Rudy, if a changeling? Perhaps we have here only a piece of writing. Perhaps the reading vision is but an hypostasis of reading. And yet one cannot be certain that it does not exist, in Bloom's mind, or in some other modality of the visible or invisible. Stephen has actually seen his dead mother in the brothel. Indeed, if Bloom is standing as Father to Stephen as Son, might this be the Holy Ghost?

What is shown to us reading gentiles, then, in this miraculous epiphany? Our century's reflections on the systems in which and by which we not only live but think and know have taught us, in Piaget's words, that the actual is only an instance of the possible.[35] In the world of a writer of fiction, then, the possible (and what is not possible?) is as actual as the real. Some such conclusion is forced on us by the most celebrated feature of *Ulysses*, its abrupt changes of style. The very medium of the novel, language, through which we know it, is simultaneously a limitless potential and yet, in any given instance, a limiting condition. In *Finnegans Wake* one would be sure of one's own interpretive responsibility as *bricoleur* artist for making something definite out of the hitherandthithering waters of language. But that is another story. In *Ulysses*, at the end of 'Circe', with Bloom standing there, and he is standing there, one cannot be so sure. This ghost is sent to conduct us to the night and water world of *Finnegans Wake*.

Notes

1   James Joyce, *Ulysses* (Penguin, Harmondsworth, 1986), p. 34.
2   Robert Scholes and Richard M. Kain, *The Workshop of Daedalus* (Northwestern University Press, Evanston, 1965), p. 29. See also Giorgio Melchiori, *Epifanie* (Mondadori, Milan, 1982), 'Introduzione' for the dating and ordering of the epiphanies.
3   Cited in Scholes and Kain, *Workshop of Daedalus*, pp. 8–9
4   See Frank Kermode, *Romantic Image* (Routledge & Kegan Paul, London, 1957), pp. 110, 114–15, 128–9.
5   Morris Beja, *Epiphany in the Modern Novel* (University of Washington Press, Washington, 1971); Sandford Schwartz, *The Matrix of Modernism: Pound, Eliot and Twentieth-Century Thought* (Princeton University Press, Princeton, 1985).
6   Hegel, *Philosophy of Mind*, trans. W. Wallace (Oxford University Press, Oxford, 1971), p. 279.
7   But see Alan D. Perlis, 'Beyond epiphany: Pater's Aesthetic Hero in the Works of Joyce', *James Joyce Quarterly*, 17 (1979–80), pp. 272–9.
8   See J. F. Danby, *The Simple Wordsworth* (Routledge & Kegan Paul, London, 1960).
9   Scholes and Kain, *Workshop of Daedalus*, p. 60.
10 See William Noon, S. J., *Joyce and Aquinas* (Yale University Press, New Haven, 1957), and several essays in *Joyce's 'Portrait': Criticisms and Critiques*, ed. Thomas E. Connolly (Meredith, New York, 1962).
11 James Joyce, *Stephen Hero*, ed. T. Spencer, rev. J. J. Slocum and H. Cahoon (Jonathan Cape, London, 1956; repr. 1969), ch. XXII.
12 See Hugh Kenner's scepticism about the validity of appeal to the unconscious in 'Tales of the Vienna Woods' *James Joyce Quarterly*, 7 (1954–5), pp. 276–85, his review of Ernest Jones's biography of Freud.
13 Scholes and Kain, *Workshop of Daedalus*, p. 13. See Bernard Benstock, 'The temptation of St Stephen: a view of the villanelle', *James Joyce Quarterly*, 14 (1976–7), pp. 31–8, for a commentary on the poem in the light of previous criticism.
14 James Joyce, *A Portrait of the Artist as a Young Man*, ed. C. G. Anderson and R. Ellmann (Jonathan Cape, London, 1964), pp. 71–2.
15 ibid., pp. 221–8 with allusions to pp. 217, 220.
16 ibid., p. 196.
17 ibid., p. 89.
18 ibid., pp. 71, 84, 226.
19 ibid., p. 71.
20 James Joyce, *Exiles* (Jonathan Cape, London, 1952), pp. 155–6; Richard Ellman, *James Joyce* (Oxford University Press, Oxford, 1965), p. 368; see pp. 450–2 for Joyce's analyses of Nora's dreams.
21 Ellmann, *Joyce*, pp. 326–7, 380–1.
22 There is an extensive literature on Joyce and psychoanalysis, in Freudian, Jungian, Lacanian and other terms. *James Joyce Quarterly*, 13 (1975–6), is a special number devoted to the subject, with a checklist by Mark Schechner. See also Frederick J. Hoffman, *Freudianism and the Literary Mind* (Louisiana State University Press, Baton Rouge, 1957), Erwin R. Steinberg, *The Stream of*

Consciousness and Beyond (University of Pittsburgh Press, Pittsburgh, 1973), Sheldon R. Brivic, *Joyce between Freud and Jung* (Kennikat Press, Port Washington, 1980), Richard Brown, *James Joyce and Sexuality* (Cambridge University Press, Cambridge, 1985).

23 Bernard Hart, *The Psychology of Insanity* (Cambridge University Press, Cambridge, 3rd edn, 8th imp, 1921), pp. 151, 145 (quoting William James), 136. Pound's celebrated definition of the image first appeared in *Poetry*, 1 (March 1913), p. 6.

24 Joyce, *Exiles*, p. 86.

25 ibid., p. 158.

26 ibid., pp. 79, 150.

27 L. L. Whyte, *The Unconscious before Freud* (Julian Friedmann, London and New York, 1978), p. 179; see also pp. 59–62, 88, 182–3.

28 Joyce, *Exiles*, p. 143.

29 Joyce, *Ulysses*, pp. 429–44.

30 ibid., pp. 48–9, 63–4.

31 Adaline Glasheen, '*Finnegans Wake* and the girls from Boston, Mass.', *James Joyce Quarterly*, 7 (1954–5), pp. 89–96, shows that Joyce knew *The Dissociation of Personality* (Longmans, London, 1905) by the American psychologist Morton Prince. This includes such speculations as: 'Of the various possible selves which may be formed out of the "mass of consciousness" belonging to any given individual, there is no particular real or normal self; one may be just as real and just as normal as another, excepting so far as one or the other is best adapted to a particular environment. If the environment were changed, another self might be the normal one', p. 233. As a doctor Prince rejects this; as an author Joyce might not.

32 Mikhail Bakhtin, *Rabelais and his World*, trans. Helene Iswolsky (MIT Press, Cambridge, Mass., 1968); C. L. Barber, *Shakespeare's Festive Comedy* (Princeton University Press, Princeton, 1959); Arnold Van Gennep, *The Rites of Passage*, trans. M. B. Vizedom and G. L. Caffee (University of Chicago Press, 1960); Victor Turner, *The Ritual Process: Structure and Anti-structure* (Cornell University Press, Ithaca, 1977); Natalie Z. Davis, *Society and Culture in Early Modern France* (Stanford University Press, Stanford, 1975).

33 Joyce, *Ulysses*, p. 495.

34 ibid., p. 497.

35 Jean Piaget, *Structuralism,* trans. C. Maschler (Routledge & Kegan Paul, London, 1975), p. 38. See also Malcolm Crick, *Explorations in Language and Meaning* (Malaby Press, London, 1976), pp. 37–42.

SUGGESTED READING

Brown, R., *James Joyce and Sexuality,* Cambridge University Press, Cambridge, 1985.

James Joyce Quarterly, 13, (1975–6): a special number on Joyce and psychoanalysis.

Eco, U., '*Finnegan's Wake*' in *The Middle Ages of James Joyce: The Aesthetics of Chaosmos,* trans. Ellen Esrock, Hutchinson Radius, London, 1989, pp. 61–90.

Whyte, L.L., *The Unconscious Before Freud,* Julian Friedmann, London and New York, 1978.

5

Primitivism and Psychology: Nietzsche, Freud, Thomas Mann

RITCHIE ROBERTSON

The influence of primitive culture on Modernism is most obvious in painting. Gauguin found in Samoa an exotic subject-matter; primitive art offered the next generation of European painters a set of new techniques. The elongated faces of the women in Picasso's *Les Demoiselles d'Avignon* show the influence of African wood-carving, while the brightly coloured, rudimentary figures in Emil Nolde's paintings reflect the journey through the Far East and Polynesia which he undertook in 1913–14. These are not isolated borrowings, but part of a modern interest in primitive culture and society which is here called primitivism. As Lionel Trilling pointed out in his essay 'On the Teaching of Modern Literature', certain canonical works of Modernism (including some discussed below) employ the primitive as a means of cultural criticism and advocate features of the primitive to alleviate the shortcomings of civilization.[1]

The inferences drawn from primitive art may be illustrated by some passages from D. H. Lawrence's *Women in Love* (1921). Gerald Crich is examining a primitive sculpture:

> [...] there were several negro statues, wood-carvings from West Africa, strange and disturbing, the carved negroes looked almost like the foetus of a human being. One was a woman sitting naked in a strange posture, and looking tortured, her abdomen stuck out. The young Russian explained that she was sitting in childbirth, clutching the ends of the band that hung from her neck, one in each hand, so that she could bear down, and help labour. The strange, transfixed, rudimentary face of the woman again reminded Gerald of a foetus, it was also rather wonderful, conveying the suggestion of the extreme of physical sensation, beyond the limits of mental consciousness.[2]

This passage contains two conceptions of the primitive, which students of the subject have called 'chronological' and 'cultural' primitivism.[3] Chronological primitivism is implied by the depiction of childbirth itself, the repeated comparison of the woman to a foetus, and the word 'rudimentary'. The carvings come from the beginning of human history. Thus the primitive is consigned to the remote past, and it is defined negatively, by lacking the constraints and complications that human life has subsequently acquired. But another concept, cultural primitivism, is implied when the carving is said to convey 'the extreme of physical sensation'. Primitive life is now seen, not simply as an earlier, rudimentary version of our own, but as qualitatively different. Primitive peoples are credited with a highly developed physical consciousness, just as we have, in Lawrence's opinion, an over-developed mental consciousness. A few pages later Lawrence's mouthpiece, Birkin, declares that the carving is the product of hundreds of centuries of development of 'pure culture in sensation, culture in the physical consciousness, really *ultimate* physical consciousness, mindless, utterly sensual'.[4]

Freud discusses modern primitivism in *Civilization and its Discontents* (1930). Why is it, he asks, that the intellectual, social, and technical achievements of civilization have not made modern man happy, but arouse envy for the simple life of primitive societies? He suggests that civilization compels its beneficiaries to repress, or at best sublimate, their instinctual urges. The advance of civilization therefore requires what Freud elsewhere calls 'the secular advance of repression in the emotional life of mankind' (*SE*, IV, p. 366). Since Freud, other writers have traced the advance of discipline and repression in diverse areas of civilized life: the growth of bodily discipline in social intercourse; of discipline as a means of punishment, education and military training; and work-discipline as a means of maximizing efficiency and productivity.[5] Hence denizens of a disciplined and rationalized society imagine the primitive as a state of instinctual freedom, in which sensation predominates over thought: a notion which bears little relation to the actual primitive (or, if you prefer, 'archaic') societies studied by anthropologists. A glance back to the eighteenth century and earlier will show how a chronological conception of the primitive as belonging to mankind's simpler past gave way to a cultural conception of the primitive as a qualitatively different, and preferable, way of life.

Europeans encountered archaic peoples in the course of colonial expansion. The discovery and exploitation of America, the exploration of the Pacific, and the gradual penetration of Africa, introduced them to very different societies which had somehow to be fitted into the European world-picture and scale of values. 'Soft' primitivists like Bougainville, in the first description of Tahiti (1771), credited these societies with the happiness of the Golden Age: 'I thought I was transported into the garden of Eden. [. . .] We found companies of men and women sitting under the shade of their fruit trees [. . .] everywhere we found hospitality, ease, innocent joy, and every appearance of happiness amongst them.'[6] 'Hard' primitivists praised the virtue and vigour of peoples uncorrupted by civilized vices: thus

there is a conflict between civilised rules and primitive desires. Greek Oedipus

Jesuit missionaries to the Canadian Hurons, while deploring their superstition, acknowledged their freedom from ambition and avarice.[7] For both types of primitivist, archaic societies could serve as instruments of social criticism. Tacitus in *On Germany* had rebuked the luxury of Imperial Rome by describing the austere virtues of ancient Germanic tribes; Diderot, in his *Supplement to Bougainville's Voyage* (1772), criticized the sexual mores of Christian Europe by contrast with the cheerful promiscuity of the Tahitians. But eighteenth-century thinkers not only criticized particular institutions: they questioned the value of civilization itself. Rousseau's second Discourse (1755) located human happiness in small, simple, early communities, and maintained that private property and the division of labour propelled man out of this happy state: 'all further progress has been, in appearance, so many steps towards the perfection of the individual, and, in reality, towards the decrepitude of the species.'[8]

In the late nineteenth century doubts about the value of civilization recurred more insistently, and again primitive life was looked to as an antidote. But this time the primitive was not sought in exotic continents: it was discovered in the midst of civilization itself. This view was propounded most influentially in Nietzsche's *The Birth of Tragedy* (1872). Nietzsche opposed the conception of Greek culture, dominant in German classicism, which stressed its serenity and found this best conveyed in the beauty of a statue or in the joyous life of the gods on Mount Olympus described by Homer. This luminous world, Nietzsche says, is only one side of Greek culture. On closer inquiry, 'the Olympian magic mountain opens itself before us, showing us its very roots.'[9] Acutely aware of the pain, horror and transience of life, the Greeks created the ideal world of Olympus as a compensation. But the strain of believing in this beautiful and harmonious ideal was so great that they had to seek relief, and hence they were attracted by the savage, orgiastic cult of Dionysus which they found among the nations further east. The festivals of Dionysus freed people temporarily from the burdens of civilization and even of individuality, and allowed them to release their pent-up impulses with the aid of music and dancing. Purged of its cruel and bestial elements, the cult of Dionysus was incorporated into Greek culture. And the highest achievement of Greek civilization, Athenian tragedy, is, Nietzsche argues, a product of both impulses – the Apolline desire for beauty and harmony, and the Dionysiac urge for intoxicating instinctual release. The artistic form of tragedy is Apolline, but the chorus is derived from the crowd of Dionysiac worshippers, and the hero is doomed to lose his individuality and perish, like Dionysus himself, who was torn to pieces by his frenzied followers. Thus the classical civilization of Athens was not a triumph of civilization over barbarism. It was rather a synthesis of civilized order with ritual practices which had previously been seen as primitive and barbaric, but which the Greeks incorporated into their civilization. When the Dionysiac element in Greek civilization weakened, the Apolline element declined too, dwindling into the narrow rationalism of

Socrates and Euripides. Dominated too exclusively by the intellect, the Greeks became incapable of tragedy.

Comparisons between the ancient Greeks and primitive peoples had already been drawn. Missionaries in North America had compared the life of the Indians to the Bronze Age culture described by Homer, and their harsh method of bringing up children to the educational practices of Sparta.[10] But it was novel to claim that elements of the primitive formed an essential part of the high civilization of classical Athens. Hence *The Birth of Tragedy* received a largely hostile reception. Almost its only defender was Nietzsche's close friend and fellow-scholar Erwin Rohde. Rohde was later to become well known for his book *Psyche*, a study of ancient Greek cults of the dead and conceptions of immortality. Although this book never mentions Nietzsche, it is clearly indebted to *The Birth of Tragedy,* particularly in the chapters on the worship of Dionysus. Later writers stimulated by Nietzsche were to turn to Rohde for more detailed and scholarly information than Nietzsche provided. Thus Hugo von Hofmannsthal and Thomas Mann, both of whom admired *The Birth of Tragedy*, drew on Rohde's Dionysus chapters for detail about ancient Greek cults. Hofmannsthal borrowed from Rohde the figure of the shamanic priest in his play *Oedipus and the Sphinx* (1906); Mann relied on Rohde for the Dionysiac orgy in Aschenbach's fevered dream in *Death in Venice* (1912).[11]

Did Nietzsche's discovery of the primitive in the midst of civilization have any effect on Freud? We know that he had read at least Nietzsche's early works, and though he was inclined to shrug off comparisons between Nietzsche and himself in some embarrassment, two affinities can be pointed out.[12]

First, Freud acknowledged that Nietzsche had anticipated him in describing dreams as a regression to a primitive mode of thought. In *Human, All Too Human* Nietzsche remarks that dream-thought is illogical and confused, and liable to invent details to cover up lapses of memory; in these ways it resembles the mental life of primitive man as described by present-day travellers. 'But in dreams we all resemble this savage', Nietzsche says; 'in sleep and dreams we repeat once again the curriculum of earlier mankind.'[13] Freud quotes Nietzsche in a passage added in 1919 to *The Interpretation of Dreams*. Having said that in dreaming the dreamer regresses not only to his own childhood but to the childhood of the human race, Freud continues:

> We can guess how much to the point is Nietzsche's assertion that in dreams 'some primaeval relic of humanity is at work which we can now scarcely reach any longer by a direct path'; and we may expect that the analysis of dreams will lead us to a knowledge of man's archaic heritage, of what is psychically innate in him. Dreams and neuroses seem to have preserved more mental antiquities than we could have imagined possible; so that psycho-analysis may claim a high place among the sciences which are concerned with the

reconstruction of the earliest and most obscure periods of the beginnings of the human race (*SE*, V, pp. 548–9).

Thus Freud discovers the primitive not only within civilization, as Nietzsche had done, but surviving within the mind of the supposedly civilized individual; and psychoanalysis becomes a method of studying primitive survivals.

Secondly, Freud had founded psychoanalysis on just such a primitive survival, namely the Oedipus complex. The view of classical Greece pioneered by Nietzsche and developed by Rohde had created an intellectual climate in which Freud could look to Greek tragedy for evidence of irrational and unconscious processes. He found these in the story of Oedipus.[14] As a child Oedipus was left by his father Laius to die, because of a prophecy that the child would grow up to kill his father. Oedipus was found and brought up by foster-parents. As an adult he met his father, without knowing who he was, quarrelled with him and killed him. He then became king of Thebes and married its queen, Jocasta, not knowing that she was in reality his mother. Sophocles' play *King Oedipus* shows this web of ignorance being unravelled, until Oedipus is revealed as unwittingly guilty of parricide and incest.

Freud's interest in this story dates from the 1890s, when he was seeking the origins of neurosis. In a paper written early in 1896, 'Heredity and the Aetiology of the Neuroses', Freud maintained that all neuroses originated from the subject's sexual life: some from current sexual disorders, others from the sexual abuse of the subject in childhood by an adult. Freud had become persuaded of this theory by the number of patients who, under analysis, had confided to him that they had been sexually abused in childhood. Yet when Freud presented this theory to a medical society in Vienna, it was dismissed as a 'scientific fairy-tale'.[15] And in September 1897 Freud himself accepted this view. In a letter to his friend Wilhelm Fliess he wrote: 'I want to confide in you the great secret that has been slowly dawning on me in the last few months. I no longer believe in my *neurotica*.'[16] That is, he no longer believed that his patients' stories of childhood seduction were true, and he found himself compelled to abandon the seduction theory of the origin of neurosis. Another letter to Fliess, written the following month, contains Freud's first formulation of what he was later to call the Oedipus complex. His self-analysis, he explained, had disclosed in himself love for his mother and jealousy of his father, and he believed that these feelings were universal. Hence the appeal of the Oedipus story: 'the Greek legend seizes upon a compulsion which everyone recognizes because he senses its existence within himself. Everyone in the audience was once a budding Oedipus in fantasy and each recoils in horror from the dream fulfilment here transplanted into reality.'[17]

By discarding the seduction theory, Freud was abandoning a theory which attempted to explain adult neuroses by actual events which had befallen the sufferer in childhood, in favour of a theory which explained neuroses as orignating within the psyche. The sexual life of the child, which Freud was to go on to explore in his *Three Essays on the Theory of Sexuality* (1905), was crucially determined by intra-psychic processes. No matter how the parents behaved, the child was innately disposed to feel sexual attraction to the mother and murderous jealousy towards the father. This theory became the cornerstone of psychoanalysis. In 1920 Freud wrote: 'Every new arrival on this planet is faced by the task of mastering the Oedipus complex; anyone who fails to do so falls a victim to neurosis' (*SE*, VII, p. 226).

There are, however, several serious objections to the theory of the Oedipus complex. First, anthropologists have not found the Oedipus complex to be a cultural universal. Second, Freud's account is based on male psychology, and can be applied to women only by positing the dubious notion of penis-envy. Third, if actual family relationships are irrelevant, the theory cannot explain why some people become neurotic and others do not. Fourth, classical scholars argue that Freud's interpretation of *King Oedipus* differs substantially from the play's probable meaning for its original Greek audience; and to reply that the explicit meaning does not matter, since Freud is concerned with the unconscious meaning, is to argue in a circle, taking for granted the universality of the Oedipal fantasies which Sophocles' play is supposed to help to prove.[18]

Moreover, the seduction theory now looks less implausible. Evidence is accumulating that sexual abuse of young children is far from rare. In 1983, interviews with randomly selected American women disclosed that 28 per cent had suffered sexual abuse before the age of fourteen.[19] As Jeffrey Masson has now shown, Freud knew of numerous instances of such abuse, which he refrained from making public.[20] It is not clear, therefore, what justification he had for assuming that his patients were fantasizing about their early experiences. Biographical researchers have noted that Freud abandoned the seduction theory soon after the death of his father in October 1896, and have scrutinized every grain of evidence about his relationships with his father and other relatives. They point out, for example, that Freud's father was forty when he was born, and his mother was barely twenty-one; the disparity of their ages might tend to arouse in a male child the sexual emotions which Freud claims are universal, and one suspects that here and elsewhere Freud is generalizing from his own early experience.[21]

It is intriguing, too, that in his discussions of the Oedipus legend Freud does not mention that Oedipus had good reasons for hostility to his father, who after all had mutilated and exposed him. Nor does he mention an earlier section of the Oedipus legend according to which Oedipus' father Laius was himself a pederast, had kidnapped and seduced a boy, and was placed under a curse for doing so. Admittedly, this part of this story is not in Sophocles, but it does occur in a well-known German collection of classical legends and could thus have been known to Freud.[22] Altogether, it seems likely that filial piety deterred Freud from maintaining a theory which blamed the actual behaviour of parents for the difficulties suffered subsequently by their children. Instead, he adopted a theory which placed the source of these difficulties within the child. The later hypothesis of infantile sexuality may be seen as an attempt to bolster this theory. By emphasizing 'the factors of constitution and heredity' at the expense of 'accidental influences derived from experience' (*SE*, VII, p. 275), Freud encouraged psychoanalysis to concentrate on studying inner psychological development rather than looking critically at the politics of the family.[23]

Over the next few years, Freud showed some discomfort with his account of psychic conflicts as originating within the patient. He wanted to find some other origin for them by tracing them back to bedrock in external reality. Their immediate origin might be within the psyche of each individual, but their ultimate origin might lie far back in the history of the human species, and they might be transmitted through the memory of the species. These speculations were founded on Freud's adherence to the now discredited Lamarckian theory of evolution which claimed that acquired characteristics could be inherited: thus a creature with a usefully elongated neck could transmit that neck to its descendants until they became giraffes. Freud applied this theory to mental as well as physical characteristics. Thus he described dream symbols as survivals of 'an ancient but extinct mode of expression' (*SE*, XV, p. 166). Eventually he managed, to his own satisfaction, to account for the Oedipus complex as another such survival, acquired by the human race in the most primitive period of its history.

This is the thesis of *Totem and Taboo* (1913), in which Freud tried to use psychoanalysis to explain two phenomena that anthropologists had found linked. Many primitive tribes, for example among the Australian aborigines, have a totem animal which is taboo: that is, members of the tribe may not kill it. At certain festivals, however, this prohibition is lifted, and they kill and cermonially eat the totem animal. Freud was struck by the resemblance between taboos and the irrational prohibitions which obsessional neurotics impose on themselves, while the ambivalence of primitives towards the totem animal was like the ambivalence of children towards their parents. He argues therefore that the totem animal symbolizes the father, and that the institution of totemism can be derived from the earliest state of human society. He suggests that in the earliest social organization, a tribe or horde was ruled by an old male who kept all the women to himself until the younger males joined together to kill him and replace him. The killing of the father in order to obtain his women was an enactment of the Oedipal conflict. It gave rise to guilt, and guilt gave rise to religion. The primal father was replaced by the totem animal, which was normally regarded as sacred; its death became a religious sacrifice, and the guilt of killing it was expiated by a communal feast, the ancestor of surviving religious ceremonies. Parricide is also the origin of art: the hero of tragedy represents the primal father; the chorus represents the company of brothers which killed him; the hero's death redeems them from their guilt. Freud refers particularly to Greek tragedy, whose subject was originally the suffering of Dionysus and the lamentation of the chorus. Thus Nietzsche's argument about the origin of tragedy is revised and fitted into a more comprehensive argument intended to prove, in Freud's words, that 'the beginnings of religion, morals, society and art converge in the Oedipus complex' (*SE*, XIII, p. 156).[24]

But if Freud is tracing all human institutions back to a primal act of parricide, is it necessary to maintain that this act was really performed? Until almost the end of *Totem and Taboo* it seems not. Freud says that, just as neurotics fail to distinguish factual from merely psychical reality, so do primitives. 'Accordingly the mere hostile *impulse* against the father, the mere existence of a wishful *phantasy* of killing and devouring him, would have been enough to produce the moral reaction that created totemism and taboo' (*SE*, XIII, pp. 159–60). But then, for no logically compelling reason, Freud complicates the analogy between neurotics and primitives. Neurotics fantasize instead of acting; primitives act instead of fantasizing. Hence Freud concludes that 'in the beginning was the Deed' (*SE*, XIII, p. 161): the violent actions of primitive people survive as the violent fantasies of the civilized. The mentality of primitives survives in our unconscious. Thus Freud has satisfied his need to trace the Oedipus complex back to the bedrock of reality, but has transferred that reality back to the beginnings of history.

Totem and Taboo ends with the scandalous claim that all the institutions that we value as the highest achievements of civilization originate from primitive fantasies. In *Death in Venice*, Thomas Mann depicts Aschenbach writing an essay on an unspecified problem in culture and taste while gazing at the body of the boy Tadzio, and offers the narratorial reflection: 'Verily it is well for the world that it sees only the beauty of the completed work, and not its origins nor the conditions whence it sprang; since knowledge of the artist's inspiration might often but confuse and alarm, and so prevent the full effect of its excellence.'[25] Here and in much of his fiction Mann is searching for a model of civilization which is strong and flexible enough to contain (in every sense) its antithesis. Acknowledging the allure of chaos and the primitive, he asks how order can contain chaos, art incorporate sensuality, health be not endangered but fortified by contact with sickness.

To these questions *Death in Venice* provides only a negative answer. Its psychology is Nietzschean, not Freudian: Mann recognized in Nietzsche a master psychologist who anticipated Freud in tracing civilized values back to their embarrassing origins. Aschenbach is an exaggeratedly Apolline figure. The Prussian rigidity of his character, and the simplistic moralism to which his art is increasingly dedicated, exclude the ironic self-questioning which would have discovered, and perhaps controlled, the contrary forces within himself. His suppressed rage for chaos is symbolized early in the story by his hallucinatory vision of a tiger-infested tropical swamp, and later by his climactic, preternaturally vivid dream of a Dionysiac orgy. Once his orderly life has been undermined, his moralism is replaced by the suicidal cynicism that makes him prefer to perish with Tadzio rather than warn other people about the cholera lurking in Venice.

Another Nietzschean figure occurs in the later story *Mario and the Magician* (1930). The deformed hypnotist Cipolla embodies the 'ascetic priest', the religious type described by Nietzsche in *The Genealogy of Morals*, who offers his flock relief from their sufferings but is himself afflicted by the same sickness as they. He compels some of his audience into a prolonged dance, parodying a Dionysiac orgy, while the rest gaze on spellbound.[26] But Cipolla's demagogic techniques suggest that by now Mann had also read Freud's *Group Psychology and the Analysis of the Ego* (1921). Here Freud argues that members of a crowd are united by shared libidinal attachment to a leader, recapitulating the original relation of the young males to the primal father that had been hypothesized in *Totem and Taboo*. If so, Mann is combining Nietzschean and Freudian psychology in a perceptive analysis of Fascist demagogy.

A similar syncretism is practised in *The Magic Mountain* (1924), written when Mann's knowledge of psychoanalysis was still almost entirely second-hand. The psychoanalyst in the novel, Dr Krokowski, is another Nietzschean 'ascetic priest'. He plays a modest but beneficial part, however, in the education of the stolid hero, Hans Castorp. Krokowski's lectures on psychoanalysis bewilder their audience by mixing conventional categories: not only in the delivery, which is scientific in language and bardic in manner, but in Krokowski's use of the word 'love', which keeps Castorp uncertain 'whether he had reference to its sacred or its passionate and fleshly aspect'.[27] Thus Krokowski helps to propel Castorp on a Nietzchean course away from his conventional assumptions and past the competing ideological systems of Settembrini and Naphta. Along the way Castorp becomes acquainted with death and disease, and is thus qualified to affirm life in full awareness of the forces threatening it.

Castorp's first brush with chaos comes at Carnival time. Carnival is traditionally a festival of indulgence in sex and food, in which the social order is temporarily suspended, a King of Misrule takes command, and irreverent joking is licensed.[28] Mann enriches the symbolic texture by heading the chapter 'Walpurgisnacht' and larding it with quotations from *Faust* that recall the orgiastic assembly of German witches on the Brocken. During the fancy-dress dance which follows the Carnival meal, Castorp defies his mentor Settembrini and addresses him familiarly as 'du'. For Settembrini, the abolition of social distances implied in this form of address is deeply menacing: 'it is an objectionable freedom,' he says, 'it is wantonly playing with the roots of things [*ein Spiel mit dem Urstande*], and I despise and condemn it, because at bottom the usage is audaciously and shamelessly levelled against our civilization and our enlightened humanity.'[29] Undeterred, Castorp rejects Settembrini's repressive rationality and speaks for the first time to the alluringly sluttish Clawdia Chauchat. Their conversation includes a eulogy of the body, taken by Mann from Whitman's 'I Sing the Body Electric' but delivered by Castorp in inspired French, and ends with an unmistakable invitation from Clawdia. Here sex and the body belong to that *Urstand* which is the permanent substratum of social as of individual life and takes no account of civilized conventions or rational misgivings. One thinks both of Freud and of the passage from *Thus Spoke Zarathustra* where Nietzsche contrasts the 'little intelligence' in the mind with the 'great intelligence' which is the body.[30] The body is the primitive and timeless foundation of civilization.

At Carnival the body is seen benignly. It may be grotesque, but not loathsome. But what about dissolution, disease, violence and death? Can any model of civilization be capacious enough to accommodate them? Castorp receives an answer in the chapter entitled 'Snow'. Having learnt to ski, he ventures into the snow-covered wilderness surrounding the sanatorium, and soon finds himself beyond all landmarks, all distinct shapes, amid the elemental indifference of the mountains. It is like chaos made manifest, and yet it has an appeal, for 'in his narrow, hypercivilized breast, Hans Castorp cherished a feeling of sympathy with the elements'.[31] Overtaken by a blizzard, he loses his way but manages to shelter in the lee of an Alpine hut. His exhaustion induces a trance in which he beholds a sunlit bay, inhabited by graceful, athletic people who treat each other with a gentle ceremoniousness. These 'People of the Sun' seem to represent an ideal civilization, reconciling nature and culture. But then Castorp realizes that the bay is overlooked by a massive temple in whose recesses he finds two hideous women tearing apart a baby and devouring it. When he has recovered from his horror, he surmises that the People of the Sun treated each other so kindly precisely because they were aware of the gruesome sacrifices going on in the temple. And he formulates the resolution which Mann's typography emphasizes as the message of the novel: '*For the sake of goodness and love, man shall let death have no sovereignty over his thoughts.*'[32] The People of the Sun know that life is always overshadowed by death, not to mention cruelty and violence. But instead of letting this knowledge license barbarism (like that advocated by the authoritarian Naphta), they have created a way of life which neither denies death (like the benevolent but shallow rationalism represented by Settembrini) nor submits to it.

This model of civilization owes distinct debts to Nietzsche. The Mediterranean setting suggests Greece, and the massive columns of the temple recall Mycenae and the civilization of pre-classical Greece whose sacrificial cults had been discussed by Nietzsche and, more fully, by Rohde. Castorp is descending to the early history of Western culture and discovering the ambivalence that marked it even then. And the primitive past is present in his own psyche. That is why, although Castorp has never been to the Mediterranean, he recognizes it, and he decides that the dream does not emanate solely from his own psyche: 'Now I know that it is not out of our single soul we dream. We dream anonymously and communally, if each after his own fashion. The great soul of which we are a part may dream through us, in our manner of dreaming, its own secret dreams, of its youth, its hope, its joy and peace – and its blood-sacrifice.'[33] Later in the novel, Krokowski organizes séances in order to explore 'connexions and associations between the lowest and least illumined regions of the individual soul and a wholly knowing All-soul'.[34]

For this notion Mann was indebted mainly to Schopenhauer's conception of the Will, a blind impelling force objectified in the physical world. Despite our illusion of separate identity, says Schopenhauer, each person, like each object, is an outcrop of the Will, and driven on by it. In the individual, the will to live manifests itself as hunger and the fear of death; in the species, as the sexual urge and as care for one's progeny. Death removes the illusion of separateness and reabsorbs the individual into the universal Will. Together with the Romantic concept of the world-soul, this was the framework into which Mann eventually fitted psychoanalysis. He read Freud between 1925 and 1929, and his annotations suggest that he was mainly interested in Freud's metapsychological and anthropological works.[35] One might add that he preferred the mythopoeic to the scientific side of Freud's work. He read, for example, *Beyond the Pleasure Principle* (1920), where Freud argues that life is based on a conflict between the life instinct and the always successful death instinct, and adds: 'We have unwittingly steered our course into the harbour of Schopenhauer's philosophy' (*SE*, XVIII, pp. 49–50). For Mann, then, Freud was a philosopher of the instincts, whose 'unconscious mind' was a restatement, with scientific credentials, of Schopenhauer's Will. Mann's scanty knowledge of Jung easily fitted this model. In 1935 Mann read the introduction to the Tibetan *Book of the Dead*, in which Jung declares that man's conscious life is dominated by the forces of his psyche and praises the *Book of the Dead* because it 'vouchsafes to the dead man the ultimate and highest truth, that even the gods are the radiance and reflection of our own souls'.[36]

Of the works by Freud that Mann read, the one that affected his own writing most directly was *Totem and Taboo*. He was attracted by Freud's explanation of the origin of religion in the projection of the image of a primal father who had been injured, was angry, and had to be appeased. This provides one of the dominant ideas of the *Joseph* tetralogy on which Mann worked from 1926 to 1942. The primal parricide is mentioned in its first part, *The Tales of Jacob* (1933), as 'perhaps the beginning of all things'.[37] But the idea that man projects his father-imago into the heavens is interpreted more optimistically by Mann than by Freud. For Freud, the primal parricide has implanted in a man a guilt which has driven him to create all the achievements of culture and forbidden him to enjoy them. Mann, however, stresses the benevolence of his father-figures. The young Joseph imagines God as 'a higher replica of his father, by Whom, Joseph was naively convinced, he was beloved even as he was beloved of his father'.[38]

Depth psychology, for Mann, descends not just into the psyche but into the depths of the past, and thus enables people to confront and master their ambivalent inheritance. Freud says in *Totem and Taboo* that social psychology requires the hypothesis of a collective mind to transmit the experience of earlier generations (*SE*, XIII, p. 158); Mann agrees, seeing the individual psyche as layered and sedimented with ancestral inheritances. *The Tales of Jacob* show characters living in accordance with earlier models stored in the unconscious. They understand their own lives as re-enactments of ancestral lives, and make no sharp distinction between reality and myth. Thus the conflict between Esau and Jacob re-enacts those between Ishmael and Isaac, between Cain and Abel, and, ultimately, between Set and Osiris. And Jacob's servant Eliezer often speaks as though he were identical with Eliezer, the servant of Abraham, who lived several generations earlier. And that, Mann suggests, is not so unreasonable, for identity is not fixed. If ancient people had a less secure sense of individual identity than we, they may have been nearer the truth, for 'is man's ego a thing imprisoned in itself and sternly shut up in its boundaries of flesh and time? Do not many of the elements which make it up belong to a world before it and outside of it?'[39]

Mann's positive acceptance of the primitive is formulated in his two essays on Freud, 'Freud's Place in the History of Modern Thought' and 'Freud and the Future', written in 1929 and 1936 respectively.[40] Both trace the genealogy of psychoanalysis back via Nietzsche and Schopenhauer to the German Romantics and the Enlightenment. Mann's purpose is to wrest the German intellectual tradition away from the reactionaries of the Weimar Republic by disclosing in it a tradition of critical inquiry which acknowledges irrational forces in order to comprehend and master them. He places Freud in this tradition by quoting the dictum 'Where id was, there ego shall be' (*SE*, XXII, p. 80). The earlier essay argues that in revealing the ubiquity of neurosis, and in proposing to dissolve neurosis through critical understanding, psychoanalysis is a socially revolutionary force. Moreover, psychoanalysis has illuminated literature, art, religion and myth. The *Joseph* tetralogy shows this illumination operating as irony, both in its presentation of character and in its many reflective passages dealing with identity and myth. The novel is intended to permit empathy with a mentality very different from the modern one, but also to apply modern insights to permit a detached understanding of the 'mythic' mentality of the patriarchs. Hence Ernst Bloch, the Marxist philosopher, wrote to Mann in 1940: 'It is clear that your powerful *Joseph* represents the most successful and illuminating instance of adapting myth to a different function.'[41]

Thus Mann has absorbed those aspects of psychoanalysis that interested him by assimilating them to the thought of Schopenhauer and Nietzsche. These diverse sources help him to articulate his conviction that the primitive is present within civilization, and within the individual psyche. Instead, however, of surrendering blindly to the primitive or trying to deny its power, he wants to explore and understand it with the aid of his modern consciousness. Hence his irony: a means of keeping the primitive at bay while acknowledging its authority and its appeal. Other writers discussed in this volume were to explore ways of accepting and mastering the revelations of psychoanalysis; few, though, were to rival the sovereign skill of Mann's literary tightrope-walking.

Notes

1 Lionel Trilling, *Beyond Culture* (Secker & Warburg, London, 1966), pp. 3–30.
2 D. H. Lawrence, *Women in Love,* ed. David Farmer, Lindeth Vasey and John Worthen (Cambridge University Press, Cambridge, 1986), p. 74.
3 See Arthur O. Lovejoy and George Boas, *Primitivism and Related Ideas in Antiquity* (Johns Hopkins Press, Baltimore, 1935).
4 Lawrence, *Women in Love,* p. 79.
5 See Norbert Elias, *The Civilizing Process,* vol. I, trans. Edmund Jephcott (Blackwell, Oxford, 1978); Michel Foucault, *Discipline and Punish,* trans. Alan Sheridan (Allen Lane, London, 1978); E. P. Thompson, 'Time, work-discipline, and industrial capitalism', *Past and Present,* 38 (1967), pp. 56–97.
6 Quoted in Bernard Smith, *European Vision and the South Pacific, 1768–1850* (Clarendon Press, Oxford, 1960), p. 25.
7 On the Jesuit Lafitau and his predecessors, see Anthony Pagden, *The Fall of Natural Man,* 2nd edn (Cambridge University Press, Cambridge, 1986).
8 *The Political Writings of Jean Jacques Rousseau,* ed. C. E. Vaughan (Cambridge University Press, Cambridge, 1915), I, 175 (my translation).
9 Friedrich Nietzsche, *The Birth of Tragedy and the Genealogy of Morals,* trans. Francis Golffing (Doubleday, New York, 1956), p. 29. For discussion, see M. S. Silk and J. P. Stern, *Nietzsche on Tragedy* (Cambridge University Press, Cambridge, 1981).
10 See Henri Baudet, *Paradise on Earth,* trans. Elizabeth Wentholt (Yale University Press, New Haven and London, 1965), p. 50.
11 On Hofmannsthal and Viennese primitivism, see Ekkehard Stärk, *Hermann Nitschs 'Orgien Mysterien Theater' und die 'Hysterie der Griechen': Quellen und Traditionen im Wiener Antikebild seit 1900* (Fink, Munich, 1987); on Mann's sources, see T. J. Reed's edition of *Der Tod in Venedig* (Clarendon Press, Oxford, 1971).
12 See Edwin R. Wallace IV, *Freud and Anthropology* (International Universities Press, New York, 1983), p. 13; more generally, Ernest Gellner, *The Psychoanalytic Movement* (Paladin, London, 1985), pp. 18–26.
13 Friedrich Nietzsche, *Human, All Too Human,* trans. R. J. Hollingdale (Cambridge University Press, Cambridge, 1986), p. 17.
14 See Peter L. Rudnytsky, *Freud and Oedipus* (Columbia University Press, New York, 1987).
15 Quoted in Ronald L. Clark, *Freud: The Man and the Cause* (Jonathan Cape, London, 1980), p. 158.
16 *The Complete Letters of Sigmund Freud to Wilhelm Fliess, 1887–1904,* ed. and

trans. Jeffrey Masson (Belknap Press, Cambridge, Mass., 1985), p. 264.

17   ibid., p. 272.

18   See Jean-Pierre Vernant and Pierre Vidal-Naquet, *Tragedy and Myth in Ancient Greece,* trans. Janet Lloyd (Harvester, Brighton, 1981), pp. 63–86.

19   See R. S. and C. H. Kempe, *The Common Secret: Sexual Abuse of Children and Adolescents* (Freeman, New York, 1984), p. 18.

20   Jeffrey Masson, *Freud: The Assault on Truth* (Faber, London, 1984).

21   See Marie Balmary, *Psychoanalyzing Psychoanalysis: Freud and the Hidden Fault of the Father,* trans. Ned Lukacher (Johns Hopkins University Press, Baltimore, 1982); Marianne Krüll, *Freud and his Father,* trans. Arnold J. Pomerans (Hutchinson, London, 1987).

22   See George Devereux, 'Why Oedipus killed Laius', in *Oedipus: A Folklore Casebook,* ed. Lowell Edmunds and Alan Dundes (Garland, New York, 1983), pp. 215–33.

23   Contrast two accounts of the Schreber case: Freud's *Psycho-Analytic Notes on an Autobiographical Account of a Case of Paranoia* (1911) (*SE,* XII; Pelican 9), and Morton Schatzman, *Soul Murder: Persecution in the Family* (Allen Lane, London, 1973).

24   For discussion, see Bronislaw Malinowski, *Sex and Repression in Savage Society* (Kegan Paul, London, 1927); Melford E. Spiro, *Oedipus in the Trobriands* (University of Chicago Press, Chicago, 1982).

25   Thomas Mann, *Death in Venice,* trans. H. T. Lowe-Porter (Secker, London, 1928), p. 75.

26   See Klaus Müller-Salget, 'Der Tod in Torre di Venere: Spiegelung und Deutung des italienischen Faschismus in Thomas Manns *Mario und der Zauberer'*, *Arcadia,* 18 (1983), pp. 50–65.

27   Thomas Mann, *The Magic Mountain,* trans. H. T. Lowe-Porter (Secker, London, 1927), p. 162.

28   See Peter Burke, *Popular Culture in Early Modern Europe* (Temple Smith, London, 1978), pp. 182–91; Mikhail Bakhtin, *Rabelais and his World,* trans. Helene Iswolsky (MIT Press, Cambridge, Mass., 1968).

29   *The Magic Mountain,* p. 415.

30   Friedrich Nietzsche, *Thus Spoke Zarathustra,* trans. R. J. Hollingdale (Penguin, Harmondsworth, 1969), pp. 61–2.

31   *The Magic Mountain,* p. 602.

32   ibid., p. 626. For comment, see Michael Beddow, *The Fiction of Humanity* (Cambridge University Press, Cambridge, 1982), pp. 265–7.

33   *The Magic Mountain,* p. 624.

34   ibid., p. 823.

35   See Manfred Dierks, *Studien zu Mythos und Psychologie bei Thomas Mann* (Francke, Berne, 1972).

36   C. G. Jung, *Collected Works,* vol. XI, p. 513.

37   Thomas Mann, *The Tales of Jacob,* trans. H. T. Lowe-Porter (Secker, London, 1934), p. 206.

38   ibid., p. 42.

39   ibid., p. 112.

40   'Freud and the Future' is available in T. Mann, *Essays of Three Decades,* trans. H. T. Lowe-Porter (Secker & Warburg, London, 1947).

41   Quoted in Dierks, *Studien,* p. 260.

SUGGESTED READING

Bell, M., *Primitivism*, Methuen, London, 1972.

Bitterli, U., *Die 'Wilden' und die 'Zivilisierten': Grundzüge einer Geistes- und Kulturgeschichte der europäisch-überseeischen Begegnung*, Beck, Munich, 1976.

Bitterli, U., *Cultures in Conflict: Encounters between European and non-European Cultures, 1492–1800*, trans. Ritchie Robertson, Polity, Cambridge, 1989.

Crawford, R., *The Savage and the City in the Work of T. S. Eliot*, Clarendon Press, Oxford, 1987.

Kuper, A., *The Invention of Primitive Society*, Routledge, London, 1988.

Leach, E. (ed.), *The Structural Study of Myth and Totemism*, Tavistock, London, 1967.

Reif, W., *Zivilisationsflucht und literarische Wunschräume*, Metzler, Stuttgart, 1975.

6

Style indirect libre to Stream-of-Consciousness: Flaubert, Joyce, Schnitzler, Woolf

NAOMI SEGAL

Freud willingly admitted that his 'discovery' of the unconscious was not new: the poets had said it all before. What he had added was the scientific dimension of analysis, an attempt to describe the laws of the mind's functioning. In the avant-garde period where, in such theories as Surrealism, the scientific analogy – the claim that an artist works as discoverer rather than maker – seems to have reached a peak of influence, it is often through Freud's theories that creative writers rediscovered what they knew already.

Association of ideas, for example, was no new aesthetic principle: Lawrence Sterne had wittily adapted Hume's philosophy of association in his *Tristram Shandy* in the 1760s. What Freud added was the idea of 'free' association, the belief that, in certain circumstances, the mind could produce an utterance less than usually censored by the ego. We shall see later how far the association patterns in stream-of-consciousness writing are free of a controlling mechanism.

Stream-of-consciousness owes no more to Freud than it does to such other thinkers as William James and Henri Bergson.[1] But it gained an extra impetus when it was perceived that within the area of the mind accessible to the waking consciousness we can find irruptions from the preconscious which are symptoms of unconscious motives. Plenty of writers had sought to represent in some way or other the more secret levels of the mind: anti-realist art has always done this, and so occasionally has realist: Nerval's *Aurélia*, Joyce's own 'Night-town' episode in *Ulysses*. Stream-of-consciousness limits itself to the level of perceived thoughts, and this is how, paradoxically, it is able to suggest the existence of the motives and the vocabulary of the unconscious. We must never forget that there is no direct access to the unconscious; indeed there is no way of knowing that it exists. The existence of the unconscious is simply a good hypothesis to explain otherwise obscure anomalies in the functioning of the conscious mind – dreams, slips of the tongue or pen, parapraxes like forgetting names, mislaying objects, losing one's way – these apparent effects of chance seem to the scientific mind to demand rational explanation. If the thought-text is obscure, then (so says the scientist Freud) somewhere it must make sense. In human affairs there is no chance and no innocence: everything is motivated, and the unconscious is the motivator of the muddled text of thought. Troubled surfaces bespeak a dark but limpid depth.

All this is to stress that, where stream-of-consciousness relies on a theory of the unconscious, it is *en abyme* only. Contrary to the obscurity of its appearance, stream-of-consciousness is not fundamentally an experimental technique. It does not play with language. It is a realist mode, used by writers of fiction with the aim of achieving ever more precisely the illusion that what appears on paper is not of the language world but of the object-world – Mr Ramsay's enquiries, Leopold Bloom's obsessions – as if they pre-existed the text. (For this reason, for all their resemblance, the texts of the Surrealists are not stream-of-consciousness: they purport to be direct transcriptions of the author's, not a character's, mind.)[2] Because it is realist, it presents thoughts in words, more or less mimetically but always unproblematically. Philosophy and psychology cannot resolve the question of whether there is sub-verbal thought; but Freud sliced the Gordian knot by realizing that all we can do is analyse the word-patterns of utterances, and thus he exchanged the Romantic love of 'unheard melodies' for the close inspection of perceptible symptoms. As far as stream-of-consciousness fiction is concerned, the words on the page matter because they serve to illustrate the levels and kinds of psyche being represented.

To speak of 'levels' is to indulge in a geological image of the mind. This need not imply gradations of value – there is nothing superior in either the 'high' or the 'deep' – but can simply suggest, as does Freud, that the further we go from the conscious organization of thought in speech the more the 'underside' of our psyche asserts itself and the less control the reason, the inhibiting censor, the conscious wish to be civilized, will exert. In this model the 'deepest' level is the most instinctual. Together with this goes an inclination to see the speech level as the most individuated. I speak; by saying 'I' I assert my subjecthood: I choose how, why and whereof I may speak. My accent, my habits of diction, my timbre or tone characterize me distinctively. The 'deeper' the level, the less it is articulated, the less individual accent and idiolect will be apparent. If it is explicitly pitched at a sub-speech level, the language used by the realist writer has no need to represent voice in this way. It can be, or pretend to be, universal, neutral, undifferentiated – it can sound as though it were no particular character's voice but simply the representation of mind.

Against this model, various objections can be made. Firstly, that at the most articulated level I am already motivated not by reason (Freud has little time for this concept) but simply by conscious rather than unconscious aims of pleasure or self-preservation. But a more important objection is that the concept of individuality is inherently unstable. In the overt transaction of speech we are at our most social. When I speak, my accent is not 'mine' but that of my region or class; my turns of phrase bespeak a history embedded in groups and places; my habits of 'hedging', stammering, misplacing words or letters belong to my gender or socio-cultural position.[3] There is nothing in my speech that I entirely control. Knowing that no utterance is ever innocent, we also know our words are only ever lent us.

The presentation of speech in pre-twentieth-century literature is instructive here. Compare the talk of Lysander and Bottom or of Don Juan and Sganarelle: the admission of proletarian characters to serious literature is conditional upon their being distinguished by regional accent and quaint locutions, so that the parallels set up between them and the heroes are safely contained. Later, in the fiction of Balzac or Dickens, the characters given recurrent turns of phrase, lisps or verbal mannerisms tend to be, or thereby become, impossible to take seriously. The more speech-patterns are idiosyncratic, then, the more the character seems *no more than* a member of a regional, class or social sub-group. This is essentially an ironic device, relying (as I shall shortly show *style indirect libre*, to rely) on a silent implied 'tone' common to the author and the reader, a 'classless accent', the Received Pronunciation of literature.

But the reader is not so safe as that may suggest. Labouring in Balzac's novels through pages of speech from Nucingen or Schmucke, in which the German accent is reproduced by a tireless exchange of Ps for Bs and Ts for Ds, we discover the only way to decipher it at speed is to read it out loud. If we are not to skip these bits altogether, we find ourselves obliged to stop being readers and become speakers instead. This casts us into an embarrassing position, producing the author's *de haut en bas* characterization by stepping down off his level.

The author alone holds the privileged position. Not for nothing does Proust observe that the frail or corrupt body of the writer is cast off when he [sic] 'becomes' text. As a speaker or even a reader I always have an accent. But as that bodiless thing the implied author, I have only style.[4] Thus the linguistic vulnerability of Joyce's Molly, Woolf's Lily or Schnitzler's Else, what makes their words revealing and interpretable, originates not in the 'rag-and-bone shop' of their unconscious but in the aspirations of their authors to be the mind in control. The character's lapse is the author's *coup*. To be the implied author is to go one better than Freud, being not so much analyst as God. And to look more closely at this old-fashioned paradox, we must go back fifty or sixty years to Flaubert.

'L'auteur dans son œuvre', he wrote in a letter of 1852, 'doit être comme Dieu dans l'univers: présent partout et visible nulle part.'[5] A visible God would be a mere doll; only the *deus absconditus* has power. The hidden author's power resides above all in irony, and to examine how that works I want to look at the central innovation in Flaubert's rhetoric — a device which later ranges itself among the resources of stream-of-consciousness writing – *style indirect libre*.

Flaubert no more invented *style indirect libre* than Freud discovered the unconscious. It had been used before him and appears in countless other languages; critics point to its use in La Fontaine, Goethe, Jane Austen.[6] It has also been observed in the Bible, where it tends to be introduced by the figure 'and behold' (*vehinneh*). Meir Sternberg quotes an example from Judges 4: 21–2:

> Jael the wife of Heber took a tent peg, and took the hammer in her hand, and went softly to him, and drove the peg into his temple and it went on into the ground. He was fast asleep and weary. So he died. And behold, Barak was pursuing Sisera. Jael came out to meet him and said to him, Come and I will show thee the man whom thou seekest. And he came into her tent, *and behold, Sisera fallen, dead, and a peg in his temple.*[7]

In the last phrase, the narrative repeats information we already have. Thus we are alerted to the fact that it is Barak who is beholding Sisera dead; we are seeing as and what he sees. The order of information (death first, peg second) also stresses Barak's viewpoint by showing his scale of priorities and order of discovery.

Style indirect libre was the name given by Charles Bally in 1912 to a form of narrative where the usual narratorial third person and preterite tense continue without use of introductory verb ('he thought that . . .', 'she felt that . . .'), but where we sense that the language represents the thoughts or speech of a character. This ambiguity leads to what some writers have called the 'double intonation' or 'dual voice'.[8] The terms used for it in German and English – *erlebte Rede*, free indirect discourse – indicate that it has a close affinity to spoken language. Indeed it is sometimes defined by the presence of speech-patterns in a written text, but it is not true that it is never found in direct speech. It may even have its origin in the sarcastic reporting of one person's discourse to another: 'she couldn't come: her feet's been playing her up again.'

Style indirect libre is not always used for reasons of irony:[9] the Biblical passage quoted above serves rather for emphasis and heightened drama. Roy Pascal takes examples from the work of Austen and George Eliot where sympathy for a character's inner turmoil dictates the 'borrowing' of her language. He chooses these instances of non-ironic *style indirect libre* to show that the device is often used, before Flaubert, on the basis of a dialect shared by author, reader and character, to shore up rather than score off social groupings. Thus Goethe's characters in *Die Wahlverwandtschaften* or Austen's village gentlefolk all talk very much alike and it seems natural that they should borrow their author-narrator's voice to think in. But I want to argue that the ironic use by Flaubert is significant for exposing and exploiting the differences always implied by similarities, and for creating distance precisely where there risks being too little, none or almost none.

Flaubert is famous also for having said to a friend, perhaps ironically: 'Madame Bovary, c'est moi.' The ironic defence may not really have been necessary, for everyone, beginning with Baudelaire, hastened to refute the 'unsexing' this analogy implies by testifying to Emma's 'masculinity'.[10] Even in Sartre, we find the phenomenon of male hysteria coming to Flaubert's rescue as it did to Freud's. However, irony or not, we now recognize that the phrase is also an admission: I am that woman, *idiot de la famille*, clumsy sub-tragic dancing bear, unable to go anywhere, even in language. Flaubert has much at stake in Emma – as have all authors in all characters – and being like her is no less a risk than making her like himself. She must at all costs be distinguished from him.

He *is* an author only by distinguishing himself from a character, just as a man is a man by not being a woman.[11] Specifically, as I shall suggest, his control depends on her uncontrol. Emma must not escape or enjoy, in order that the pleasure and free play of the text remain in the author's hands. This battle is engaged most seriously in the question of style, as Flaubert clearly perceived when he expressed his desire to create 'un livre sur rien, un livre sans attache extérieure que se tiendrait de lui-même par la force interne de son style'.[12] In this paradox, the ideal book has no content, and style comes into its own, unreferential, as matter becomes less. Subject matter cannot, of course, be wished away. But the greatness of authorship requires the events and characters to be diminished, reductive, disappointing; and Flaubert does this by an extreme strategy of realism 'behind' which the author will seem to disappear.

We know well how urgently Flaubert tried to hide his authorial presence. He does it, or tries to do it, by making the narrative position unstable so that it is impossible to figure a character we might call the narrator or, worse, the author-narrator. But *style indirect libre*, like the other devices of realism, depends on the formation of an author-narratorial 'tone' from which we distinguish the character's implicit voice. It is not so much the narrator as the implied author who is at stake here – our sense of the difference between this tone and this voice depends on our distinct images of two persons, the 'author' and the character. What happens in *Madame Bovary* is that when we infer the presence of an Emma whose idiom 'cannot be Flaubert's we are forming a 'Flaubert' who cannot be Emma.

Let us begin by looking at some examples from *Madame Bovary*:

> Est-ce que cette misère durerait toujours? Est-ce qu'elle n'en sortirait pas? Elle valait bien, cependant, toutes celles qui vivaient heureuses![13]

> Elle allait donc posséder enfin ces joies de l'amour, cette fièvre du bonheur dont elle avait désespéré. Elle entrait dans quelque chose de merveilleux où tout serait passion, extase, délire . . . N'avait-elle pas assez souffert! Mais elle triomphait maintenant, et l'amour si longtemps contenu, jaillissait tout entier avec des bouillonnements joyeux. (pp. 473–4)

L'histoire de la nourrice était la pire excuse, tout le monde sachant bien à Yonville que la petite Bovary, depuis un an, etait revenue chez ses parents. D'ailleurs, personne n'habitait aux environs; ce chemin ne conduisait qu'à la Huchette; Binet, donc, avait deviné d'où elle venait, et il ne se tairait pas, il bavarderait, c'était certain! (p. 477)

[Would this unhappiness last for ever? Would she never get through it? And yet she was certainly the equal of all those women living in happiness!

At last now she would possess those delights of love, that fever of bliss that she had almost ceased to hope for. She was entering a wonderful state where all would be passion, ecstasy, delirious joy . . . Had she not suffered enough? But now she was triumphing, and love, so long held back, burst forth in a bubbling of happiness.

The wet-nurse was the worst possible pretext to give, since everyone in Yonville knew the Bovary child had been back at her parents' house for the past year. For that matter, nobody lived around here; this path led only to la Huchette; so Binet must have guessed where she had been, and he would never keep quiet, he would spread it to everyone, that was certain!]

What are the indices of *style indirect libre* here? One can point to the instances of speech-idiom interrupting the text (rhetorical questions, repetitions, 'donc', 'enfin', 'ce', 'maintenant') or of typographical hints also suggestive of speech (exclamation marks, or, elsewhere, italics). Thus, in my last example, the phrase 'la petite Bovary' signals that we have one indirect quotation within another; or the use of 'maintenant' in the last sentence of my second example resolves what could be a genuine ambiguity. But something else seems to be going on too. The simplest response puts it thus: 'It must be Emma here because Flaubert wouldn't have put it like that.' Yet if we pursue a few examples, we find that there is no consistent stylistic or thematic reason for the distinction: sometimes it seems her thoughts clothed in his too-fine prose, sometimes the clichés are hers, the sensibility his.[14] What is constant is the distinction of this His and Hers and the hierarchical relation between the two. *Style indirect libre* depends on a concept of stupidity as reliably enshrined in language. Flaubert wouldn't − because he wouldn't care to − talk like that, much less write like it.

This irony is not directed only towards a female character − Charles Bovary, Frédéric Moreau, Bouvard and Pécuchet are also damned by their garbled blinkeredness. But the quintessential figure is Emma because it is in her that Flaubert comes nearest to loving the foolish double. She comes in for none of the rough distaste we see in Frédéric, nor the bare contempt directed at Charles. She is the exact reverse of Homais, whose thoughts are never presented through *style indirect libre* (though his flatulent direct speech is), and who is the only man in the text who never desires Emma. Thus when Emma, who on one level represents Flaubert's own narcissism, is 'opened up' in style indirect libre, she must release the host by seeming stupid. She is stupid above all in her thoughts: here she must lack the grace she effortlessly shows elsewhere. For the brake on her subjectivity is the crucial thing: she must not be creative. Like many another foolish Romantic hero, Emma has read so many books that she is unfitted for life. Flaubert's wise creative male writer can only be implied by a stupid and derivative female reader.

Emma has fed on clichés and these are all she can be allowed to give forth. In Joyce there are two instances of a very similar ironic usage wherein a silly girl is implied by the artful use of cliché: the eponymous heroines of the short story 'Eveline' and the 'Gerty MacDowell' episode of *Ulysses*. Here, exactly as in Emma's passages of *style indirect libre*, we infer the thoughts of the woman through language that seems hers – or, more precisely, we sense the controlling presence of a Joyce or a Flaubert who knows her clichés better than she does herself. Critics may spill ink over whether the word 'mused' in the narrative of 'Eveline' belongs to the heroine or the implied author.[15] But it can easily be seen that Eveline's naiveté ends where Joyce's sophistication begins. For it is the cultured, controlled implied author who is the real object of narcissistic desire. To reverse an old myth, where she is body, he can be soul.

There are many important points that such critics miss. One is that the certainty of what vocabulary she 'would' use ignores the whole question of how our passive vocabulary (the words we know but do not use, that fund that is so massive in the pre-linguistic infant) might be the language we readily think in; another that their confidence in knowing how a young working-class female feels and thinks might attest less to the breadth than to the narrowness of their sensitivity. But this kind of reading rarely admits the political dimension of realism.

Nevertheless as a consequence of this sexual-political deal the reader of the text is again placed in an awkward position. As Wayne Booth's *Rhetoric of Irony* has shown, irony depends for its success on another, more nearly overt transaction: the reader infers the intention of the implied author and becomes that author's implied reader by agreeing to a shared laugh at the follies of characters. In the Emma/Flaubert structure I am taking as the model of *style indirect libre*, this is complicated by an equation between reading and gender: by the very act of reading, we are cast in the role of the female character. Much as we might like to be clever authors, what we are doing makes us foolish girls.

The habit of conferring male gender along with authority on the apparently sexless narratorial voice is shown up in two passing remarks by critics of these texts. Both find themselves uncomfortable with the possibility that a female writer's narrator could be gendered female. Roy Pascal on Jane Austen: 'so truly is this impersonal narrator the "spirit of the story", that one cannot ascribe him/her a sex, and it is misleading to use either "him" or "her" for this function; I use "him" throughout this study in the same way one uses "man" for "mankind" (in Jane Austen's case it

usefully makes a clearer distinction between the author and the narrator)'
(*The Dual Voice*, pp. 45–6); Seymour Chatman on Dorothy Richardson's
Miriam: 'these are her direct impressions, not some narrator's account, in
his words' (*Story and Discourse*, p. 187, italics Chatman's). Pascal actually
reinforces the argument about gender by his anxiety to distinguish Austen
from her 'male persona': such scruples do not seem to affect the pronouns of
critics dealing with male authors. This problem highlights, for it is simply
one example of the transaction of reading, how far involved sexual politics
is in our patterning of texts.

In the stream-of-consciousness writing of Joyce, Schnitzler and Woolf, we
find the technique applied to three different levels of the mind, with the
corresponding loosening of mimetic specificity in the representation of
'voice'. I shall examine some examples from each, looking everywhere for
the position of the implied author and, especially, seeing how differently
male and female characters are represented.

In *Ulysses* (1922) the clever, evasive implied author is ubiquitous. He of
course has put together the endless stylistic play, the ever new angles, the
monstrously complex web of references. The reader can never catch up: the
best we can do, given a long spell on a desert island, would be to read and
reread until we almost attained the heights of the *scriptible*. Yet it is Joyce,
of my three authors, who uses stream-of-consciousness in the most
conventional speech-level way, as one of a range of realist techniques that
distinguish characters from each other. Compare these two passages:

> Ineluctable modality of the visible: at least that if no more, thought through
> my eyes. Signatures of all things I am here to read, seaspawn and seawrack,
> the nearing tide, that rusty boot. Snotgreen, bluesilver, rust: coloured signs.
> Limits of the diaphane.[16]

> Yes. Thought so. Sloping into the Empire. Gone. Plain soda would do him
> good. Where Pat Kinsella had his Harp theatre before Whitbread ran the
> Queen's. Broth of a boy. Dion Boucicault business with his harvestmoon face
> in a poky bonnet. Three Purty Maids from School. (p. 167)

Both are obscure, if by obscurity we mean difficulty of understanding what
is meant. But the first is obscure in the usual sense of intellectually
over-demanding, the second because its references are specific to the time
and place or to the individual's life. Both have accent and ideolect: compare
'broth of a boy' to 'limits of the diaphane'. As these two phrases show,
Stephen is characterized by his polysyllabic, Bloom by his monosyllabic
diction. Both register what is in front of them and both think intertextually;
but we immediately recognize a difference of socio-economic class, interests,
age perhaps. It has often been noted that authorial irony is directed much
more at Stephen than at Bloom; like Emma, the autobiographical function
of the former makes him need to be distanced, while the latter, already

established as outsider and cuckold, gradually elicits a second-degree respect.

Molly's more or less autonomous monologue is at another level of generality. This is immediately signalled by the look of the text: no punctuation, full stops or paragraphs. The image of the stream is as closely represented as it can be on the page. Now we must not forget that no one thinks (or even speaks) in 'sentences': just as the division of written language into phonemes and morphemes is a typographical convenience. But if we remember that Stephen and Bloom, for all their other distinguishing marks, both have their thoughts broken up by full stops, we might ask what is being done differently with the woman's character.

Molly is only half-awake. As Dorrit Cohn points out, such autonomous monologues as this tend to begin or end with sleep; this one is throughout at a level very close to that of unconsciousness. She is almost continuously immobilized in bed. Recumbent, she roams in time and desire, but always around her body's senses. Now this 'lower-level' narrative suggests three things: the sleepy state of the moment; a personal lazy sensuality; the river-like flow of mythical woman. These are not three choices but all equally produced by the effect of the typography, and all together implied by the figure of Molly – like that of Anna Livia Plurabelle after her, wife, narrator and River Liffey.

Within the familiar oedipal triangle the woman is isolated as pure function: she is neither desiring child nor authoritative parent. Molly occupies a strange hinterland for, while Bloom replaces the son who haunts him, Stephen does not find a mother. The cuckold is given back his potency, the boy joins the fathers and the woman's last word is 'the female word *yes*'.[17]

The author's place is correspondingly different in the stream-of-consciousness of the two sexes. In the men's sections, a narratorial voice intervenes to place the character as he moves around, while Molly's rare movements are represented with great ingenuity through a series of plausible reactions in her voice. In this passage she gets up to put on a sanitary towel and use the chamber-pot; the italicized phrases mark her movements:

> O *patience above its pouring out of me like the sea* anyhow he didn't make me pregnant as big as he is *I dont want to ruin the clean sheets* the clean linen I wore I brought it on too *damn it damn it* and they always want to see a stain on the bed to know youre a virgin for them all thats troubling them theyre such fools too you could be a widow or divorced 40 times over a daub of red ink would do or blackberry juice no thats too purply O *Jamesy let me up out of this* pooh sweets of sin whoever suggested that business for women what between clothes and cooking and children *this damned old bed too jingling like the dickens* . . . *wheres the chamber gone easy Ive a holy horror of its breaking under me* (pp. 690–91).

Dorrit Cohn analyses this section and concludes: 'we search in vain through "Penelope" for a first-person coupled with an action verb in the present tense – precisely the combination that creates the most jarring effect in less well-executed interior monologues' (p. 227). The absence of implied-author intrusion is skilfully achieved here, whereas in the men's passages Joyce does not seem to need it. The effect is to deprive the woman of all use of the first person coupled with an action verb in the present tense. The author is, like Flaubert, playing the hidden God.

Molly's position is both more singular than the men's – she is all voice – and entirely plural – pure murky flow, all her individuality types her as 'the sex'. It is where she is potentially the most individuated (coping with the start of her period, drifting in and out of memories, assenting) that she is the most identified as archetypal woman, in a way that is quite distinct from Bloom's function as Everyman or Stephen's as Christ/Hamlet. Penelope does not weave but is woven.

Schnitzler's two autonomous stream-of-consciousness narratives, *Leutnant Gustl* (1901) and *Fräulein Else* (1924) were written almost a quarter of a century apart. The latter shows far more that fascination with the hysterical psyche that made the author seem to Freud a veritable double, although this is no simple case of influence as is attested by Schnitzler's clairvoyantly early study of hypnosis, *Paracelsus* (1897).[18] The two eponymous protagonists are young Viennese, speaking in the dialect of their region and class. They are distinguished by the diction and preoccupations typical of the upper-class officer:

Aber was geht mich denn das alles an? – Was scher' ich mich denn um solche Sachen? – Ein Gemeiner von der Verpflegsbranche ist ja jetzt mehr als ich . . . ich bin ja überhaupt nicht mehr auf der Welt . . . es ist ja aus mit mir . . . Ehre verloren, alles verloren! . . . Ich hab' ja nichts anderes zu tun, als meinen Revolver zu laden und . . . Gustl, Gustl, mir scheint, du glaubst noch immer nicht recht daran?[19]

[*What's all that got to do with me anyway? – What do I care about things like that? – The lowest private in the supply corps is higher than me now . . . I've got no business on earth any more . . . it's all up with me . . . Lose your honour, you lose everything! There's nothing left for me but to load my pistol and . . . Gustl, Gustl, you haven't really taken it in yet, have you?*]

and of the middle-class Jewish girl:

Wenn er mir nur nicht so unsympathisch wäre. Auch die Art, wie er mich ansieht. Nein, Herr Dorsday, ich glaube Ihnen Ihre Eleganz nicht und nicht Ihr Monokel und nicht Ihre Noblesse. Sie könnten ebensogut mit alten Kleidern handeln wie mit alten Bildern. – Aber Else! Else, was fällt dir denn ein. – Oh, ich kann mir das erlauben. Mir sieht's niemand an. Ich bin sogar blond, rötlichblond, und Rudi sieht absolut aus wie ein Aristokrat. (p. 253)

[*If only I didn't dislike him so much. Even the way he looks at me. No, Herr Dorsday, you can't fool me with your elegant ways or your monocle or your nobility. You could just as easily be a dealer in old clothes as old paintings. – But Else, Else, what are you thinking of? – Oh I'd get away with it. No one can tell with me. I've even got blond hair, red-gold, and Rudi looks exactly like an aristocrat.*]

And they are 'overheard' at a particular moment of their daily lives, as are the figures in *Ulysses*. But for Gustl and Else, there is no suggestion that the moment is arbitrarily chosen. It is a moment of crisis, reminiscent in many ways of the twenty-four hour crux of classical tragedy. Both are forced to rethink everything they live for, fail to learn from the crisis and have a brush with death. But whereas Gustl is rescued from a suicide of honour by the timely death of the baker who has insulted him, Else dies of the poison swallowed on impulse, while uttering unheard pleas to save her life.

The different endings of the two texts distinguish them as versions of comedy and tragedy. *Leutnant Gustl* is a comic satire; the protagonist is stupid and absurd but his mistaken values are presented as dangerous chiefly to himself. The recurrent strains of anti-semitism and sexual casualness typify a vulgarity that complements his blindly conventional attitude to military honour. He comes close to, but never has to pursue, thoughts of his own mortality, and he never faces the significance of the offence to his narcissism in having his sword gripped by a man calling him 'stupid boy'. His sloppiness with language and ideas combine to make us disinclined to take him seriously, so that while we share the sense of shock and absurdity at a young life almost cut off, we scarcely rise to a concern for his safety.

Else is a much more complex case, not least because the issue of sexuality is here right to the fore, and the passivity into which she is cast makes her foolish death particularly painful. She dies, like so many heroines of fiction, not out of masochism but because of the *impasse* of her gender position. Her active desire to be seen becomes parodied by the impotent gaze that Dorsday offers her. Without ever suffering the display he has demanded and which she is both repelled and tempted by, she fails to reverse it into something she controls, so that when she exposes herself she is immediately cast into the immobility of the hysteric, carried upstairs, laid on her bed. Like Molly, she co-exists in physical stillness and mental rage, and here the dramatic ironies of stream-of-consciousness multiply, as she hears her doctor cousin and his mistress call her name, replies, and is not heard. Cissy teases Paul with Else's nakedness, and embraces him while Else implores him inaudibly to save her and he merely remarks 'Scheint dir nicht, daß sie lächelt?' ('doesn't she look as though she's smiling?', p. 298). Finally, the others realize something is wrong, but by this time Else has begun to float out of consciousness and we infer her death when the narrative ceases mid-word: 'Ich fliege . . . ich träume . . . ich schlafe . . . ich träu . . . traü –

ich flie . . . [*'I'm flying . . . I'm dreaming . . . I'm sleeping . . . I'm drea . . . drea – I'm fly . . .'*] (p. 299, ellipses Schnitzler's).

This is perhaps the most extreme use of stream-of-consciousness to imply that the mind is co-extensive with its utterance. Else emits first-person action verbs in the present tense when she is at the very end of a life in which her impulses and wishes had no place except mediated through others' demands. Dorsday was only a version of the imperatives of her father's fecklessness: he had squandered the family's resources for the nth time, and it was up to her to buy a loan with her beauty. At this point, Else is fascinated not so much by the fulfilment of an exhibitionistic fantasy as by the chimera of power over the men who think they are using her. But – very much like Freud's 'Dora' – it turns out that this is never a real option. The nearest either young woman gets to being heard (as opposed to being looked at) is by falling into silence: Dora leaves analysis, Else dies. Silence is only one step beyond the 'female word yes'.

Fräulein Else is many things: it partakes of the comic satire of *Gustl*, for it too is a portrait of a superficially spoilt, simple youngster; it has the stifling atmosphere of a tragedy, but also the apparent lightness of a story with a nasty twist at the end; it is an exploration of the limits of consciousness; but it is most of all a fictional case history. In case histories, names are disguised but everything else is supposed to be scrupulously truthful (as if the rest could stay in place with the identifying aspects removed, or as if any written text were not, as Freud admits in 'Dora', already fiction) and presented as an exemplary scientific report. The individual and the typical meet in the case history as they are supposed to meet in the realist novel. Thus, exactly as in Molly Bloom's monologue, although the last word is so different, every detail of Else's specificity goes towards a portrait of her sex.

Both these women characters are drawn with considerable sensitivity and a kind of sympathy – as is Emma Bovary – but the doom of all three is their restriction in the face of a world they cannot act in. This is shown by the power of the language they finally only waste. It brings them nothing. Only we perceive what it means and even then, what it 'means' is only ever signification, never a willed intention. Intention, like style, belongs to the author who, however generously, holds the keys.

A woman's relation to authorship is always problematic. There is now no lack of research in the area of what Elaine Showalter calls 'gynocritics'.[20] The problem lies not just in the crude but very real traditional identification of pen with penis,[21] but in questions of women's access to the media of communication and to a public voice. Woolf pointed out in *A Room of One's Own* (1929) that a writer needs a regular income and private space, necessities rarely available to women; she also deplored, as many others have since, how the female creative tradition tends to fall out of recorded history. While the 'strong poets' of Harold Bloom battle it out on the gloomy ground of their oedipal ambition, women writers have found themselves motherless. They have, in other words, no valid relation with authority; to be a writer is to be less a woman. Woolf takes this argument a stage further:

> For we think back through our mothers if we are women. It is useless to go to the great men writers for help, however much one may go to them for pleasure. [They] never helped a woman yet, though she may have learnt a few tricks of them and adapted them to her use. The weight, the pace, the stride of a man's mind are too unlike her own for her to lift anything substantial from him successfully. The ape is too distant to be sedulous. Perhaps the first thing she would find, setting pen to paper, was that there was no common sentence ready for her use.[22]

She gives an example of the male sentence and women writers' problems with it, and goes on to suggest that the conventional genres too are man-made:

> The novel alone was young enough to be soft in her hands – another reason, perhaps, why she wrote novels. Yet who shall say that even now 'the novel' (I give it inverted commas to mark my sense of the words' inadequacy), who shall say that even this most pliable of forms is rightly shaped for her use? No doubt we shall find her knocking that into shape for herself when she has the free use of her limbs; and providing some new vehicle, not necessarily in verse, for the poetry in her. For it is the poetry that is still denied outlet. And I went on to ponder how a woman nowadays would write a poetic tragedy in five acts. Would she use verse? – would she not use prose rather? (p. 74)

The new poetry or drama would be in prose, and use a 'female sentence', whatever that might turn out to be. Dorothy Richardson, looking back on how she began her novel-cycle *Pilgrimage* around thirty years earlier, wrote in 1938:

> since all [the authors of modern realist novels] happened to be men, the present writer, proposing at this moment to write a novel and looking round for a contemporary pattern, was faced with the choice between following one of her regiments and attempting to produce a feminine equivalent of the current masculine realism.[23]

This identification of the new technique with female consciousness and a uniquely female utterance is not theirs alone; both contemporary and recent critics have endorsed it.[24] It has to do, though, less with the supposed special interest of women in the emotions or the hitherto secret truths of women's experience than with the politics of the character/implied author relation. Writing from within a world where her utterance has never had authority, it is perhaps possible for a female author to deal differently with the character whose voice she 'borrows'. Richardson in a sense by-passed this possibility by creating a huge novel cycle, like Proust, on the autobiographical model. If her protagonist Miriam exults "'I wouldn't have a man's – *consciousness* for anything'",[25] the author has avoided the real problem of stream-of-consciousness, which is how to represent the consciousness you do not have.

Let me make one more theoretical contrast. Both Joyce and Woolf stress the importance of the everyday as subject-matter. Joyce points out that 'most lives are made up like the modern painter's themes, of jugs and pots and plates, back-streets and blowsy living-rooms inhabited by blowsy women'; Woolf speaks of 'the cotton wool of daily life' in which 'a geat part of every day is not lived consciously. One walks, eats, sees things, deals with what has to be done; the broken vacuum cleaner; ordering dinner; writing orders to Mabel; washing; cooking dinner; bookbinding.'[26] The viewpoint in the first of these quotations is that of an artist freely looking: what he sees are the shapes in a Cézanne or a Bonnard. The viewpoint of the second, much of it in a quasi-first person with active verbs in the present tense, is of the detailed living out of a frustrating routine of work inside which she will seek her material. 'There is a pattern hid behind the cotton wool' (p. 84), Woolf concludes.

In Woolf's first major stream-of-consciousness novel, *Mrs Dalloway* (1925), there are two main centres of consciousness: the society hostess Clarissa Dalloway, whose outward activities culminate in a party, and the shell-shocked Septimus Smith who on the same afternoon commits suicide. The common element between them, apart from time and space simultaneity, is the bitterly satirized psychiatrist Sir William Bradshaw, a man's man entirely out of sympathy with his patient and more or less directly responsible for his death. As Elaine Showalter comments: 'it remained to Virginia Woolf . . . to connect the shell-shocked veteran with the repressed woman of the man-governed world through their common enemy, the nerve specialist.'[27] Whereas Woolf had herself suffered from physicians like Bradshaw, she chose to represent the entrapment of the patient through the voice of a man 'castrated' into a passive position by the male version of hysteria. Smith's mind wanders through fantasy and memory unreached, like Emma's and Else's, by the sympathy of others, and he too succumbs to death. In the meantime, the women make aesthetic objects: Rezia's garnished hat, Clarissa Dalloway's party. 'Let us not take it for granted that life exists more fully in what is commonly thought big than in what is commonly called small', writes Woolf.[28] Women's creativity, confined to the apparently trivial, is the only activity of this work. As understated as it is – and after all the text ends on Clarissa misread as the beautiful centrepiece of her party – the gender burdens of active and passive have been reversed.

To the Lighthouse (1927) begins as *Ulysses* ends, on 'the female word *yes*'. But this is not the view of a blowsy woman fantasized by a man, it is a reconstruction of the mother who died when the author was adolescent. The yes is not sexual but maternal. It is addressed in speech, not thought, to the woman's child, and is a tacit rebuke to the father's literal-minded no. James wants to visit the lighthouse; his philosopher father insists the weather will not be good enough; his mother allows him to hope. These two versions of truthfulness – answering the question or answering the child – typify the paternal and the maternal in the novel. Moreover, as we quickly see, Mrs Ramsay's creative nurturing includes the man as well as the eight children: all of them rely for their continuance and success on the fountain of her care. She is, like Julia Stephen, 'central . . . the whole thing' (*Moments of Being*, p. 96).

The stream-of-consciousness narrative moves lightly in this text from character to character. One of the most important innovations is Woolf's use of the pronoun 'one'. We have already seen its significance in describing her own daily life. Used in a character's thoughts, it sits equidistant between the first and third persons and has an ambiguity of general and particular that, unlike a similar ambiguity in the figures of Molly and Else, is not implied but chosen. Ungendered, it has a certain generous imprecision that is perhaps one key characteristic of the 'female sentence' or 'the poetry in her'. Here are some examples from a passage of Mrs Ramsay's thought:

> No, she thought, putting together some of the pictures he had cut out – a refrigerator, a mowing machine, a gentleman in evening dress – children never forget. For this reason, it was so important what one said and what one did, and it was a relief when they went to bed . . . Not as oneself did one find rest ever, in her experience (she accomplished here something dexterous with her needles), but as a wedge of darkness . . . It was odd, she thought, how if one was alone, one leant to things, inanimate things; trees, streams, flowers; felt they expressed one; felt they became one; felt they knew one, in a sense were one; felt an irrational tenderness thus (she looked at the long steady light) as for oneself.[29]

Here the most remarkable thing is the way in which Mrs Ramsay, who is that quintessential other the recollected figure of a beloved mother, is presented from within. The implied author, a middle-aged woman herself, has as much reason as Joyce and Schnitzler to represent the woman from a distance. The whole text is indeed about the darkness that comes over the scene when the mother parenthetically dies; and, as we shall see in a moment, a critique of Mrs Ramsay is made through a very different woman who aspires to established genres of art. But here the impossible is achieved. Through the use of 'one', an epiphanal blurring of the symbol-object and its beholder, and above all in the blending of the mystical with the everyday (cut-out pictures, skilful knitting, trees and flowers), Mrs Ramsay's mind is kept both productively autonomous and emblematic without satire.

This is an exceptional book in many respects. Where else do we find such assurances of the beauty of a fifty-year-old woman? Or the adoration of a mother by the figure of a daughter? Mrs Ramsay's beauty does not objectify her; she never rests long enough to become either decorative or narcissistic. She gives forth to the point of exhaustion – 'there was scarcely a shell of herself left for her to know herself by; all was so lavished and spent' (p. 39) – yet precisely in spending herself she is, like the lighthouse, replenished. Many critics suggest that Woolf's key technique in *To the Lighthouse* is the use of symbols to convey feeling; but what happens here is rather a surpassing of the central symbol so obviously present as phallic. In her 'moment of being' Mrs Ramsay uses the lighthouse to recognize and love herself. Similarly in the crisis between her and her husband initially perceived by James as a sort of rape, she ends by taking over the fecundating role of male sexuality: 'there throbbed through her, like the pulse in a spring which has expanded to its full width and now gently ceases to beat, the rapture of successful creation' (p. 40).

The other key centre of consciousness in the text is the younger woman Lily Briscoe. Lily as displaced daughter, doubly bereaved by Mrs Ramsay's death, finds herself in love with a woman she cannot altogether respect: it is with her head in the mother's lap that she laughs 'almost hysterically at the thought of Mrs Ramsay presiding with immutable calm over destinies which she completely failed to understand' (p. 50). In particular, the incorrigible match-maker – this like her dinner-party is Mrs Ramsay's aesthetic project – fails to understand Lily's aspiration to serious (that is, public, men's) art. But through the persona of Lily, the homage has no trace of bitterness. If the last stroke of the painting in which Lily has her vision and accomplishes her creative work as the others reach the lighthouse balances the crucial blur of the mother-and-son icon, it is the mother-daughter couple that is finally made complete, and the presence of the implied author brings them together without irony.

Woolf's ultimate 'experiment' in stream-of-consciousness is *The Waves* (1931) and it is here most clearly that she fulfils her aim of recording 'the atoms as they fall upon the mind in the order in which they fall, [and tracing] the pattern, however disconnected and incoherent in appearance, which each sight or incident scores upon the consciousness'.[30] To see how far she has gone from a directly mimetic representation of mind, compare the following:

> Once upon a time and a very good time it was there was a moocow coming down along the road and this moocow that was coming down along the road met a nicens little boy named baby tuckoo. . . . .
>
> His father told him that story: his father looked at him through a glass: he had a hairy face.
>
> He was baby tuckoo. The moocow came down the road where Betty Byrne lived: she sold lemon platt.
>
> *O, the wild rose blossoms*
> *On the little green place.*
>
> He sang that song. That was his song.
>
> *O, the green wothe botheth.*

When you wet the bed, first it is warm then it gets cold. His mother put on the oilsheet. That had the queer smell.

'I see a ring,' said Bernard, 'hanging above me. It quivers and hangs in a loop of light.'

'I see a slab of pale yellow,' said Susan, 'spreading away until it meets a purple stripe.'

'I hear a sound,' said Rhoda, 'cheep, chirp; cheep chirp; going up and down.'

'I see a globe,' said Neville, 'hanging down in a drop against the enormous flanks of some hill.'

'I see a crimson tassel,' said Jinny, 'twisted with gold threads.'

'I hear something stamping,' said Louis. 'A great beast's foot is chained. It stamps, and stamps, and stamps.'

'Look at the spider's web on the corner of the balcony,' said Bernard. 'It has beads of water on it, drops of white light.'

'The leaves are gathered round the window like pointed ears,' said Susan.

'A shadow falls on the path,' said Louis, 'like an elbow bent.'[31]

These passages both come from the openings of texts organized chronologically. The first, from Joyce's *A Portrait of the Artist as a Young Man* (1916) represents Stephen in his infancy by reproducing his world of sensations and language: the repetitive diction of fairytales he is told, the song he lisps, impressions of smell, sight and touch. It is mimetic like the men's passages in *Ulysses:* we quickly identify the essential here, which is the age of the protagonist. With the second passage, from *The Waves*, we are likely to remain puzzled much longer. Only after reading further, probably, will we realize that the first six sentences are supposed to be spoken by preverbal infants. Two conclusions follow. First, that here and elsewhere the use of 'said' and inverted commas is not to be taken literally: the thoughts are not uttered. Second, that this is no reproduction of speech-without-voice but imitative of some other 'level' of thought. As we move into the second set of sentences, we perceived that the children have grown a little: they do not just see and hear but make comparisons, use imperatives and register complex relations within the visible. Progress in time is thus rendered by a change in the impressions registered and a correspondingly developed syntax; but at no time are these presented as the words 'they would use'.

By this major change in what is still a realist usage, Woolf again avoids an effect of irony. There is no suggestion of the implied author as controlling the 'voices'. (With one exception: Neville, especially on his first day at school, is lightly satirized as polysyllabic.) On the whole, we find exceptionally little in the texture of the language that might distinguish one character from another: they are individuated instead through their manners of seeing and through recurrent motifs that build up each's store of mental patterns. And this brings us full circle to the 'sympathetic' use of internal monologue observed in the writing of Austen and Eliot by Roy Pascal. It seems that Woolf and her six are linguistically of a group.

Paradoxically, such freedom from the usual social satire of stream-of-consciousness brings its own problems. Where Woolf aspires presumably to presenting, in no one's voice, in the direct speech of the psyche, a level of thought in which there are no idiolects, we can easily perceive the upper-middle-class accent of Bloomsbury. Like the nagging sense, at least to modern readers, that her use of 'one' places her and her characters transparently in a class that gives orders to Mabel rather than preparing the *bœuf en daube* itself, the unity of voices makes her fictional position parochial precisely where it seeks universality. This is, however, to say no more than can be said of most of the universalist stances of literary men.

The Waves has a certain lyrical monotony; it perhaps goes so far from realist plotting that its very linearity feels static. But its use of a stream-of-consciousness that eschews individuation of accent shows that Woolf has taken mimesis beyond irony. In *style indirect libre* we have seen how realism depends on a politics of us-and-them: readers and writers play power-games with the images of each other and of characters. The very necessity of trust that Booth stresses (or what Sartre calls the freedom that writer and reader mutually invest in the work) is based on an exclusion of the other, as happens in the resolved oedipus with the mother who is a third party whom one must not desire to have or to be. The implied reader as son and the implied author as father unite to exclude and control. In *The Waves*, stream-of-consciousness is still mimetic but it is no longer realistic in the mode of the *style indirect libre*. The implied author is present everywhere but she is not God.

Notes

1   For full-length studies of stream-of-consciousness see R. Humphrey, *Stream of Consciousness in the Modern Novel* (University of California Press, Berkeley, Los Angeles and London, 1954); M. Friedman, *Stream of Consciousness: A Study in Literary Method* (Yale University Press, New Haven, and London, 1955); and E. R. Steinberg, *The Stream of Consciousness Technique in the Modern Novel* (National University Publications, Port Washington, and London, 1979). See also R. Scholes and R. Kellogg, *The Nature of Narrative* (Oxford University Press, London, and New York, 1966); S. Chatman, *Story and Discourse* (Cornell University Press, Ithaca and London, 1978); and the excellent D. Cohn, *Transparent Minds*, (Princeton University Press, Princeton, 1978).

2   They also fail to see what Freud insists on, that the unconscious is inaccessible and cannot be 'explored'; least of all can one go hunting there for the big game and buried treasure they claim to 'bring back' in the form of poems. Their texts are ends in themselves, true aesthetic objects; Freud's are data to be used in the cure; those of stream-of-consciousness writers are devices to make us suspend our disbelief.

3   On the relation of language and gender see D. Cameron, *Feminism and Linguistic Theory* (Macmillan, London, 1985), and J. Coates, *Women, Men and Language* (Longman, London and New York, 1986).
4   For an analysis of the phantasy of the bodiless implied author see my *The Banal Object* (Institute of Germanic Studies, London, 1981).
5   Letter to Louise Colet of 9 December 1852, G. Flaubert, *Correspondance II*, ed. J. Bruneau (2 vols, Bibliothèque de la Pléiade, 1973 and Paris, 1980), p. 204.
6   For general studies of *style indirect libre* see M. Lips, *Le Style indirect libre* (Payot, Paris, 1926); R. Pascal, *The Dual Voice* (Manchester University Press, Manchester, 1977); and B. McHale, 'Free indirect discourse: a survey of recent accounts', *PTL*, 3 (1978), 249–287. See also Scholes and Kellogg, *The Nature of Narrative*, Chatman, *Story and Discourse*, and *Transparent Minds*. For discussions of *style indirect libre* in Flaubert see S. Ullmann, *Style in the French Novel* (Blackwell, Oxford, 1964); V. Brombert, *The Novels of Flaubert* (Princeton University Press, Princeton, 1966); C. Perruchot, 'Le Style indirect libre et la question du sujet dans *Madame Bovary*', in C. Gothot-Mersch (ed.), *La Production du sens chez Flaubert* (10/18, Paris, 1975). pp. 253–85; S. Haig, *Flaubert and the Gift of Speech* (Cambridge University Press, Cambridge, 1986).
7   M. Sternberg, *The Poetics of Biblical Narrative* (Indiana University Press, Bloomington, 1985; repr. 1986), p. 52; italics Sternberg's.
8   The first phrase is from Voloshinov, see McHale, 'Free indirect discourse', p. 266; the second forms Pascal's title.
9   Though in the broadest view, as Scholes and Kellogg point out, 'the narrative situation is . . . ineluctably ironical' (*The Nature of Narrative*, p. 240) because of the inevitable distance between the teller and the tale, and the teller and the audience.
10   C. Baudelaire, *Œuvres complètes*, ed. M. A. Ruff (Seuil, Paris, 1968), pp. 451–2; for a less excusable reaction a century or so later, see Brombert, *Novels of Flaubert*, p. 91: 'it does not matter whether we believe with Baudelaire that Flaubert infused his virile spirit into the veins of Emma, or whether we are convinced by Sartre's less flattering notion that in *Madame Bovary* Flaubert disguised himself as a woman' . . .
11   Recent feminist psychoanalytic studies, such as D. Dinnerstein, *The Mermaid and the Minotaur* (Harper & Row, New York, 1976), and N. Chodorow, *The Reproduction of Mothering* (University of California Press, Berkeley, Los Angeles and London, 1978), stress the significance for both sexes of growing away from the mother, showing however that this is less complete and less aggressive on the part of a daughter. In a different context, orthodox Jewish men say a prayer daily thanking God 'for not having made me a woman'; this might be understood not simply as a repetition of contempt but rather as a repeated compulsion to shore up a difference from the mother (and from the repressed female deity) that is never more than precarious.
12   Letter to Louise Colet of 16 January 1852, *Correspondance II*, p. 31.
13   Quotations from *Madame Bovary* are from G. Flaubert, *Œuvres I*, ed. A. Thibaudet and R. Dumesnil (2 vols, Bibliothèque de la Pléiade, Paris, 1958–9); this reference, p. 386; translations are my own.
14   In all these cases, the sometimes deplored 'presence of the artist' is sensed in any piece of fine writing; see Lips, *Le Style indirect libre*, p. 192, Pascal, *The Dual*

Voice, p. 105–10; Chatman detects narrators by their 'superior diction' (*Story and Discourse*, p. 156), 'elegant terms' (p. 157) or '"well-spoken" style' (p. 200).

15 For this debate, between Chatman and Clive Hart, see Chatman, *Story and Discourse* p. 153 n.9. The latter argues that while the 'maudlin sentiments' are Eveline's, the 'tawdry clichés' are used parodistically by the narrator.

16 James Joyce, *Ulysses* (Penguin, Harmondsworth, 1960, repr. 1971), p. 42.

17 Letter from Joyce to Frank Budgen of 16 August 1921, quoted in R. Ellmann, *James Joyce* (Oxford University Press, Oxford, 1982), pp. 501–2. The full passage indicates the limits of Joyce's sympathy: '*Penelope* is the clou [star turn] of the book. The first sentence contains 2500 words. There are eight sentences in the episode. It begins and ends with the female word *yes*. It turns like the huge earth ball slowly surely and evenly round and round spinning, its four cardinal points being the female breasts, arse, womb and cunt expressed by the words *because*, *bottom* (in all senses bottom button, bottom of the class, bottom of the sea, bottom of his heart), *woman*, *yes*. Though probably more obscene than any preceding episode it seems to me to be perfectly sane full amoral fertilisable untrustworthy engaging shrewd limited prudent indifferent *Weib. Ich bin der* [sic] *Fleisch der stets bejaht*'; italics Ellmann's.

18 See letter from Freud to Arthur Schnitzler of 14 May 1922, in E. L. Freud (ed.), *Letters of Sigmund Freud 1873–1939*, trans. T. and J. Stern (Hogarth Press, London, 1961), p. 344.

19 Quotations from both texts are from A. Schnitzler, *Casanovas Heimfahrt*, (Fischer, Frankfurt, 1950; repr. 1986); this reference, p. 40; ellipses Schnitzler's; translations are my own.

20 See 'Toward a feminist poetics', repr. in E. Showalter (ed.), *The New Feminist Criticism* (Virago, London, 1986), pp. 125–43.

21 See S. M. Gilbert and S. Gubar, *The Madwoman in the Attic* (Yale University Press, New Haven and London, 1979; repr. 1984), pp. 3–44.

22 Quotations are from V. Woolf, *A Room of One's Own* (Triad/Panther, Glasgow, 1977); this reference pp. 72–3.

23 From the Foreword to *Pilgrimage*, quoted in Steinberg, *The Stream of Consciousness Technique*, p. 78.

24 J. C. Powys, for instance, in *Dorothy Richardson* (Joiner & Steele, London, 1931): 'what she has done has never been done before. She has drawn her inspiration neither from man-imitating cleverness nor from narcissistic feminine charm but *from the abyss of the feminine subconscious*', quoted with italics in Friedman, *Stream of Consciousness*, p. 187; or Scholes and Kellogg, *The Nature of Narrative*, p. 183: 'the inner life of the female of the species contemplating her erotic situation has been a focal point of narrative concern with the psyche from Medea and Dido to Anna Karenina and Molly Bloom'; see also pp. 194–5. In neither of these comments, though, do we see much belief in women's creativity.

25 D. Richardson, *The Tunnel*, vol. II of *Pilgrimage* (4 vols, Dent, London, 1967) p. 149; quoted in G. Hanscombe and V. L. Smyers, *Writing for their Lives* (The Women's Press, London, 1987), p. 52.

26 Joyce in conversation with Arthur Power, quoted in Steinberg, *The Stream of Consciousness Technique*, p. 74; Woolf in J. Schulkind (ed.), *Moments of Being* (Granada, St. Albans, 1978), pp. 83 and 81–2. For a discussion of the

difference between the two authors' use of the trivial, see my 'Sexual politics and the avant-garde'; in E. Timms and P. Collier (eds), *Visions and Blueprints* (Manchester University Press, Manchester, 1988), pp. 246–9.

27 E. Showalter, *The Female Malady* (Virago, London, 1987), p. 192.

28 V. Woolf, 'Modern Fiction', *The Common Reader*, quoted in Steinberg, *The Stream of Consciousness Technique*, p. 67.

29 V. Woolf, *To the Lighthouse* (Granada, St Albans, 1977), pp. 60–1.

30 'Modern fiction', in Steinberg, *The Stream of Consciousness Technique*, p. 67.

31 Joyce, *A Portrait of the Artist as a Young Man* (Granada, London, 1977), p. 7; ellipses Joyce's; V. Woolf, *The Waves* (Granada, St Albans, 1977), p. 6.

SUGGESTED READING

Brombert, V., *The Novels of Flaubert*, Princeton University Press, Princeton, 1966.

Coates, J., *Women, Men and Language* Longman, London and New York, 1986.

Cohn, D., *Transparent Minds*, Princeton University Press, Princeton, 1978.

Dinnerstein, D., *The Mermaid and the Minotaur*, Harper & Rowe, New York, 1976.

Ellmann, R., *James Joyce*, Oxford University Press, Oxford, 1982.

Lips, M., *Le Style indirect libre*, Payot, Paris, 1926.

McHale, B., 'Free indirect discourse: a survey of recent accounts', *PTL*, 3 (1978), pp. 249–87.

Pascal, R., *The Dual Voice*, Manchester University Press, Manchester, 1977.

Perruchot, C., 'Le Style indirect libre et la question du sujet dans *Madame Bovary*', in C. Gothot-Mersch (ed.), *La Production du sens chez Flaubert*', 10/18, Paris, 1975.

Steinberg, E. R. *The Stream of Consciousness Technique in the Modern Novel*, National University Publications, Port Washington, NY, and London, 1979.

7

The Word and the Spirit: Explorations of the Irrational in Kafka, Döblin and Musil

DAVID MIDGLEY

The literary writer need fear psychoanalysis as a rival power only as long as he has little understanding of it and it presents itself as a seductive blend of scientific genius and popular journalism.

Robert Musil[1]

By 1912, the theories of Freud had become such common knowledge in the German-speaking world that Kafka could note in his diary that 'thoughts of Freud' had come to mind as a matter of course – 'natürlich' – as he reflected on one of his own compositions. *The Interpretation of Dreams*, originally published in 1900, had appeared in expanded and revised editions in 1909 and 1911. Freud had effectively popularized his own ideas with *The Psychopathology of Everyday Life* (1901), giving currency to the notion that we all betray our unconscious impulses through unwitting language acts. And he had pursued some of his central ideas further in his book on jokes, and in his essays on sexuality, both published in 1905. These four publications, more than any others of the period, helped to focus intellectual attention on aspects of mental activity which came to be reflected directly in literary writing, whether this took the form of stream-of-consciousness narrative or of the associative techniques fostered by the French Surrealists.[2] But in the German-speaking world, psychoanalytic thought presented itself at an early date as a new theoretical canon which literary writers consciously sought to resist, as much as to exploit. This chapter examines three distinct forms of literary response to the challenge of new thinking about the unconscious mind, as exemplified in the works of German and Austrian writers during the early decades of the twentieth century.

The diary entry alluded to above records Kafka's immediate reflections on the short prose text 'Das Urteil' ('The Judgement') which he had written in the space of a single night in September 1912. The same note expresses his conviction that this particular composition represented a breakthrough to a new kind of literary achievement for him, and in the context of his writing career 'Das Urteil' does indeed appear as the first kafkaesque story that he wrote. Thoughts of Freud might well have been prompted by the content of the story, for it tells of how the attempt of a son to assert his independence – and marry – is thwarted by the contempt and wilful scorn of his elderly, but still powerfully authoritarian, father. This 'Judgement' is a condemnatory one, pronounced by the father on the son, but executed by the son himself in an act of suicide. The course of the narrative is thus an intensely bleak expression of an *internalized* paternal injunction, activated to prohibit the fulfilment of sexual desire; in this we may recognize something very similar to Freud's idea of an Oedipus complex in the male infant, and of the power this can still exert in adult life. Kafka's diary note appears to acknowledge this close parallel between his text and the Freudian theory, although it should be stressed that Kafka's sense of father/son rivalry as an irredeemable source of individual guilt was no theoretical concept, but an intensely personal experience which he later described autobiographically in his 'Letter to My Father'. But the sense in which Freud's theories may have assisted Kafka in the process of self-recognition extends beyond the content aspect of his text and into elements of the narrative technique that he recognizes here as signalling a personal breakthrough. 'The Judgement' is the first of Kafka's stories in which abrupt dreamlike transitions and verbal ambiguities profoundly determine the utterance of the text. They affect especially the image of the father in the story, who is capable of expressing totally contradictory sentiments towards the son's mysterious friend in Petersburg, and whose vehement response to the prospect of being 'covered up' (in bed) signals the sudden resurgence of his patriarchal dominance. These are aspects of the text which challenge the reader to pursue the psychological implications of the narrative in ways which can draw fruitfully on Freud's methods of analysing dream imagery.

Such features were to become characteristic of Kafka's subsequent writing, and it has long been an established critical practice to apply Freudian techniques to the textual interpretation of his works.[3] Kafka himself described the dominant purpose of his literary writing in 1914 as 'the presentation of my dreamlike inner life',[4] and it may be said that his most characteristic technique is to articulate intractable mental states by visualizing them as external, and therefore describable, situations. Gregor Samsa, in 'The Metamorphosis' (1912), does not merely feel like a parasite on the body of his family, but actually finds himself transformed into a verminous creature. Joseph K., in *The Trial* (begun in 1914), pleads his case in a courtroom which he knows he will find at the top of whichever tenement staircase he climbs, and which generally appears devised to answer the inner promptings of his own undefined guilt. But the text which goes further in simulating the seemingly illogical discontinuity of the dream is undoubtedly 'Ein Landarzt ('A Country Doctor') of 1917.

The doctor himself is the first-person narrator of this story, and the fluctuation of the narrative between imperfect tense and historic present helps to give it the feel of a partially rationalized reconstruction of something that has been dreamed. The account begins with the doctor being called out one winter's night and sending his housemaid to search the village for a horse to pull his carriage, since his own has died. Subsequent developments suggest, however, that this information is itself an attempt (what Freud would call 'secondary revision') to rationalize the imagery that the dream itself has initially presented. For the doctor suddenly finds himself kicking open the door of a delapidated pig-sty, in which he finds a strange man with vivid blue eyes and starkly 'open' face. This is the first of several images in the text which present themselves abruptly and without explanation, as if they constituted the concentrated dream images for which the narrative seeks to provide rational connections. The stranger crawls out on all fours, assumes the role of stable lad, and conjures up a pair of horses which squeeze out through the same low door and emerge as powerful beasts, strong in the loin. The housemaid at this point comments that 'you never know what you're going to find in your own house',[5] a remark which is received as a joke by the doctor.

All this has been described in the first concise paragraph, and as we glance back over it, it becomes obvious how the choice of imagery associated with the muscular horses, reinforced in the German by the stable boy's seemingly innocent use of the term 'anspannen' (to put the horses into harness, but also suggestive of muscular tension), contains intimations of 'displaced' sexual arousal, which are also acknowledged in the housemaid's innuendo. Edward Timms has demonstrated elsewhere how the image of the pig-sty itself, in a German context, prompts verbal associations with obscene behaviour rather than the mere squalor it might suggest in English.[6] The further course of the narrative reinforces the impression that (in Freudian terms) the manifest imagery of this dream experience is giving distorted expression to a formerly suppressed sexual urge which is being transferred onto the figure of the stable boy and the objects associated with him. For it is he who now exhibits violently demonic tendencies, biting the housemaid on the cheek, and pursuing her into the house in order to exact what the text acknowledges as the purchase price for enabling the doctor to make his night call. Again the reader experiences an abrupt transition as the doctor finds himself immediately at the patient's house, where the logic of medical rationality appears temporarily to supervene. He has been summoned to tend a boy whom he finds in good health, until his attention is drawn to an open wound in the boy's pelvic region. This, too, is an image which intrudes abruptly upon the narrative, the magnitude of it – the wound is 'as big as the palm of my hand' – lending further emphasis to its irrational potency. The likely significance of the wound as a female genital symbol is moreover highlighted by verbal association: the sentence in which the wound is described is so constructed that the adjective 'rosa' (pink) appears as the first word, and is thus capitalized, making it indistinguishable from the proper name by which the housemaid has earlier been referred to. The fact that diagnostic rationality again seems to assert itself in the doctor's discovery of a 'complication' involving maggots 'as long and as thick as my little finger' might in turn be viewed as the onset of revulsion triggered by his repression of the primary sexual urge. This long central section of the text continues, indeed, with the doctor being ceremoniously undressed and laid in bed 'beside the wound', as if in grotesque modulation of some blatant marriage rite.

Through such suggestive imagery, the distorted sexuality in Kafka's text becomes so palpable that it would not surprise us perhaps to find the doctor subsequently waking in a lather in his own bed. But that is not how the text concludes, and important as the sexual motifs are to its overall meaning, it is also constructed in such a way as to resist reduction to such a clinical interpretation. There is indeed a further abrupt transition in the narrative, which brings the doctor not to his bed, but to his carriage. And in this carriage he now sees himself as destined to proceed on a never-ending journey towards the 'home' from which the night-call (and all that has been associated with it) has seduced him, exposed to the frosts of a profoundly disconsolate era. His nakedness has come now to symbolize a cosmic loneliness and metaphysical despair which we may recognise in retrospect as exercising every bit as strong an influence on the imagery of the central section of the text as does the sexual impulse. The conversation which the doctor has had with the boy pointed up the significance of the wound as a symbol of mortality; the consummation for which the boy himself yearns is that of death. And the grotesque marriage ritual is couched in terms which express not so much transferred sexuality, but rather a pseudo-messianic expectation in which the function of medicine, and of scientific rationality generally, as a surrogate religion in the post-Enlightenment age is openly acknowledged: 'the parson sits at home and unravels his vestments, one after another; but the doctor is supposed to be omnipotent with his merciful surgeon's hand.'

This theme of the lost assurance of religious faith, and of the cosmic anxiety that remains, is one that Kafka treats more distinctly in various texts that draw on the imagery of the Great Wall of China, and of the Chinese imperial regime. There the notion of a grand scheme whose significance has become lost, or of a message from the Emperor that is destined never to be delivered, lends itself to the simpler and more playful articulation of metaphysical uncertainties. In 'A Country Doctor' (and incidentally also in *The Trial* and the 'Letter to My Father') the metaphysical anxiety appears inseparable from a more clinical form of anxiety with evident sexual origins. An awareness of Freud's theories can positively assist the reader not only in recognizing manifestations of the latter, but also in appreciating the manner in which the material of Kafka's highly condensed text is organized. In the language of *The Interpretation of Dreams*, the imagery of 'A Country Doctor' is 'over-determined': the test gives unified expression to what the analysing mind perceives as a plurality of (latent) ideas. What we see Kafka cultivating here as a distinctive literary technique is above all the ability to convey the sense of a condition of being in its undifferentiated entirety, whereas rational discourse (including that of Freud himself) seeks always to differentiate between various determining factors.

In one of his later letters to the Czech writer Milena Jesenká, Kafka explicitly rejects the notion of psychoanalysis as a therapeutic method on the grounds that spiritual anguish is often precisely what gives a person their particular identity and their sense of being 'anchored' in the cosmos.[7] The pursuit of an enhanced sense of spiritual identity is a dominant feature of German writing during the early decades of our century, which is loosely grouped together under the title 'Expressionism'. And as a literary impulse it often gave rise to an ethical utopianism or to apocalyptic visions that lack the tight stylistic discipline of Kafka's more introspective scenarios.[8] The writings of Alfred Döblin, on the other hand, distinguish themselves by virtue of their very concreteness and extravert quality from the general trend of the times. A trained neurologist, Döblin was highly sceptical of the Freudian concentration on the putative psychic origins of physiological effects; in an autiobiographical essay of 1927 he stressed that his personal medical opinion had always been guided rather by what is known of the influence of hormones and metabolic process.[9] And in his writings, human identity is presented as something inseparable from the vast realm of Nature upon which life in general depends.

Döblin's literary career began in earnest in 1911 when he qualified as a medical practitioner, and he may fairly claim to be one of the most self-consciously Modernist German prose writers of his time. As a student in Berlin he had sought the company of avant-garde writers associated with Else Lasker-Schüler and Herwarth Walden, and published his early compositions in their journal *Der Sturm*. It was here that the German version of the Futurist Manifesto appeared in March 1912, and it was here also that Döblin reviewed the exhibition of Futurist art which opened in Berlin the following month. He sympathized with the dynamism and the anti-academic thrust of the Futurists' programme, but he also sensed the superficiality of the cult of technology that he found in Italian Futurism, and was severely critical of Marinetti's *Mafarka* novel for its resort to arbitrary syntax and wilful metaphor, which did nothing, he felt, to fulfil the proper function of literary writing in conveying the essence of things.[10] This comment again suggests, perhaps, an affinity between Döblin's intentions and the visionary techniques developed by German Expressionist painters on the eve of the First World War. But when he published his own 'Berlin Programme' in 1913, Döblin distinguished himself from the general trend towards intuitive vision and abstraction by calling for the cultivation of a 'stone-hard style' that he conceives as a kind of heightened Naturalism. In a later essay, indeed, he speaks of the modern age generally as a 'naturalistic' one in the sense that its dominant impulse is to extend the inquiry into biological and environmental factors beyond the limits of what was achieved by the Naturalist movement of the late nineteenth century, in the hope of effecting a Copernican shift in the awareness of Nature's mysteries that will transcend the traditional boundaries of western rational thought.[11] His dismissive attitude towards psychoanalysis is of a piece with his repudiation, in the 'Berlin Programme', of the conceptualized psychology to be found in much of the popular fiction of his time (and ours). It is for the closeted eroticism of this 'atelier' literature, as he calls it, that his brand of Naturalism is to provide the cold shower. And when he speaks in the same context of a need for literature to learn from psychiatry, it is the technique of precise observation and clinical description that he has in mind.

The implications of Döblin's programme are already apparent in his earliest published story, 'Die Ermordung einer Butterblume' ('The Assassination of a buttercup').[12] In clinical terms, the text describes the onset of a schizophrenic condition. A tubby middle-aged businessman, Michael Fischer, finds himself viciously assaulting a buttercup with his walking-stick. 'Finds himself' is the only appropriate way to describe his own experience of this action, because the narrative makes him the unwitting accessory to his own involuntary actions from the outset. Döblin does not write 'He walked', but 'The trees strode past him.' As a character sketch, the text draws its vitality and humour from the progressive dissociation between a man's conscious identity and his own motor reflexes. In his attempt to regain self-control, Fischer reaches for the sort of authoritarian clichés we might imagine him applying to his employees: he wants to show his own thoughts 'who is boss', to put his own feet 'in their place'. And the obsessive remorse he subsequently displays towards the deceased buttercup is expressed in acts which similarly transfer the assumptions of his social ambience directly onto the world of non-social existence. He gives the buttercup a decent burial and conveys his condolences to her next-of-kin ('Blume' is feminine in German); he names her Ellen and hypnotically transfers money to her account; and he does penance by carefully digging up another plant and putting it in a pot, inscribing on the bottom a reference to the legal statute on civil liabilities. Fischer is liberated from this fixation when the pot is accidentally smashed by his housekeeper and thrown out with the rubbish, but the sense of release that ensues does not lead to his re-integration into social conventionality. On the contrary, he interprets this occurrence for which he bears no responsibility as licensing him to murder as many buttercups as he likes, and he disappears with a manic laugh into the depths of the forest.

The interest of the text lies not in the diagnosis, but in the vivid depiction of an unstable mental condition. It does not interpret Fischer's behaviour in any terms other than those which express the character's own immediate sense of motivation. It presents visual and olfactory sense-data in as direct and undiluted a fashion as possible. And it achieves a sense of recognizable structure and of relation to the familiar world of the reader by its ironic confrontation of Fischer's impulsive behaviour with the mental habits of his business routine. The apparent slightness of Döblin's fable is belied by the wit and skill with which he frees his language, and thus the perceptions of his reader, from any schematic preconceptions.

It is in his best-known work, *Berlin Alexanderplatz* (1929), that Döblin takes full advantage of various experimental narrative techniques that had been explored during the Expressionist period in German literature.[13] The complexity and dynamism of modern city life are evoked here by stark and vibrant images, by the invocation of mythological and visionary elements, but above all by the constant interplay of voices and motifs suggestive of the diverse forces that determine human behaviour. The novel is famous for its use of montage – montage of the sights and sounds of Berlin streets, of news items and advertisements, of official documents, of kitsch novels. But montage becomes a fundamental compositional principle here not simply in order to suggest the fragmentary nature of urban existence, but rather out of an awareness of the limitations imposed on consciousness by any single form of discourse. The result is a protean narrative stance which has quite justifiably invited comparison with Joyce's *Ulysses*, but which pursues purposes of its own that are independent of any straightforward 'influence'. As a contemporary reviewer noted, Döblin uses styles in much the same way that ordinary people use the tramcar, letting each one take him just as far as he wants to go, then leaping off and selecting a new one.[14] Already on the opening page we find his narrative sliding freely from authorial reportage, through indirect free style, into interior monologue, and out again into a montage of apparently random street impressions. Even the authorial voice itself is a highly adaptable entity. It frequently mimics the argot of Berlin working life, its jocular irony, its comforting and cajoling, according to the needs of the situation. The narrative proper is prefaced with a summary of the plot in which Döblin adopts the idiom of the fairground ballad-monger (the German Moritat[15] tradition exploited by Brecht, too, in his song of 'Mack the Knife') and spices it with the jargon of the boxing commentator. At the climax of the action, on the other hand, the authorial voice can equally well affect the grandiloquence of high Romantic drama, when a very different purpose is entailed.

By contrast with the grotesque dissolution of personality in 'The Assassination of Buttercup', which could be interpreted as expressing a somewhat nihilistic impulse, the plot of *Berlin Alexanderplatz* has a discernible moral purpose. Here we have moved on from the pre-war avant-garde questioning of all conventional social values to the challenge of political responsibility posed by the post-war Weimar Republic, and amongst many other things Döblin's novel highlights the competing demands for political allegiance placed on the individual in a parliamentary democracy.[16] His protagonist, Franz Biberkopf, is admittedly a marginal figure, an ex-convict who is trying to go straight, and the plot summary informs us explicitly that Biberkopf will eventually have to learn that the source of all his problems really lies within himself. The story-line is constructed around the series of hard knocks which are dealt out to him as he tries to re-establish his social identity, and it ultimately becomes clear that the 'old Biberkopf' will have to die in order for a new, self-aware and self-critical personality to emerge. The relevance of Döblin's montage technique to this moral theme lies in the fact that he is not depicting character development in any traditional sense, but rather evoking material factors and social contraints which together determine the limits of Biberkopf's behavioural possibilities and his potential for self-knowledge. There is a sexual dimension to the forces which constrain the emergence of a 'new Biberkopf', but it is treated largely as a matter of physiological fact which merits no special attention except in so far as Biberkopf conceives his personal identity in terms of sexual prowess. His self-assertion in this domain is linked with motifs reminiscent of his wartime military service – a bugle call, fragments of patriotic songs – not primarily to effect a crude association between male sexuality and physical aggression, but because the 'old Biberkopf' is organizing his sense of identity in either instance with reference to regressive and illusory images of harmony and loyalty. The naivety of his ideal of sexual partnership is underscored by frequent invocations of simple mythical models: Adam and Eve, Hansel and Gretel. It is the extension of this domestic idyll into the political sphere that makes him susceptible to the appeal of reactionary and irrational forces.

The emergence of the 'new Biberkopf' is prepared in the reader's perception not by any intimation of self-denial on the character's part, but by a competing set of leitmotifs associated with the presence of a serpent in paradise, and more importantly with the all-pervasiveness of death. Biblical quotations which emphasize human mortality are interpolated into a section describing the functioning of a city abattoir, and the image of a repeatedly swinging axe which is also introduced there becomes associated later with the traditional figure of Death the Reaper. The climactic battle for Biberkopf's soul is in fact played out as an allegorical confrontation between Death on the one hand and the Whore of Babylon, who represents the seductive appeal of the city and of Biberkopf's sensual habits of mind, on the other. Biberkopf's conversion is depicted as a process by which Death scythes away at his obstinate former identity, reducing it to some core of primal vitality that is better able to adapt to the external reality against which life in Berlin has pitted him.

The complex network of images which Döblin develops in *Berlin Alexanderplatz* makes its appeal to the domain of public discourse by evoking traditional representations of the human condition and its moral implications. In the early work of his Austrian contemporary Robert Musil, by contrast, we find the elaboration of imagery as a means to express pre-conscious, or at least pre-verbal impulses. A trained mathematician and engineer, Musil develops a technique for the literary representation of the flow of psychic energies which might be described as high-resolution approximation.

In his first novel, *Die Verwirrungen des Zöglings Törleß* (1906, translated as Young Törless), Musil explored the experiences of adolescence with a peculiar sensitivity towards emotional states that tend to be trivialized by conventional discourse. To take a simple example from early in that work, the withdrawn and phlegmatic cast of mind that Törless displays in the remote seminary where he is being educated is interpreted by those around him, and indeed by himself, as 'homesickness'; but the narrating voice inquires more closely, observing that the image of his 'beloved parents' is not directly the object of Törless' yearning, but rather the pretext for exciting a state of longing which appears to be primarily egoistic or narcissistic in character. The novel explores a dark world of adolescent sensuality and self-discovery, presenting insights which can be related to the contemporary theories of Freud and Weininger. But with his emphasis on the narcissistic, Musil is arguably pushing his psychological investigation into areas which Freud was only later to integrate into his psychoanalytical system, and as an important new study of the Törless novel has shown, Musil is here presenting erotic interest and the quest for knowledge as interrelated potencies which are devalued by any attempt to separate them out into rational, analytical categories.[17]

The technique of evoking elusive emotions by estranging them from conventional preconceptions was pushed further by Musil in a pair of short stories published in 1911 under the title *Vereinigungen* (*Unions*). The inherent ambiguity in this title highlights once more the intimate connection beween sexual desire on the one hand and a quasi-mystical self-recognition on the other. The first of these texts, 'Die Vollendung der Liebe' ('The Perfecting of a Love'), presents us with a paradox. A married woman leaves the familiar ambience of her home and a secure relationship with her husband in order to visit her daughter, the offspring of an earlier, casual relationship. On the journey she becomes snowbound and a prey to the unsolicited attentions of a somewhat bestial stranger. It is in these disorientating circumstances, under the threat, indeed, of sexual humiliation, that she momentarily experiences a heightened perception of her love. This simple outline does nothing to convey the subtle texture of Musil's narrative, in which a complex fabric of similes has been developed to suggest the play of subliminal impulses and emotions at work in the heroine's mind.[18] But it is the second of the two compositions, 'Die Versuchung der stillen Veronika' ('The Temptation of Quiet Veronica'), which is better suited to an exposition of Musil's purpose in our present context, because its well-charted textual history shows particularly clearly how a literary technique has developed in conscious interaction with psychoanalytic theory.

The collected works of Robert Musil contain two earlier drafts of the Veronika text, as well as the final version of 1911.[19] The first of these operates entirely within the conventions of nineteenth-century Realism, and the tone of its opening might be compared with a tale by Maupassant. An omniscient narrator tells how Veronika, the notary's daughter, is helping Cäcilie, the chemist's daughter, to prepare for her wedding. The conversation between these young ladies is presented in a jovially naturalistic fashion. They call each other by pet names and exchange superficial pleasantries, to which the bride's mother also contributes sentimental clichés befitting the occasion. The bride's father finally adds his avuncular humour, evidently to hide his own embarrassment, and his remark creates an opening for the narrator to give an extended character sketch of Veronika who, at the age of twenty-eight, seems destined to become an old maid. The psychological description of her gradually becomes intensely intimate, evoking the concealed emotional potency of Veronika's introverted personality; but the perspective remains external to the emotional experience itself, and the reader receives comforting indicators that this is how the character herself looks back on her own personality development. The draft also contains an account of Veronika's conversation with Cäcilie's brother, a young priest, whose powerful (and implicitly sensual) expression of his religious conviction evidently has a disturbing effect on her. It is clearly indicated that the priest's departure is to become a significant turning-point in Veronika's inner life, but the manuscript breaks off with only a brief sketch of the mystical relationship to the world at large that she is intended to achieve.

The second version is one that Musil prepared for publication in the literary journal *Hyperion* in 1908, giving it the title 'Das verzauberte Haus' ('The Enchanted House'). In this version the latent sensuality of the character (who is here called Viktoria) is made explicit by the introduction of a narrative frame involving a lustful young Hungarian army officer by the name of Demeter Nagy. It is he who overhears the conversation in which Viktoria denies herself to the priestly figure; he falls to wondering how such a dowdy creature could rouse anyone to the heights of passion; and he finally proceeds to do what he takes to be expected of him when he finds her rolling on his own bed in some kind of frenetic trance. It is frequently the case in Musil's writings that he seeks to off-set the investigation of heightened states of awareness with allusions to the mundane materiality of human existence, but the dominant – and domineering – presence of the Demeter figure in 'The Enchanted House' has the unfortunate effect of overshadowing the finer texture of his narrative with the blunt directness of a mess-room yarn. For contained within that framing narrative is a sensitive depiction of the fluid mental state of Viktoria herself in the interval beween the two moments registered by Demeter, together with an apodictic paragraph which comments provocatively on the nature of an individual 'soul' (or psychic identity) as a hindrance to a loving relationship with another person. In this particular textual context, the account of Viktoria's inner life appears limited to a description of her behaviour in terms that will make her emotional continuum between moment A and moment B plausible to the reader.[20]

The final version of 1911 dispenses with all such concessions to conventional narrative structure, together with the conventional expection that the goal of the narrative will be some form of sexual consummation. The very dialogue in which Veronika denies herself to Johannes (as her priestly friend is now called) has not only become detached from the eavesdropping perception of Demeter, but from any concrete social setting at all. It is presented in the opening paragraph as something to be imagined, possibly taking place not as a conversation at all, but as a juxtaposition of 'voices' on the pages of a diary, with the suddenly urgent utterance of the woman enfolded (in an erotically charged image) within the mellow continuum of a masculine disquisition.[21] Not content with this difficult mental construct, the paragraph continues with an alternative image in which these entwined voices are being propelled towards a point of clarity and determinacy by a force which is as yet only perceptible as a vague perturbation. This studious detachment of the subject-matter from a material context, together with the further elaboration of the imagery deployed in this opening paragraph, gives the text a densely involuted quality which can appear irritatingly precious to the uninitiated reader. But it is precisely the decontextualization of imagery in this text that enables Musil to push ahead of the theorists of his day in his exploration of pre-verbal psychic activity.

It is possible to understand this text as organized around the problem of Veronika's difficulty in accepting another person as a love-object and a focal point for one's own existence. The discursive paragraph from 'The Enchanted House' on the 'soul' as a hinderance to a loving relationship is here fully integrated into the depiction of Veronika's thoughts and perceptions during the most significant night of her life. Johannes has departed, apparently with the intention of killing himself for love of her, and her thoughts revolve around him as the absent centre of her emotional life – to which she can relate with greater intensity as an introjected figure than she ever could in the flesh. The dead have no soul; that is, they have yielded up that personal identity of the living which holds something back from a relationship and directs feelings back onto oneself. They are as empty vessels into which the energy of dreams can be poured. This emptiness and receptivity is something which the dead share with children and with animals (p. 215 / 99 f).[22] Her love can dream of Johannes as an internalized dead entity (p. 217 / 103), the thought that she has killed him presents itself undisturbingly to her (p. 219 / 107). It is in this fantasized fashion that she can experience her moment of 'mysterious spiritual union', even as the encroaching daylight begins to dispel the notion of Johannes's romantic suicide, and even if the arrival of a letter from Johannes describing his recovery from morbid illusions leaves her savouring only the faded promise of sensual fulfilment (pp. 220–3 / 107–12).

Animality, which clearly holds a terrifying fascination for Veronika, is represented in this final version again by the presence of Demeter; the mythical resonances suggested by the detached use of this forename serve now to underscore the earthiness of the figure. A bond of kinship between the characters is intimated in order to explain their presence in the same house together, and Veronika is clearly preoccupied with the thought of Demeter and Johannes as alternative sexual partners. But the network of images associated in the text with the animal realm is not confined to the sensual intimacy that Veronika fears specifically from Demeter. The 'emptiness' which she perceives in the soulless state of animals and dead persons is something that she has previously accused the living Johannes of displaying, seeing it indeed as the link between animality on the one hand and the denial of manhood entailed in becoming a priest on the other (pp. 198–9 / 74–5). Images of animal sensuality – hens and a cockerel in the yard, a peasant woman whose only companions are her dogs – intrude obsessively upon her conversation. Such a combination of an insistent denial of one's own sexuality with obsessive manifestations of sexual desire had been highlighted by Freud, in his publications of 1905, as an indicator of the psychosexual origins of hysteria.[23] There is much in Veronika's responses that seems to echo this theory. But the imagery of Musil's text develops a multivalency which suggests a more complex system of impulses and resistances than this simple clinical interpretation would accommodate.

Images of hardness and erectness in this text can carry a patently phallic association when they are invoked in connection with dogs or the eruptive and unrestrained sex drive of Demeter (pp. 197, 199–200 / 73, 76–7). But they can be applied equally to the firm contours of the emotional experience itself, as Veronika recalls it from her encounter with Demeter in particular (pp. 196 ff. / 72). Indeed, what she ostensibly fears in a descent to animality is a kind of aimless insouciance, which is expressed in an opposing set of images suggestive of softness and formlessness (p. 197 / 73). Erectness can be associated with a positive goal that might redeem her from the indeterminacy of her adult life, such as the firmness and lucidity of rational discourse which Johannes consciously strives for, and which is evoked authorially at the end of the opening paragraph (pp. 194–5 / 68–70). Softness, in contradistinction to this, expresses Veronika's disappointment in Johannes's humility and lack of backbone on an occasion when he has been struck in the face by Demeter (pp. 198 ff. / 74). But the firm rationality of Johannes's disquisition can appear equally to Veronika as something threatening and potentially wounding – 'as hard and solid as a stone flung at me' (p. 201 / 79) – and in this way it amalgamates itself in her mind with that threatening encounter with Demeter that has remained in her consciousness like a foreign body, and also with her later sense of her own person as being like a knife plunged into Johannes's life (p. 212 / 96).

Lisa Appignanesi has given an interpretation of Veronika's situation in terms of a quest for the complementary principle that Johannes appears to incorporate for her.[24] The text does indeed indicate that Johannes brings the promise of definition into Veronika's indeterminate existence (pp. 207ff. / 89), and the theme of sexual complementarity is a recurrent feature of Musil's writings in general. But to emphasize the significance of male and female 'roles', as Appignanesi does, both elevates a subordinate theme in this particular text to undue prominence, and leads to an over-simplification of Musil's achievement. (By presenting Veronika as performing a Salome role vis-à-vis Johannes, she gives a quite misleading impression of what the necrophilia motif signifies in Musil's text.[25]) The apparent self-contradiction in Musil's application of hard and soft imagery enables him to sustain a sense of the abiding tension between Veronika's desire for completeness on the one hand and her internal resistance to it on the other. Hardness can suggest the firmness of a positive goal, but also the pain of experiences (with or without an explicit sexual dimension) which lodge in the mind like foreign bodies; softness can suggest the open potentiality of a fluid existence, but also the vulnerability that arises from the absence of purpose.

This ambivalence in Veronika's emotional life is expressed most poignantly at the actual moment of Johannes's departure. Here it is the leave-taking itself which appears as something erect that accompanies the two human bodies stiffly on their way. The experience that lodges painfully in her consciousness (like an internal calcification rather than a foreign body) is her own act of refusal which has brought about this separation. Her perception in the present moment is one of disintegration, of slanting and sliding, which makes the trees round about seem unnaturally perpendicular by contrast.

> And something came over her that made her small and weak, reducing her almost to nothingness, until she was like a small dog whimpering and limping on three legs, or like a tattered pennant fluttering but droopingly in a very faint breath of wind: so utterly did it dissolve her. And there was a yearning in her to hold him – a yearning that was like the softness of a broken-shelled snail faintly twitching in its search for another, yearning to stick to it tightly even as it dies. (p. 210 / 92)

And in this moment of separation and extreme vulnerability her feelings for Johannes himself become submerged beneath a surge of more primary emotion which has hitherto been pent up within her, and which now opens the way for that moment of exaltation that the ensuing text describes and which she can only experience autistically (pp. 209ff. / 91–2).

Clearly there is an erotic dimension to Musil's imagery which shows clear affinities with Freudian theory. But equally clearly, Musil's elaboration of this imagery between 1908 and 1911 shows a marked divergence from the way Freud's thinking was developing during the same period. Contrary to popular supposition, Freud approached the subject of sexual *symbolism* in dreams only gradually and cautiously, adding extensive comments on the subject to the 1909 and 1911 editions of *The Interpretation of Dreams*, and providing his famous catalogue of symbols only in the *Introductory Lectures* he gave in 1915–16. Musil's use of rigid and fluid imagery incorporates an erotic dimension, but is also resistant to any interpretation that would seek to reduce Veronika's pre-conscious impulses to the sexual. The tentative manner in which the description of these impulses is presented (frequently in the form of an 'as if' or 'as when' construction), together with the multivalent nature of the imagery itself, appears calculated to forestall the assimilation of Veronika's experience to the categories of psychoanalysis or any other conceptual system. If the term 'phallic' can be applied to the *system* of imagery in Musil's text, it is only in the sense developed much later by Jacques Lacan, namely as a (veiled, elusive) 'signifier' for the desire arising out of a process of differentiation *within* the economy of the individual psyche.[26]

It is in the writings of Lacan, indeed, that recent scholarship has found useful orientation for a theoretical understanding of Musil's works. Lacan's conception of a 'mirror stage' in early personality development provides the terminology to describe the self-directed eroticism depicted in Musil's early writings. But it is Lacan's sensitivity to the elusiveness of meaning behind the written or spoken word, his awareness of the slippery relationship between 'signifier' and signified', that can perhaps be most instructively applied to the approximative technique for suggesting pre-verbal mental activity that Musil develops in these early works.[27] Musil, like Lacan, treats even the symptom as a metaphor for impulses in the unconscious which are not directly discernible or communicable.[28] He is the most assiduous amongst Modernist writers in his pursuit of the unstructured *spirit* at work in the mind, which the *word* of conventional discourse seeks to impound. And it is in 'The Temptation of Quiet Veronica' that he comes closest to realizing the project he had intimated in one of his earliest diary notes: 'As long as we think in sentences with full stops there are certain things which cannot be said – at best they can be vaguely felt. But it might be possible to learn to speak in such a way that certain infinite perspectives which lie as yet on the threshold of the unconscious become comprehensible.'[29]

The anticipation of historically later theoretical insights is not in itself a criterion for artistic merit. The three authors examined here command our attention by virtue of their creative application of language to the articulation of aspects of human experience which could not be more adequately expressed in any other way. Kafka makes discriminating use of

Freudian insights, and exploits the logic of dreams, in order to convey the interconnected anxieties besetting the rational consciousness of modern humanity. Döblin is dismissive towards psychoanalysis, and pursues his own intimate inquiry into the nature of human identity in ways which exploit and enrich the terms of public discourse. And Musil enters into a half-effaced dialogue with Freud, developing the finesse of a radically figurative language in order to suggest the autonomous nature of pre-verbal impulses. Each of these literary strategies is very different, but each seeks in its way to protect an awareness of the irrational dimension of the human mind from precipitate conceptualization.

Notes

1   *Gesammelte Werke*, ed. Adolf Frisé (2 vols, Rowohlt, Reinbek, 1978), vol. II, p. 1404.

2   See the contributions to this volume by Naomi Segal and Peter Collier. Also Edward Timms, *Freud and the Aesthetic of the Dream: The Impact of Psychoanalysis on Modern European Literature*, (Polity Press, Cambridge, forthcoming).

3   See Hartmut Binder, *Motiv und Gestaltung bei Franz Kafka*, (Bouvier, Bonn, 1966). pp. 92–114; Edward Timms, 'Kafka's expanded metaphors: a Freudian approach to "Ein Landarzt" ', in *Paths and Labyrinths*, ed. J. P. Stern and J. J. White (Germanic Institute, London, 1985), pp. 66–79.

4   Franz Kafka, *Diaries*, 6 August 1914; 2 vols, trans. Martin Greenberg (Secker & Warburg, London, 1949), vol. II.

5   Quotations from the Kafka text are taken from the translation by Willa and Edwin Muir: Franz Kafka, *In the Penal Settlement. Tales and Short Prose Works*, (Secker & Warburg, London, 1949), pp. 132–40.

6   Timms, 'Kafka's expanded metaphors', pp. 71ff.

7   Franz Kafka, *Letters to Milena*, trans. T. and J. Stern (Secker & Warburg, London, 1953), pp. 217ff.

8   cf. *Prosa des Expressionismus*, ed. Fritz Martini (Reclam, Stuttgart, 1970); Wilhelm Krull, *Prosa des Expresssionismus*, (Metzler, Stuttgart, 1984).

9   Alfred Döblin, *Aufsätze zur Literatur*, (Walter-Verlag, Olten, 1963), p. 362.

10   ibid., pp. 9–15.

11   ibid., pp. 15–19, 62–83.

12   See *Die Ermordung einer Butterblume*, (Walter-Verlag, Olten, 1962), pp. 42–54).

13   For a fuller discussion of Döblin's 'modernist' techniques, see Alan Bance, 'Alfred Döblin's *Berlin Alexanderplatz* and literary Modernism', in *Weimar Germany. Writers and Politics*, ed. Alan Bance, (Scottish Academic Press, Edinburgh, 1982), pp. 53–64.

14   Axel Eggebrecht, 'Alfred Döblin's neuer Roman *Berlin Alexanderplatz*', *Die literarische Welt*, 8 November 1929.

15   The *Moritat* was a popular ballad on a sensational theme.

16   cf. Herbert Scherer, 'The individual and the collective in Döblin's *Berlin*

Alexanderplatz', in *Culture and Society in the Weimar Republic*, ed. Keith Bullivant, (Manchester University Press, Manchester, 1977), pp. 56–70.

17   See Andrew Webber, 'Sexuality, Discourse and the Self in the Works of Georg Trakl and Robert Musil', dissertation, University of Cambridge, 1987, pp. 79–107. Freud's article 'Introducing Narcissism' first appeared in 1914.

18   A close analysis of contrasting sets of images in this text is provided by Osman Durrani, ' "Die Vollendung der Liebe": Apocalypse or Utopia?', in *Musil in Focus*, ed. Lothar Huber and John J. White (Germanic Institute, London, 1982), pp. 12–22. See also Jürgen Schröder, 'Am Grenzwert der Sprache: zu Robert Musils *Vereingungen'*, *Euphorion*, 60 (1966), pp. 311–34.

19   For these revisions of the Veronika text, as well as *Unions*, see *Gesammelte Werke*, vol. II. Other drafts and fragments are extant in addition to these. For a full discussion of the textual history, see Karl Corino, *Robert Musils 'Vereinigungen'. Studien zu einer historisch-kritischen Ausgabe*, Musil-Studien 5 (Fink, Munich, 1974).

20   This appears to have been Musil's conscious purpose in this phase of working with the material: see Corino, *Robert Musils 'Vereinigungen'*, pp. 81ff., 151.

21   ibid., pp. 169–231, reproduces and discusses a manuscript version of 1910 which had indeed been written in diary form.

22   Page references given in the text in this way are firstly to Musil's *Gesammelte Werke*, vol. II, and secondly to the standard translation by Eithne Wilkins and Ernst Kaiser, *Tonka and Other Stories*, (Secker & Warburg, London, 1965).

23   Sigmund Freud, *SE*, VII, pp. 7ff., 113–15, 164–5. See also Corino, pp. 128–30.

24   Lisa Appignanesi, *Femininity and the Creative Imagination. A Study of Henry James, Robert Musil and Marcel Proust*, (Vision Press, London, 1973), pp. 87–105.

25   ibid., pp. 100, 102.

26   Jacques Lacan, *Ecrits: A Selection*, trans. Alan Sheridan (Tavistock Publications, London, 1977), pp. 282–91.

27   Peter Henniger, *Der Buchstabe und der Geist. Unbewußte Determinierung im Schreiben Robert Musils*, (Peter Lang, Frankfurt and Bern, 1980), emphasizes this aspect of the Veronika text in particular, although his developed argument dwells somewhat reductively on the 'phallus' as the thing signified by Musil's equibocal imagery. Webber, 'Sexuality, Discourse and the Self', pp. 108–22, follows Henninger in this particular, although he is generally more circumspect in his application of Lacanian insights. Dieter Heyd, *Musil-Lektüre: der Text, das Unbewußte*, (Peter Lang, Frankfurt, 1980), examines Musil's concern with the deconstruction of logocentricity in his magnum opus *Der Mann ohne Eigenschaften*.

28   cf. Lacan, *Ecrits*, pp. 59, 166.

29   Robert Musil, *Tagebücher*, ed. Adolf Frisé (2 vols, Rowohlt, Reinbek, 1981), vol. I, p. 53.

SUGGESTED READING

Bance, A. 'Alfred Döblin's *Berlin Alexanderplatz* and literary modernism', in *Weimar Germany. Writers and Politics,* ed. Alan Bance, Edinburgh, Scottish Academic Press, 1982, pp. 53–64.

Binder, H., *Motiv und Gestaltung bei Franz Kafka,* Bouvier, Bonn, 1966.

Corino, K., *Robert Musil's 'Vereinigungen'. Studien zu einer historisch-kritischen Ausgabe,* Musil-Studien 5, Fink, Munich, 1974.

Durrani, O. ' "Die Vollendung der Liebe": Apocalypse or Utopia?', in *Musil in Focus,* ed. Lothar Huber and John J. White, Germanic Institute, London, 1982, pp. 12–22.

Henninger, P., *Der Buchstabe und der Geist. Unbewußte Determinierung im Schreiben Robert Musils,* Peter Lang, Frankfurt and Bern, 1980.

Heyd, D., *Musil-Lektüre: der Text, das Unbewußte,* Peter Lang, Frankfurt and Bern, 1980.

Krull, W., *Prosa des Expressionismus,* Metzler, Stuttgart, 1984.

Martini, F. (ed.), *Prosa des Expressionismus,* Reclam, Stuttgart, 1970.

Schröder, J., 'Am Grenzwert der Sprache: zu Robert Musils *Vereinigungen*', *Euphorion,* 60 (1966), pp. 311–34.

Timms, E. 'Kafka's expanded metaphors: a Freudian approach to "Ein Landzart" ', in *Paths and Labyrinths.* ed. J. P. Stern and J. J. White, Germanic Institute, London, 1985, pp. 66–79.

Webber, A., 'Sexuality, Discourse and the Self in the Works of Georg Trakl and Robert Musil', dissertation, University of Cambridge, 1987.

8

Following the Stranger: Narratives of the Self in Svevo and Pirandello

JUDY DAVIES

In 1923 Ettore Schmitz published *La coscienza di Zeno (The Confessions of Zeno)*, last of three novels to appear at his own expense and under the pseudonym of Italo Svevo. The rescue operation that gave Svevo recognition began two years later, through the agency of Schmitz's former English teacher, James Joyce, who alerted his literary contacts in Paris. During the period of Svevo's nascent fame, in 1926, Luigi Pirandello's *Uno, nessuno e centomila (One, No One and a Hundred Thousand Others)* was published. These two works, though written by men of vastly different temperament, and born at opposite ends of the Italian peninsula, profoundly altered the scope and direction of the Italian novel. Pirandello was Sicilian, from an inevitably Catholic background. Always a man of letters, he was at first best known for novels and short stories, while the 1920s brought him international recognition as a playwright. Schmitz, by contrast, was Jewish and a business-man. A resident of Trieste, he was not even an Italian citizen until the First World War dismantled the Austro-Hungarian Empire. He had been educated for commerce in Germany, and often claimed to regard literary activity merely as an innocuous private vice. Far subtler discriminations might be made almost *ad infinitum* between the two. Yet Pirandello and Svevo — men of the same generation after all — share the sense of individual alienation and the spirit of scepticism that makes them so distinctively 'moderns'. They have in common an abiding curiosity about the mind's activities, and they are fascinated in particular by its tendency to distort perception in order to function more adequately in an alien external world: both cast doubt on the ability of the intellect to know itself.[1]

I shall sketch out some points of comparison (and divergence) between these two pioneering novels, and then go on to explore what may seem a paradox: that *La coscienza di Zeno* — the major part of which purports to be the autobiography of a man preparing for psychoanalysis – ultimately refuses to be deciphered in psychoanalytic terms (nor is it to be understood as *merely* parodying the analytic process); while *Uno, nessuno e centomila* might profitably be read precisely within the sort of framework offered by Freud and his followers. But first it will be as well to say something about these writers' relationship to Freud. In considering their common pursuit of what Pirandello calls the 'stranger', the elusive self, it is worth noting from the outset that the 'models of mind' that underpin *La coscienza* and *Uno, nessuno* owe a great deal to Freud on the one hand and to Alfred Binet on the other (see chaper 12).

According to Svevo's own testimony, he began to read (unspecified) Freudian texts in 1908. Moreover, he became involved with psychoanalysis in a personal and practical way. His brother-in-law Bruno was in analysis with Freud, no less, by 1914 (and subsequently with the 'wild' analyst Groddeck, most famous for his contribution to Freud's concept of the id); and Svevo himself, inspired no doubt by Freud's undertaking as revealed in *The Interpretation of Dreams*, later attempted some self-analysis. When writing on the subject of psychoanalysis in 1927–8 Svevo none the less proved ambivalent and self-ironic. What surfaces – in letters to Valerio Jahier or in his autobiographical piece *Soggiorno londinese (London Sojourn)* – is the desire to safeguard the 'illness' that makes him different from other men, and so keeps alive his vocation as a 'confessional' writer. While Jahier (about to resume analysis with Marie Bonaparte) worried about his mental state and looked to Svevo for advice, Svevo assumed that he and Jahier had been merely 'talking literature'. Freud is supremely interesting from a *literary* point of view, he tells his correspondant; and an analysis with the great man would have resulted in a 'more complete' version of *La coscienza*. When finally he registers Jahier's anxiety, he counsels autosuggestion. Freud's summary dismissal of an uncured Bruno had 'disgusted' Svevo, and no doubt conditions his advice to Jahier; but Svevo also betrays the fear – shared by so many artists subsequently – that successful analysis erodes creativity: whereas, he assures Jahier, practitioners of autosuggestion 'won't change your personal "ego". So don't despair. *I'd* despair if they managed to change mine.'[2]

Writing towards the end of the 1920s, and cannily protective of his hard-won success, Svevo, however, had further likely reasons for taking up a relatively independent stance with regard to the theories emanating from Vienna. Not only had psychoanalytic narratives begun to proliferate, but in Italy Crocean idealism was in the ascendent, and so was a Regime which abhorred the uncertainties of introspection. It was not unnatural that despite Svevo's familiarity with Freud's work – despite friendship for instance with Edoardo Weiss (Freud's first Italian disciple) or acquaintance with Wilhelm Stekel – he chose to treat Freud as 'no more important for literature' than Nietzsche or Darwin (I, p. 863). At the same time, as we shall see, his contention that novelists simply 'play about with the great philosophies'

(III, p. 686) cannot be dismissed solely as a piece of defensive self-irony.[3]

For Pirandello there was no experience remotely similar to Svevo's. The gestation period of *Uno, nessuno* was a long one (witness 'preparatory' short stories such as 'Stefano Giogli, uno e due' ('The Two Stefano Gioglis') of 1909 or 'Canta l'Epistola' ('He-Sings-the-Epistle') of 1911); and the result by common consent is quintessentially Pirandellian. Yet Cesare Musatti (doyen of Freudian psychoanalysis in Italy) has commented that when he read or watched a Pirandello play during the inter-war years he 'felt he was breathing the very air of psychoanalysis'. 'It may be', Musatti speculates, 'that between 1920 and 1930, like so many other cultured people, [Pirandello] got wind of Freud's writing, but his mode of thinking . . . had been formed long ago.'[4]

Certainly the typical Pirandellian character lacks what Laing called 'primary ontological certainty',[5] the sense of a central identity capable of enjoying stable relationships with the reality of others. As far back as 1893, confronting the demise of scientism, Pirandello recorded the dolorous absence of certainty that would mark all his subsequent thinking: 'In the minds and consciences of men an extraordinary confusion reigns. . . . Never before, it seems to me, has life been so lacking in unity, ethically and aesthetically . . . We wait – and wait alas! in vain – hoping that someone will finally arise to announce the New Word . . . We are at the mercy of life.'[6] The Pirandellian *personaggio*, the clairvoyant madman spoken of in *L'umorismo (On Humour)*, is party to the secret shared with Binet, that the human personality is dicontinuous, fragmented, multiple, held together for the purposes of interpersonal relating only in the most precarious manner: whence the 'mask', the 'construct', the 'empty forms' that imprison life. And in Pirandello there is an instinctive attraction towards the breaking point through which the nocturnal self will burst. That self is the murderer in *Henry IV*; it is the Father who nearly commits incest in *Six Characters*; the lawyer in the famous story 'La carriola' ('The Wheelbarrow') who can sustain his public persona only by secretly indulging the ludicrous impulse – whence the story's title – to walk the family dog on its forepaws.

Beneath the untroubled surface there lies an unknown continent. The amoral, disordered, contradictory impulses of the secret self bear comparison with Freud's libidinal drives, and Pirandello's dualism with Freud's 'first topography' of the psychic apparatus which divided unconscious from preconscious/conscious. Perazzetti, from a story of 1909, 'Non è una cosa seria' ('No serious matter'), is aware of:

> just how different the deepest part of each man's being is from the spurious versions of it that he automatically creates for himself, either in an unconscious pretence – out of the need to believe, or have it believed, that he is different from what he really is – or in emulation of others, or for reasons of necessity and social propriety.

This deepest part Perazzetti terms 'the lair of the beast' – 'the primitive beast crouching inside each of us, beneath the layers of consciousness that have superimposed themselves one after the other over the years.' After warning of the dangers of goading the beast ('Out springs the thief, the scoundrel, the murderer') he modifies his developmental model somewhat, conceding that 'after so many centuries of civilization, the beast that many people now keep in their lair is a mortified creature.'[7] The phylogenetic view, in which the individual is somehow 'lived' by forces emanating from ancient racial history, and contained by his 'culture', may owe something to the influence of Lombroso and possibly of Nietzsche. All the same it is oddly compatible with phylogenetic tendencies in Freud's thinking (as in *Totem and Taboo* of 1912), another aspect of Pirandello that helps to explain Musatti's sensation of familiarity.

No doubt as a consequence of their insight into man's lack of psychological fixity, both Pirandello and Svevo entrust their narratives to 'men without qualities', adrift on the surface of existence, dependent for their sense of identity on the perceptions of others. In both authors there is considerable deviation from traditional modes of narrative communication; the structured unfolding of the story fades into relative insignificance; the way is opened to reverie and digression; novelistic closure becomes problematic or illusory. The use of the first person – already rehearsed by Pirandello in *Il fu Mattia Pascal (The Late Mattia Pascal)* (1904) and *Si gira (Diary of a Cameraman)* (1915), and arrived at by Svevo via the narratorial ambiguities and collusions of *Senilità (As a Man Grows Older)* (1898) – is no guarantee of a stable viewpoint. It is rather, at least in the first instance, a refusal of the techniques of the realist novel which reify and alienate the protagonist, leaving potential gaps for an authorial voice to speak more or less directly to the reader from over his shoulder. Here Svevo's neurotic (Zeno Cosini) and Pirandello's 'madman' (Vitangelo Moscarda), beset by problems in their contact with the external world, swamp the entire narrative space with their subjectivity and so reassert their singularity as 'characters', as speaking subjects within a form.

Ceaselessly verbal, the hero becomes, as it were, a rationalist critic of his own subjective feelings. His word (as Biasin remarks of Svevo) is 'at one and the same time remedy and poison – a word that cures disease while establishing and positing it'.[8] Zeno's 'word-sickness' may cause him to distort things and people as soon as he opens his mouth, yet utterance without that distortion seems 'pointless' (II, p. 659). For Pirandello's characters, including Moscarda, language may be the tool of reason, but it is also the straitjacket which attempts to contain the chaos of being. Against the disintegration of self that Moscarda experiences, he pits a writerly control most obvious in the succession of ironic chapter titles: 'Here we are, you and I', 'What then?', 'With your permission', 'Forgive me, yet again' . . . For Pirandello and Svevo, given the instability of the subject, the communication of private experience is problematic. But neither seeks to offer anything analagous to the sinuous monologues of a Joyce or a Woolf. Communication for them is always to the other (to the analyst or to Moscarda's supposedly obtuse reader) and always faulty: the narratives we are considering are discourses *about* flux, not discourses *of* flux. In the final paragraphs of *Uno, nessuno* Moscarda-Pirandello, it is true, develops a form of writing that seeks to imitate the flowing open-endedness of a consciousness that is no longer self-aware. But as the text acknowledges, where there is no subject called 'I', there is no 'you' either: the text might continue infinitely in its naming of objects – 'I am this tree. Tree, cloud, to-morrow book or wind'[9] – but communication has ended.

The invading subjectivity of these novels also involves a repudiation of those criteria against which the nineteenth-century bourgeois hero had so often been measured. Both Zeno and Moscarda are economically passive, for instance, for both have been provided by their fathers with administrators who prevent them from participating in flourishing business enterprises. In their enforced leisure, introspection tends to replace action. And before they begin to trace their thoughts in writing, both their fathers have died. The effect of this is to suggest that, even where the protagonists manage to engage with the real world, all their activity is more symbolic than real. The novel has become, so to speak, spectral: no longer a story of how people make (or fail to make) their mark in the world of their fathers, but a record of the struggle to find, and to speak, the self in the looming shadow of the internalized Oedipal Other.

These narratives subvert the solemnity of the traditional 'real'. Moscarda's entire *récit*, his journey into madness, derives from a moment of disorientation before the mirror, when his wife casually remarks on the rightwards tilt of his nose, which he had not previously noticed. Zeno's account of himself is set in motion by the memory of a particular brand of cigarette unavailable since the outbreak of war. The progression of his thoughts – first on his smoking, then on his father's death, his marriage, adultery and business partnership, and finally (in diary form) on his abandoned analysis – is not entirely uninhibited: for his initial attempt at free association simply resulted in peaceful slumber. The material he produces – the bulk of it in anticipation of his analysis and in the light of some cursory analytic reading, and the remainder against the grain of an actual experience as analysand – has the broad shape of a developmental history of the individual, from infancy to middle age. But Svevo also causes the text gradually to reveal its own unconscious: an involuntary spiralling counter-structure – patterns of recurrence chief of which is the substitution of persons along Oedipal lines.

If what Svevo seems to be holding up for inspection are the layerings of the psyche, Pirandello insists most obviously on its fragmentation. Moscarda splinters into a hundred thousand unknown versions of himself reflected back by others; and his narrative shatters into brief paragraphs: meditations, explanations, summaries, lists, digressions.

In these two narratives the centre of consciousness is also the object of its own enquiry. The subjectivities called Zeno and Moscarda are narrators and narrated in that special sense. In *La coscienza* there is constant interference between the two dimensions. Thus, for instance, Zeno recounts the distant trauma of his father's death – the old man's final gesture that might have been a slap, an angry protest at Zeno's attempt to constrain him to his death-bed; and it is in narrative-time ('last night') that he experiences the 'very vivid' dream (II, p. 640) that inverts the positions of himself and the doctor-in-attendance, Coprosich, concerning the appropriate treatment of the sick man. The wish-fulfilling dream offers a complex gloss on the past, an expression of Zeno's perpetual desire for innocence as well as an indirect re-expression of his unconscious hostility. The past in Svevo's novel becomes elusive, subject to the intrusions of the present, to the timelessness of the Oedipal unconscious. Recollection never restores to light what took place. As the older Zeno implies (in a text that should have formed part of the sequel to *La coscienza di Zeno*) the past is only past in as far as it is freed of affect, of those particulars that made it unique: 'When memory has succeeded in eliminating from events everything about them that might produce surprise, fear and disarray, one may say that they have moved into the past' (III, p. 138). To recollect is also to forget. And Svevo chooses to make of Zeno's text not so much the occasion for an accurate recording of experience, as an opportunity for Zeno to reprocess the contents of his psyche.

The narrative plane of Zeno's text is indeed studded with locutions suggesting that the recovery of the past is not so much re-creation as creation, full of surprises and discoveries that occur at the moment of the text's emanation. After he has deposited his memoir with the analyst, and stopped his analytic sessions, Zeno's final diary entry records a triumphal success in business, and continues:

> When my doctor has received this last part of my manuscript, he should give me back the whole thing. I could re-do it all with real clarity – for how was I in a position to understand my life before I knew anything about this recent period? Maybe I lived all those years merely in preparation for it (II, p. 954).

Like a psychoanalysis in which patient and analyst move towards ever more adequately explanatory versions of the patient's story, in a process which risks being – to use Freud's word – interminable, Zeno's story is infinitely retranscribable. But with the difference, as we shall see more clearly in a moment, that this particular narrator is not seriously in search of a cure, of a single, adequate narrative.

In Pirandello, by contrast, the elusiveness of the self provokes profound disquiet. He looks for definitive answers. Whereas the narrating self in *La coscienza* is itself marked by the passage of time, perpetually 'on the run' because subject to the impact of events, the Moscarda who narrates has no physical location and no temporal extension. Zeno finds himself recounting stories that often he does not 'perfectly know' (II, p. 655); but Moscarda is from the beginning in perfect possession of his narrative, and knows its outcome. Pirandello's narrator is, as it were, disembodied: pure mind exercising anxious control over the chaos of selfhood. Gone is Svevo's fluid interplay between narrator and actor. In Pirandello the latter philosophizes in the same way as the former and his activity in the 'real' world, accompanied as it is by endless intellectualization, tends to constitute itself as a demonstration of theses shared with the narrator-self. The close of the book makes explicit the fundamental identity of the two 'voices': they perfectly coalesce, in anonymity and total isolation, outside time, beyond yesterdays and to-morrows. There is no suggestion in *Uno, nessuno e centomila* that the past, in its passage though the psyche and into recall, undergoes distortion: representations of completed events, as well as the contents of memory, have the haunting clarity and the strangeness of hallucination. But then Moscarda's outward adventure – the one that concerns abandonment by a wife, a new sentimental entanglement and the renunciation of wealth – is not the *true* story. What this latter relates is a regressive movement into the archaic and pre-social, a 'schizoid' flight back to the point where language itself is on the verge of extinction.

La coscienza di Zeno, in contrast, involves a neurotic – a case primarily of 'conversion hysteria' as Freud would have called it;[10] and it traces Zeno's progress until the moment when he can assert that he feels 'absolutely healthy' and socially integrated. We may now try to see in more detail what part the discourse of psychoanalysis plays in this process.

La coscienza opens on the convolutions of the analyst's Preface, which warns the reader that the text which follows is a mass of 'truths and lies' (II, p. 599). The authority of Dr S's implicit reference to the effects of repression and resistance on the narration is rather undermined by his piqued tones and by his outrageous contravention of professional standards in publishing his patient's manuscript: analytic readings of texts, Svevo implies, are not essentially different from other kinds of reading, in that all interpretation is defined – and limited – by the subjectivity of the interpreter. None the less Svevo has chosen to establish a psychoanalytic framework for his novel. And he appeared indeed to want the analytic aspect of his work recognized, pointing out to Jahier, for example, the significance of Zeno's famous lapsus on the occasion of his brother-in-law's funeral (I, p. 863).

What the analytic approach reveals are the unmet desires and the unconscious hostilities, not only of the Oedipal phase but of an earlier oral stage, which continue to shape adult behaviour. Viewed from this perspective, the 'characters' in *La coscienza di Zeno* lose their fixity. Guido, to take a single example, marries the unattainable Ada and cuts off Zeno's access to perfect health. In so doing he becomes both a castrating sexual rival *and* a usurper of the maternal breast that gives life, or 'health'. At this second (and earlier) level the brother-in-law is the brother. He is the younger sibling, for instance, who cannot be allowed to consume the undissolved sugar at the bottom of his coffee cup because of Zeno's greedy desire to keep the mother-breast entirely to himself; he is the brother who figures in Zeno's desire as absence ('I look at the place [where the brother should be], but it appears empty to me' (II, p. 603)). Like the (dead) brother, Guido too will be eliminated from the text. It is not, however, my purpose to look at *La coscienza* analytically (though certainly there are rich pickings for the analyst/reader postulated by Svevo):[11] a 'diagnostic' reading is only *one* response to this extraordinarily complex text; and perhaps, as I suggested earlier, it is not the only, or even the best, response we can find when attempting to define the sense of self as it emerges from Svevo's novel.

One reason for the sensation that the analytic approach is somewhat problematic lies in the cunning circularity with which Svevo has arranged his text. The tempting Oedipal diagnosis comes from an analyst whose mishandling of the therapeutic enterprise seems manifest. On the other hand, except as 'author' of the Preface, Dr S is a creation of Zeno's narrative: reports of his ineptitude come to us from the strenuously resisting and contemptuous patient. And then again the negative transference which conditions the report is pre-emptively taken into account by the very person it aims to discredit. 'Anybody who knows anything about psychoanalysis', says Dr S in his Preface, 'knows what to make of the animosity that the patient feels towards me.' A knowing *letterareità* of Svevo's, by providing two conflicting (and suspect) sources of narrative authority, witholds interpretability and gives *La coscienza* a particular resilience.

Furthermore, this is a text in which *other* explanatory models of being-in-the-world proliferate. Where Moscarda subscribes to the radical scepticism theorized by Pirandello in *L'umorismo*, and regards all intellectual constructs as mendacious attempts to contain the disorderliness of experience, Zeno's story is perpetually generating its own systematizations of life, and being seduced by each of them in turn.

This *esprit de système* may appear as a minor symptom, in the form of Zeno's brief fables or gnomic pronouncements on human behaviour, proffered tongue-in-cheek. But more particularly there are what I shall term his 'Darwinian parables', those idiosyncratic, pseudo-objective accounts of human existence such as the one stimulated by his obsessive study of Basedow's (Graves's) Disease. They include the meditation triggered by Zeno's chance combination of words on life (which suddenly seems 'neither good nor bad but original' (II, p. 869)); his disquisition on the 'law of nature', deemed ignorant of 'calculation' and proceeding by 'empirical experiment' (II, p. 899); and the final paragraphs on man as an aberration in the smooth unfolding of the evolutionary process. Zeno, ex-student of chemistry, contemplates scientific certainties with self-ironic longing. Persistently he attempts to inscribe private anxiety within the public institution of medical science – hence his enthusiasm for the panaceas of Drs Beard and Niemayer, or for what seems to him the gloriously simplified existence of the diabetic.

One of Zeno's parables features what he calls the 'comestible object'. On this, he says, the human parasite feeds, reproducing or dying off in an oscillating cycle which constantly tends to establish an equilibrium between the entity of the eatable and the number of eaters. Mechanistic models of the world such as this are always embedded within other discourses which make suspect Zeno's apparent aspiration to an objective style of thought. Patches of intellectual exuberance, when referred to their context, turn out to be the by-products of psychic energy formerly 'bound' by trauma, but now released by developments in Zeno's interpersonal world which promise to reverse his past 'defeats'. The context for this particular fable is Guido's financial ruin. Zeno's apparently gratuitous inventions require the disguise of their pseudo-objective language so that their real motivation in 'cry of triumph' remains safely concealed, even from their author, Zeno.

Also straining against the hidden story of unconscious aggression is another overt tale that merits brief mention. It is a tale of chance. Zeno sees himself as the 'croupier' at the gaming table of life, the man who follows his 'inspirations', and is surprised by the way life functions, distributing health and sickness, success and failure, profit and loss, in a highly unpredictable way. Zeno's role as the gambler seems justified by the disappearance of proportion or expected linkage between cause and effect. War offers the ultimate example; and not just because, seen from the point of view of Zeno's ineradicable levity, its first effect is to separate him from the cup of breakfast coffee which now lies the wrong side of the Austrian patrols: it actually makes possible the 'impossible' business deal. As shortages bite, Zeno – with great profit and satisfaction – sells incense as a resin substitute. Increasingly self-confident, Zeno at last feels able to grasp a total situation, and offers the verdict that 'business will be restored to health when peace comes' (II, p.952). Once again, however, the intimate Oedipal story impinges. Referring to his administrator – now resident in Switzerland but still in anxious communication with his protégé – Zeno is dismissive: 'If only he knew how wide of the mark his advice is in this totally changed environment' (II, p.952). His own successful adaptation depends precisely on taking risks Olivi 'wouldn't have allowed' (II, p.953). At this late stage in the text, 'original' life is well on the way to being reconstrued as life-that-is-illness, its dangers surmountable only by experts in the field like Zeno; and the grand Darwinian ending, with its vision of an explosion which annihilates the human race, in reality offers only a mimicry of novelistic closure. For in terms of Zeno's Oedipal struggles the hidden purpose of these last paragraphs is to elaborate a system capable of explaining the survival of the unfittest, thereby relieving the survivor of his guilt. And yet, as the dangers of the future are laid out before the reader, Svevo also seems to celebrate the capacity of the thinking, agile self to survive amid a confusion that lies without as well as within.

In *La coscienza* narratives overlap and jostle. If there is an overarching psychoanalytic story it is only perceptible in the margins of Zeno's alternative narratives; and even then it is allowed to tell no more than that chapter of the self which sees the unconscious as infinite – and infinitely productive. While Dr Paoli tests his urine for sugar, Zeno toys with the 'sweet' prospect of effortless integration into the world 'outside', a final release from the precariousness of subjectivity; and as he watches, a comparison with psychoanalysis suggests itself:

> Nothing happened in the phial that could remind me of my behaviour with Doctor S when, to please him, I invented more details of my childhood to back up Sophocles's diagnosis. Here, instead, all was truth. The substance to be analysed was imprisoned in the test-tube and, for ever identical with itself, awaited the chemical reagent. When that came, it always pronounced the same word. In psychoanalysis, the same images and the same words never recur. It should be called something else, psychical adventure, let's say (II, p. 938).

Any psychoanalytic narrative will have its share of gaps and contradictions. It will continue to change for a long time so that, as Freud remarked, 'it is only toward the end of the treatment that we have before us an intelligible, consistent, or unbroken case history'.[12] Where *ultimately* the unbroken case history aims to take the patient is, however, to the full-stop of an objective truth about himself. And what Zeno-Svevo really requires is not a cure, but surprises and discoveries, extensions of life, 'the roses of May in mid-winter' (II, p. 929), that 'more complete' version of the novel. Beyond the truth there is nowhere to go, nothing to write. That is why Zeno keeps superimposing one whimsical systematization of the world on another, and why all systems, including psychoanalysis, *must* be ironized and relativized by the text, perceived as discourses, cultural artifacts that guarantee the narrativity of the self-in-its-world.

While Zeno's narratives multiply, the self remains a stranger, slipping away to a place of safety, still undefined. Although Svevo appears to suggest that at the root of Zeno's evasive story-telling lies Freud's unconscious, he refuses to limit his own creative enterprise to what he sees as the truth-seeking impulse of psychoanalysis. He makes Zeno represent the intelligence that in striving to speak its catastrophes, engages with uncertainty. *La coscienza* acknowledges that even if the true and the false are inextricably bound together so that confession can produce only more or less fictional traces of an individual's life, what remains is not only the pleasure of the endlessly proliferating text, but also the hope that a thinking self can resist in times of epistemological crisis.

Moscarda also raises questions about the grounds of his self-knowledge. But the perception that there are infinite different versions of himself is only a starting-point: the whole thrust of the novel is towards the discovery of an underlying principle of unity in the self.

Uno, nessuno e centomila is as apparently rich in Oedipal material as *La coscienza di Zeno*. Again there is a father who arouses ambivalent feelings, and a long-dead mother whose appearances in the text are significant for their rarity. But while Zeno's oral-erotic relationships to female figures such as Ada always include a father-brother, and are thus triangular, Moscarda's relationships are essentially dyadic. We may say that what Zeno suffers from is jealousy, 'which is mainly concerned with the love that the subject feels is his due and is being taken away, or is in danger of being taken away, by a rival'; and that Moscarda instead appears to experience envy, 'which implies the subject's relation to one person only and goes back to the earliest relation with the mother'.[13] (In fact Pirandello makes no significant distinction between father and mother.) Where Zeno offers his interlocutor the seductions – the invitations to collusion – of his wit, Moscarda argues and confronts. Whether on the metanarrational plane – where the Other is the reader postulated by the text – or in the context of the protagonist's interactions in the story, the presence of the Other invariably produces a sense of conflict.

In *Uno, nessuno* we find the familiar Pirandellian topos of the mirror as an image of the mind's self-consciousness. The narrative dwells obsessively on the problem of the self's relating to itself. It is a process subject to interference from outside, for a sense of identity depends on the reflecting-back of the other; and that perceiving other tends to fragment the personality of the subject along with his body, reducing them to the status of scattered objects appropriated into the external world. They cannot be reassembled because it is impossible to be both inside the self and outside it, to be both the agent of consciousness and the object of its activity. Yet to be looked at is the very condition of the self's social existence. This is the dilemma that Moscarda probes with demented curiosity. I wish to draw on some aspects of psychoanalytic thinking, not so much to illuminate Moscarda's 'pathology' as to provide one way of bringing to light a fundamental coherence in Pirandello's organization of his material, and of arriving at an explanation for some of the text's more bizarre insistences and inclusions.

Uno, nessuno e centomila might usefully be examined in the light of Laingian, or more generally 'existential' analysis, but Melanie Klein's work also suggests itself, and for two main reasons. The novel, from an analytic point of view, deals with early, narcissistic material, and it was Klein who extended Freudian research back into the very first months of life. Secondly, whereas Freud's notion of the death instinct, introduced in 1920 in *Beyond the Pleasure Principle*, provoked doubt in many analytic quarters, it found full acceptance with Klein, informing her extraordinary descriptions of the raging, envious infant at the breast. In her view, the death instinct seeks the return to a state of total quiescence, and is thus self-destructive; but the immature ego when faced with the anxiety of its own urge towards annihilation defends itself by projecting the destructive parts of itself onto the external world. Klein's staring baby with his 'evil eye' is a prey to persecutory fantasies, unable to distinguish between anxiety and aggression, self and other. Moscarda seems to inhabit just this kind of world, where on the one hand external reality is perceived as hostile, and needs to be destroyed; on the other, it is experienced as the source of negative versions of the self, 'bad' introjects, which produce anxiety against which ego-disintegration may be the last defence.[14]

It is the father who is the agent of the most striking instance of Moscarda's being dispossessed of himself. In the mirror of his father's 'glassy blue eyes', the idle son 'full of errant thoughts' (pp. 790, 789) is used to reading tenderness tinged with pity and derision. But a moment of distraction and inattentiveness inevitably comes: the confirmatory function of the paternal glance ceases. Then, for Moscarda, fathers become the other, the enemy:

> Suddenly the person who was so close to us is miles away: catching sight of him we see a stranger. And our lives feel utterly torn to shreds, except at one point which still connects them to that man. It is a point of shame – the fact of our birth, detached and cut off from him, as though it were an everyday happening. Perhaps not unforeseen, but involuntary, in the life of that stranger – the evidence of a gesture, the fruit of an action, something in short that now, oh yes! makes us feel shame, that arouses resentment and almost hatred in us (p. 792).

The 'child' who is speaking here depends on the parent for his sense of self and cannot tolerate the perception of father and child as fatally separate. Moscarda can only react with a projection, construing the father's otherness as persecutory and seeking to survive it by his own acts of aggression.

This is the emblematic episode that will organize the rest of the text. Pirandello's narrative goes on to chart a regressive process which eliminates the other from a series of dyadic relationships. Moscarda's story presents itself most obviously as one of rebellion against the social order of the fathers: his activity culminates in the total renunciation of his paternal legacy, both monetary and cultural. But he becomes involved not only in the progressive renunciation of the hundred thousand selves-for-others – from the 'usurer's son' to the 'Gengé'-Moscarda who is Dida's husband – but also in a final renunciation of the self-for-me, the unitary self.

The journey towards the roots of being first thrusts aside the social definitions of self. It then looks at the possibility of being 'one', a self anterior to the processes of splitting and fragmentation initiated by the presence/absence of the other. But here at the centre of being the text seems to see only destructiveness. Dida's uncomprehending laughter wounds what Moscarda calls the 'live place' (p. 855) within him. Later he redefines that live place as the 'God-within' (comparing it to the 'God-without' who needs the 'constructs' of organized religion) (pp. 880–1). The implication seems to be that there is an indestructible and sacred self which Dida wounds at her peril, something comparable perhaps to the tenuous post-natal ego seen by Klein as 'called into operation by the life instinct' which deflects the 'threat of annihilation by the death instinct' towards the outer world.[15] Dida's annihilating laughter leads into the momentarily exhilarating experience of becoming one, finally oblivious of the other, 'as deaf and as shut in on itself as a stone' (p. 858). But Moscarda achieves this oneness only by an act of aggression against Dida, and is then horrified at the 'blind way feeling and will had risen up inside me and *given me body*, a bestial body that has caused fear and made my hands violent' (p. 859). Oneness is inseparable from destructiveness.[16] It de-peoples the world and in so doing threatens the very existence of the 'I' it aimed to preserve:

> I thought: 'I'm free! She's gone! . . . But where was the wound now? Was it in me? . . . When I touched myself, or squeezed my hands together, yes, I could say 'I'; but to whom, 'I' for whom? I was alone, alone in all the world, alone-for-myself. I shuddered and in that instant . . . felt eternity and the chill of this infinite solitude (pp. 861,862).

A glacial sense of disembodiment and loneliness accompanies Moscarda to the end of his maniacal experiments. Given the dangerousness of being one, this story of schizoid flight will go on to examine the possibility of being 'no one'. This is the closing area of the text and the one which includes Anna Rosa, the 'revolver among the flowers', and the shooting of Moscarda. It includes, that is to say, the most perplexing clashes between the 'real' story, which still clings perversely to the everyday textures of provincial life, and the 'hidden' narrative of the unconscious. Anna Rosa and the events surrounding her are, in fact, best regarded as symbols, subject to a species of condensation, to overlapping time-schemes of the self, oblivious certainly of common-sense chronology. Anna Rosa for instance is potential lover, but she is also female Narcissus and Mother. In this last guise she seems to hold out the possibility that Moscarda can abdicate selfhood altogether. Just before he reaches out his arms to her, Moscarda recalls:

> I said things to her that I can no longer remember, words in which she must have felt my consuming desire to give all the life that was in me, everything that it lay within my power to be, so that I could become the one she might desire of me, and for myself no one, no one at all (p. 893).

But then, in the vaguely uterine penumbra of the rose-coloured room, the gun explodes, and the dream of merging is shattered. A Freudian such as Svevo, one imagines, would have avoided that too-phallic revolver. But Pirandello, in his innocent and yet luminous intelligence of inner worlds, can produce a seeming sample of Klein's fantasized 'combined parent'.[17] Yet we seem to be dealing with a representation not so much of the sexual theories of children, as of the infant's discovery that it can never fully meet the desire of the mother, since that desire is always tending elsewhere, towards a father. So it is that in the final phase of the book Moscarda makes a last retreat from all relatedness with the denying other. In the closing

'Non-Conclusion' he seems to inhabit a limbo between existence and non-existence. As Dombroski puts it, 'in losing his specific and autonomous identity through submersion in the landscape, Moscarda certainly 'loses' the self that was endangered by the scrutiny of others; and thus paradoxically he avoids "non-being" by avoiding "being".'[18]

In chapter 12 of this book Ann Caesar explores a parallel between the creative process in Pirandello and the receptiveness of the medium to his 'voices'. In a similar fashion Moscarda has run the risk of 'possession'. He is infinitely suggestible, inhabited contemporaneously and successively by other selves – rather as Klein's infant ego is made up of part-objects. He becomes the Moscarda who thieves from himself, or is jealous of the Gengé loved by Dida, or is persuaded that there exists a Moscarda in love with Anna Rosa. 'Doubts in the possession of the good object and the corresponding uncertainty about one's own good feelings', such as Moscarda experienced in relation to his father, 'contribute to greedy and indiscriminate identifications,' writes Klein: 'such people are easily influenced because they cannot trust their own judgement.'[19]

It is also in terms of part-objects that we may begin to account for some of the unexplained and quasi-hallucinatory images that occur in the text. There is for instance an oddly over-elaborated passage (a reworking of a passage from a story entitled *Ritorno* ('Home-Coming') of 1913), which describes the gradual appropriation by villagers of the courtyard in front of Moscarda's house. It seems important that the father never finished building the wall which should have protected the area, and that the invaders – who inspire feelings of intense physical revulsion in Moscarda – become bold only after his death. The passage, surely, describes an inner landscape. The courtyard is a self deprived by the 'absent' father of confirmatory mirroring, of narcissistic gratification, and so exposed to the attacks of its 'bad objects'. Before the fear of being visible there was indeed the desire to be constantly in view. It is this desire that explains the abrupt surfacing of another strange memory – a memory:

> of when I was a boy walking preoccupied in the country and suddenly realized I was lost, far away from any pathway, in a solitude dark with sunlight and stupor; of the terror I felt and could not then explain. It was this: the horror of something that at any moment might be revealed to me alone, out of view of others (p. 844).

The self-destructiveness and the hostility of Klein's death instinct interweave in Moscarda's narration. Just as he himself is fragmented, turned into a succession of objects-for-others, so the other is ruthlessly dismembered, deprived of its persecutory vitality: the father is perceived merely as hands or 'shiny cranium', Dida is a 'broken doll', the father-in-law a 'tailor's dummy' or the 'head in a barber's shop-window' (pp. 791, 859, 864). Just as Moscarda's philosophizing is a defence against anxiety, so his omnipotent impulses deny the psychic reality of dependence on the object.

When interviewed in 1930, Pirandello glossed the close of *Uno, nessuno* optimistically. Leone De Castris, for one, sensed an evasion. He saw Moscarda's 'reintegration into the universal' as a sudden forced inversion of the dissolution of the individual that had been in progress; and attributed it to a 'voluntaristic use of Bergsonian vitalism' unrepresented anywhere else in Pirandello's oeuvre.[20] Yet Pirandello's interpretation makes sense. The text undoes what has been done to an individual in the course of a lifetime; and it arrives finally not at the atomization of that individual, though it has indeed passed through that stage, but at a pristine self replete with undefined potentiality. Which is why Pirandello's final lyrical paragraphs repeatedly allude to newness and rebirth.

Pirandello tells a developmental story backwards, so to speak: he works on the mature individual to discover the infant within; he is anxious as always to distinguish the face from the mask, final truths from 'later' encrustations of falsehood. In this respect he operates like the pioneer psychoanalysts who claimed scientific status for their investigations; and the overall structure of the novel – with its oneiric, sexually-charged detailing – aligns Pirandello's work with the concerns of the psychoanalytic consulting-room, and invites an analytic approach. But there is an important difference. For Moscarda, unlike the analytic patient, is not returned to life. Pirandello makes the end of *Uno, nessuno* coincide with a beginning that is only potential. From such a threshold between being and non-being the nascent individual might perhaps one day emerge to reattempt the perilous business of constructing a self in the world of others.

But in Moscarda it is formlessness and unknowability alone that keep alive that possibility of confronting some day the conflicting thought-systems and the impingements of the world. In Pirandello, as in Svevo, there is a price to be paid for survival. Whether the self resists through an ability to play with systems of signification, or whether it manages to slip away through the meshes of interpretation into silence, the implication is surely the same. Where there is no one system of thought that can succeed in encapsulating the intrapsychic and interpsychic experience of the self, that self is condemned to remain a stranger.

Notes

1   For comparative work on the two authors see Renato Barilli, *La linea Svevo-Pirandello* (Mursia, Milan, 1963), and Renato Barilli et al. *Il romanzo di Pirandello e Svevo* (Vallecchi, Florence, 1984).

2   See *Epistolario*, vol.I, *Opera omnia*, ed. Bruno Maier, 6 vols (Dall'Oglio, Milan, 1966–78), pp. 859–60. The critical edition of Svevo's work being still

incomplete, I shall use Maier's edition, and specifically vol.I: *Epistolario*; vol.II: *Romanzi*; and vol.III: *Racconti, saggi e pagine sparse*. References to this work, giving volume number and page, will be included in the text. *La coscienza di Zeno* is easily available in translation as *Confessions of Zeno*, trans. Beryl de Zoete (Penguin Books, Harmondsworth). All translations in the chapter are my own.

3 For additional biographical information about Svevo and psychoanalysis see Enrico Ghidetti, *Italo Svevo: la coscienza di un borghese triestino* (Editori Riuniti, Rome, 1980) pp. 224–36, and John Gatt-Rutter, *Italo Svevo: A Double Life* (Clarendon Press, Oxford, 1988), pp. 247–51.

4 Cesare Musatti, *Mia sorella gemella la psicoanalisi* (Editori Riuniti, Rome, 1985), pp. 213–14.

5 See R. D. Laing, 'Ontological Insecurity', ch. III, *The Divided Self* (Tavistock Publications, London, 1960, and Pelican, Harmondsworth, 1977).

6 See *Saggi, poesie, scritti varii*, ed. Manlio Lo Vecchio-Musti, 3rd rev. edn (Mondadori, Milan, 1973), pp. 900, 901, 903.

7 See *Novelle per un anno* vol.II, 8th edn (2 vols, Mondadori, Milan, 1969), pp. 366–7.

8 Gian Paolo Biasin, *Literary Diseases* (University of Texas Press, Austin and London, 1975), p. 87.

9 See *Uno, nessuno e centomila*, vol.II, *Tutti i romanzi*, ed. Giovanni Macchia (2 vols, Mondadori, Milan, 1986), p. 901. All page references given in the text are to this edition of Pirandello's novel. It has been translated by Samuel Putnam as *One, None and a Hundred Thousand*, repr. of 1933 edn (Howard Fertig, New York, 1983).

10 A conversion hysteria is involved when a psychical conflict is transposed or converted into a bodily symptom. See for instance Freud's *Studies on Hysteria* (1895), *SE*, II; Pelican 3.

11 See for instance Elio Gioanola's *Un killer dolcissimo* (Il Melangolo, Genoa, 1979), which is particularly alert to the 'oral' dimension in *La coscienza*.

12 'Fragment of an Analysis of a Case of Hysteria' ('Dora'), *SE*, VII, p. 18.

13 See Melanie Klein, *Envy and Gratitude and Other Works*, 3rd imp. (Hogarth Press and Institute of Psycho-Analysis, London, 1984), p. 181.

14 Compare Hanna Segal, *Introduction to the Work of Melanie Klein*, new enlarged edn (Hogarth Press and Institute of Psycho-Analysis, London, 1982): 'Disintegration is the most desperate of all the ego's attempts to ward off anxiety: in order to avoid suffering anxiety the ego does its best not to exist, an attempt which gives rise to a specific acute anxiety – that of falling to bits and becoming atomized' (pp. 30–1).

15 Klein, *Envy and Gratitude*, pp. 190–1.

16 Compare for instance Harry Guntrip, 'The Schizoid Problem, Regression, and the Struggle to Preserve an Ego', ch. II, *Schizoid Phenomena, Object Relations and the Self*, 5th imp. (Hogarth Press and Institute of Psycho-Analysis, London, 1983): '*The frustration of libidinal need for good object-relations both arouses aggression and intensifies libidinal needs till the infant fears his love-needs as destructive towards his objects*' (p. 167; italics in original).

17 For this concept see J. Laplanche and J.-B. Pontalis, *The Language of Psychoanalysis*, 4th imp. (Hogarth Press and Institute of Psycho-Analysis, London, 1985), pp. 70–1.

18   Robert S. Dombroski, *Le totalità dell'artificio; ideologia e forma nel romanzo di Pirandello* (Liviana Editrice, Padua, 1978), p. 128.
19   Klein, *Envy and Gratitude*, p. 187.
20   Arcangelo Leone De Castris, *Storia di Pirandello* (Laterza, Bari, 1962), p. 201.

SUGGESTED READING

Barilli, R. *La linea Svevo-Pirandello*, Mursia, Milan, 1963.
Barilli, R. et al. *Il romanzo di Pirandello e Svevo*, Vallecchi, Florence, 1984.
Corsini, G. *Il romanzo inevitabile*, Mondadori, Milan, 1983.
Gioanola, E. *Un killer dolcissimo. Indagine psicanalitica sull'opera di Italo Svevo*, Il Melangolo, Genoa, 1979.
Gioanola, E. *Pirandello. La follia*, Il Melangolo, Genoa, 1979.
Lavagetto, M. *L'impiegato Schmitz*, Einaudi, Turin, 1975.

For reference
David, M. *Letteratura e psicanalisi*, Mursia, Milan, 1967.
David, M. *La psicanalisi nella cultura italiana*, 2nd edn, Boringhieri, Turin, 1970.

9

Proust's 'Livre intérieur'

ROBIN MACKENZIE

In November 1913, just before the publication of *Du côté de chez Swann*, Proust gave an interview to *Le Temps* in which he outlined some of the central themes and preoccupations explored in his work. He discusses voluntary and involuntary memory; impressions and their transformation into art; the question of style, as vision rather than technique. But before he develops all these characteristic themes we find Proust making this statement: 'my book could perhaps be seen as a series of 'Fictions of the Unconscious.'[1]

It is rather a surprise to find the unconscious present as a leitmotiv, an organizing principle, in Proust's projected novel, especially at such an early stage in its composition. Unlike memory, art or the impression, the unconscious is not the subject of extended narratorial comment in *A la Recherche*. Its importance is implicit, its conceptual boundaries uncertain. There are, however, indications of its place in Proust's imaginative vision in some of his critical and theoretical writings. It should of course be emphasized that Proust's readings of his own work are not necessarily authoritative, or even privileged; but they can indicate fruitful areas of investigation and methods of enquiry.

In the interview for *Le Temps* Proust makes connections between the unconscious and those other salient themes: the impression, memory, art. The impression seems to be the main repository of the Proustian unconscious: 'Not only will the same characters reappear in different guises during the course of the work, as they do in some of Balzac's novel cycles, but even within a single character (. . .) certain deep, almost unconscious impressions will also recur' (*CSB*, pp.557–8). The self would seem to be constituted from these deep-rooted impressions; their periodic resurgence would structure both subjective time and the work of fiction itself. These recurrent impressions would be memory traces, although not every memory would belong to the set of 'impressions profondes'. Hence the distinction between voluntary and involuntary memory, which Proust sees as absolutely central. Voluntary memory is a surface phenomenon, depending on will and conscious rationality; involuntary memory (which is rooted in sensation as much as in perception) emerges from deeper unconscious levels of the mind.

The connection between art and the unconscious processes is complex. Involuntary memory would furnish the raw material ('la matière primaire') of the work of art, and would somehow ensure its aesthetic balance. Thus unconscious processes would be seminal in the creative process, relegating conscious intelligence to a secondary position. Proust in his critical writings – like the narrator of *A la recherche* – frequently sets up an opposition between intelligence or reason and other less rational modes of mental functioning, sometimes called intuition or instinct, sometimes 'the impression' and occasionally 'the unconscious'. In a letter to Jacques Rivière, Proust writes: 'Ahead of the intellect I place the unconscious, which the intellect will eventually clarify, but which itself provides the reality and the originality of a work.'[2] This makes the interdependence of ordering intelligence and unconscious material quite explicit (as well as indicating their relative importance). In the interview for *Le Temps*, Proust is less sanguine about their complementarity: 'At first I perceived [the finer details of my work] in my inner depths, without understanding them, finding it just as difficult to convert them into something comprehensible as if they had been as alien to the world of the intellect as, say, a musical motif' (*CSB*, p.559). This introduces a final element, or opposition, into the thematic force-field of the Proustian unconscious. The real of the intelligible is contrasted not only with the unconscious but also with music, which (by assimilation) would presumably stand in some homologous relation to the unconscious. This connection may be little more than an aside at this stage of Proust's writing, but it is one that Proust will develop and elaborate on in *A la recherche*, where he shows first Swann, and then the narrator, attempting to grasp their inmost feelings through the stimulus of a musical motif.

In spite of its putative importance, the unconscious remains difficult to define in Proust's novel. This is in part due to the rare occurrences of the word in the text: according to Brunet's concordance, 'l'inconscient' as a substantive appears only seven times in the whole of *A la recherche*.[3] The distribution is interesting, incidentally: the word occurs only in the last four volumes, and four out of the seven occurrences are in *La Prisonnière* and *La Fugitive* – the last sections of the work to be written. This would seem to indicate that Proust's interest in unconscious processes was increasing as he grew older, with consequences both thematic and formal (such as the increasing discontinuity of the narrative which Genette has commented upon in *Figures III*).[4]

The paucity of explicit reference to the unconscious is not the only reason for these difficulties in definition. The notion of the unconscious was in a phase of conceptual turmoil around the turn of the nineteenth century, before it was adopted – or colonized – by Freud and the psychoanalytic movement. There were two very divergent currents of thought in which the unconscious played an important part. The first was the rising science of psychology, whose major representative in France was the neurologist Charcot (with whom both Freud and Proust's father worked). French psychologists carried out quite extensive research into some of the more irrational aspects of human behaviour, such as dual personality, using hypnosis as a tool to explore zones of the self which were otherwise inaccessible. The unconscious was never perhaps a very clearly defined part of their conceptual scheme, but positivist psychology nevertheless focussed attention on unconscious mental processes to an unprecedented degree.

A more rigorously defined and much less empirically based notion of the unconscious was developed in the very different intellectual tradition of German Idealism. German Idealism was showing clear signs of decline, not to say demise, by the later years of the nineteenth century – at least in Germany – but one of its last flourishes came with Edouard von Hartmann's massive *Philosophie des Unbewussten* (1869), in which he expounded a metaphysical system centred on an Unconscious which owed a great debt to the notion of the 'Will' developed by his precursor Schopenhauer. Hartmann's Unconscious was a kind of cosmic force or energy, which bore little resemblance bar the name to the neurological unconscious of the French psychologists. But Hartmann's work was quickly translated into French (1877 – the title, *La Philosophie de l'inconscient*, containing the first recorded use of 'inconscient' as a substantive), and had an influence on at least one notable writer, Laforgue, whose poetry in the 1880s gave a pessimistic interpretation of desire in terms of this cosmic Unconscious.

The emergence of psychoanalysis in the early years of the twentieth century saw the notion of the unconscious take on a prominence and a precision hitherto unknown. There is little evidence, none of it conclusive, that Proust was aware of Freud's work, and the narrator's remarks about the unconscious in *A la recherche* show no indubitably Freudian features.[5] Nevertheless, a comparative study of Proust and Freud on unconscious (and (and other) mental processes reveals many interesting convergences (and divergences) in areas like dream, desire and memory.

The most elaborate description of a 'substantive' unconscious in *A la recherche* occurs in the so-called 'aesthetic theory' section of *Le Temps retrouvé*. As the ageing Marcel is waiting to be admitted to the Guermantes salon, a series of involuntary memories comes flooding over him, triggered by the uneven surface of the Guermantes courtyard, the texture of a napkin, the sound of a spoon on a plate. He resolves to explore the causes, deep-rooted he suspects, of the felicity the memories bring him. The result of this exploration is a theory of art closely linked to the 'privileged moments' of memory and perception which every so often punctuate

Marcel's existence. The unconscious is introduced at a crucial point, just after Marcel grasps the connection between memory and artistic creation:

> As for the inner book of unknown symbols (symbols carved in relief they might have been, which my attention, as it explored my unconscious, groped for and stumbled against and followed the contours of, like a diver exploring the ocean-bed), if I tried to read them no one could help me with any rules, for to read them was an act of creation in which no one can do our work for us or even collaborate with us.
>
> (III,p.879; KIII,p.913)[6]

There are two major isotopies, or metaphoric clusters, here: the topographical motif, and the metaphorics of reading and textuality. The topographical motif may seem rather obvious: the unconscious is presented in terms of surface and depth, on a vertical axis, with the unconscious as the deeper region of the mind and consciousness (in the figure of the diver) making occasional forays below the surface in its interpretative mission. This pattern of surface and depth is something of a faded metaphor, a catechresis (as in 'depth psychology', for instance) but it does suggest links between the unconscious and specific mental processes (like memory and dream) in *A la recherche*. The interplay of surface and depth characterizes the 'madeleine' episode, in which the taste of a cake dipped in an infusion triggers a resurgence of forgotten impressions in the narrator's mind, thus allowing him imaginatively to recreate his Combray childhood:

> I feel something start within me, something that leaves its resting-place and attempts to rise, something that has been embedded like an anchor at a great depth; I do not know yet what it is, but I can feel it mounting slowly; I can measure the resistance, I can hear the echo of great spaces traversed.
>
> (I,p.46; KI,p.49)

As in the 'livre intérieur' passage, the pattern of surface and depth is linked to an image of water, of the sea ('désancré'). This metaphoric strand also appears in passages describing sleep and dreams: 'one cannot properly describe human life unless one bathes it in the sleep into which it plunges night after night and which sweeps round it as a promontory is encircled by the sea' (II,p.85; KII,p.83). The metaphoric affinities suggest a thematic link between memory, dream and the unconscious: all are 'depth' phenomena, not obviously accessible to the more transparently rational faculties. Involuntary memory and dreams are in fact probably the two poles of the Proustian unconscious, but this is nowhere made explicit in the narrator's commentary. The other salient feature of the Proustian topography, the imagery of water and the sea, also carries interesting implications for the thematics of the unconscious: 'Perhaps the unconscious well-being induced by this summer day came like a tributary to swell the flood of joy that had surged in me at the sight of Elstir's 'Carquethuit Harbour''

(I,p.842; KI,p.901). This tributary image is somewhat reminiscent of one of Freud's pervasive metaphors of mental process, the so-called 'hydraulic' model, in which the operations of desire are represented in terms of flow and blockage, the damming up of libidinal currents, etc. But often the water images in *A la recherche* evoke stasis rather than the dynamics of Freud's model: they form a topography rather than an energetics.

Freud of course also proposed a topography of the psyche (two in fact: the first centring on the conscious-unconscious opposition, with the pre-conscious as liminal area; the second providing a triadic model of ego, superego and id). In contrast to Proust's image of the diver moving between surface and depths, the Freudian topography of mind is frequently represented along a horizontal rather than a vertical axis. In the *Introductory Lectures*, for example, we find a description of the mind as a house with two rooms: the unconscious is like a large entrance hall where many separate mental impulses swarm around, while the pre-conscious mind is compared to a smaller drawing-room, in which rather more sedate behaviour is expected.[7] In between, guarding the drawing-room door in case any undesirables try to enter, is a watchman who goes by the name of 'resistance' (a kind of intrapsychic bouncer). This model points to one crucial difference between Freudian and Proustian views of the mind. In the Freudian model, conflict is much more in evidence — 'resistance' will not hesitate to use some muscle against the more unruly elements in the unconscious. In the 'livre intérieur' passage the conscious mind encounters obstacles, but there is no suggestion of an intrapsychic battle between conscious and unconscious forces. Even in other Proustian metaphors, where the unconscious has a less passive role, it usually works in collaboration with the conscious rather than in opposition to it: 'I suffered to the very depths of my being, in my body and in my heart . . . from this curiosity to which all the force of my intelligence and my unconscious contributed' (III,p.526; KIII,p.536). There is occasionally a conflict of memory and perception, of past and present moment, in Proust's narrative of mind: the effect of involuntary memory is described in a rhetoric of struggle — as a mental wrestling bout — in *Le Temps retrouvé*:

> Always, when these resurrections took place, the distant scene engendered around the common sensation had for a moment grappled, like a wrestler, with the present scene. Always the present scene had come off victorious, and always the vanquished one had appeared to me the more beautiful of the two.
>
> (III,p.875; KIII,p.908)

But the psyche is not presented in *A la Recherche* as the zone of unremitting conflict between impulses or forces we see in Freud.[8]

The second focal metaphor of the *Temps retrouvé* passage — also to be found in Freud, incidentally — is that of textuality, of reading and writing (what Derrida in 'Freud and the scene of writing' called the 'graphological' motif).[9] It is a pivotal metaphor here, because it provides a link between the unconscious as represented or described in *A la recherche* and the poetics of the work, between the thematics of mind and the techniques of writing. It is an interface of theme and form, of paradigm and poetic process.

The 'livre intérieur' passage presents us with one account of the link between writing and the unconscious, which could be designated the 'expressivist' model. This model is explicitly formulated by the narrator and has consequently – in various stages of paraphrase and re-ordering – formed the basis of much Proust criticism. It essentially presents the mind as (or as containing) a network or structure of signs – the 'livre intérieur' – which seem to solicit interpretation or deciphering, this process of interpretation being at the same time the creation of the work of art. The motif of deciphering is a recurrent one:

> already at Combray I used to fix before my mind for its attention some image which had compelled me to look at it, a cloud, a triangle, a church spire, a flower, a stone, because I had the feeling that perhaps beneath these signs there lay something of a quite different kind which I must try to discover, some thought which they translated after the fashion of those hieroglyphic characters which at first one might suppose to represent only material objects.
>
> (III,p.878; KIII,p.912)

The unconscious as a collection of hieroglyphic inscriptions is to be found in Freud as well, particularly in connection with the dream-work (which is also compared to cuneiform and Chinese ideographic scripts),[10] and in connection with the psychoanalyst himself, whom Freud tends to compare to an archaeologist. But whereas Freud tends to deduce rules of method from these comparisons – for instance the antithetical meaning of identical elements in the dream, resulting from the suppression of logical relations, such as negation, in the unconscious – Proust's narrator frequently expresses a distrust of method (as in the 'livre intérieur' passage). But in both writers deciphering the signs of the unconscious is of central importance.

However, this process of interpretation by the Proustian narrator also involves the danger of misreading, of error. There are for instance several episodes in *La Fugitive* where Marcel fails to register Gilberte's name. The first occurs when Marcel, visiting Mme de Guermantes, meets a young woman whose name he hears as 'Mlle d'Eporcheville'. He immediately identifies her as the young aristocrat whom Saint-Loup claimed to have encountered in a house of ill repute. Saint-Loup however informs him that the young woman in question was actually called 'Mlle de l'Orgeville'. Subsequently Marcel finds out that the woman he had met was 'Mlle de Forcheville', i.e. Gilberte. This tissue of error, of misprision, might appear fortuitous; but Marcel fails to recognize Gilberte's name once again, this time in writing, when he receives a telegram in Venice which he imagines is from Albertine. The idiosyncracies of Gilberte's signature provide a satisfactory explanation for the narrator:

> We guess as we read, we create; everything starts from an initial error; those that follow (and this applies not only to reading of letters and telegrams, not only to all reading), extraordinary as they may appear to a person who has not begun at the same starting-point, are all quite natural.
>
> (III,p.656; KIII,p.671)

But a suspicious reader might well take this error as less fortuitous and 'natural' than the narrator maintains. Unconscious (mis)perception may well be more structured than it appears; it is tempting to construct a Freudian narrative around these episodes, a narrative of repression of the name of Gilberte, of denial of the death of Albertine, of unwitting revelation of their sexual ambiguity (in Saint-Loup's and Marcel's readings, for instance, half-hidden 'orgies' and 'porcheries' emerge; Proust might also be illustrating Freudian jokes or parapraxes). A subterranean intelligence seems to be at work in Marcel's mode of perception.

But this 'perceptual unconscious' is not always a source of error and distortion, of projection and hallucinated wish-fulfilment, of repression and negation, as in Freud. Much aesthetic ordering and registering of impressions operates below the threshold of conscious attention:

> There was in me a personage who knew more or less how to look, but it was an intermittent personage, coming to life only in the presence of some general essence common to a number of things, these essences being its nourishment and its joy. Then the personage looked and listened, but at a certain depth only, without my powers of superficial observation being enhanced.
>
> (III,p.718; KIII,pp.737–8)

This subliminal recording of details is connected to the expressivist model of writing, since the perceptions thus recorded form the store of internal signs which have to be deciphered in the production of a work of art. But the expressivist model is counterbalanced by the idea that deciphering is also a form of creation. This somewhat paradoxical notion occurs quite frequently in the narrator's discourse, in the 'madeleine' episode for example, which (as so often) prefigures the subsequent explicit description of the unconscious: 'What an abyss of uncertainty, whenever the mind feels overtaken by itself; when it, the seeker, is at the same time the dark region through which it must go seeking and where all its equipment will avail it nothing. Seek? More than that: create' (I,p.45; KI,p.49). Among the compromise for-m(ul)ations through which the narrator explores the interpretation-creation polarity is the motif of translation, which may not seem very different from interpretation but does at least acknowledge a change of medium between 'livre intérieur' and material work of art: 'I realised that . . . the essential, the only true book, though in the ordinary sense of the word it does not have to be 'invented' by a great writer – for it exists already in each one of us – has to be translated by him. The function and the task of a writer are those of a translator' (III,p.890; KIII,p.926). An opposition between translation and invention has been set up which is very similar to the interpretation-creation one, except that translation and invention are presented as mutually exclusive rather than paradoxically conjoined.

But the crux of the interpretation-creation problematic is provided by metaphor, the figure around which the narrator's poetics – indeed aesthetics – resolve. Metaphor links the theory of art and the theory of self or mind in *A la recherche*:

> truth will be attained by the writer only when he takes two different objects, states the connexion between them – a connexion analogous in the world of art to the unique connexion which in the world of science is provided by the law of causality – and encloses them in the necessary links of a well-wrought style; truth – and life too – can be attained by us only when, by comparing a quality common to two sensations, we succeed in extracting their common essence and in reuniting them to each other, liberated from the contingencies of time, within a metaphor.
>
> (III,p.889; KIII,pp.924–5)

This is a climactic passage in the narrator's aesthetic theory, and also a convoluted one. For metaphor clearly functions as the verbal – or indeed aesthetic – analogon of the propensity for connection which characterizes involuntary memory and the hermeneutics of the impression. Metaphor reveals a resemblance between two apparently unrelated elements – a fish as 'une polychrome cathédrale de la mer' (I,p.695) for instance – just as a similar sensation discloses an unsuspected connection between two moments far apart in time (tripping on a paving stone at the Guermantes' recalls for Marcel the feeling of the uneven floor of St Mark's in Venice). But there is perhaps more implied: metaphor may be not only analogous to involuntary memory in its operation (i.e. a formal model) but also the transcription of a particular memory or impression, the record of an event in Marcel's experience (as when the vision of Combray arising from the patterns formed by lime leaves in Marcel's tea structures as well as transcribes the overlap of experience between the young and the old Marcel drinking the infusion). The convergence between privileged moments and the process of writing itself becomes clear, a convergence dramatized (with a hint of ironic distance) in the Martinville episode when the young Marcel composes a description of three steeples he sees while riding in a carriage near Combray:

> Without admitting to myself that what lay hidden behind the steeples of Martinville must be something analogous to a pretty phrase, since it was in the form of words which gave me pleasure that it had appeared to me, I borrowed a pencil and some paper from the doctor and . . . composed the following little fragment'
>
> (I,p.181; KI,p.197)

This suggests both an expressive element in writing – the steeples provide the stimulus, for which Marcel must find a verbal equivalent – and something more like a general model of mental functioning, based on the activity of one of the 'petits personnages' who (in a recurring metaphor) comprise Marcel's personality. This 'personnage' – 'a certain philosopher who is happy only when he has discovered between two works of art, between two sensations, a common element' (III,p.12; KIII,p.4) – is clearly present in the Martinville passage, since the young Marcel's exercise in writing produces essentially a series of metaphors, transforming the steeples into birds, flowers, trees, maidens.

But the centrality of metaphor – at least in the restricted sense, of a figure based on resemblance – began to seem problematic with the publication of Genette's analysis of Proust's writing in *Figures III*.[11] This demonstrated quite convincingly that metaphor, far from being the foundation of all art and tyle in *A la recherche*, was very often itself motivated by metonymy; it showed that the random contiguity of sensations was often at the root of an apparent resemblance. For example, when Marcel catches sight of the hawthorns growing near Tansonville, the text proliferates with religious imagery:

> I found the whole path throbbing with the fragrance of hawthorn-blossom. The hedge resembled a series of chapels, whose walls were no longer visible under the mountains of flowers that were heaped upon their altars; while beneath them the sun cast a checkered light upon the ground, as though it had just passed through a stained-glass window.
>
> (I,p.138; KI,p.150)

The narrator gives no immediate explanation, though the attentive (or retentive) reader may have grasped that the first time Marcel had seen hawthorns was in the church in Combray. Contiguity, then, has played a major part in generating the metaphor. If we integrate this rhetorical procedure into the narrative of *A la recherche*, if we assume some correspondence between the movement of the narrator's discourse and that of Marcel's mind, then a dynamics of language, perception and consciousness begins to emerge. Metaphor, instead of being an *a posteriori* expression of an impression, actually anticipates the emergence into consciousness of a buried or forgotten memory or perception. Metaphor would then be – in almost Lacanian manner – a product of unconscious, or not-yet-conscious connections and processes, and the deciphering – or indeed recuperation – of metaphor becomes a 'prise de conscience'. The narrator – 'das erzählende Ich', as Jauss puts it [12] – would be a split subject, since the meanings, the metaphorical ramifications of his discourse would at least initially elude the scrutiny of his conscious mind. The next question would be whether the narrator's retrospective explanation actually accounts for the force of the metaphor, whether the narrator's interpretations are in any way privileged or authoritative.

The model of self emerging from these speculations on metaphor may be reminiscent of the 'split subject' of psychoanalytic theory, but in spite of the affinities between Freudian and Proustian accounts of the mind, we should perhaps re-emphasize the specificities of Proust's version, and recall some of the elements in the 'livre intérieur' passage which resist assimilation into a psychoanalytic framework – for instance the static aspect of the unconscious, its role as a repository of signs rather than as an agent in the creative process.

But if the unconscious in the 'livre intérieur' passage is figured as a book, a text, we find a more active unconscious at work in an episode in *La Prisonnière*. Marcel is trying to complete an ominously unfinished sentence of Albertine's – which he imagines will furnish information about her concealed feelings and desires:

> But while she was speaking there continued within me, in that curiously alive and creative sleep of the unconscious (a sleep in which the things that have barely touched us succeed in carving an impression, in which our sleeping hands take hold of the key that turns the lock, the key for which we have sought in vain), the quest for what it was that she had meant by that interrupted sentence, the missing end of which I was so anxious to know.
>
> (III,p.339; KIII,p.345)

The unconscious here is figured not as text but as reader. And quite a sophisticated reader too, according to the narrator's retrospective analysis of the unconscious mind's *modus operandi*: it is a two-track apparatus, scanning both the verbal content of Albertine's conversation and the gestural expressive accompaniment, and it is sensitive to contextual indications.

But the perspicacity of unconscious interpretations is open to question. Many of the signs of dissimulation and unadmitted desire which Marcel thinks he sees in Albertine's speech and behaviour creep into his own discourse. The obvious example would be the disjunctive figures – for example, anacoluthon – which Marcel considers particularly revelatory: 'Albertine . . . employed, not by way of stylistic refinement, but in order to correct her imprudences, abrupt breaches of syntax not unlike that figure which the grammarians call anacoluthon or some such name' (III,p.153; KIII,p.149). There are perhaps indications in *La Prisonnière* that projection (to use the Freudian term), the distortion which desire visits on perception and explanation, is a pervasive feature of the narrator's discourse. Traces of the unconscious would be discernible in the syntactic and lexical and metaphorical texture of the narrator's prose, and also in the sequence of cognitive and perceptual moves he makes, revealing unexamined patterns and recurrences – and contradictions.

The other feature of the 'sommeil vivant' passage that I want to discuss involves – a little tangentially perhaps – the initial metaphor. The unconscious as sleep, but intellectually active sleep – the link is nowhere explicit, but there is surely a suggestion of dreaming here, especially since dreams are rather important – 'la seconde muse' – in the argument of *A la recherche*. (Indeed, the opening pages of *A la recherche* show Marcel deriving his whole experience of self-discovery from his experience of self-dispersal at moments of half-sleeping and half-waking). There is, however, an important reversal involved as we move from the deciphering unconscious to the dream. The unconscious of the 'livre intérieur' resembled a text; that of the 'sommeil vivant' functioned as a reader. The unconscious operations at work in the dream are, I would suggest, more like those involved in artistic creation: the unconscious as writer. In which he perhaps comes close to the position of the Freudian dreamer, with his 'secondary revision', motivated by the need to create a coherent narrative out of disturbing images, perceptions and sensations. And there are various images drawn from writing, and indeed all the arts, to corroborate this contention. The metaphoric interplay of writing and dreaming perhaps provides a model of writing and the unconscious which modifies and supplements the more well-known and oft-expounded memory-metaphor nexus.

The importance of dreams as an aesthetic model is made quite explicit in various places in *A la Recherche*, most notably in *La Prisonnière*:

> I was still enjoying the last shreds of sleep, that is to say of the only source of invention, the only novelty that exists in story-telling, since none of our narrations in the waking state, even when embellished with literary graces, admit those mysterious differences from which beauty derives.
>
> (III,p.124; KIII,p.119)

This is the strongest statement of the influence of sleep and dream on fictional techniques, the basis of the so-called 'oneiric optic' which is in evidence in the form of *A la recherche*. [13] It is a tantalizingly vague statement of Proustian aesthetics: we would have to examine other more figurative passages to find out what these 'mystérieuses différences' might be. Many of the operations of the dreaming mind are in fact metaphorical, i.e. based on connecting operations. The dream which has probably the closest links with art and the imagination in *A la recherche* – the dream of the 'cité gothique' – displays various broadly metaphoric devices: 'One of my dreams was the synthesis of what my imagination had often sought to depict, in my waking hours, of a certain seagirt place and its mediaeval past' (II,p.146; KII,p.147). 'Synthesis' may seem to be a very general mode of connection which, like condensation in the Freudian dream-work, can link any pair of elements or images, but, in fact, the 'cité gothique' dream presents not just an amalgam of an ideal landscape with its cultural history. The allegorizing capacities of this dream are impressive. Its Venetian vision seems to provide an allegory of various possibilities of beauty, art, and travel which confuse the conscious Marcel. This provides further evidence of the creative activity of the unconscious: the dreaming mind solves a problem which has defied the powers of waking consciousness.

The other connecting operation in the dream is more contingent perhaps, insofar as it is generated by the somatic condition of the sleeper (a phenomenon noted by Freud who linked it to the use of the day's events in creating the dream's manifest content):

> So, my eyes blinded, my lips sealed, my limbs fettered, my body naked, the image of sleep which my sleep itself projected had the appearance of those great allegorical figures (in one of which Giotto has portrayed Envy with a serpent in her mouth) of which Swann had given me photographs.'
>
> (II,p.146;KII,p.148)

But this too in Proust moves out to form a vast allegorical figure, linking Swann's gifts of Giotto reproductions to the narrative paralysis caused in Swann and Marcel by jealousy.

Another variety of the metaphoric experience – another form of linking operation – which occurs in dreams, and also in their interpretation by the waking mind, is 'association' – of ideas, of memories, of impressions. One of the more inventive examples is the assimilation of Forcheville to Napoleon III in Swann's dream:

> As for Napoleon III, it was to Forcheville that some vague association of ideas, then a certain modification of the baron's usual physiognomy, and lastly the broad ribbon of the Legion of Honour across his breast, had made Swann give that name; in reality, and in everything that the person who appeared in his dream represented and recalled to him, it was indeed Forcheville.
>
> (I,p.379–80; KI,p.413)

The narrator's reductive interpretation hardly does justice to the polysemic possibilities of the image: ideas of dominance, of 'empire' over Odette's affections, of virility, even, are hinted at in the figure of Napoleon III, as well as social ambition. But later on the narrator himself explores a chain of associations in his deciphering of the Gilberte dream – surely one of the most 'Freudian' episodes in Proust's novel in its combination of associative method and libidinously charged memory:

> I remembered then that, the last time I had seen her . . . she had, whether in sincerity or in pretence, declined, laughing in a strange manner, to believe in the genuineness of my feelings for her. And by association this memory brought back to me another. Long before that, it was Swann who had not wished to believe in my sincerity, or that I was a suitable friend for Gilberte. In vain had I written to him, Gilberte had brought back my letter and had returned it to me with the same incomprehensible laugh. She had not returned it to me at once: I remembered now the whole of that scene behind the clump of laurels.
>
> (I,p.630; KI,p.678)

(The laurel bushes in the Champs-Elysées gardens had been the scene of some erotic play between Marcel and Gilberte.)

A passage like this makes it tempting to reorder the narrator's descriptions of dreams within the framework of Freud's dream-work, with its central categories of condensation – the fusion of two disparate images or elements in the manifest dream – and displacement – the accentuation in the dream of a detail which is relatively insignificant for the interpretative process. But in spite of the economy and analytic power of Freud's paradigm of the primary processes of the unconscious, it can lead us to neglect the specific emphases of the Proustian vision, which has its own oneiric rhetoric.

This oneiric rhetoric is not restricted to metaphor and similar devices. It also includes an embryonic narratology of dreaming, presented mainly in a sequence of metaphors taken from fictional and dramatic technique – focussing on the ordering of events or the representation of time. Swann's dream contains several good examples: 'like certain novelists, he [[Swann]] had distributed his own personality between two characters, the one who was dreaming the dream, and another whom he saw in front of him sporting a fez' (I,p.379; KI,p.413). As with the 'cité gothique' it is Proust's whole novel which provides the context for the creation and interpretation of the dream: the pathologically jealous Swann is fascinated by Gentile Bellini's portrait of Mahomet II, whom he sees as the epitome of jealousy.

This 'double' motif suggests tantalizing, though incomplete, parallels with the dual figure of Marcel (as protagonist) and the narrator of *A la recherche* – 'celui qui fait la narration' – though of course Marcel and the narrator are temporally, rather than spatially, separated unlike Swann and his alter ego in the dream. The hint of reflexivity is also present, though less obviously perhaps, in the peripeteia alluded to in the following passage; 'and out of feelings and impressions of which he was not yet conscious he [Swann] brought about sudden vicissitudes which, by a chain of logical sequences, would produce, at specific points in his dream, the person required to receive his love or to startle him awake' (I,p.380; KI,p.413). Swann may be one of the 'célibataires de l'art', condemned to creative sterility in his waking existence, but in dreams he is an artist, not just a novelist or dramatist even, but also a sculptor, for instance. Marcel when dreaming calls on an even greater range of artistic techniques: he is a theatrical producer, a musician, even a magic lantern operator. This breadth of metaphoric reference should have dissolved any last doubts about the creative and transformative capacities of the unconscious in *A la recherche*. But here I want to focus on those operations and techniques which have some relevance to writing and literary form. The image of the magic lantern certainly has; it provides a model of discontinous narrative, a combination of static image (as in painting) and dynamic narrative (as in fiction): 'on the contrary we bring to bear on the spectacle of life only a curious vision, extinguished anew every moment by oblivion, the former reality fading before that which follows it as one projection of a magic lantern fades before the next as we change the slide' (I,p.820; KI,p.878). Significantly, the magic lantern metaphor re-enacts the child Marcel's first experience of narrative art, as he watched the story of Golo of Brabant unfold on his bedroom wall.

Perhaps the most fertile source of narrative innovations is music. The musical metaphors in the dream passage tend to accentuate either the general aesthetic effect of changes of rhythm or interval – waking is compared to 'those drastic changes of rhythm which, in music, mean that in an andante a quaver has the same duration as a minim in a prestissimo' (III,p.121; KIII,p.117) – or the idea of repetition:

> Often it was simply during my sleep that these 'reprises,' these 'da capos' of one's dreams, which turn back several pages of one's memory, several leaves of the calendar at once, brought me back, made me regress to a painful but remote impression which had long since given place to others but which now became present once more.
>
> (III,p.538; KIII,p.549)

The first point to make here is that music in *A la recherche* is very often associated with repetition, theme and variation, the motif. The presence of Wagner is pervasive: the narrator mentions him more often than any other composer (apart from the fictional Vinteuil) in *A la recherche*, and the leitmotiv provides a powerful if not always very precisely defined model for Proust's own composition. Wagner's music also seems to form a bridge between aesthetic form and emotional (even corporeal) reality:

> I was struck by how much reality there is in the work of Wagner as I contemplated once more those insistent fleeting themes which visit an act . . . so internal, so organic, so visceral, that they seem like the reprise not so much of a musical motif as of an attack of neuralgia.
>
> (III,p.159; KIII,p.156)

This suggestion – reminiscent of Schopenhauer's idea that music was in some sense an analogon of the affects and their movement – [14] is echoed and indeed developed in the 'da capo' passage, in which the outlines of a grand unified theory of self and art, of aesthetics and subjectivity, are sketched in. Moreover, at a key moment in *A la recherche*, recognition of Vinteuil's 'petit air' and its analogy to a de Hooch painting tantalizes Swann with a confused grasping of his inner self. Modulated repetition seems to provide a 'deep structure', a general principle, of mental process and aesthetic form in *A la recherche*. It underlies the occurrences of memory and dream, subsumes them under the overall narrative pattern of intermittence. It also provides a formal model for art and writing, and in particular for *A la recherche* itself, though the leitmotiv technique, the repetition with variation of an image or episode or narrative configuration. It can even be harmonized with metaphor, the other great structural principle of Proust's work. Metaphor is based on resemblance, which is itself a form of modulated repetition, and it is associated with that paradigmatic phenomenon of intermittence, involuntary memory.

But there is something not quite satisfactory about such a totalizing reading of *A la recherche*. The narrator's grand aesthetic theory is after all relativized and subtly subverted by the sudden awareness of time – and its effects – which overcomes him at the Guermantes matinée:

> For I had decided that this [my book] could not consist uniquely of the full and plenary impressions that were outside time, and amongst those other truths in which I intended to set, like jewels, those of the first order, the ones relating to Time, to Time in which, as in some transforming fluid, men and societies and nations are immersed, would play an important part.
>
> (III,p.932; KIII,p.974)

This passage suggests that – in spite of the narrator's confident tone – the other face of intermittence, its discontinuity and the constant threat it harbours that time will prove irrecuperable, even by art and involuntary memory, cannot be altogether suppressed. Intermittence can be inscribed in a totalizing interpretation of *A la recherche*; but it can also undermine the notions of self-identity on which such a project is based. Metaphor is similarly ambiguous. The narrator regularly describes metaphor as a mode of apprehending essences and transcending time; but another equally justifiable reading would take it as a heuristic device, a piecemeal exploration of divergent models which never finally merge into a single coherent system. This would work even for such an assertive passage as the 'livre intérieur' one, shifting as it does from topographical to scriptural metaphors. This indeterminacy is built into *A la recherche*, in the thematics of intermittence, in the poetics of the narrator's discourse and in the reading process itself, as is only natural in a work which aims not to describe the self from a fixed position, but to build a dialectical model constantly evolving between conscious and unconscious modes.

Notes

1 *Contre Sainte-Beuve*, ed. P. Clarac and Y. Sandré (Gallimard, Pléiade, Paris, 1971), p. 558; hereafter cited as *CSB*.
2 P. Kolb (ed.), *Correspondance de Marcel Proust avec Jacques Rivière* (Gallimard, Paris, 1956), p. 52
3 E. Brunet, *Le Vocabulaire de Proust* (Slatkine, Geneva, 1983).
4 G. Genette, *Figures III* (Seuil, Paris, 1973), p. 128.
5 E. Czoniczer, *Quelques antécédents de 'A la Recherche'* (Ambilly-Annemasse, Geneva, 1957), chs. 2 and 4.

6   References to Proust are to the following editions: *A la recherche du temps perdu*, ed. P. Clarac and A. Ferré (3 vols, Gallimard, Pléiade, Paris, 1954), hereafter cited by volume and page number, e.g. I, p. 93; and *Remembrance of Things Past*, trans. C.K. Scott-Moncrieff and Terence Kilmartin (3 vols, Penguin Classics, Harmondsworth, 1985), hereafter cited as K followed by volume and page number, e.g. KI, p. 91.

7   S. Freud, *Introductory Lectures on Psycho-Analysis* (1916–17), prt III, ch. 19, *SE* XVI; Pelican 1.

8   Rivière contrasts Freud's dualistic and conflictual paradigm with the more pluralist multiple self of *A la Recherche*. cf. J. Rivière, *Quelques progrès dans l'étude du coeur humain* (Gallimard, Paris, 1985).

9   J. Derrida, *L'écriture et la différence*, ch. 7, 'Freud et la scène de l'écriture' (Seuil, Paris, 1967).

10 S. Freud, *Introductory Lectures on Psycho-Analysis* (1916–17), prt II, ch. 15, *SE*, XV; Pelican 1.

11 G. Genette, 'Métonymie chez Proust', in *Figures III*, pp. 41–63.

12 H. R. Jauss, *Zeit und Erinnerung im Werke Marcel Prousts* (Heidelberger Forsch., 3, Heidelberg, 1955).

13 W. S. Bell, *Proust's Nocturnal Muse* (Columbia University Press, New York, 1962), ch. 5.

14 cf. A. Henry, *Marcel Proust: théories pour une esthétique* (Klincksieck, Paris, 1981).

SUGGESTED READING

Bell, W. S., *Proust's Nocturnal Muse*, (Columbia University Press, New York, 1962.

Bellemin-Noël, J., ' "Psychanalyser" le rêve de Swann?', in *Poétique*, no.8 (1971), pp. 447–69.

Bersani, L., *Marcel Proust: Fictions of Life and Art,* Oxford University Press, New York, 1965.

Bowie, M., *Freud, Proust and Lacan: Theory as Fiction*, Cambridge University Press, Cambridge, 1987.

Genette, G., *Figures III*, Seuil, Paris, 1973.

Lacan, J., *Ecrits*, Seuil, Paris, 1966, esp. 'Fonction et champ de la parole et du langage en psychanalyse' and 'L'instance de la lettre dans l'inconscient ou la raison depuis Freud'.

Miller, M. L., *Nostalgia: A Psychoanalytical study of Proust*, Gollancz, London, 1957.

Richard, J.-P., *Proust et le monde sensible*, Seuil, Paris, 1974.

Rivière, J., *Quelque progrès dans l'étude de coeur humain*, Gallimard, Paris, 1985.

10

Hesse's Therapeutic Fiction

EDWARD TIMMS

Historians of psychoanalysis and its literary significance tend to ignore the creative anarchy of the early years. Early psychoanalysis was not an intellectual system. It was a cornucopia overflowing with new ideas and ancient myths arrestingly reformulated. It was not until 1916–17 that Freud attempted to systematize his theories into a coherent doctrine. His earlier publications had dealt – in exhilaratingly unpredictable sequence – with the benefits of cocaine and the significance of dreams; with jokes and slips of the tongue; with homosexuality and the erotic fantasies of infants; with a novella by Jensen and paintings by Leonardo; with primitive anthropology and the passion for war; not to mention a series of case histories so imaginatively reconstructed that they read like works of fiction.

The territories charted by his early disciples were equally extraordinary. C. G. Jung, after beginning as an orthodox experimental psychologist, plunged into the realms of alchemy and the occult, comparative anthropology and matriarchal myth. Otto Rank devoted himself to the incest motif in literature and legend, to hero-worship and the figure of the *Doppelgänger*. Stekel demonstrated the links between dreaming and the fear of death, Bleuler devoted books to schizophrenia, and Otto Gross initiated a cult of erotic self-fulfilment. And although the majority of Freud's followers had emerged from orthodox medical schools, their theories of the unconscious seem to owe more to literary sources than to clinical experience.

German authors had the advantage of being able to dip into this cornucopia at first hand. Even before 1900 authors like Schnitzler were immersing themselves in Freud's early writings. And around 1910 we find the ideas of the early psychoanalysts filtering into the work of the most innovative authors of the German-speaking world: Musil and Thomas Mann, Kafka and Rilke, Hesse and Werfel, Kokoschka and Kubin, Stefan Zweig in Vienna and Arnold Zweig in Berlin, not to mention Döblin and the Expressionists. Kafka spoke for his generation when (in a diary entry of 1912) he associated an extraordinary burst of creativity with 'thoughts of

Freud, naturally'.[1] The authors of this precocious generation (as Joyce put it in a cryptic reminiscence) 'were yung and easily freudened'.[2]

Between Freud and Jung: Hesse's Psychotherapy

Hermann Hesse provides the extreme case. More completely than any other writer of his generation he immersed himself in psychoanalysis, not merely as an intellectual theory but as a therapeutic experience. Although most accounts date his encounters with psychoanalysis from 1914, it seems likely that he had a foretaste of the new therapeutic methods in 1909, when he underwent a first course of treatment with Dr Albert Fraenkel at the spa of Badenweiler in south-west Germany. At that date Hesse, a married man in his early thirties with two small children, had already won literary success, especially through his early novels *Peter Camenzind* (1904) and *Beneath the Wheel* (1906). The vivid reworking in these novels of the travails of his youth suggest that from an early stage the writing of fiction had for Hesse a therapeutic value. But he also felt a strong need for more systematic forms of psychotherapy – he returned to Badenweiler for further treatment in 1912. He seems to have accepted Fraenkel's view that his symptoms were not physical in origin, but arose from 'his whole spiritual disposition'.[3] More systematic treatment, involving both psychoanalysis and electrotherapy, followed in 1916–17 with Dr Josef Bernhard Lang at a sanatorium near Lucerne. The two continued their psychoanalytic dialogue well into the 1920s. Lang, a pupil of Jung's, had wide-ranging interests in oriental languages and gnostic religions which also contributed to Hesse's philosophical reorientation. After further treatment in 1918 by a less well-known analyst, Johannes Nohl, Hesse finally turned in 1921 to Jung himself.

Hesse was evidently convinced that these successive courses of psychotherapy brought him great personal benefit. He described Lang as 'a loyal, intelligent and very sensitive man whom I can trust – he has really become my friend'. Above all he praised Jung for 'conducting my analysis with an exceptionally sure touch, indeed with genius'.[4] This is not to say that he found psychotherapy an enjoyable experience. His consultations with Jung are described in 1921 as 'the deep disturbance' of analysis. 'It cuts to the quick and causes pain', Hesse added. 'But it's helping.'[5]

The absence of medical records makes it difficult to ascertain the source of Hesse's distress. But it is clear that he experienced a protracted midlife crisis, which seems to have been precipitated by his father's death in 1916 and lasted until the publication of *Steppenwolf* in 1927. His career had been profoundly disrupted by the First World War, which he spent in Switzerland, becoming an outspoken pacifist. Denounced in a flood of newspaper articles and hate-mail as a traitor to the German cause, he felt radically alienated from his earlier readership. Meanwhile his apparently secure domestic life was also disintegrating. Separated from his wife and children (and later divorced), he married again in 1924, this time a woman twenty years younger than himself. But within three years his second wife was also petitioning for divorce. During this same period he was plagued by recurrent physical afflictions – problems with his eyesight, severe headaches, intestinal infections, sciatica and gout (exacerbated by bouts of heavy drinking). And in his letters he repeatedly refers to suicide as the only solution.

Psychotherapy provided him with a lifeline. It may not have cured his neurosis, but it helped him to come to terms with it and to transform it into a source of renewed creativity. Since childhood Hesse had been afflicted by a sense of an irreconcilable division within the self. A letter written by his elder sister in 1881, when Hesse was four years old, vividly records how completely the boy's animal spirits were at odds with his puritanical Christian upbringing. At one moment he would behave like a 'buffalo' and go wildly on the rampage; the next he would be contritely saying his prayers, as docile as a 'dormouse'.[6] The strictness of Hesse's upbringing as the son of a Protestant pastor exacerbated this contradiction. His parents found his wild spirits unmanageable and decided to send him to boarding school. But in May 1892, at the age of fourteen, he ran away from school. And a month later he disappeared again, this time leaving a suicide note. The heart-rending letters which he wrote home show how bitterly he was torn between the imperatives of moral authority and the impulses of the emotional self. With self-lacerating sarcasm he describes himself as 'an orphan whose "parents" are still alive'. 'Dear little Hermann' has been transformed into a 'hater of the whole world'.[7]

These same dualisms recur in the correspondence of the forty-year-old author, after the traumas of his father's death and the break-up of his first marriage. In a revealing letter of autumn 1919 he still shows himself to be obsessed with the conflict between his 'moral self' and the 'animal and criminal within me'. But through psychoanalysis he has gained the insight that these destructive impulses cannot simply be denied (a defence mechanism which he defines by means of the concept of 'repression'). Instead he envisages a radical revision both of his moral values and of his literary style. In place of the spurious harmonies of his earlier writings he must develop new, more discordant tones.[8] Psychoanalysis may not have cured him, but it has helped him to gain a certain self-detachment – to see the agonies of the divided self not simply as a personal affliction, but as a 'symptom for the spirit of the age'.[9]

This radical reorientation was based not only on personal therapy, but on the systematic study of psychoanalytic writings. A book review of autumn 1914 shows that he was already familiar with the work of Freud and Adler. And in 1916, at the time of his therapy with Lang, he read Jung's *Symbols of Transformation*, a book which evidently impressed him through its redefinition of Freud's concept of 'libido' in mythopoeic terms. In 1920 he reviewed the German editions of two of Freud's most comprehensive publications, the *Introductory Lectures on Psycho-Analysis* and the *Five*

Lectures originally given at Clark University. And a year later he reviewed Jung's *Psychological Types* (*MB*, pp.355–60).[10] Hesse was in the exceptional position of having immersed himself in psychoanalysis during a decade of turbulent debate between Freudian and Jungian tendencies.

The impact of all of this on Hesse as a writer can hardly be overstated. Coinciding as it did with the emotional traumas of his private life and the historical rupture of the First World War, it led him to embark on a radically new style of fiction, based on psychological principles which (as he put it in a letter of 1920) had been 'completely reorientated by psychoanalysis'. [11] This new attitude to narrative, with its emphasis on the articulation of the unconscious, was also announced in Hesse's essays of the period around 1918. The aim, as Hesse puts it in an essay on 'Language' (1917), is to gain access to what may be called 'the abyss of the soul or the unconscious'. Where 'the average citizen has placed a watchman between himself and his soul, . . . the artist secretly comes and goes between this side and that, between conscious and unconscious, as though at home in both houses' (*MB*, pp.26–9).

The value of psychoanalysis, Hesse continues in the essay 'Artists and Psychoanalysis' (1918), is that it provides a 'key' to the observation of the unconscious through its interpretation of psychic mechanisms such as 'repression, sublimation and regression'. And by giving these concepts a 'scientific formulation', psychoanalysis can significantly aid the poet. Through its 'confirmation of the value of fantasy', psychoanalysis justifies the claims of art against those of bourgeois pragmatism. But for the person who has actually undergone the 'experience' of analysis, as opposed to having merely an 'intellectual interest' in it, there are more 'permanent' gains. Through the 'path of analysis' he gains 'what may be called the "inner relationship to *his own unconscious*" . . . a warmer, more fruitful and passionate interchange between conscious and unconscious' (*MB*, pp. 46–51).

In the dozen years which followed the publication of this essay, Hesse produced a rich sequence of psychoanalytically informed writings, including the novels which have gained him a worldwide reputation: *Demian* (1919), *Siddhartha* (1922), *Steppenwolf* (1927) and *Narcissus and Goldmund* (1930). They are novels inspired by the principle of 'passionate interchange', not merely between conscious and unconscious but between a series of interrelated dualisms: the instinctual and the moral self, man and animal, action and contemplation, immanence and trascendence. Hesse has often been criticized for a facile over-reliance on such dualistic categories. But in the argument that follows it will be suggested that this principle of dialogue between identities is one of the essential sources of his fiction. Hesse had experienced aspects of both the Freudian 'talking cure' and Jungian 'art therapy' with its pictorial representations of the unconscious. In *Demian* he introduces one of the first fictional images of a therapist, albeit in disguised form. But Hesse did not draw on psychoanalysis as a closed system. He was inspired precisely by the contradictions it left unresolved – by the tensions between individual psychology and occult myth, between the sexual emphasis of Freud and the mysticism of Jung. 'Psychoanalysis today', Hesse wrote in a letter of May 1921, 'can fundamentally have hardly any other goal than the creation of a dimension within us in which we can hear the voice of God.'[12] The question is: which God? And the answer will depend whether we assign greater significance to *Demian* – the most Jungian of Hesse's therapeutic fictions, or to *Steppenwolf* – the most Freudian (or indeed post-Freudian).

Demian – The Jungian Matrix

Demian was written during 1916–17, the period of Hesse's analysis with Lang. It was in this same period that Hesse was introduced to Jung's speculations about gnostic religions, probably through discussions with Lang. He may also have had first-hand knowledge of Jung's *Septem Sermones ad Mortuos*, privately published under a pseudonym in 1916. And it was certainly in 1916 that he read his *Symbols of Transformation* – that cornucopia of matriarchal myths interwoven with a 'case history'. It was clearly this aspect of Jung's theorizing that most appealed to Hesse at that crucial juncture in his development. Indeed, reviewing Jung's work fifteen years later, in 1931, Hesse was to lament the fact that the psychologist's tone had become so 'professorial' in subsequent writings. He had evidently been most strongly attracted by what he called 'the eccentricity and otherworldliness of the former "occult" Jung' (*MB*, p.359).

It is *Symbols of Transformation* which provided Hesse with his master-plot for *Demian*. Summing up the three extraordinary chapters in which he analyses the symbolism of the 'Mother' and of 'Rebirth', Jung writes:

> Man leaves the mother, the source of libido, and is driven by the eternal thirst to find her again, and to drink renewal from her; thus he completes his cycle, and returns again into the mother's womb. Every obstacle which obstructs his life's path, and threatens his ascent, wears the shadowy features of the 'terrible mother', who paralyses his energy with the consuming poison of the stealthy, retrospective longing. In each conquest he wins again the smiling, love- and life-giving mother – images which belong to the intuitive depths of human feeling . . .[13]

It is this model of an existential quest, linking the realms of individual unconscious and archetypal myth, which gives *Demian* its overall structure. But there are many further aspects of theme, characterization and symbolism which betray Jung's influence. The most striking is the leitmotif of the 'heraldic bird', inscribed above the entrance to the hero's home. The 'gigantic egg' from which this 'sparrow-hawk' is struggling to liberate itself

– a Jungian symbol of rebirth – provides a keystone for the whole novel.[14]

In Hesse's first-person narrative, published under the pseudonym Emil Sinclair, a young man recalls the painful evolution of his personality between the ages of ten and eighteen. He frames his experience within a series of dualisms, beginning with the antithesis between the 'light world' of his secure family home and the 'dark world' outside. The world of his parents is governed by 'order, tranquillity, duty and good conscience' – in sharp contrast to the 'loud and shrill, sullen and violent world' beyond the family circle (*D*, p.10). The most sinister representative of that darker world is Franz Kromer, a raffish schoolboy from a poorer background who blackmails Sinclair by threatening to expose his – largely imaginary – misdeeds. But as the narrative unfolds we begin to suspect that Kromer is not simply to be read as a 'character' in a realistic novel, but as a 'projection' of an aspect of Sinclair's personality. 'I could not escape him', Sinclair recalls. 'He haunted my dreams like my own shadow' (*D*, p.33).

In casting Kromer as Sinclair's 'shadow', Hesse is obliquely inviting us to read the relationship between them in Jungian terms. The 'shadow', as defined in Jung's early writings, represents the unconscious self with its less than creditable motives.[15] In this sense Kromer externalizes an aspect of Sinclair's inner self – his secret fascination with the dark world he is supposed to despise. But Hesse's use of the Jungian metaphor is all the more effective because it is unobtrusive. Kromer remains an all too plausible bully, even after we have recognized that the source of his power lies within the personality of his victim – in Sinclair's moral ambivalence.

The Jungian sub-text becomes more prominent with the introduction of the figures of Max Demian and Beatrice. Demian is the idealized older schoolboy who rescues Sinclair from Kromer's clutches. But from the start Demian is invested with an aura of mystery as the spokesman for some inner wisdom towards which Sinclair must aspire. He speaks with what Sinclair recognizes as 'a voice which could only emanate from myself' (*D*, p.38). As a result the encounters within Demian lack narrative vividness and appear to take place on a plane of disembodied spirituality. The same is true of the Beatrice episode in chapter 4. 'Beatrice' is the name Sinclair gives to a girl glimpsed from afar who inspires him to renounce the dissolute habits into which he has fallen at boarding school. But he never speaks to her, never even learns her real name, but is content with the cult of her image.

Where Kromer was Sinclair's ambiguous 'shadow', Demian and Beatrice are his 'imagos' – in the Jungian sense of being 'more an image of a subjective function-complex than of the object itself'.[16] They are projections of an idealized higher self. So overt does this psychoanalytic concept of image-making become in the novel that Sinclair, following Jungian principles of art therapy, tries to get more closely in touch with these images welling up from his unconscious by expressing these visions in pictorial terms. In states of consciousness heightened by ecstatic dreams, he paints a picture in which Beatrice becomes indistinguishable from Demian: 'the face somehow expressed my life, it was my inner self, my fate or my daimon' (D, p.79). It becomes clear that Demian is not so much a character as a Jungian construct, echoing the *Septem Sermones*: 'The daemon of spirituality descendeth into our soul as the white bird. It is half-human and appeareth as desire-thought.'[17] Demian (Sinclair's 'daimon') does indeed make the impression of being 'half-human', lacking the vitality of an imaginatively realized character. And Hesse's hero is left stranded among the 'desire-thoughts' of the unconscious self, whose mask-like faces acquire the archaic features of Jungian archetypes: 'that pale, stone mask . . . the real Demian' (*D*, p.63).

Demian's hypnotic appeal, both on the psychological and the mythic plane, is that he has no father. Sinclair feels trapped within the paradigms of his 'paternal home' ('Vaterhaus', cf. *D*, p.9), with its strict imperative of duty and rigid conception of guilt. His personality bears the indelible stamp of a patriarchal and puritan upbringing. But Demian has grown up under the aegis of a widowed mother who reportedly never goes to church – perhaps they are even Jews or Mohammedans (*D*, p.32). And she comes to embody a matriarchal principle which transcends the simplistic Christian categories of good and evil by embracing experience in its perplexing extremes: tenderness and violence, light and darkness, mother and lover, indeed male and female. She becomes 'Frau Eva' – the ultimate fulfilment of Sinclair's existential quest.

This development from a patriarchal to matriarchal universe is signalled by two of the most significant of Sinclair's numerous dreams. In the first, a recurrent nightmare conceived under the influence of his 'shadow', Sinclair feels himself under a terrifying compulsion to carry out a 'murderous attack' on his own father (*D*, p.33). But as he moves beyond the influence of Kromer into the sphere of Demian, parricidal impulses are displaced by maternal yearnings, expressed in the following dream:

> I was on my way to my parents' home and over the main entrance the heraldic bird gleamed gold on an azure ground. My mother walked towards me but when I entered and she was about to kiss me, it was no longer she but a form I had never set eyes on, tall and strong with a look of Max Demian and my painted portrait – yet it was somehow different and despite the robust frame, very feminine. The form drew me to itself and enveloped me in a deep, shuddering embrace.
>
> (*D*, pp.89–90)

The dream is recorded in Jungian terms, with the natural mother being superseded through the agency of the bisexual daimon/Demian by the archetypal mother from the 'intuitive depths'. The symbolic motif of the heraldic bird has already been decoded for us to ensure that we don't miss the point: 'The bird is struggling out of the egg. The egg is the world. Whoever wants to be born must first destroy a world. The bird is flying to God. The name of the God is called Abraxas' (*D*, p.86).

It is this violent rebirth out of the egg/womb/world which forms the climax of the novel. The final chapter records the response of Demian and Sinclair to the outbreak of the First World War. Far from being inspired by their matriarchal wisdom to stand out against the patriotic euphoria of the 'herd', they too are soon in uniform. And Sinclair's narrative, supposedly completed on his sick-bed after he has been wounded in battle, culminates in a final vision:

> A great town could be seen in the clouds and out of it poured millions of men who spread in hosts over vast landscapes. In their midst strode a mighty, godlike form with shining stars in her hair, as huge as a mountain but having the features of Frau Eva. The ranks of men were swallowed up into her as into a gigantic cave and vanished from sight. The goddess crouched on the ground, the 'sign' shone on her brow. She seemed to be in the grip of a dream. She closed her eyes and her great countenance was twisted in pain. Suddenly she called out, and from her forehead sprang stars, many thousands of them which leaped in graceful curves across the dark heavens.
>
> (*D*, p.153)

The stars are exploding grenades which wreak destruction on all sides. The vision suggests that a new world will be born from the destruction of the old.

It is hardly surprising that the novel (particularly its final chapter) strongly appealed to Jung. In December 1919, at a time when its authorship was still a closely guarded secret, he wrote to Hesse saying that he had seen through his pseudonym and recognized the contribution made by his own teachings. 'Your book has the best possible conclusion,' he continued, 'that is to say the birth and awakening of the New Man. The great Mother has become pregnant through the solitude of the quester. She has (through the exploding grenades) borne the old man into death and impregnated the New with . . . the mystery of individuality.'[18] But Jung's effusive tribute unwittingly draws attention to the major defect of the novel. *Demian* is too heavily Jungian in conception to be entirely convincing as a work of fiction.

Hesse does not draw on the cornucopia of Jungian mythology in a controlled and discriminating way. He allows his narrative to become swamped by Jungian motifs. The image of the 'great mother' is only the most obtrusive example. It is never integrated into Sinclair's personal development, for example through a searching reassessment of his relationship with his actual parents (who remain insubstantial figures). Nor does it interact with the sexuality of the developing adolescent. The problem of masturbation is projected by Sinclair onto a scapegoat figure, Knauer, a schoolboy whose sexual urges generate suicidal despair. Sinclair copes by means of cold baths in the mornings and dreams of his idealized Beatrice at night, until carried beyond the realms of physical desire by his longing for Frau Eva. This desexualization of libido is a further indication of how heavily the novel is indebted to Jung (as opposed to Freud).

It is difficult to assent to Jung's judgement (echoed by many subsequent critics) that *Demian* portrays a development towards 'individuality'. The claim that Sinclair has discovered his true 'self' and inner 'destiny' rings hollow, not least through repetition. And the return to the maternal embrace, however alluring, seems like a narcissistic self-indulgence which precludes independence of thought and feeling. Moreover, the fact that within the Jungian scheme there can be no clear distinction between the 'terrible' and the 'life-giving' mother undermines the suggestion that Sinclair is ascending towards some higher morality. In this novel the matriarchal values of tenderness and intuition are not presented as challenging alternatives to the patriarchal imperatives of rationality and domination. On the contrary, Frau Eva actually embodies in Sinclair's final vision the destructive force of war itself. The all-purpose Jungian myth so completely obscures the moral issues raised by the outbreak of the First World War that no reader could possibly have guessed that the author of *Demian* was an outspoken pacifist.

This helps to explain the immense popularity of *Demian* at the time of its publication in 1919. It seemed to offer a spiritual justification for the destructiveness of the War and the collapse of social and moral values. In place of the simplicities of Christianity, with its pious belief that good can be distinguished from evil, we are offered a more glamorous and dynamic religion. The God whose voice becomes audible in Hesse's therapeutic fiction is Abraxas. Here again he is dependent on Jungian sources (although Nietzsche too lurks in the background). The reinterpretation of the biblical story of Cain and Abel, which sets the ethical tone of the novel by suggesting that Cain was the 'strong man' who slew a 'weakling' (*D*, p.30), owes something to each of these thinkers.[19]

Hesse was initiated into the cult of Abraxas during his psychotherapy with Lang in 1916–17. This dimension of Jung's thinking became just as crucial to the conception of *Demian* as the psychodrama of the return to the womb. So impressed was Hesse by what he learnt from his encounters with Lang that he took the unusual step of transposing the psychoanalyst into his novel as a fictional character, Pistorius the theologian and musician. Pistorius, who dominates the central chapters of the novel (chapters 5 and 6) does not at first sight remind one of a psychoanalyst. This is partly because modern psychoanalysis tends to be clearly distinguished from the occult speculations which inspired some of the earliest investigators. For Hesse, however, psychoanalysis was important precisely because it offered something like an alternative religion – a challenge to the puritan rigidities in which he had found himself trapped since early childhood.

Pistorius's analysis relates the claims of this alternative religion to the impulses of the unconscious self:

'Our god, my dear Sinclair, is called Abraxas and he is both god and devil; he contains in himself the world of light and the world of darkness. Abraxas has nothing to object to in any of your thought or any of your dreams . . . If something that seems quite mad or sinful enters your head in the future, should you feel like murdering somebody or committing some enormity, remember for a moment that it is Abraxas at work in your imagination!'

(*D*, pp.104–6)

The idea is evidently that Sinclair should be liberated from his puritan conscience by accepting the aggressive and erotic impulses of his physical self as a godlike endowment. This creed closely echoes the doctrines enunciated in Jung's *Septem Sermones*: 'The world of the gods is made manifest in spirituality and in sexuality', proclaims Basilides of Alexandria (Jung's prophetic persona). 'Abraxas begetteth truth and lying, good and evil, light and darkness, in the same word and in the same act.'[20] The problem is that Hesse's hero, even under the spell of Abraxas, is unable to free himself from the dualistic categories of his Christian upbringing. Hesse has not yet found the new language he sought: a language that could break down the barriers between 'conscious and unconscious, as though at home in both houses' (*MB*, p. 31). *Demian* is thus a hybrid and ultimately unsatisfying achievement: a novel overloaded with Jungian borrowings which have not yet been integrated into a new mode of fiction. There are hints in the novel that Hesse was uneasily aware of this, especially at those points where Sinclair distances himself from the 'antiquarian' learning of Pistorius/Lang: 'We were studying a Greek text together about Abraxas and he read out extracts from the *Vedas* and taught me how to speak the sacred "Om". But it was not these bits of occult learning that provided my inner substance' (*D*, p. 114). These reservations are not adequately worked out in *Demian*, which remains too heavily indebted to the 'occult' Jung in theme and structure. But they point ahead to the more sophisticated treatment of depth-psychological themes in *Steppenwolf*.

'Wolf Man' and 'Anima': A Therapeutic Synthesis?

The development from 'occult learning' to 'inner substance' took ten full years – years of intense intellectual activity and emotional turmoil. *Steppenwolf*, published in June 1927 to mark Hesse's fiftieth birthday, is by far the most complex of his therapeutic fictions. Hesse describes himself in his letters as an author who has 'made his own neurosis (because it is a symptom of the age) into the subject of fiction'. In this novel the raw nerves of the author show through more painfully than in any other. Even the hero's intention to commit suicide on reaching the age of fifty is one which Hesse had recorded in a private letter.[21] All the more impressive is the degree of detachment which is achieved by means of highly original formal techniques. The most original of these techniques are the use of an unreliable narrator and a symbolic language which discredits the traditional dualisms.

This language of deconstruction is evident even in Hesse's title.

'Steppenwolf' (literally: 'prairie-wolf') is the name the narrator, Harry Haller, applies to himself because he feels 'half wolf, half man'. In an earlier autobiographical text, *Psychologia Balnearia* (1924), an ironic account of his treatment for sciatica at the spa of Baden near Zurich, Hesse had already identified himself as 'Steppentier' ('prairie-beast'). He was clearly looking for a term that would express his own sense of 'split' or 'schizophrenic' identity. In the introduction to *Psychologia Balnearia* he even borrows Bleuler's new-coined medical concept, identifying himself as 'a tolerably gifted solitary from the family of the schizophrenics, not in need of being interned'. In this text, which is inspired by the sense that his physical symptoms are psychosomatic in origin, he experiments with a series of devices for expressing dual identity, with the conscious self caustically mocking the physical self as it goes through the motions of taking the waters. But the linear, realistic narrative of *Psychologia Balnearia* clearly left Hesse dissatisfied with what he calls the 'failure of my linguistic experiment'. He had not yet found the 'double melody' he was looking for, a language in which the physical and the spiritual would be so closely intertwined that – like a musician – he would be able to make 'melody and counterpoint simultaneously visible'.[22]

The very title of *Steppenwolf* announces the breakthrough to this new, more complex language with a multiplicity of associations. The linguistic code it most explicitly invokes is that of Nietzsche, whose writing had contrasted the 'predatory animal' ('Raubtier') of the primitive, instinctual self with the enfeebled spirit of the 'herd'. But Hesse may also be echoing Freud's celebrated case history of the 'Wolf Man', which had been published – under an austerely medical title – in 1918. Freud's case history too is constructed around the 'werewolf' motif, which had haunted his patient since childhood. And its theme (like that of Hesse's novel) is 'the contrast between the patient's agreeable and affable personality, his acute intelligence and his nice-mindedness on the one hand, and his completely unbridled instinctual life on the other'.[23]

The title *Steppenwolf* accentuates this contrast by means of a Freudian play-on-words. The prefix 'Stepp-' does not simply denote the 'steppes' or 'prairies' inhabited by a primitive predator. It also alludes to the central sequences in the novel in which the hero learns to dance. 'So you can't dance?' he is asked. 'Not even a one-step?' (*S*, p.105). Hesse's letters, which describe his own experience of learning to dance at the age of almost fifty, show that he is consciously punning on the words 'one-step' and 'Steppenwolf'. In a letter of March 1926 he transcribes the name of the modish American 'one-step' phonetically into the German neologism 'Wonne-Stepp' (literally 'ecstasy-step'). In another letter written a year later he describes a masked ball in which he had again 'stepped it out and wolfed it up' ('habe ... wieder gewolft und gestept').[24] The soubriquet 'Steppenwolf' thus denotes not simply a 'wolf that can walk' but a 'wolf that can dance', with dancing signifying transcendence of the mind/body antagonism by means of ecstatic and even mystical experiences.

Steppenwolf thus takes us beyond the Jungian mode of allegory and immerses us in a Freudian multiplicity of meanings. This is already evident in the ironic distancing of the first-person narrative. The main body of the novel consists of 'notebooks' ('Aufzeichnungen') left behind by the mysterious Harry Haller. They are presented to us by an 'editor' who claims to have found them in Haller's flat and cannot vouch for their authenticity. *Demian* had made its impact through its tone of confessional authenticity (the patriotic young German writing his spiritual testament while apparently dying from war-wounds). The disconcerting power of *Steppenwolf* derives from the overt way it parades its fictitiousness.

The tension between the 'tangible' and the 'spiritual', between 'fictitious' form and 'lived' experience (*S*, pp.25–6), is sustained throughout the novel. There is no withdrawal into a Jungian realm of disembodied spirituality; the Freudian reality principle continuously reasserts itself against the subjective claims of fantasy and hallucination. Where *Demian* is set in the timeless realm of the romantic Bildungsroman, the narrator of *Steppenwolf* remains trapped in the abrasive, nerve-wracking world of the 1920s, with its political and economic crises, its jazz-culture and its sensational journalism. We are continuously reminded of the self-inflicted wounds suffered by Germany during the First World War; one of the sources of Haller's despondency is that his warnings about the dangers of a new war arising from unresolved aggressiveness and recrimination fall on deaf ears.

This new realism is reinforced by the vividness with which Haller records the experiences of the body. He is palpably a narrator with a physical presence, his middle-aged body wracked by gout and by fiendish headaches, accompanied by intense bouts of depression leading to suicidal impulses. Existential anguish over the sterility of modern civilization is shown to be inextricably involved with physical pains which neither alcohol nor sleeping-pills can subdue. All of this is reflected in a tortuous syntax which avoids the simplistic dualisms of Hesse's earlier style and gives full weight to the physical oppressiveness of psychosomatic disorders. All the more exhilarating, by contrast, are the later passages describing the experience of dancing – the sensuous rhythms of the saxophone and the erotic sensations brought about by physical embrace. Melody and counterpoint do indeed become 'simultaneously visible', as Hesse shows how physical sensation can lead to spiritual transfiguration.

Only at one point does the novel lapse into a more abstract conceptual language. This is in the celebrated 'Treatise on the Steppenwolf', which Haller claims to have had thrust into his hands by a stranger encountered in the street. But even this highly contrived document contains a subversive self-irony. It begins by lamenting, in Nietzschean terms, that the Steppenwolf has 'two natures, a human and a wolfish one', 'bourgeois' and 'outsider' (*S*, pp.52, 65). But two-thirds of the way through the 'Treatise' a more critical voice intervenes to point out that this division of the self into dualisms is a 'fundamental delusion'. It is a 'mythological simplification' to believe that his identity is divided into 'two hostile and opposed beings'. Harry consists of 'a hundred or a thousand souls, not two. His life oscillates . . . between innumerable poles' (*S*, pp.69–70).

Thus the Treatise itself deconstructs the Faustian lament about the 'two souls' within the human breast, emphasizing instead the 'multiplicity' ('Vielspältigkeit') of the self, which medical science designates as 'schizophrenia': 'If ever the suspicion of their manifold being dawns upon men of unusual powers and unusually delicate perceptions, so that, as all genius must, they break through the illusion of the unity of the personality and perceive that the self is made up of a bundle of selves, they only have to say so and at once the majority puts them under lock and key, calls science to aid, establishes schizophrenia and protects humanity from the necessity of hearing the cry of truth from the lips of these unfortunate persons' (*S*, p.71).

Steppenwolf thus anticipates the anti-psychiatry of the 1960s. But its true originality lies in the fact that it finds a new fictional mode through which to convey not simply the collapse of the classical concept of personality, but also therapeutic impulses towards reintegration. This is not, however, to be achieved by the orthodox Freudian method of becoming conscious of repressed material and thereby regaining equilibrium. Haller's problem is that he has already seen his situation 'so clearly' and is 'so very conscious of it'. And in a passage which seems to express Hesse's own scepticism about the over-cerebral emphasis of classical psychotherapy, Haller continues: 'I might have made the most intelligent and penetrating remarks about the ramifications and causes of my sufferings, my sickness of soul, my general bedevilment of neurosis. The mechanism was transparent to me. But what I needed was not knowledge and understanding. What I longed for in my despair was life and resolution, action and reaction, impulse and impetus' (*S*, pp.124–5).

The novel thus takes us beyond both Freud and Jung, imaginatively anticipating a range of alternative therapies: encounter therapy, bioenergetics, dance therapy, psychedelic experience, sex-therapy and hallucinogenic liberation. The anarchic substructure of early psychoanalysis is brought to the surface of Haller's narrative, as the clinical tone of the 'Treatise' becomes subordinated to scenes set in seedy night-clubs and glamorous masked balls. The vivid foreground narrative is thronged with prostitutes and call-girls, jazz musicians and transvestites. But the language they speak echoes that of Freud advocating the invigorating effects of cocaine, Otto Gross arguing for sexual liberation and Jung insisting that fulfilment is only possible through the bisexual encounter with the anima.

This 'double melody' becomes most resonant in Haller's account of his experiences with the call-girl who teaches him to dance. The essential aim is to overcome the rigid mind-body dualism by putting him in touch with the libidinous energies dammed up within his physical self. He has to relearn the simplest bodily functions – to eat, drink and sleep, to touch and be touched, above all to dance and laugh. But the call-girl who reaches out to him to help him break free of his male, middle-class persona can only succeed because she corresponds to his own repressed 'feminine' self. She is both a vividly realized 'character' and a Jungian 'projection', corresponding to his anima.

Haller is even able to guess her name, Hermine; for she reminds him of a boy named Herman, to whom he had been emotionally attached in childhood. Her boyish features and fondness for wearing male clothes also draw attention to the bisexual associations of her name. Hermine's counselling thus touches answering chords deeply inhibited since childhood. But Hesse, in this sophisticated narrative, strikes a balance between subjective and objective perspectives. Hermine is not a narcissistic imago of femininity (like the ethereal Beatrice in *Demian*); she continuously challenges the hero's – and the reader's – expectations.

Steppenwolf shows how far Hesse's concept of therapeutic counselling had advanced since the writing of *Demian*. There is a far more overt acceptance of sexuality, indeed the hero is tempted to sleep with the counsellor who has reactivated the repressed forces of his libido. But just as we begin to feel that this is the inevitable outcome, the hero discovers that another call-girl, Maria, has been deputed by Hermine to carry through his sexual reawakening. Hermine, he realizes, 'stood in too close a relation to me'. (*S*, p.147) One cannot make love to one's analyst (particularly if she is a projection of one's anima!). What is necessary is that the patient should be capable of breaking his dependence on the therapist when the time comes. This is the ultimate significance of Hermine's warning, during an early encounter, that Haller's final obligation will be to 'kill' her (*S*, p.131).

Hesse's technique of giving 'tangible' form to 'spiritual' events (*S*, pp.25–6) culminates in the 'Magic Theatre', a sequence reminiscent of the 'Circe' episode in Joyce's *Ulysses*. This 'Magic Theatre', as Haller had been warned, is 'For Madmen Only!' – 'Nur für Verrückte!' (*S*, p.41). The secondary meaning of 'verrückt' alludes to a 'displacement' of blocked emotions. Once this has been achieved through Hermine's bioenergetic interventions, Haller is ready for the psychedelic ministrations of his second counsellor, Pablo, the jazz musician. His methods, so much more drastic than those of his predecessor Pistorius, involve smoking 'cigarettes whose smoke was as thick as incense' and sipping an equally hallucinogenic 'aromatic liquid' (*S*, p.204). By this method Haller is put in touch with unconscious fantasies which he subsequently records in a series of surrealistic tableaux. Each door in the 'Magic Theatre' corresponds to one of the innumerable facets of his 'multiplicity' of selves, from the destructive drives of a glorified death instinct to the erotic fantasy that 'All Girls are Yours'. The aspirations of Haller's cultural self are equally vividly conveyed, as Pablo is transformed into the figure of Mozart, inviting him to join in the timeless laughter of the Immortals.

Haller's sense of stable personality disintegrates like the innumerable chess-pieces in a game whose rules he only dimly apprehends. He finally tries to kill Hermine in a fit of sexual jealousy, not realizing that he has confused the 'beautiful picture gallery' of the unconscious with 'so-called reality' and therefore 'stabbed to death the reflection of a girl with the reflection of a knife'. The novel is thus open-ended. After experiencing the deconstruction of his bourgeois personality, Haller has not yet succeeded in reintegrating the 'hundred thousand pieces of life's game' (S, p.250). But he is now in a position to reflect upon the rich gamut of his experiences – and to begin the game again with enhanced understanding.

Conclusion

The conclusions to be drawn from this novel depend upon the viewpoint of the reader. For the theory of psychotherapy, the implications of *Steppenwolf* are that orthodox analysis, which relies on the methods of the 'talking cure', tends to leave untouched the more turbulent dimensions of the instinctual self. Classical analysis is too cerebral. It needs to be enriched by alternative therapies which create a 'Magic Theatre', in which unconscious impulses can be acted out through bioenergetic and psychedelic means. But the danger is that this artificial 'picture gallery' may be treated as an alternative 'reality' into which one may retreat under the seductive influence of hallucinogenic drugs. The open ending of *Steppenwolf* suggests that far more strenuous efforts are needed to achieve psychological re-integration.

For Hesse himself the writing of *Steppenwolf* seems to have had a therapeutic value – a form of artistic-emotional discharge which enabled him to gain detachment from the traumas of his middle years. It was a work begun in a mood of self-lacerating confession, reflected in the 'Steppenwolf' poems which Hesse originally intended to incorporate in the novel.[25] But the distancing use of a persona resulted in a more benign self-irony, comparable to the writing-out of emotional traumas within a psychoanalytic framework in Italo Svevo's *Confessions of Zeno* (1923). Hesse even read a section from his novel to Jung's psychological club in Zurich, prior to publication – a further indication of the reversal of roles through which the erstwhile patient had become the active author of his own imaginative therapy.

The publication of the novel confirmed its value as an original literary experiment. It proved controversial, particularly among conservative readers and reviewers, who were affronted by its overt treatment of sexuality, of the razzmattazz of the 1920s, and of the threat of war arising from unresolved tensions in the German psyche. But precisely this controversy confirmed that Hesse had achieved his underlying aim of transforming a 'personal neurosis' into a 'symptom of the spirit of the age'. In his image of the 'Steppenwolf' Hesse dramatizes the split between the 'two Germanies': the cultural superstructure epitomized by Mozart and Goethe, and the predatory aggressions lurking beneath the surface of civilisation. He shows that the divorce between mind and instincts, between culture and technology, can have the most devastating consequences. But he also envisages processes of re-integration – not through the cult of some new 'God', but through an acceptance of the pluralism of modern civilization and the 'multiplicity' of the self which is its inevitable concomitant. Spiritual harmony may yet be attainable if the wolf can learn to dance.

Notes

1   Franz Kafka, *Tagebücher* (Fischer, Frankfurt, 1967), p. 210 (entry for 23 September 1912).
2   James Joyce, *Finnegans Wake* (Faber, London, 1939), p. 115.
3   See Hermann Hesse, *Haus im Frieden. Aufzeichnungen eines Herrn im Sanatorium* (1910), repr. in Hesse, *Prosa aus dem Nachlass*, ed. Ninon Hesse (Suhrkamp, Frankfurt, 1965), pp. 353–77 (p. 366).
4   For a detailed documentation of Hesse's experience of psychotherapy, see Johannes Cremerius, 'Schuld und Sühne ohne Ende: Hermann Hesses psychotherapeutische Erfahrungen', in *Literaturpsychologische Studien und Analysen*, ed. Walter Schönau (Rodopi, Amsterdam, 1983), pp. 169–204.
5   Quoted in Cremerius, 'Schuld und Sühne', pp. 174 and 178–9.
6   Letter of 26 July 1881 from Marie Hesse to her parents, quoted in *Hermann Hesse 1877–1977. Stationen seines Lebens, des Werkes und seiner Wirkung* (Munich, 1977: Catalogue of the Schiller Nationalmuseum, Marbach), p. 35. All translations except those cited in n. 10 are mine.
7   Hermann Hesse, letter to his father of 14 September 1892, quoted in *Hermann Hesse 1877–1977*, p. 37.
8   Hermann Hesse, letter of (?) autumn 1919 to Carl Selig, in Hesse, *Gesammelte Briefe*, ed. Ursula and Volker Michels, 4 vols (Suhrkamp, Frankfurt, 1973–86), vol. I, pp. 422–4.
9   Hermann Hesse, letter of 13 October 1926 to Hugo Ball, in Hesse, *Gesammelte Briefe*, vol. II, p. 152.
10   Page references to currently available editions of Hesse's writings in English translation are identified in the text as follows: *MB* Hermann Hesse, *My Belief: Essays on Life and Art*, ed. Theodore Ziolkowski, trans. Denver Lindley and Ralph Manheim (Triad/Panther, London, 1978); *D* Hermann Hesse, *Demian*, trans. W. J. Strachen (Grafton Books, London, 1969); *S* Hermann Hesse, *Steppenwolf*, trans. Basil Creighton, rev. Walter Sorrell (Penguin, Harmondsworth, 1965).
11   Hermann Hesse, letter of 5 January 1920 to Ludwig Finckh, in Hesse, *Gesammelte Briefe*, vol. I, p. 436.
12   Hermann Hesse, letter of May 1921 to Emmy and Hugo Ball, in Hesse, *Gesammelte Briefe*, vol. I, p. 474. For a judicious summary of Hesse's attitude to psychoanalysis, see Joseph Mileck, 'Freud and Jung, psychoanalysis and literature, art and disease', *Seminar*, 14, 2 (May 1978), pp. 105–16.
13   C. G. Jung, *Psychology of the Unconscious: A Study of the Transformations and Symbolisms of the Libido*, trans. Beatrice M. Hinkle (Kegan Paul, Trench, Trubner, London, 1917), p. 427.

14   Jung, *Psychology of the Unconscious*, p. 469: 'Indra, who as a falcon has stolen the soma, . . . brings . . . the souls to the entrance into the maternal egg . . .' – 'the shells of the egg of the world'.
15   C. G. Jung, *Psychologische Typen* (Rascher, Zurich, 1921), p. 233; trans. by H. Godwin Baynes (Kegan Paul, Trench, Trubner, London, 1923; repr. 1944), p. 203.
16   Jung, *Psychologische Typen*, p. 674 (English trans., p. 600).
17   [C. G. Jung], *Septem Sermones ad Mortuos* (The Seven Sermons of the Dead written by Basilides in Alexandria, the City where the East toucheth the West), trans. H. Godwin Baynes (privately printed, 1925), p. xxv.
18   C. G. Jung, letter of 3 December 1919 to Hermann Hesse, in Jung, *Briefe 1956–1961 und Nachträge*, ed. Anilla Jaffé (Walter, Olten and Freiburg, 1973), pp. 384–5.
19   For more detailed accounts of the Jungian sources of *Demian*, see Uwe Wolff, *Hermann Hesse: Demian – Die Botschaft vom Selbst* (Bouvier, Bonn, 1979), esp. pp. 15–22; and Walter Jahnke, *Hermann Hesse: Demian – Ein erlesener Roman* (Schöningh, Paderborn, 1984), esp. pp. 132–47: 'Der geliehene Mythos'.
20 · [Jung], *Septem Sermones*, pp. xiv and xxi.
21   For the autobiographical background to *Steppenwolf*, see *Materialien zu Hermann Hesses 'Der Steppenwolf'*, ed. Volker Michels (Suhrkamp, Frankfurt, 1972), esp. pp. 115–6 (on his second divorce).
22   Hermann Hesse, *Psychologia Balnearia* (1924), repr. under the title *Kurgast: Aufzeichnungen von einer Badener Kur* in Hesse, *Gesammelte Schriften*, 8 vols (Suhrkamp, Frankfurt, 1968), vol.IV, pp. 9–115 (pp. 10, 76 and 113).
23   Sigmund Freud, 'From the History of an Infantile Neurosis' (The 'Wolf Man'), *SE*, XVII, p. 104; Pelican 9, p. 345.
24   Quoted in *Materialien zu . . . 'Der Steppenwolf'*, pp. 65 and 109.
25   See Hermann Hesse, *KRISIS: Ein Stück Tagebuch* (1928), repr. in *Materialien zu . . . 'Der Steppenwolf'*, pp. 161–98.

SUGGESTED READING

Boulby, M., *Hermann Hesse: His Mind and his Art*, Cornell University Press, Ithaca, 1967.

Freedman, R., *Hermann Hesse – Pilgrim of Crisis : A Biography*, Abacus, London, 1979.

Serrano, M., *C. G. Jung and Hermann Hesse: A Record of Two Friendships*, trans. Frank MacShane, Routledge & Kegan Paul, London, 1966.

Ziolkowski, T., *The Novels of Hermann Hesse: A Study in Theme and Structure*, Princeton University Press, Princeton, 1965.

Ziolkowski, T. (ed), *Hesse: A Collection of Critical Essays*, Twentieth Century Views, Prentice-Hall, Englewood Cliffs, NJ, 1973.

PART III

The Image in Performance

11

Secrets of a Soul: 'A Psychoanalytic Film'

SORLEY MACDONALD

Freud was courted by the cinema on two occasions. He was first approached by Samuel Goldwyn, the famous producer, who came to Europe on a publicity tour in the early months of 1925 to sign up talent for export to Hollywood. Freud's financial difficulties were well known, and augmented at this time by the crisis affecting the *Verlag*, the International Psychoanalytic Press, in which he had a personal stake. Goldwyn may have hoped to induce Freud to embark on a second voyage to America, his first having been the celebrated lecture tour of 1909. This time the visit would be to California. Goldwyn is reported to have offered $100,000 for Freud's participation in a film 'depicting scenes from the famous love stories of history, beginning with Antony and Cleopatra'.[1] If Freud was amused at the ingenuousness of the attempt to exploit the sensational associations of psychoanalysis, he refused to meet Goldwyn or discuss the matter further. There was hearsay that a telegram of rejection created a greater sensation in New York than that which greeted the English translation of *The Interpretation of Dreams*.[2]

A second approach followed soon after, through the mediation of Karl Abraham, a prominent psychoanalyst in Berlin who was a member of the 'Committee', the Freudian inner circle, and a past-President of the International Psychoanalytic Association. Abraham had been contacted by Hanns Neumann, a documentary producer for UFA (Universum Film Aktion-Gesellschaft, the nearest European equivalent to Metro-Goldwyn-Mayer) who sought the authorisation and collaboration of Freud and his colleagues in the production of 'a popular, scientific film about psychoanalysis'.[3] Freud did not wish to be involved personally. Acknowledging, but not concurring with, Abraham's arguments in favour of co-operation, Freud approved the suggestion that the latter remain with the project as scientific advisor. Abraham however was about to succumb to lung cancer and his role in the project was taken over by another analyst and colleague, Hanns Sachs, who began a long and active association with the film world.[4]

Hanns Neumann had proposed a *Lehrfilm*, a part-documentary, educational film with metaphors and illustrations derived from Freud's public lectures.[5] But the film that finally resulted from his initiative was to turn out very differently. *Secrets of a Soul (Geheimnisse einer Seele)* is a feature film, a dramatization of the onset, manifestation and treatment of a neurosis that accommodates a potentially 'difficult' subject in one of the staple forms of fiction films of the period: the marital, domestic drama or *Kammerspiel*. Allegedly based on a case of knife phobia recorded and treated by Freud, [6] the film is a singular and uneasy compound of naturalistic observation, melodrama and narrative exposition – with exposition coming a poor third: a story about a bourgeois marriage threatened by the husband's compulsive behaviour and saved by the benign intervention of psychoanalytic therapy, which discloses a dynamic of unconscious motivation and induces an affective – and dramatic – catharsis (see plate 1).

The film is known as G. W. Pabst's *Secrets of a Soul*, but the Austrian director joined the production after the script had been written by Neumann, Colin Ross (a well-known travel writer of the day), Abraham and Sachs, and the type of film determined. Pabst was chosen by UFA on the strength of his success with *The Joyless Street (Die Freudlose Gasse)*, a film about the effects of inflation in post-war Vienna, which was noted for a penetrating social and psychological realism. *Secrets of a Soul* was to be the second important film in Pabst's career, and a stepping stone in a progress which elevated him to the top rank of European film-makers in the inter-war period – a position which was later compromised by his ambiguous accommodation with Hitler. The stars of the film, Werner Krauss, Ruth Weyher and Ilka Gruning, were leading film actors of the day. The role of the psychoanalyst was played by Pavel Pavlov, an emigre Russian actor and former associate of Stanislavsky at the Moscow Art Theatre.

Secrets of a Soul opened in Berlin in March 1926. Reviews were favourable [7] and the film was a considerable success, running for many months at the Gloria Palast, still one of the largest and most prestigious cinemas in West Berlin. (The engagement coincided with the famous run of *Battleship Potemkin* in the same city.) Release followed in Germany, America, Britain and France. Prints for foreign consumption were re-edited in various ways, a common practice at the time. Changes affected names of characters, intertitled dialogue, narrative and dramatic structure. It is evident that re-editing and interpolation in British and American prints served to reinforce spurious claims that this was an 'authorized' psychoanalytic film.[8] Although the film is notoriously evasive on the question of erotic factors the French release was known as *Au seuil de la chambre à coucher*!

Secrets of a Soul is a silent film, but a film produced towards the end of

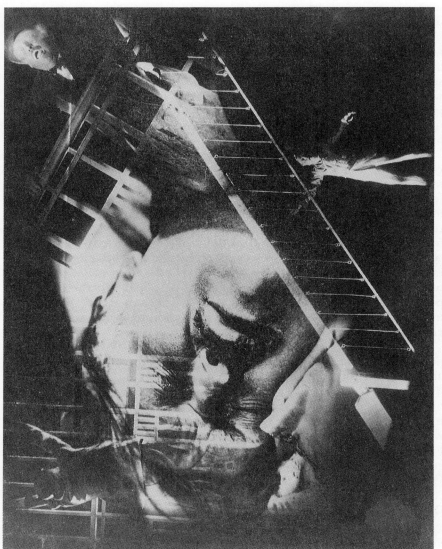

Plate 1 Still from film *Secrets of a Soul*: the cinematic depiction of psychic disorder (© Transit Film, Munich. Photograph courtesy of National Film Archive, London).

the silent era and, paradoxically, a silent film about what Freud called his 'talking cure'. It is chiefly remembered on account of its celebrated dream sequence, in which the hero's significant dream is depicted unmediated, with great technical virtuosity. But by his own account Pabst was concerned to depict the process and experience of analysis, an occurrence which involves the internal, subjective factors of memory, conceptualization and verbalization. To depict and evoke this process in images (the subjectivity and point-of-view of these and other sequences is a question which requires separate consideration), Pabst invented visual codes and narrative formulae which have been inaccurately described in published accounts of the film. He was also constrained by the limits of conventional, realistic, representational film language; we shall find that the climax to the analytical sequence has been crucially misunderstood.

If the film is a curious, as it were perverse anomaly in the history of the cinema, it is also a significant, almost forgotten chapter in the history of psychoanalysis. The production and release of *Secrets of a Soul* became the focus of a violent rupture in the psychoanalytic community. On an immediate level this was related to the current fortunes of the *Verlag*, but it reflected profounder, fundamental tensions: between the fast consolidating orthodox and heterodox factions in the analytic movement, between the competing claims for analysis as science or therapy, between opposing factions on the question of lay analysts. The film represents a crucial moment in the exposition of psychoanalysis to a lay public; perhaps the first popularizing account of a relationship that had been previously considered uniquely intimate and unpublishable, a relationship between two individuals that was necessarily conducted in secret.

By nature of its very success the film was one of the first signficant popularizations of psychoanalysis. But it aroused deeper and more complex antagonisms than those described by Ernest Jones in his famous biography of Freud. One reason may well be that it contains the earliest, and still one of the most detailed cinematic accounts of what actually occurs in analytic treatment. To Bernard Chodorkoff and Seymour Baxter, American analysts writing in 1974, the film is a valuable historic record of a style of therapeutic practice, of the interventionist, direct tenor of analytic technique current in the 1920s.[9]

There is no print of *Secrets of a Soul* available for screening in this country: this account is based on a viewing copy kindly lent by the Deutsches Institut für Filmkunde.[10] One can be confident that this represents an 'authentic' print of the original release version, but one qualification needs acknowledgement. The print under review is a 16mm copy of a 35mm original, and the process of transferring the film on to a convenient format involved the revision and editing of intertitles; from a transcription and translation document which accompanied the print it is clear that fully half the intertitles were omitted. This may have affected dialogue (and exacerbated the paucity of 'explanation' in the scenes of analysis); it certainly affected captions which elucidated the action of the film. Characters become anonymous, early sequences are difficult to read and so on. The print differs from the script (which need not be regarded as a blueprint) and from other descriptions of the film in the omission of an important piece of information: when the hero wakes from his dream he remembers the terror but not its substance – his impulses remain obscure to him; but after sharing his nightmare experience a contemporary audience might assume that he remembered the content of the dream, that he was aware of his desire to murder his wife. The difficulty of narrating the repressed, or articulating the unsaid, was not easily resolved in this first attempt at screening the dynamics of the unconscious.

In an attempt to reproduce the archaeological layering of the mind as posited by Freud, Pabst created a film of contrasting visual textures and representative modes. The objective, social world, limited to the home, place of work and the psychoanalyst's consulting room, is a succession of constricted and confining interiors, encumbered with solid, upholstered late-nineteenth century furniture and filmed by a static camera in close-up and medium shot. *Bürgerlich*, claustrophobic, but in 1926 slightly archaic, the settings abstract the drama from a strongly defined sense of period or location, though the script indicates that the action is set in a suburb of Vienna – information omitted in the print under review. The few exterior scenes occur at moments of emotional extremity in the hero's conscious-ness: they are moments of disturbance, anxiety or delirious joy, and feature a striking use of hand-held camera and oblique angles of vision. The evocation of mental life – the depiction of dreams and mental processes – is marked by a bold visual stylization in which space and time are distorted or rendered ambiguous. Some sequences are influenced by the visual conven-tions of Expressionism, or of other German films of the silent period; others feature visual schemata which seem to have been invented by Pabst, his designer and cameraman. The variation and differentiation of visual texture are parallelled by a modulation of acting styles in Werner Krauss's performance. Early sequences of domestic life, or scenes illustrating parapraxis (the tell-tale expression of psychic disorder by mistakes affecting everyday conscious actions) are enacted in a low-key, naturalistic manner and informed with an almost clinical observation. But sequences of melodrama (and of analysis) feature a violent agitation of facial and bodily gesture that seem more familiar from an actor famous for his anti-naturalistic and radically stylized performance in *The Cabinet of Doctor Caligari*. Krauss invests his role in *Secrets of a Soul* with a genuine pathos that still involves a modern audience.

Secrets of a Soul begins with an extended intertitle: a preamble which connects the occurrence of neurotic symptoms to the struggle of conflicting desires in the unconscious mind. 'Mysterious disorders result from these struggles, the outcome of which is the actual work of psychoanalysis. The work of University Lecturer (*Dozent*) Dr Sigmund Freud is regarded as important in the treatment of such illness.' [11] This declaration contrasts with the story that follows in that it emphasizes the academic and scientific resolution of conceptual problems, rather than the medical treatment of abnormality and distress which the film actually shows.

The action then begins in the house of Matthias Fellman, [12] a stolid, solemn but wistful figure. It is a bright morning and he is shaving in front of the mirror; he hears his wife's call and moves through to her bedroom to shave the nape of her neck, provocatively revealed by her boyish 'twenties hairstyle. Matthias is about to apply the razor when he is startled by a scream from the street outside: a murder has been committed in a neighbouring house. He cuts his wife's neck (held in almost obsessive close up by the camera) and drops the razor. Pabst cuts to events in the street, the arrival of the police and an ambulance, the reactions of the curious and the prurient. When we return to the house, Matthias is dressed and ready to leave for work. His svelte, glamorous wife cradles a puppy, one of a litter given birth by the household pet, and looks at her husband longingly and accusingly; he avoids her gaze and departs. We learn that Matthias is a chemist in charge of a medical laboratory. The visit of a little girl shows that Matthias is demonstrably fond of children but his effusiveness reveals a previously unsuspected sentimentality and infantilism in his own behaviour that is noticed by his attractive assistant (see plate 2). These opening scenes establish the essentials of the drama: the frustration underlying superficial domestic happiness; Matthias's impotence (suggested by shots of his wife caressing curtains and looking wanly unfulfilled) and subconscious fear of sharp objects; his emotional disequilibrium in the face of a violent intrusion from the outside world.

On his return home Matthias is disturbed by a brief police interrogation – he is wrongly but symptomatically connected with the neighbouring murder. He also throws a newspaper account of the incident into the fire; but a letter from his cousin Eric, announcing his impending visit, apparently cheers him. Eric, Matthias and Frau Fellman had been playmates in childhood. Eric is now an explorer and archaeologist and he encloses with his letter two gifts: a ceremonial dagger and an oriental statue of a fertility goddess, which looms large as a direct allusion to the couple's childlessness. During the night a storm breaks and Matthias is wracked by an anguished dream.

This famous extended sequence of the dream employs a battery of special effects: superimposition, subjective camera movement, negative exposure, optical distortion, slow motion and miniature sets surrounded by a dark, enveloping space. In favourably comparing the sequence with effects in Douglas Fairbanks's *Thief of Baghdad*, contemporary German reviewers were, in effect, describing Pabst as a Steven Spielberg of the silent cinema – and ensuring the film's commercial success. [13] It is worth remembering that

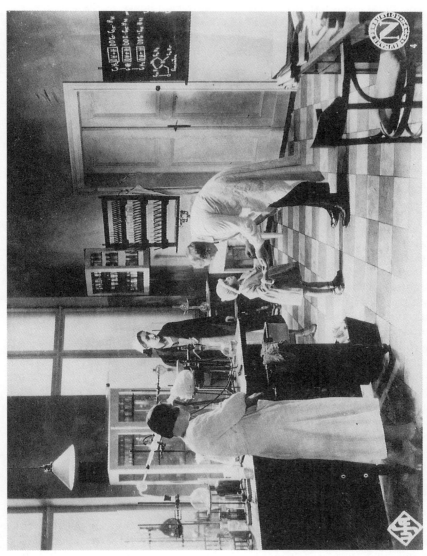

Plate 2 Matthias in his laboratory: production still (© Transit Film, Munich. Photograph courtesy of National Film Archive, London).

before the invention of the optical printer such effects were created entirely in the camera and a period of six weeks – half the production schedule of the film – was given over to their creation.[14]

The dream is presented unmediated: the audience is shown directly, without explanation, the events that take place in Matthias's mind. In recreating the disjunctive continuity and rhythm of the dream experience, the sequence falls into six episodes or narratives. As the sequence proceeds, some episodes are separated by shots of Matthias turning restlessly in bed suggesting both violent degrees of agitation and varying levels of sleep and consciousness. Later episodes, however, flow into one another or are punctuated by symbolic imagery. In the last episode Pabst creates an effective sense of dislocation: at first we think that the dream has ended and are seeing Matthias at work the next day. Much of the imagery is readily intelligible in conventional symbolic terms. Images of potency and fertility which surround Matthias in waking life take on monstrous, threatening dimensions.

The dream narrative proceeds in the following sequence:

Episode One   We see an exterior shot of Matthias' house at night. Eric, dressed in tropical gear, squats in a tree outside. Matthias emerges in his pyjamas, and finds that he is locked out. Unable to bear Eric's derisive laughter, he flies into the air (a subjective shot shows the forecourt of the house receding under his feet). Eric shoots him down (with a toy pop-gun) and salutes mockingly as Matthias crashes to the earth. In real life Matthias continues sleeping (see plate 3).

Episode Two   Still dressed in his pyjamas, Matthias walks towards an oriental shrine situated in a cave. His progress through an ambiguous dark space is suddenly interrupted by a descending barrier and a train rushes past. In distorted and superimposed images of the train we see Eric leaning out of a carriage and waving joyfully. The barrier lifts, Matthias goes on to the shrine and we recognize the fertility statue given by Eric. With a puzzled expression he throws a piece of paper on the ground and it bursts into flame. Matthias finds he is able to bound through the shrine and the walls of the cave. The sequence ends with a shot of churning pistons.

Episode Three   Matthias is dressed in his suit, with bowler hat and cane, but he walks through the same dark environment. Houses and a bell tower erupt out of the ground. The tower spirals like a revolving ziggurat, dwarfing the diminutive figure of Matthias at the bottom of the frame. Matthias looks up, and on to the image of swinging bells are superimposed the laughing faces of Matthias's wife, his maid and his (female) laboratory assistant. With great effort Matthias rushes up the tower but finds no one there. In rage and frustration he beats his cane against the parapet. We see an image, distorted through an anamorphic lens, of people whom we have earlier seen at the scene of the murder. Lightning illuminates the bedroom as Matthias tosses in his sleep.

Plate 3 *The Dream*: Matthias 'shot down' by Eric: production still (© Transit Film, Munich. Photograph courtesy of National Film Archive, London).

Episode Four   Matthias passes a house with lighted windows and is confronted with the silhouette of his wife and Eric in a passionate embrace. He beats on the railing with childlike impotent rage and the railings rise up to enclose him like prison bars as lightning flashes in the sky. Eric gesticulates mockingly and the scene changes.

Episode Five   A scene of trial and execution is depicted with distorted 'Expressionist' imagery. Matthias is again reduced to a diminutive presence in a lower corner of the frame, dwarfed by close-ups of a beating drum, pointing fingers and the silhouette of a guillotine blade. Matthias's wife bares her neck with a gesture similar to that in the opening scene of the film. A train rushes directly towards the camera. Again we see Matthias in bed, this time calmer than before.

Episode Six   Dressed in a white coat, Matthias seems to be back at work, standing in a brightly lit room accompanied by his assistant. He is disturbed by some sound outside the window and he piles books and equipment on the floor in a frantic attempt to look outside. Peering down through constricting bars he sees his wife and Eric in a rowing boat, floating on a dark lake. Frau Fellman takes a baby doll, which miraculously emerges – is given birth – from the water, and gives it to Eric who receives it tenderly (see plate 4). They become aware of Matthias screaming at them and row away from him waving and laughing in friendly mockery. Inside the room Matthias grabs the ceremonial dagger and stabs repeatedly at a phantom of his wife – superimposed transparently against surrounding objects – while his assistant laughs derisively. At this point the dream ends.

In accordance with Freudian dicta on the content of dreams, the sequence mixes material from the previous day, from the precipitating events, with content related to the dreamer's personal history. The script, and other accounts of the film, indicate that this content was to receive a fuller explanation than that given in the print under discussion. The ominous, phallic bell tower which erupts from the ground in the third episode, for example, represents the campanile of the hill town where Matthias spent his honeymoon: the implication of this grotesque symbol is clear – Matthias has been impotent since the start of his marriage.[15]

Certain images are also understandable in Freudian terms as negations or condensations subject to the processes of displacement characteristic of mental activity in dreams. The episode with the pop-gun and Matthias's unhappy attempt to fly vividly express Matthias's desire and fear of masculine potency. But an awareness of his condition, wittily implied in the dangling cork after the gun has been 'fired', could also encompass displaced violent feelings towards his cousin. This apparent urge towards self-destruction (bordering on a desire for self-castration?) might disguise a fear of Eric that is hostile, violent and repressed. The scene of trial and execution will later be interpreted as a desire for self-punishment by the dreamer

Plate 4 *The Dream, sixth episode:* frame enlargement (© Transit Film, Munich. Photograph courtesy of National Film Archive, London).

because of a guilt complex with regard to his wife, no doubt connected with his impotence and failure to give her a child. But this episode occurs *before* we see him attempting to murder her phantom and is linked in our mind with the murder that opens the film: the event whose fortuitous occurrence precipitated the action and concurred with the hidden dynamic of Matthias's unconscious mind. The sequence with the boat on the dark waters clearly illustrates Matthias's jealousy and inadequacy, but the sinister aura of the dark waters also seems to indicate ambivalent feelings towards birth and natural processes. The significance of the doll will emerge under analysis.

Matthias wakes up screaming, instantly forgetting the content of his nightmare but traumatized by its horror.[16] He is comforted by his wife: sobbing uncontrollably he puts his head in her lap – for Siegfried Kracauer an exemplary gesture 'through which most males of the German screen express their immaturity' (see plates 5 and 6).[17] In waking life the dreamer is increasingly anxious and preoccupied and his difficulties proliferate: now unable even to hold a razor he must go to a barber's to be shaved (where he is further distressed by another newspaper account of the murder); at work he cannot force himself to use a letter opener and he drops a test tube on receiving word of his cousin's arrival.

That evening Matthias returns to a happy and animated reunion though he is briefly and mysteriously troubled on seeing a photograph which shows the three protagonists as children (Matthias and Eric in sailor suits flanking the future Frau Fellman in a party frock). Apart from reminding the audience that the triangular relationship extends back into childhood, the photograph clearly indicates that Matthias and Eric are of similar age; the grown-up Eric, however – played by an English actor, Jack Trevor, who bears a resemblance to Leslie Howard, the quintessential 'aristocratic' matinée idol of the 1930s – is so much more handsome, vigorous and *youthful* than the unglamorous, sedentary Matthias that the difference seems pointed to the extent of caricature. The audience might read this scene as being filmed from Matthias's point of view, and assume that Eric's charisma and vigour express Matthias's sense of inferiority and justify his unconscious feeling of being threatened, a feeling which was so graphically revealed in the dream. But an earlier, presumably 'objective' scene, showing Eric arriving at the house, in which Matthias is not present, is played in the same way. This scene occurs before Matthias is told of the event and there is no indication that it is mediated through his imagination. The episode indicates that Eric and Matthias's wife have retained a strong mutual affection, perhaps an attraction; there is a hint that Matthias's anxieties may have some basis in reality. But the narrative of the film is didactic and conformist and demands that the apparent threat of real adultery be dispelled. Eric is subsequently shown to be a loyal and proper friend to both Matthias and his wife.

The evening proceeds smoothly until Matthias is faced with the necessity

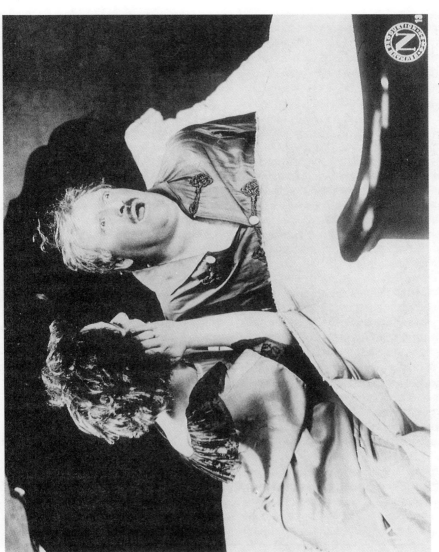

Plate 5 *Matthias awakes from his dream*: production still (© Transit Film, Munich. Photograph courtesy of National Film Archive, London).

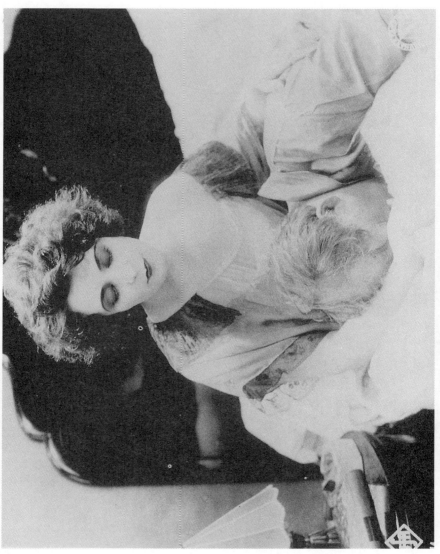

Plate 6 *Matthias seeks comfort in his wife's lap*: production still (© Transit Film, Munich. Photograph courtesy of National Film Archive, London).

of using a knife at the dinner table. After an agitated struggle to control his feelings he is overcome by the phobia and rushes from the house leaving his bewildered companions behind. The scene changes to a smoky, cavernous *Bierkeller*, where Matthias sits alone with a drink, surreptitiously observed by a powerful, thick-set man at a neighbouring table. The watcher notices that Matthias leaves his key behind when he pays and leaves; he follows him into the street, a place of shadow and spatial ambiguity, similar to the enveloping darkness which surrounded events in Matthias's dream. We might be watching an early thriller by Fritz Lang and the scene embodies 'the menace of the street', the threat of violence implicit in the social flux which Kracauer defined as a characteristic theme of German films of the inter-war years. Matthias stops at his gate and fumbles for his missing key. His observer emerges from the darkness, smiling (directly at the camera, breaking one of the central conventions of narrative cinema) holding out what Matthias is looking for. The unknown man asks – or suggests – whether Matthias may have a reason for not wishing to enter, a motive that might explain an act of apparent forgetfulness. He explains his diagnosis – 'I am a psychoanalyst, it is part of my work' – and continues on his way. In this episode Pabst wittily combines illustration of Freudian parapraxis – Matthias's unconscious appeal in leaving the stranger his key – with a more conventional symbolism: the key to unlock the mystery.

The thriller mode continues as Matthias is greeted by his wife in the flickering light of the fireside. Over her shoulder he catches sight of Eric's gifts from the previous day: the fertility symbol and the Japanese dagger. His eyes fix on the blade and he nearly succumbs to a murderous impulse to plunge it into her neck (see plate 7). This sequence, in its figure placement, lighting, angles of vision and striking image of a flare of light gliding down a blade, closely anticipates a similar scene which *does* end in murder in Pabst's most celebrated film: the killing of Lulu in *Pandora's Box* (1928). Matthias, however, restrains himself with a violent effort and for the second time that evening rushes wildly from the house. He takes refuge with his widowed mother for whom it becomes evident he has retained an intense emotional attachment, with the implication that his sexual and emotional impulses may have always been complicated. As his mother comforts him Matthias confesses to 'strange passions . . . confused thoughts'. His reflection in a polished table dissolves into the face of the psychiatrist holding out the key, the solution to his incomprehensible and terrifying predicament. Conscious now of his violent impulses, Matthias decides to seek help (see plate 8).

He tracks down his interlocutor, Doctor Orth, and calls on him at a large, well-appointed consulting room. Troubled and anxious, Matthias explains something of his situation: the doctor smiles reassuringly, even cajolingly, as if to a child, and declares with an unequivocal confidence: 'I can help you, there is a method. It is called psychoanalysis.'

Orth accepts Matthias as a patient and imposes emotional and physical

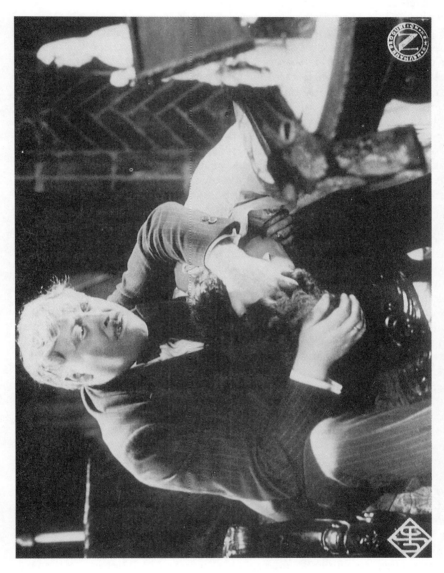

Plate 7 *The dreamer gripped by a murderous compulsion: frame enlargement* (© Transit Film, Munich. Photograph courtesy of National Film Archive, London).

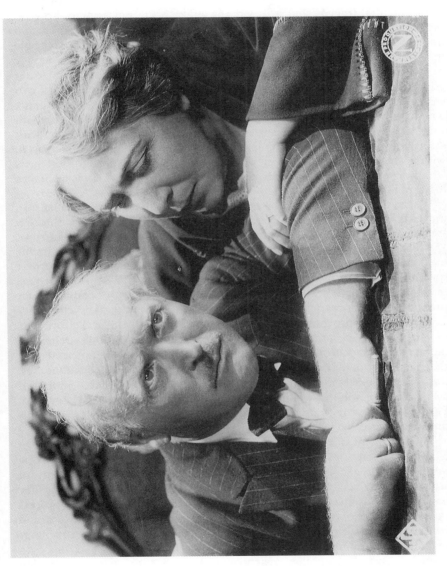

Plate 8 *Matthias comforted by his mother*: production still (© Transit Film, Munich. Photograph courtesy of National Film Archive, London).

parameters, requiring him to live away from his wife for the duration of the analysis. Matthias moves in with his mother. The analyst recommends this course of action in response to the extremity of the situation, in order to avert potential tragedy, but it is perhaps unlikely, an indication of how far the situation, allegedly based on a real event, has been fictionalized and (melo)dramatized for cinematic narration. While he thought it advisable that the analysand should refrain from major decisions affecting marriage or career, Freud thought it 'much more advantageous' that the vast majority of patients 'remain during treatment in the conditions in which they have to struggle with the tasks that face them'.[18] The doctor telephones Matthias's wife to inform her of the situation and also to ask her to pack a suitcase with some of his things. His tone is genial but he seems to be sparing with information because Frau Fellman's bewilderment is evidently increased, with a suggested addition of emotional hurt. As treatment progresses she is left in the dark: a short sequence shows her spying on Matthias as he makes his way between his mother's house and the analyst's couch.

What Freud described as 'the tedious labour' of psychoanalysis takes up the last third of the film. (There is one respite: about midway through treatment, Matthias walks to his mother's house – surreptitiously observed, as we have seen. He eats a meal with a spoon after his mother has cut up his meat and removed the 'dreadful knife', cited by Kracauer as a further striking illustration of retrogressive behaviour.)[19] The analysis is condensed into four discernible sessions, building to a single moment of catharsis that probably owes more to the demands of dramatic cogency than psychoanalytic veracity. The process is shown to comprise essentially mental effort: acts of memory, conceptualization and interpretation. Matthias rehearses moments of shock from the recent past which prompted, or coincided with the manifestation of his debilitating symptoms (the phobia, the parapraxes, the onset of anxiety and compulsion), and recovers long-buried memories of events from childhood which reveal the cause and genesis of his neurosis. Finally – and most dramatically – he is led to recall the substance of his dream and discovers its meanings (see plate 9).

The treatment in the film depends on the discovery of the 'meaning' of Matthias's symptoms and the solution to the mystery involves a painstaking unravelling of a complex skein of memories and associations, many of which have to be retrieved from the patient's unconscious to which they have been consigned by his repressive psychic mechanisms. The process operates on an interplay of three planes of memory: that of immediate and conscious events; the content of the significant dream; the buried memory of childhood trauma. Within each session Matthias follows a tortuous path from one strand to another, reaching back further into the past, digging deeper into hidden strata of unconscious repression. The clarification of each strand is a necessary part of the treatment, discovery on one plane leading to association and further elucidation on another. Enlightenment is achieved at a point of convergence.

Plate 9 *Matthias and Dr Orth in the consulting room*: production still (© Transit Film, Munich. Photograph courtesy of National Film Archive, London).

But the 'explanation' posited by the film is incomplete and disingenuous – in both psychoanalytic and dramatic senses. Memory and association eventually lead the patient to confront an incident in childhood that reveals the significance of the photograph of the children and of the action with the doll in the dream episode. In Matthias's mind the circumstances of the photograph are restaged, prefaced by a striking shot of a man, Matthias's father (his only appearance in the film), pointing a camera at the audience. It becomes clear that the event took place at Christmas when the three children were playing in the nursery surrounded by elaborate Victorian toys. A brother or sister to Matthias has just been born and the boy has been told that his mother has 'given the baby as a present to his father'.[20] In imitation of the adults the children play with their dolls, but while Matthias is preoccupied with his new sibling the girl gives the doll to Eric, excluding Matthias, her usual partner in play and future husband. We are asked to believe that this incident represents the 'kernel of the neurosis', that it establishes Eric as a rival and threat and instils in Matthias a repressed anger and desire to punish the girl.

This resolution avoids an explicit acknowledgement of childhood sexuality, or of the motivating force of libidinal factors. Arguably these factors are implicit in the visual information that is conveyed by the scene. The presence of the baby is surely significant. Matthias would no longer be an exclusive recipient of his mother's affections; his feelings towards his sibling would be ambivalent, torn between welcome, resentment and fear of rejection. The absence of any other reference to the father is itself suggestive of a repressed Oedipal jealousy that is never acknowledged by script or film. The cinematic account of analysis stops just at the point where the real work might begin. One might wish to speculate that Matthias had witnessed his parents in the act of intercourse some time before. A banal, minor incidence of childhood jealousy is clearly inadequate to explain the development of a neurosis which results in impotence and near catastrophe.

The photograph is an important device in the film. On a single viewing it is easy to miss the fact that the image and Matthias's memory of it are quite different. His recollection has the girl in the centre holding the fateful doll and the expressions of the trio display markedly differing emotions. But in the actual picture the doll is absent; poses and expressions are emotionally neutral.

In this account of analysis it is worth asking exactly *what* is being dramatized (and from whose perspective). The answer seems to be three distinct aspects of the event. The first, and most important, is the representation of Matthias's subjective experience of the process – *his* memories, fantasies and ideas, represented through a strikingly varied visual schema. Secondly, Pabst and his scriptwriters present analysis as an interactive process, involving analyst and patient in mutual effort; the film may also be a valuable record of past therapeutic styles and technique, though in this respect the presentation is prone to dramatic distortion and misinterpretation. Thirdly – and, as we have seen, least convincingly – the film offers an 'explanation', an exposition of the genesis, dynamics and meaning of the patient's neurosis.

When Matthias commences the treatment, lying prone on the couch, he expresses his sense of pain, confusion and bewilderment. He is evidently asked to recount the onset of his problem, because we return to the shaving incident which opened the film. Apart from an introductory close-up of shaving brush and mirror, the scene is presented entirely differently, enacted against a neutral, bright white ground, with simplified, stylized gestures and viewed from different angles of vision. The scene is abridged to its essentials: a woman screams, husband and wife jump in alarm, passers-by talk excitedly. From Kracauer onwards, commentators have suggested that Pabst uses the white ground in flashbacks of dream and reality in an undifferentiated manner 'to characterise them as stray recollections'[21] but I disagree with this assessment. Re-enactments against a white ground also occur in the third session of analysis (when Matthias recalls the visit of the little girl to his laboratory and his dropping the test tube), by which time it is clear that Pabst is employing different visual conventions in a consistent way to distinguish different psychic events and different categories of recollection. When Matthias begins to remember his dream (in sessions three and four) we see fragments of it in their original form, in direct flashback. The shift in visual modes also serves to destabilize the narrative image. The original shot of the cut on Frau Fellman's neck may seem now, in retrospect, to have been as much a fantasized wound as a real occurrence: she seemed remarkably unaffected and unharmed (see plate 10).

Through free association Matthias pursues other levels of thought which in turn are evoked through other visual conventions. He explains or conceptualizes his marital situation, focusing on the triangular emotional configuration of husband, wife and cousin. This is represented in the form of theatrical tableaux of which there are echoes in other German films of the silent era (for example the introduction of the archetypal characters in Arthur Robison's *Schatten (Warning Shadows)* or the dance of the false Maria in Fritz Lang's *Metropolis*) and which bring to mind the themes and imagery of E. T. A. Hoffman, the writer who exercised an enduring fascination for many intellectual and artistic founders of modernism, including Freud. The theatrical mode also allegorizes the processes of psychic enactment, which is distinct from other processes of dream and memory. At one point the sense of Eric as an absent but potent threat is evoked by his shadow falling across Frau Fellman's white dress. Matthias indulges in lurid and masochistic fantasies where he is the impotent observer of Eric and his wife in compromising situations, similar to the fourth episode of the dream. One fantasy, particularly extravagant, installs wife and cousin in a harem, watched behind an ornate grill by Matthias; at first this scene seems realistically framed but a reverse angle shot distorts the spatial relationship between observer and observed. One further and

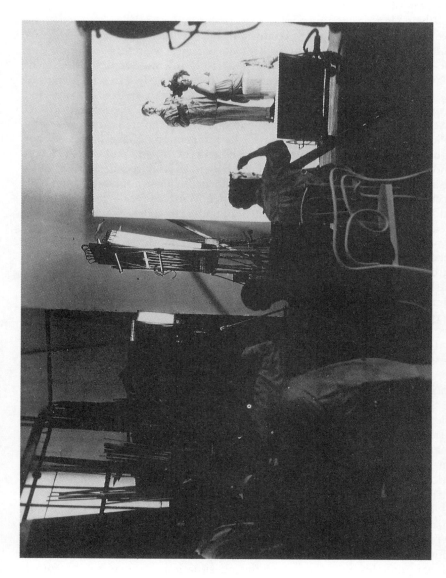

Plate 10 Filming *Secrets of a Soul* at UFA Studios, Berlin, autumn 1925.

extended sequence begins with the married couple facing each other on the brow of a hill, silhouetted against the sky. Together they plant a tree, a ritualized expression of their mutual desire for a child. Matthias and his wife then enter an empty room which they imagine fitted out as a nursery; the husband is then shown alone in the room which is now darkened and denuded. Matthias leaves the room and locks the door. The episode is eloquent and expressive, but its precise status (memory, fantasy or an imperceptible blending of the two?) is left unclear, perhaps intentionally, to suggest the evasive attitude of the patient to his impotence, the problem which underlies his neurotic crisis.

Throughout the analysis Dr Orth interjects frequently and vigorously, interrogates and provides interpretations with some degree of agitation. When Matthias begins to recall his dream his attention is drawn to the powerful and sinister image of the train: for a second time stalled pistons churn furiously, the engine rushes directly towards the spectator or, in profile, describes a half circle through the distorting prism of the anamorphic lens. Eric, dressed for the tropics, again embarks, waving joyfully. But however authentic the recreation of oneiric content and experience, the essential Freudian argument that dreams, even anxiety dreams, are to be understood as the disguised fulfilment of repressed wishes is left almost unexplored. One exception is Dr Orth's interpretation of this recurring image: that it represents Matthias's repressed desire for the death or departure of his cousin.

In explaining to Matthias that the image represents his repressed wish that his cousin depart (a disguised death wish?) the doctor bends towards his patient expostulating vigorously and seems to shout in excitement. Matthias is sufficiently startled to raise himself on one elbow and look his analyst in the face. Again, when Orth defines the emotional dynamics of Matthias's childhood trauma (explained in an intertitle after the subject's violent abreaction) he seems to impose a formulation which is immediately and passively accepted by the patient: there is little evidence of the latter making his own intellectual contribution, of Matthias playing that active role in a process of (assisted) self-discovery, which Freud described as an essential feature of treatment. Matthias's mental exertion is both strenuous and painful but seems limited to the activities of memory and recapitulation.

In character and behaviour Dr Orth is very different from more modern cinematic portraits of the psychoanalyst. In part this difference may be coloured by the authority with which he is uncritically invested in the film, but Orth's exuberance, geniality and forcefulness are in marked contrast to the qualities of gentle, calm equilibrium conveyed by the off-screen voice of Frank Finlay (as Freud) in Hugh Brody and Michael Ignatieff's *Nineteen Nineteen*, or the provocative emotional and professional reserve of Ian McKellen in *Zhina*. But there is no need to assume that the image of the psychoanalyst in *Secrets of a Soul* is *necessarily* less 'authentic', that Pavlov's performance is a function of the film's inherent tendency to melodrama. The actor and director were reportedly coached in analytic practice by Hanns Sachs for a period of several weeks before filming began (in Pavlov's case this must have been indirectly, through translation: he could not speak German) and Lee Atwell reports that Pavlov was later contacted by American therapists who assumed he was a practising analyst and wished to engage him for a lecture tour, so convincing had they found his performance.[22] There is also an account by the American poet Hilda Doolittle of her analysis with Freud in the years 1933–4 in the course of which the analyst several times expressed exasperation and frustration, at one point furiously pounding the back of the couch on which she was lying.[23]

On this last point it is perhaps legitimate to speculate as to whether in some respects Dr Orth represents a disguised portrait of the discoverer of psychoanalysis. One notes the heavy consumption of cigars, even in consulting hours, and the Persian covers on the cushions. To be sure Orth's consulting room is considerably more spacious than the cramped facilities at Berggasse 19 and his wide Slavic features bear little resemblance to Freud's (or to the caricatured Jewish features with which the profession would be characterized in Germany in the 1930s). But the heavy woollen suit and neck-tie affect the style worn by Freud all his professional life and Orth's thick-set build is not dissimilar to that of Freud in middle age.

However, our first sight of Orth, in the café, is of an ambiguous, perhaps sinister figure, an external correlative of the wishes and anxieties that crowd in on Matthias's psyche. From this point on the film becomes a kind of thriller with Orth cast in the role of detective, a confident, competent negotiator who guides and protects a helpless *ingénu* in his progress through the shadowy, dangerous world of the unconscious. In *Secrets of a Soul* it is Orth who solves the mystery and tracks the enigma to its source; his expertise and strength of character confers mastery of a threatening and violent situation. He anticipates the part played by psychoanalysts in Hollywood thrillers of the late 1940s (Ingrid Bergman in *Spellbound*, Lee J. Cobb in *The Dark Past*), as characters who are imbued with a similar benign and competent authority, who also solve mysteries and confront and defuse violent situations. John Huston's *Freud: The Secret Passion* may be one of the last instances in which psychoanalytic enquiry is dramatized within the conventions of the mystery thriller (the dream episodes also feature a quasi-Expressionist visual design). By 1962, however, the image of the practitioner is very different: Montgomery Clift's Freud is a figure of vulnerable human complexity whose insight springs from recognizing and confronting his own neuroses.

Secrets of a Soul presents an abridged account of analysis, both as event and as process. When Matthias retrieves from memory his childhood experience of rejection and humiliation he releases his repressed violent emotions, leaps to his feet like a man possessed, grabs the paper-knife from the doctor's table and acts out in mime the murder he has long and unknowingly wished to commit. Dr Orth puts out a restraining hand and explains the meaning and real intent of his violent actions and fantasies. The film then cuts to the final scene of joy and fulfilment with Matthias as a happy father on a second honeymoon. The occurrence of abreaction is thus implicitly identified with the completion of cure, rather than as a stage pointing to its achievement. This is misleading. Matthias's reaction has been induced by Dr Orth and is a function of transference, the development of a strong emotional attitude (in this case positive) on the part of the patient towards his analyst which Freud defined as the fulcrum of psychoanalytic therapy. He held that this development was a necessary precondition of a patient's ability to fight through the conflicts which were revealed by analysis, but he also insisted that a successful outcome had been achieved only when the subject had realized and overcome his emotional dependency; if the patient failed to resolve his transference there was no guarantee that he had gained sufficient mental strength to have been permanently liberated from his neurosis, and was no longer chained to 'the compulsion to repeat'.

The film makes no explicit acknowledgement of this crucial difficulty of transference nor, by extension, of a tragic dimension inherent in psychoanalysis. This omission, quite apart from the film's attitude towards infantile sexuality, lays it open to charges of bowdlerizing Freud. The 'primal scene' of childish jealousy depicted in the film is naively civilized, far removed from the elemental Oedipal scenario posited by Freud. It contradicts Pabst's own assertion that he was anxious to 'avoid being seduced by the idea of psychoanalysis as panacea'.[24]

Yet it would be possible, however, to argue that the occurrence of transference is implicitly stated in the visual presentation. Apart from the stylized shot of laughing faces superimposed on the swinging bells in the campanile in Matthias's dream, two characters in the film look directly at the camera, breaking a central convention of cinematic narrative and warning the audience that we are seeing events directly from Matthias's perspective: Dr Orth, when he holds out the key (as the event takes place, and then again in his patient's memory); and Matthias's father recalled in analysis, about to take the photograph that will 'fix' in memory the patient's childhood trauma. We have already noted the cajoling, reassuring way that Orth deals with Matthias when the latter goes to him for help; the striking similarity of the shots seems to confirm that the patient views his analyst as a (singularly benign and comforting) father-figure.

Transference is a problematic issue also because it raises the question of suggestion by the analyst, a charge acknowledged by Freud in the final chapter of the *Introductory Lectures on Psycho-Analysis*.[25] The degree of suggestion and intervention that is employed by the fictitious analyst in *Secrets of a Soul* is ambiguous and has led to inaccurate description and misunderstanding. Lee Atwell's critical biography of Pabst, the only English-language monograph on the director, describes Orth as hypnotizing

Matthias to induce the final disclosure and abreaction. This would be impossible. A quarter of a century before, around 1900, Freud had explicitly repudiated hypnosis as an analytic or therapeutic technique; but the behaviour of Matthias makes Atwell's interpretation understandable. At certain points he lies on his side, he closes his eyes, he looks inwards, he might even be going to sleep. This contradicts Freud's recommendations for the genuine inducement of free association on the part of the patient (the patient should lie flat on his back; eye contact with the analyst should be avoided and his eyes should remain open, fixed on a distant point) which he included in the 1925 edition of *The Interpretation of Dreams,* contemporaneously with the production of the film. Atwell's misunderstanding might also be connected with Kracauer's description of the film which compared *Secrets of a Soul* closely with *Warning Shadows,* 'another analytic or quasi-analytic film' in which psychic healing is effected by hypnosis.[26]

Though there is little indication that contemporary audiences – or analysts – found Orth's therapeutic behaviour *objectively* unrealistic, the analytical sequences can be consistently read as an expression of Matthias's infatuation and of his wish-fulfilment for protective care. Bernard Chodorkoff and Seymour Baxter thought that Orth was presented as too involved with his patient; considering the episode of the key and the original meeting of analyst and patient they speculate as to whether it represents a transference fantasy on the part of Matthias – but it seems odd that this interpretation is not extended to scenes on the couch. By this token the final sequence of the film, the lyrical second honeymoon, which has always been adversely criticized (and can reduce modern audiences to incredulous laughter), can be read as representing a healthy fantasy in the mind of a patient on the road to recovery. It need not necessarily depict a real event.

In his biography of Freud, Ernest Jones refers to a campaign of vilification conducted by the Viennese psychoanalysts Josef Storfer and Siegfried Bernfeld which attempted to deprecate the value of the film before it was released. Storfer was the director of the *Verlag* and he may well have taken umbrage at Hanns Neumann's original suggestion that he publish 'an easily comprehensible and non-scientific pamphlet on psychoanalysis . . . [which] may present an opportunity of helping the fortunes of the *Verlag* publishing company.'[27]

In the event the pamphlet was published by a film publishing company in Berlin.[28] Bernfeld composed a film script of his own as a counter to the project in Berlin, but it remained unrealized and unpublished due to contractual prerogatives imposed by the production of *Secrets of a Soul.* This script is discussed in a recent paper by Barbara Eppensteiner, Karl Fallend and Johannes Reichmayr.[29] Bernfeld may have anticipated some of the problems discussed in this chapter; in any case his idea for 'a film with psychoanalytic perspectives'[30] concentrated on analysis as a means to understanding and not as a therapeutic technique. In his story a young man's dreams mirror acute difficulties in love and work. He becomes interested in dreams and is aided in his understanding of them by a psychoanalyst. He does not, however, become a patient. Bernfeld also set out to give some reference to Oedipal conflict and the existence of childhood sexuality, and also to encapsulate Freud's structural model of the mind incorporating the concepts of Ego, Id and Superego. The topical model of Unconscious, Pre-conscious and Conscious first publicly formulated by Freud in *The Interpretation of Dreams*, and implicit in *Secrets of a Soul*, was already out of date by 1925.

Eppensteiner, Fallend and Reichmayr also relate the controversy that greeted the film to larger issues that divided the analytic community at this time. In Berlin in the 1920s the institutional and professional advance of psychoanalysis developed relatively unhindered. University clinics (*psychoanalytische Poliklinik*) had opened shortly after the First World War and psychoanalytic therapy was practised by non-medical analysts. The situation was very different in Vienna, the founding city of the new science, where psychoanalysis was not readily accepted by a conservative academic establishment. Notwithstanding Freud's qualified approval of the enrolment of lay analysts, most practitioners in Vienna jealously guarded their medical status and vehemently opposed lay therapeutic involvement. The situation was complicated by laws which protected against professional malpractice (*Kurpfuscherei*), and the production of *Secrets of a Soul* coincided with events that were to culminate in the prosecution of Theodor Reik. Freud and many of his colleagues deplored the growing popularization and discussion of psychoanalysis and Berlin was regarded with a good deal of suspicion as a centre of 'wild analysts' and heretical developments. A particular animus was reserved for Hanns Sachs as an enthusiastic popularizer of the science. Freud was apparently distressed that the film was attacked in some quarters as an advertisement for a therapeutic technique which had not been accorded universal endorsement and acceptance.[31]

For Eppensteiner and her colleagues *Secrets of a Soul* is an early instance of psychoanalytic 'Trivialkino', a prototype for the integration of psychoanalytic themes in popular film genres, as in American thrillers of the 1940s and 1950s. The film is undoubtedly evasive and misleading with regard to some of the central concerns of psychoanalysis in both its theoretical and therapeutic dimensions. Further problems reside in the treatment of the Frau Fellman character. Not only is she relegated to the periphery of the drama, but in a film in which symbols affect the viewer by a process of linkage certain episodes and images seem to be coloured by Freud's now notorious, embarrassing iconography of the feminine. But the film remains of interest, not so much as a coherent cinematic exposition of psychoanalysis, but as a bold and sophisticated dramatization and articulation of different categories of thought and psychic experience in purely visual terms. It might be argued that the brilliance of invention in Pabst's direction did not so much transcend his material as throw into sharper relief the evasions and simplifications of a compromised script. But *Secrets of a Soul* was a unique experiment in silent film, an attempt to dramatize and expound complex and controversial material in a form that strained against the limits of conventional film narrative.

Notes

The author would like to thank Dina Gordon-Brown, Peter Collier, Hannelore Kraus, Helga Rulf, Rick Rylance, Peter Schoenberg, Michael Shortland and Anna Zacharewicz for their help; and to acknowledge the assistance of the British Film Institute (Stills Library), the Deutsches Institut für Filmkunde (Wiesbaden), the Goethe-Institut (London) and Transit-Film-Gesellschaft mbH (Munich).

1   Ernest Jones, *The Life and Work of Sigmund Freud* (Hogarth Press, London, 1957); vol. III, pp. 121–2. Jones refers to *Secrets of a Soul* as *The Mystery of the Soul.*
   Slightly variant accounts of Goldwyn's overtures to Freud can be found in *The Goldwyn Touch: A Biography of Sam Goldwyn*, by Michael Freedland (Harrap, London, 1986), and *Goldwyn: The Man Behind the Mask*, by Arthur Marx (The Bodley Head, London, 1976).
2   Jones, *Life and Work of Sigmund Freud*, p. 121.
3   Letter from Karl Abraham to Freud, 7 June 1925: Karl Abraham and Sigmund Freud, *A Psychoanalytic Dialogue: The Letters of Sigmund Freud and Karl Abraham 1907–26* (Hogarth Press and The Institute of Psychoanalysis, London, 1965), p. 382.
4   Hanns Sachs was a notable contributor to the influential film magazine *Close-up* (1927–33) and became widely known for a psychoanalytic reading of *Battleship Potemkin*. The title of this chapter is derived from one of two pamphlets written by him to accompany the original release of the film: *Secrets of a Soul: A Psychoanalytic Film (Geheimnisse einer Seele: ein psychoanalytischer Film)* (Berlin: Lichtbildbuhne, 1926). Copy kindly lent by the Deutsches Institut für Filmkunde, Wiesbaden.
5   Abraham and Freud, *A Psychoanalytic Dialogue*, p. 383.
6   According to Bernard Chodorkoff and Seymour Baxter, '*Secrets of a Soul: an early psychoanalytic film venture*', *American Imago* 31, 4 (1974), pp. 319–34. Chodorkoff and Baxter had access to an unpublished biography of G. W. Pabst by M. Pabst in Vienna.
7   Contemporary German reviews lent to the author by the Deutsches Institut für Filmkunde include *Ahnung und Aufbruch*, S. 14, *Berliner Boursen-Courier*, 27 March 1926, *Deutsche Allgemeine Seitung*, 27 March 1926, *Der Film*, 1926 (13), *Die Film Woche*, 1926 (15), and *Vossiche Zeitung*, 26 March 1926. All these reviews are favourable or respectful and accept *Secrets of a Soul* on the value of its own publicity. Several note parallels with the detective thriller; none gives a penetrating reading of the film.
8   The print of *Secrets of a Soul* screened in London in July 1927 evidently began

with a portrait of Freud, preceding the introductory intertitles. Reviewed in *Bioscope*, 7 May 1927. Publicity surrounding the film outside Germany also served to reinforce the impression that this was an 'authorized' film treatment of psychoanalysis. Jones, *Life and Work of Sigmund Freud*, mentions an article in *Time Magazine* before filming began that sparked off the furore in the analytic movement. A later publicity article *According to Freud* by John S. Cohen trumpeted the film as 'the first combination of drama and mental science, the first utilisation on the screen of psychoanalysis which is, perhaps, the most important contribution to psychology that has yet been made': *Photoplay*, August 1926, pp. 73 and 98.

9 Chodorkoff and Baxter, *'Secrets of a Soul'*, pp. 329–31.
10 This print of *Secrets of a Soul* received a public screening at the Arts Cinema, Cambridge, on 10 February 1988. The film was a centrepiece of a short season entitled *Screen Memories: Aspects of Freud in the Movies:* other films in the series included John Huston's *Freud: The Secret Passion*, Hugh Brody's *Nineteen Nineteen*, Arthur Robison's *Warning Shadows (Schatten)*, Nicolas Roeg's *Bad Timing* and Bernardo Bertolucci's *La Luna*. The season was presented by the Arts Cinema with the assistance of the Judith E. Wilson Fund (University of Cambridge), The Goethe Institut (London) and MCA Television.
11 Quoted from an intertitle on the print under review. All subsequent quotes from film text derive from this print.
12 As the leading character is called in the script and original cast list. In the American print discussed by Lee Atwell (see n. 14) he is called Martin. In the print under review the characters are listed anonymously: Der Mann, Die Frau, Der Arzt and so on, with the exception of Eric who has always been designated with an English spelling.
13 *Vossiche Zeitung*, 26 March 1926.
14 Lee Atwell, *G. W. Pabst* (Twayne Publishers – Theatrical Arts series, Boston, Mass., 1977), pp. 37–42. This is the only English-language monograph on the director.
15 This information is made clear in Sachs's pamphlet *Secrets of a Soul: A Psychoanalytic Film*. It is unclear if it featured in an original print of the film.
16 This crucial information – on which the plot hinges – was clear to contemporary reviewers: see Siegfried Kracauer, *From Caligari to Hitler: A Psychological History of the German Film* (Princeton University press, Princeton, 1947; (5th edn, 1974), or the *Bioscope* review of 7 July 1927.
17 Kracauer, *From Caligari to Hitler*, p. 171.
18 Sigmund Freud, *Introductory Lectures on Psycho-Analysis*: (1916–17), Lecture 28, *Analytic Therapy*, SE, XVI, p. 461; Pelican, p. 515. Chodorkoff and Baxter, *'Secrets of a Soul'*, mention the consternation among practising analysts (both in the 1920s and the 1970s) over Dr Orth's action in removing Matthias from the matrimonial home.
19 Kracauer, *From Caligari to Hitler*, p. 171.
20 This explanation is given in Sachs's pamphlet, which elaborates that given in the film without discussing Oedipal or infantile erotic factors.
21 Kracauer, *From Caligari to Hitler*, p. 172. See also Atwell, *G. W. Pabst*, and Paul Rotha's *The Film Till Now: A Survey of World Cinema* (Jonathan Cape, London, 1930 and subsequent editions with additional material up to 1967). Once a seminal text on film history, Rotha's book gives a good example of

changing critical perspectives on Pabst, moving from keen appreciation in the early 1930s to bitter disappointment in the 1940s and after.

22 Atwell, G. W. *Pabst*, 42.

23 Doolittle's account, from her book *Tribute to Freud* (McGraw-Hill, New York, 1956), is contained in Janet Malcolm's *Psychoanalysis: The Impossible Profession* (Picador, London, 1982), p. 166. In discussing the degree of Freud's professional detachment towards his patients Malcolm adds that Freud differentiated between therapeutic and didactic analyses and that he considered Doolittle to be a pupil rather than a patient.

24 Chodorkoff and Baxter, '*Secrets of a Soul*', p. 320, who seem to be quoting from the unpublished biography of Pabst.

25 Freud, *SE*, XVI, pp. 452–3; Pelican 1, pp. 505–7.

26 Kracauer, *From Caligari to Hitler*, p.171.

27 Abraham and Freud, *A Psychoanalytic Dialogue*, p. 383.

28 This would be the other, apparently more general, pamphlet written by Sachs and published by the same company to accompany the release of the film: *Psychoanalysis: Riddle of the Unconscious (Psychoanalyse: Ratsel des Unbewussten)* (Berlin, Licthbildbuhne, 1926). This document has not been seen by the present author. It is alluded to in Barbara Eppensteiner, Karl Fallend and Johannes Reichmayr, *Psychoanalysis and Film in the 20th Century (Berlin and Vienna). The Idea in the Image and the Image of the Idea (Psychoanalyse und Film in den Zwanziger Jahren (Berlin, Wien). Die Idee im Bild und das Bild der Idee: Vorstellbarkeit und Anschauung); Studies in the History of Psychology and the Social Sciences*, 4: *Proceedings of Cheiron, the European Society for the History of the Behavioural and Social Sciences* (Psychologisch Institut van de Rijksuniversiteit Leiden, Leiden, 1987, pp. 411–19).

29 ibid.

30 ibid.

31 Jones, *Life and Work of Sigmund Freud*, p. 121.

SUGGESTED READING

Atwell, L., G. W. *Pabst*, Twayne Publishers – Theatrical Arts series, Boston, Mass. 1977.

Browne, N., and McPherson, B., 'Dream and photography in a psychoanalytic film: *Secrets of a Soul*', *Dreamworks*, 1, 1 (1980), pp. 36–45.

Chodorkoff, B., and Baxter, S., '*Secrets of a Soul*: an early psychoanalytic film venture', *American Imago*, 31 (1974), pp. 319–34.

Fleming, M., and Manvell, R., *Images of Madness: The Portrayal of Insanity in the Feature Film*, Associated University Press, London, 1985.

Kracauer, S., *From Caligari to Hitler: A Psychological History of the German Film*, Princeton University Press, Princeton, 1974.

Shortland, M., 'Screen memories: towards a history of psychiatry and psychoanalysis in the movies', *British Journal for the History of Science*, 20 (1987), pp. 421–52.

12

Pirandello and the Drama of Creativity

ANN CAESAR

After an inauspicious première in Rome on 10 May 1921 *Sei personaggi in cerca d'autore* (*Six Characters in Search of an Author*) soon won international acclaim with performances in Milan, London, Paris and New York. Luigi Pirandello was already well known in Italy as a writer of short stories and novels, but during the years of the First World War he turned increasingly to drama, finding in the problematical relationship between audience, actors and literary characters an appropriate vehicle for his own ideas. In 1925, having written a further six plays, Pirandello took the opportunity provided by the fifth reprinting of *Six Characters in Search of an Author* to add a preface which explains *a posteriori* the circumstances under which this 'play in the making' ('commedia da fare') came into being and, in so doing, he offers a clarification of some of the issues it raises.[1]

In the preface Pirandello takes us back to the play's genesis, the startling and paradoxical idea of a literary character who is in search of an author. The title is in fact something of a misnomer, for the play opens at the point when the characters, having already given up their fight to persuade an unknown author to adopt them, invade a theatre where another Pirandellian play is in rehearsal and try to re-enact their story themselves; the writer's role is entrusted to the prompter turned stenographer, whose task it now is to take down the lines as they are spoken. By using the preface to present a retrospective autobiographical account of those earlier unhappy meetings between himself, as the recalcitrant author, and the insistent characters, Pirandello writes himself back into the script, so reasserting the authority that he had apparently abjured ('play in the making') over the text and its meanings. But he also uses the preface to deny all responsibility for the torrid family drama that is unleashed on stage, in which a father who gives his wife away to another man, inadvertently buys the sexual services of the daughter of that union when they meet in a brothel. Pirandello's description of the circumstances that gave rise to the story, of how the characters came to him, imploring him to give them the opportunity to re-enact their drama, affords him some protection against the psychological implications of this bleak scenario of sexual and domestic misery.

For Pirandello character and plot are inseparable in the conception and gestation of a literary work, so in rejecting the tale they have to tell, he has refused the characters access to a literary existence. But the continuous battle they have waged with him has confirmed their autonomy; they won't go away, he refuses to accede to their demands. The situation is impossible to sustain; for having ensnared him the characters now haunt him, until the solution comes, and with it liberation. The play will be the enactment of that rejection and its consequences. In one sense the characters win, since the author has to articulate their feelings in order to release himself from them, in another sense the author does, for the understated but nonetheless inevitable conclusion is that literary characters cannot make it alone, the author stands between the character and chaos. Writing becomes the art of controlling the uncontrollable.

> I wanted to represent six characters who are searching for an author. The drama cannot be performed precisely because the author for whom they are searching is missing; and the play that we see is the story of their unsuccessful attempt, with all the tragedy that arises from the fact that these six characters have been rejected.[2]

The preface to *Sei personaggi in cerca d'autore* is in its turn a postscript to three of Pirandello's short stories; the little-known *Persone* (*Persons*) of 1906, *La tragedia di un personaggio* (*The Tragedy of a Character*) of 1911 and *Colloqui coi personaggi* (*Conversations with the Characters*) of 1915. Although written over a period of sixteen years, the protagonists nonetheless speak with one voice: words, phrases, indeed entire paragraphs are handed down from one character to the next so they stand as a distinctive group. Each of these tales is about a confrontation between a character and the author, in which the character eventually leaves, his request unfulfilled. Where the play, however, presents the events from the characters' point of view and the preface describes them as the author experienced them, the stories try to do justice to both parties in the dispute. The setting is always the same; the author's study, but run along the lines of the many provincial lawyers' offices that appear so frequently in Pirandello's work. On the closed door with its brass plaque are hung the hours when the author is available for consultation; outside the clients queue respectfully, patiently awaiting their turn. Once summoned, they are closely questioned and note is taken of their personal details; although status and trappings align the writer's activity with the lawyer's the proceedings within the office suggest something else again – a doctor perhaps, or a psychiatrist. The characters who dominate these stories are more determined than their peers; a spiritualist, Leonardo Scotto, and a philosopher, Dr Fileno, protagonists respectively of the first two tales, force their way to the front of the queue, while in the third story a half-blind individual pushes his way past a sign announcing in a *pastiche* of bureaucratic Italian that audiences have been suspended because of the war and characters unable to wait are invited to collect their letters of application, before seeking assistance from other quarters. They resemble each other in personality traits too; they are all three obsessive, insistent, humourless and garrulous.

It is a commonplace for writers to discuss their literary characters as though they were living beings, with the suggestion that they themselves are givers of life; culture's attempt to rival nature. And Pirandello is no exception, as we can see in a speech Dr Fileno makes in *La tragedia di un personaggio* where he extols the condition of eternal life offered by a literary paternity over the fugacity of mortal life afforded by maternal nature:

> . . . we are living beings, more alive than those who breathe and wear clothes: less real perhaps, but more true! There are so many ways of coming into existence, dear sir; and you are well aware that nature uses the instrument of human imagination to pursue her work of creation. And those who are brought into existence by that creative activity which resides within the human spirit are ordained by nature to a life far superior to that of creatures born of mortal woman. He who is born a character . . . may scorn death.[3]

What makes Pirandello's representation of the creative act singular, however, is that his characters are shown as having a complete existence of which they are fully cognizant before they meet with the author. Dr Fileno is a typical case. After an ill-conceived appearance in another writer's novel, he pushes his way to the front of the queue and demands an audience with Pirandello. Our author is already familiar with his circumstances, having spent the previous night reading the novel in question; and he has seen that Fileno's problem is that his potential for self-realization as a character has been crushed by the counter-demands made of him by the plot. What is interesting is that Pirandello discusses the relationship between plot and character in terms of psychology rather than aesthetics; by refusing to relinquish control of the narrative, the author has denied the literary character a life of his own. In Pirandello's presentation of creativity, the writer becomes the medium through which the character can materialize and give expression to himself. Even the protagonist of *Colloqui coi personaggi*, who seems to have no previous literary embodiment, appearing as if from nowhere, is none the less fully himself: as a character ('personaggio') he is a 'creature enclosed within his ideal reality, outside the transitory contingencies of time'. Although these scenes bear some resemblance to a Romantic idea of the figure of the artist, they offer a radical revision of what creativity itself means. By presenting in a literary work the characters as they were when he first visualized them, Pirandello shows us that they remain at the same stage of ideation. Gone is the view that the artist is effecting a process of transformation with the materials to hand, and in its place is a model in which the author intuits, without attempting to intervene or change, the characters as they present themselves to him. (It is another matter entirely that we, as readers, may suspect those characters of representing so many aspects of Pirandello's own psyche, neatly 'characterized' in order to lend them distance.)

Given that such are the conditions of their coming into being, one might well ask in what sense it is possible to describe these creatures as 'living', in the way Pirandello does when he refers to them as 'more alive than those who breathe' (see above). Once again we have to return to Pirandello's representations of creativity to understand the significance of the word. Behind the title *Sei personaggi in cerca d'autore* is the supposition that a literary character can exist without an author and indeed without a text; the six who appear on stage are in a worse situation than their predecessors in the short stories, for they have been denied a textual existence by their original author. They are literary rejects, kept alive by their determination to find someone 'who would let them enter the world of art'. Individuated by the author as completely independent beings, unamenable to change, they demand of Pirandello representation, not realization. Theirs is not so much a birth as a re-birth. So urgent is their need to be inscribed in the literary text that they lay siege to Pirandello in his study; the Stepdaughter recalls those occasions in the play using exactly the same imagery as Pirandello adopts for his encounters in *Colloqui coi personaggi*; the evening draws in, the author too weary to turn on the light . . .

> It's true, I would go, would go to tempt him, time after time, in his gloomy study, just as it was growing dark, when he was sitting quietly in an armchair not even bothering to switch a light on but leaving the shadows to fill the room: the shadows were swarming with us, we had come to tempt him.[4]

Again, there is a covert suggestion that these obsessive temptations are shadowy psychic figurations of areas of the author's own persona, constantly threatening to overrun his normal repressive vigilance.

Although the quality of consciousness and the events that go to make a character's life are of the same order as human life, their existence is in other ways not comparable; for they live lives that are uncircumscribed by the constraints that operate on us. They live outside time, and beyond history. It is brought home to us when in *Colloqui coi personaggi* the character asks impassively of the author who is anxiously perusing the newspapers for reports on Italy's declaration of war against Austria, 'War! What war?'. Untouched by the contingent, they are inaccessible to change – they are outside time: fixed, immutable presences. In his *Interpretation of Dreams* (1900), Freud had argued that the world of the dream and the unconscious were free from temporal logic. But what is remarkable here is the transformation of a raw, psychological imperative into a fully-fledged theory and practice of creativity. In his paper on *Repression* (1915), Freud describes the repressed as being quite simply that which is kept away from the conscious, and it may be that Pirandello's theory of creativity accommodates this idea, as well as Freud's view of art as a kind of wish-fulfilment. His *personaggi* become the vehicles whereby the unacceptable and the censored can return to the surface. They play out a drama that Pirandello, by insisting on their alterity, disowns. In *Sei personaggi in cerca d'autore* stage directions emphasize the great divide that exists between the 'us', the actors, and the 'them', the characters; their otherness is communicated visually by masks and stiffened, heavy dress:

> The characters must not appear as *phantoms* but as *artificial realities* created out of unvarying fantasy. In this way they appear more real and consistent than the changeable naturalness of the Actors. Masks will help to give the impression of figures created through Art, each fixed unvaryingly in the expression of his or her basic feeling.[5]

But if there is no possibility of development or change, why should characters desire so urgently a literary existence? The characters note in no uncertain terms that where we are born to die, they aspire to eternal life; in the same way that artistic failure is the death of a character, success creates the conditions for its immortality. Morality and virtue are unimportant in the quest for eternal life, and Fileno points his finger at Don Abbondio, the fearful, cowardly village priest immortalized by Manzoni in his historical novel *I promessi sposi* (*The Betrothed*). But their circumstances also reveal other reasons for desiring a life in art that neither they nor their author mention. Only when we compare their lives to the human condition do we see what they are spared. Injustice, misunderstanding, incomprehension is their lot as much as it is ours, but living in an immobile reality, the catastrophe is always foreknown. For those of us living in historical time, as Pirandello never tires of showing, life is a concatenation of arbitary events which are as unpredictable as they are far-reaching; in *Enrico IV*, a nameless young aristocrat falls from a horse and for the next twelve years believes that he is the German Emperor; in *Cosi è (se vi pare)*, (*So It Is (if That's How You Think It Is)*), the woman survivor of an earthquake becomes an enigmatic presence with a mislaid identity; in *Il fu Mattia Pascal* (*The Late Mattia Pascal*), a suicide's corpse is wrongly identified and the protagonist has the chance of a new life. Pirandello's work is not about evolutionary processes, the slow unfolding of a life, but about change that is as capricious as it is sudden, or perhaps about the sudden revelation of hidden aspects of the self.

In Pirandello's fiction and drama, the individual has no secure, stable being in and of itself, and the social dispossesses him of all personality. When the mystery woman in *Cosi è (se vi pare)* is trapped by a local inquisition of worthy townspeople who can no longer contain their impatience to know who she really is, she tells them infuriatingly, that she is indeed *both* of the conflicting roles claimed for her; as for herself she has no identity other than that which others attribute to her. In Pirandello's dramatizations of the human condition a unitary self can only be achieved through psychosis; both Henry IV and Vitangelo Moscarda of *Uno, nessuno e centomila* (*One, No One, and a Hundred Thousand Others*) have to rupture all contact with reality before they can enter into possession of a self. Any fond lingering illusions we care to entertain about our coherence as self-determining subjects are firmly dispelled by Pirandello's fictions, but it is a nice irony that only through the cracks produced by a discontinuous psyche can his perfectly realized and centred literary characters emerge.

So far our attention has been on the modes of being that belong to the occupants of Pirandello's mind, and when we turn to look at the mechanisms which brought them into literary life, we find his customary clarity gives way to some perplexity. In the preface to *Sei personaggi in cerca d'autore*, as Pirandello reflects on how he hit on a solution to the problem the characters presented him with, his exposition yields to the acknowledgement that in reality he has little to recount: what took place obeyed its own laws and he can only stand back and marvel:

> If I think about it now, the fact that I sensed this necessity, that I found, unconsciously, the way to resolve it with a new perspective, and the way in which I achieved it, strike me as miraculous. The fact is that the play was really conceived in a moment of spontaneous illumination of the imagination when, by a miracle, all the elements of the spirit come together and work in divine harmony.[6]

This was not the first time Pirandello had described the creative mind at work. In the same year as *La tragedia di un personaggio* (1911), he published a *roman à clef* entitled *Suo marito* (*Her Husband*) (shortly before his death in 1936, he began working on a revised edition with a new title, *Giustino Roncella nato Boggiòlo*) based, much to her displeasure, on the Sardinian novelist and Nobel prizewinner Grazia Deledda. As an entertaining satire on the pretensions and greed of Roman *letterati* it anticipates the more sombre analysis of the nascent film-industry at Cinecittà in *Quaderni di Serafino Gubbio operatore* (first published in 1915 under the title *Si gira* (*Diary of a Cameraman*)). As a portrait of an artist, his choice of a protagonist at two removes from himself, another writer of the other sex, allows for a less defensive study of what is singular about the creative personality. Although he shows himself in the preface to *Sei personaggi in cerca d'autore* to be the losing side in the battle with his characters, through the protagonist Silvia Roncella the novel emphasizes another aspect: the dimension of fear. What were later to become 'miracles', 'divine harmony' and 'flashes of insight', are perceived here as malevolent presences beyond her control; the divine is demonic, illumination is possession. Silvia is incapable of sustaining a sense of selfhood; in the absence of any fixed psychological identity, she finds herself living 'with great anxiety, the extraordinary, disordered mobility of her inner being', where the strangest ideas 'darted through her mind and frightened even her'.[7]

Fear attendant upon the absence of knowledge or certainty about the self and its relation to the world motivates Pirandello's early essays written after a period in Bonn, 1889–91, where he studied philology. His growing familiarity with modern German culture exploded any residual belief in the existence of a given reality whose characteristics could be commonly agreed on, and notwithstanding his deep admiration for his fellow Sicilian writer Giovanni Verga, he found his aesthetics of *verismo* (realism) philosophically untenable. Pirandello was too influenced by idealist thinking to share Verga's confidence in a verifiable reality. But coming from Sicily with its highly codified, authoritarian structures where Church, family and community practised an effective and rapidly internalized social and moral control that went unchallenged, Nietzschean relativism held out no heady promises to Pirandello. Quite the contrary; in those early essays we see all the signs of what Robert Brustein recently diagnosed as 'Cartesian anxiety', namely 'that dread of madness and chaos where nothing is fixed, where we can neither touch bottom, nor support ourselves on the surface'.[8] In 'Arte e coscienza d'oggi' ('Art and consciousness today') (1893),[9] Pirandello paints a bleak picture of the crisis that has hit modern consciousness; exacerbated, he argues, by the intellectual and scientific pusillanimity of his age which has sent the older generation scuttling back to the consolations of religion, while the younger, trapped in the crossfire of conflicting philosophies, sinks ever deeper into the quagmires of neurosis. An interest in recent theories of the self did not help him out of his pessimism, but it was to provide him with the basis for his understanding of the human psyche. Physiological and materialist accounts of genius by Cesare Lombroso in *Genio e follia* (1864) and Max Nordau in *Entartung* (1892), among others, which argued that genius and insanity were related through a common ancestry in pathological degeneration, were dismissed by Pirandello as insensitive and stupid. What he does share with them, however, is the unstated assumption that the creative disposition has physical properties that are unique to it; what he dissociates himself from is the belief that these are in any way 'abnormal'.

Pirandello was an intuitive and practical thinker who always looked to theory for a confirmation of what he had experienced. Although just three years separate Freud's *Jokes and their Relation to the Unconscious* (1905) from Pirandello's own *L'Umorismo* (*On Humour*) (1908),[10] and Pirandello had an excellent knowledge of German, there are no indications at any stage in his career that if he knew Freud's work, it held any interest for him. Only in 1934, while revising *Suo marito*, did he add Freud to Nietzsche and

Bergson, three indispensable names for a lady of fashion to refer to. Unlike Freud's work where humour is related primarily to language and is connected obliquely to that which cannot be said, Pirandello shares with Bergson, whose own study *Le Rire* appeared in 1900, the view that comedy is provoked by emotional insensibility on the part of the spectator, but he goes on to distinguish it from his real interest, humour, which he argues develops from an understanding of, and therefore empathy with, the subject's plight. In a sense Pirandello never needed Freud; the preceding phase of dynamic psychiatry not only provided what he found to be a valid interpretation of the psyche, it also gave him the basis for a theory of creativity – an area of enquiry where Freud proved himself to be notoriously unsatisfactory, when in a more sophisticated re-working of positivist theories he aligned the artist with the neurotic; both engaged in finding imaginary consolations for a disappointing reality.

It was in Alfred Binet's remarkable account of polypsychism or multiple personality , *Les Altérations de la personnalité*, [11] that Pirandello found the catalyst to his future writings. On the basis of his experiences with hysterics, Binet argued that we each of us harbour within ourselves a colony of sub-personalities, any one of whom might at any time take over from the conscious self. The idea of a precariously perched self, ready at the drop of a hat to be jettisoned in favour of another personality with its own intelligence and consciousness, was one that captivated Pirandello. Although it has often been claimed that Pirandello was first made aware of the fragility of the psyche when, after the birth of their first child in 1903, his wife Antonietta manifested signs of an instability which gradually became chronic and led to her confinement in an asylum in 1918, her condition only confirmed what he had been arguing in his essays over a decade earlier. She did, however, provide him with the painful first-hand experience of how others effectively dispossess us of our personality, for she was victim of a jealousy so pathological that her husband and later her children were unable to recognize themselves in her projection of them. The suffering that the gap between our own perception of ourselves and the personality projected on to us by others can cause is articulated by the Father in *Sei personaggi in cerca d'autore*.

In Pirandello's fiction metaphysical insecurity is wedded to psychological instability; and even the most pragmatic and down-to-earth of personalities can fall victim to other selves. Bobbio, protagonist of the short story *L'avemaria di Maria* (1912) suffers like many of his author's characters from a chronic, recurrent toothache (in one of Pirandello's letters, he attributes Schopenhauer's misanthropy to toothache: experience here too, one suspects, has had a hand), and under the stress, another self emerges; the atheist is replaced by a pious churchgoer. Appalled at this other self he rushes to the dentist to have all his teeth extracted. Bobbio does not lack insight into the mysteries of the self, he simply cannot apply it to his own circumstances. What he demonstrates is that while one can live with the knowledge of one's own psychic instability, it is of no help when one undergoes the experience of its disintegration. The provincial Bobbio finds a parallel for the relationship between 'conscious' and 'unconscious selves' in the image of the well whose watery surface hides inaccessible depths. His simile is framed by a translation of one of Binet's most repeated observations and the narrator's own elaboration of it:

> What we know about ourselves is however only a part, perhaps a tiny part, of what we are without realizing it. Bobbio in fact was in the habit of saying that what we call consciousness is comparable to the little bit of water that is visible in the shaft of an unfathomable well. And perhaps he meant by this that there are perceptions and actions beyond the limits of memory that remain unknown to us because really they are no longer ours, but belong to us as we once were, with feelings and thoughts long forgetfulness has already dimmed, effaced, extinguished in us, which on being unexpectedly brought back by a sensation, be it taste, colour or sound, can still give signs of life and show that within us there lives on a different unsuspected being.[12]

Not only is Binet's voice heard in the above extract, but Pirandello's reference to involuntary memory, stimulated by 'taste, colour or sound' anticipates Proust and *A la recherche du temps perdu*, and so draws together Paris and Sicily, two social and cultural realities separated by geography and chronology. Many of Pirandello's ideas derive from the positivist and spiritualist writer Gabriel Séailles who was in turn a major influence on Henri Bergson; both the writer and the philosopher took from Séailles the concept of a self made up of 'fluid inner processes', a succession of selves which flow, or as Bergson expresses it in *Essai sur les données immédiates de la conscience* (1888), 'melt into one another'.

An important distinction has to be made, however, between Modernist writers such as Proust, Svevo, Joyce and Woolf, who offer the reader subtle descriptions of the fine shifts of personality that we undergo according to the people and the circumstances we encounter, and the solitary road Pirandello takes us down where identity vanishes under pressure from other beings who have taken up residence within us, like parasites on their host. As these presences often come from elsewhere, they can neither confer on us a history, nor offer us self-knowledge.

Behind Pirandello's phantasmagoric world lies one disturbing image which is of the mind we possess but do not control. In his early essays he describes it as a space invaded by what at one point are opposing armies locked in battle under cover of darkness, at another are figures weighed down with despair. A few years later, these scenes give rise in his fiction to a paradigm of the mind as a habitat for an eclectic and motley assortment of occupants of unknown provenance. Sometimes they take over completely: in the short story *Quand'ero matto* (*When I was Mad*) (1901), the brain is presented as a private dwelling-house which becomes in moments of insanity a public lodging-place: 'I had in fact become an inn open to everyone. And if I tapped my forehead, I felt that there were always people lodging there.'[13] In *Suo marito* a serious writer, Maurizio Gueli, describes his mind as being the victim of 'the usual farce of the four or five or ten or twenty argumentative beings, that each man, according to his capacity lodges within him'. In *Il fu Mattia Pascal* and *Quaderni di Serafino Gubbio, operatore* the inn becomes the *piazza* – an open space accessible to all-comers. The imagery is shared by the leading spiritualist writers of his day; here is Annie Besant describing the same phenomenon in her *A Study of Consciousness* (1904): 'Some of the queer spectres and dainty figures that arise from the sub-conscious in us do not belong to us at all, but [. . .] are our guests, inhabiting our body as a lodging-house.'[14]

One does not have to look far for the sources of Pirandello's own interest in spiritualism. On his return to Rome after two and a half years in Bonn, he found himself among a circle of friends who occasionally gathered around a fellow Sicilian, the writer Luigi Capuana, whose own wide-ranging study of psychic and metaphysical phenomena *Spiritismo?* had been published in 1884, and whose *La scienza della letteratura* (1902) includes a discussion of the analogies that can be made between spiritual communication and the creative process. Other sources are acknowledged in *Il fu Mattia Pascal* when we are introduced to the small but discriminating theosophical library belonging to Anselmo Paleari, kept in the Roman apartment where Mattia rents a room. (It is, incidentally, Anselmo who destroys Leonardo Scotto's hopes of becoming a literary character in the meta-story *Persone*, for when Scotto appears with a spiritualist work under his arm Pirandello tells him that having just finished with a character such as he, there is no possibility of his repeating the experiment: 'I remember very well just how much trouble I had to take not to let him appear boring.') Not only are the authors included in Anselmo's library listed, but in the first serialized version of the novel, chapter V, 'Maturazione', opens with a long extract from C. W. Leadbeater's *The Astral Plan*. This passage, omitted in subsequent editions, suggests that ideas and desires can be so strongly projected by an individual that they then acquire an embodied life of their own, which is fully independent of the generating mind:

> I have just recently read in a book that our thoughts and desires are incorporated in a plastic essence in the invisible world that surrounds us and soon are modelled into shapes of human beings, whose appearances correspond to their inmost nature, and once they are formed these beings are no longer under the control of he who generated them, but enjoy their own life, whose duration depends on the generating thought or desire.[15]

The idea that a psychological state can be projected on to 'a plastic essence [. . .] whose appearance corresponds to its inmost nature' brings to mind the stage directions that accompany the Characters when they first appear in *Sei personaggi in cerca d'autore*: each one is to wear a mask which expresses their fundamental emotional trait – so the Mother appears with the mask of suffering, the Father with that of remorse and so on. And later in the play the Father will apply the same concept to his condition as character when he describes how, once ideated, he is free of authorial control:

> When a character is born, he immediately acquires such a degree of independence of his own author that he can be imagined by everybody in many other situations where the author never thought of putting him. Sometimes he may also acquire a meaning that the author never dreamt of giving him.[16]

With the unconscious humour that characterizes much spiritualist writing, Leadbeater goes on to express relief at the thought that most of us are incapable of the intellectual tenacity needed to produce these forms. According to Pirandello, too, the distinction between the creative and the non-creative mind is that the former has the capacity to accommodate and sustain a much richer and more varied psychic life. In an early essay written in response to current positivist thought which saw genius as a manifestation of a degenerate mind, Pirandello presents an alternative portrait of the artist who, as active control over consciousness gives way, is ready to capture in pen and ink the newly emergent creatures:

> The elements that make up the artistic spirit are considerably more numerous and more various than those of an ordinary spirit. And when, in the moment of inspiration, the artist's normal consciousness loses its bearings, and breaks down in turmoil, then he truly composes, constructs and creates from elements of his own spirit, other characters, other individuals in himself, each with its own consciousness and living, active intelligence.[17]

Leadbeater also suggests that if the thought-form is powerful enough it can separate altogether from its generating mind and is capable of attaching itself to other beings who live in the material world; an insight which helps to explain the origins of the literary characters who queue outside Pirandello's study door in his three meta-stories.

So far we have looked behind the scenes of one of the most astonishing dramatizations of creativity this century, but an aspect of *Sei personaggi in cerca d'autore* has yet to be considered. When the family act out their drama on stage, one crucial figure is missing – the brothel-keeper, Madama Pace. Father and Stepdaughter prepare for her arrival in an episode which Pirandello called in the preface 'a break, a sudden shift in the scene's level of reality', where all semblance of theatrical convention is abandoned to allow for the representation of the author's 'imagination, in the act of creation'. Up to this point the whole play has involved staging the creation of an illusion of reality, now shattered by the introduction of another plane of reality. The company of actors mirrors the audience's incredulity as the garish and substantial Madama Pace materializes in the theatre and moves towards the set, attracted by the trappings of her trade. The procedures adopted in this *mise-en-abyme* bear more than a passing resemblance to a séance; the concentrated mental effort of the participants, the use of familiar objects from the spirit's past, her materialization *ex nihilo*; yet the scene also bears the hallmarks of the hyper-realism of the dream, where the image is overdetermined, a point of confluence for multiple emotional impulses.

Pirandello was not suggesting that the artist and the medium exercise identical skills; he clearly did not believe that the author was simply in the business of lending his pen to the spirits within him. On the contrary, all the representations of the relationship between author and character show it to be a matter of tough, sometimes even bitter negotiating, where both sides are struggling for supremacy. In the preface to *Sei personaggi in cerca d'autore* Pirandello argues that it is through their adversarial relationship that the characters acquire alterity; in layman's language, they learn to stand on their own two feet. Once they have outgrown their dependence on the helping hand extended to them in narrative, they can move straight to the stage. In the following description of the birth of a character, Pirandello can be seen putting to literary use a psychological process known as 'splitting' (*Spaltung*) discussed by Janet, Freud and Klein among others. It is an area in which Freud's links with preceeding dynamic psychiatry are more marked, for the term refers to the splitting of the content of consciousness into separate psychical groups which often occurs under hypnosis; it recalls the self-induced trance-like state of the medium:[18]

> They have already split off from me; they live on their own; they have acquired voice and movement; so they have already become themselves in this battle for life that they have had to wage over me, dramatic characters, characters that can move and speak on their own; already see themselves as such; they have learnt to defend themselves against me; they will continue knowing how to defend themselves against others. And so, here we are, we can let them go where dramatic characters usually go to have a life: on a stage. And let's see what will happen.[19]

It is impossible to judge how far Pirandello accepted the claims made by spiritualism. In *Il fu Mattia Pascal*, in what he calls the 'ashtray' of Italy, post-Umbertine Rome, spiritualism offers consolation to the helpless and the powerless. As in Svevo's *La coscienza di Zeno*, the séance presented here is a richly comic episode in which the activities of the beyond provide a cover for other less unworldly activities – kisses are exchanged, money is stolen – but none the less the disbelieving protagonist finds he cannot explain in rational terms some of the phenomena that do occur. After he has abandoned his wife and native village, he learns that a corpse has been mistakenly identified as his, freeing him to start a new life, reborn as Adriano Meis. He also discovers in the pages of a theosophical book an explanation for his own condition. But the auspicious beginnings soon peter out as he painfully learns that like the 'living dead', he is alive but not living, attracted to life's margins but unable to participate. Paleari's library teaches him that 'the dead, the truly dead, found themselves in an identical condition to mine, in their shells of *Kâmaloca*.' Literally 'place of desire', *Kâmaloca* refers to the destination of those who are as yet unable to sever their emotional ties with this world. It was the subject of Pirandello's one-act spiritualist play *All'uscita* (1916), whose title refers to the gateway at the back of the cemetery that the spirits pass through on their way to the next world, having left their bodies behind. The cast includes a child with a half-eaten pomegranate, a woman murdered by her lover, a philosospher too concerned for the land he once tended – characters who have been ejected violently or abruptly from life and yet who retain strong attachments to it.

The concern for how a play comes into being that characterizes *Sei personaggi in cerca d'autore* has vanished in Pirandello's other great testament to the creative mind, his last, unfinished play *I giganti della montagna* (*The Mountain Giants*). If one judges a man's life by external events alone, it should have been a relatively tranquil time for him. Acclaimed internationally, respected even in his native Italy, he had publicly joined the Fascist party in 1924, and so enjoyed favour with the regime as well. Fortunately, and typically, the myth-cycle that makes up his last three plays convey an altogether different mood. Pirandello's plays are often structured to appear unfinished; the play the actors are rehearsing in *Sei personaggi in cerca d'autore* is abandoned, *Ciascuno a suo modo* (*Each in His Own Way*) breaks off after two acts because of disruptions by members of the audience, in *Questa sera si recita a soggetto* (*Tonight We Improvise*) the actors are unable to complete the play as they come to identify with the story they improvise. *I giganti della montagna* was left unfinished because of the author's death in 1936; none the less it was a play he had been working on for some eight years (which was much longer than was customary for him) and it is a play of immense difficulty for both producer and audience. In his novel *Suo marito* Pirandello still held to the belief that some kind of dialogue, however tenuous, was possible between author and audience; a hope that was he was later to lose. In his last play, the public is represented on stage by the 'giants' who have an appetite for entertainment, not theatre, and in a play-within-a-play a tragic attempt to perform before them leads to the slaughter on stage of the leading actress and the dismemberment of two of the company. Giorgio Strehler, who directed the play for the first time in 1945, summed it up as 'pure theatre' showing 'the creative spirit as it springs straight from the poet's mind', but unlike Pirandello's previous representations of creativity the fantasies are now persecutory and beyond a return to reality. The play's principal protagonist, Cotrone, is sorcerer and artist, the necromancer's cave has become the artist's laboratory where this world and others meet. An exile from life, he lives in a world of phantasms and dreams 'on the edge' of life: his villa, like the brain, is 'an arsenal of apparitions': 'All those truths that consciousness rejects, I bring them forth from the secret places of the senses: or, they are from the caverns of instinct, when they are most dreadful.'[20] The writer unable to serve notice on life walks the tightrope between sanity and madness, control and chaos, one step back to safety and his literary creations slip away into the shadows, one step too far forward and he himself is precipitated down into the 'black abyss' inhabited by the 'gloomy phantasms'. Cotrone's words are Pirandello's too:

> And the true miracle, believe me, will never be the performance, it will always be the imagination of the poet in which these characters are born, living, so living that you can see them, even if they do not exist in the body.[21]

Notes

1 Pirandello's complete works, originally published in ten volumes as the *Opera omnia* (Mondadori, Milan, 1941), is gradually being replaced by a new definitive edition with textual variants, *Opere di Luigi Pirandello* ('I Meridiani', Mondadori, Milan, 1973-). My references will, where possible, be to the new edition.

2 *Opera omnia, Maschere nude*, vol. I, p. 18. All translations, unless stated otherwise, are mine. Although the play is always accompanied by its preface in Italian, English translations do not, unfortunately, include it.

3 *Opere, Novelle per un anno*, vol. I, tomo 1, p. 821. For a selection of Pirandello's short stories in English which includes 'The Tragedy of a Character' see F. May, *Short Stories* (Oxford University Press, Oxford, 1965).

4 *Opera omnia, Maschere nude*, vol. I, pp. 108–9. Translation from Pirandello, *Three Plays* (Methuen, London, 1985), pp. 124–5.

5 *ibid.*, p. 35

6 *ibid.*, p. 18

7 *Opere. Tutti i romanzi*, vol. I, p. 783.

8 R. Brustein, *Beyond Objectivism and Relativism* (Blackwell, Oxford, 1983), p. 18.

9 See L. Pirandello, *Saggi, poesie, scritti varii* (a cura di Manlio Lo Vecchio-Musti, Milan, 1977), pp. 891–903.

10 *ibid.*, pp. 17–160. Pirandello, *On humor*, introduced, trans and annotated by A. Illiano and D. P. Testa (University of North Carolina Press, Chapel Hill, 1974).

11 A. Binet, *Les Altérations de la personnalité* (Félix Alcan, Paris, 1892). Outstanding as an introduction to the early years of dynamic psychiatry is Henri F. Ellenberger, *The Discovery of the Unconscious. The History and Evolution of Dynamic Psychiatry* (Allen Lane, London, 1970).

12 *Opere, Novelle per un anno*, vol. I, tomo 1, pp. 507–8. The original from Alfred Binet reads: 'et ce que nous connaissons de nous-même n'est qu'une partie, peut-être une très faible partie de ce que nous sommes': Binet, *Altérations*, p. 243.
13 *ibid.*, vol. II, tomo 2, p. 785.
14 Annie Besant, *A Study in Consciousness* (Theosophical Publishing Society, London, 1904), p. 213.
15 *Opere. Tutti i romanzi*, vol. I, p. 1010. Leadbeater's actual words were: 'The thought seizes upon the plastic essence, and moulds it instantly into a living being of appropriate form – a being which when once thus created is in no way under the control of its creator, but lives out a life of its own the length of which is proportionate to the intensity of the thought or wish which called it into existence. It lasts, in fact, just as long as the thought-force holds it together.' The Astral Plan (Theosophical Publishing Society, London, 1895), p. 34.
16 *Opera omnia, Maschere nude*, vol. I, p. 96.
17 'Scienza e critica estetica', *Marzocco*, 1 July 1900 (not included in the collected essays).
18 See J. Laplanche and J.-B. Pontalis, *The Language of psychoanalysis* (Hogarth, Press London, 1985), pp. 427–9.
19 *Opera omnia, Maschere nude*, vol. I, p. 16.
20 *ibid.*, vol. IV, p. 635.
21 *ibid.*, p. 635.

SUGGESTED READING

Bentley, E., *The Pirandello Commentaries*, North-Western University Press, Illinois, 1986.
Donati, C., *La solitudine allo specchio: Luigi Pirandello*, Lucarini, Rome, 1980.
Macchia, G., *Pirandello o la stanza di tortura*, Mondadori, Milan, 1981.
Vicentini, C., *L'estetica di Pirandello*, Mursia, Milan, 1970.

13

Antonin Artaud:
'Madness' and Self-Expression

DAVID KELLEY

Artaud is perhaps one of the most remarkable figures in recent cultural history. Known and read only by a small circle in his lifetime, he managed nevertheless to hit the pages of the English society magazine *The Tatler* with his production of *The Cenci*. Recognized in the 1950s and 1960s as one of the major influences on modern European drama, he had never really succeeded in putting his own ideas into practice (he himself admitted that *The Cenci* was only a step towards the realization of his notion of 'le théâtre de la cruauté'). Man of the theatre, actor and director, but also an extremely prolific poet, critic and essayist – his complete works run into sixteen volumes, few of which are widely read, even now; madman – he was commited to an asylum from 1937 to 1946; martyr, Christ figure, 'cabotin', paradigm of avant-gardist integrity and purity, retarded Romantic, theorist of the theatre whose ideas went beyond the possibilities of the theatre of his time, Artaud is a man of centrifugal, but ultimately illuminating, contradictions.

The problem is perhaps to decide why he remains so disquieting and disturbing. Are the attacks which he makes on Western culture, the whole tradition of European art and thought, those of a radical revolutionary, or do they derive from a misplaced nostalgia which has fundamentally misunderstood the necessary relationships between language, thought and feeling? Is the mental sickness of which he speaks systematically throughout his writings a personal and private affliction which separates him from 'normal' society, or is it a social phenomenon? If the first proposition is true, can this mental sickness be in some way related to artistic 'genius'? And if so, why should we think of it in such a way? If we are 'sane' and he is 'mad', why is it that we cannot simply dismiss his writings as the rantings of a madman? And this leads to the second question. Is Artaud driven into 'insanity' by the even more profound mental sickness of modern European society, or does he perceive his own problems as being a particularly acute manifestation of that sickness?

I do not here intend to enter a debate about what might constitute the tenuous frontier between 'normality' and 'madness', and even less to take issue on the question of whether it was right to commit Artaud or not, whether the doctor who was responsible for him at Rodez was a benevolent protector or a sadistic torturer – partly because I am not qualified to do so, but more importantly because it is precisely the ambivalence to be found in Artaud's own work in relation to the kind of questions enumerated above which makes him perhaps the most subversively disturbing writer of modern literature, eroding simultaneously our values and counter-values, our confidence in rationality and any faith which we might be tempted to place in the irrational and the unconscious as alternative modes of thought.

One theme is central to almost everything that Artaud ever wrote, and that is an extreme sense of ontological insecurity. It is, for example, at the basis of the correspondence with Jacques Rivière, which constitutes one of the opening texts of the complete works.[1] In this rather strange exchange of letters between a young poet and the editor of a review who had rejected his poetry, but who was prepared to publish instead the resulting correspondence, Artaud insists constantly on the sense of inner emptiness which dominates his experience: 'I would like you to understand clearly it is not a matter of the sort of partial-existence which comes from what is commonly called inspiration, but from total abstraction, from true wastage' (5 June 1923, CW, I, 28). And in *Umbilical Limbo*, published in 1925, he expresses this feeling even more acutely:

> You have to know the void as really finespun and organless. Opium's void has a form like a thinking brow which has determined the location of the black pit.
> I am talking about the lack of a pit, a sort of cold pictureless [*sans images/* unimaged] suffering, unfeeling, like the undescribable shock of abortions'
> (CW, I, 62)

The inner void is so profoundly empty that it can express itself only in terms of an *absence* of pit, a void of absence.

But it is perhaps worth looking more closely at these early definitions by Artaud of his mental state. His intense feelings of anxiety are intimately connected with problems of thinking and writing. In the correspondence with Jacques Rivière, he defines his problem, the fundamental lack of being, from which he feels himself to suffer, as a sense of dissociation from his own thought:

> I suffer from a fearful mental disease. My thought abandons me at every stage. From the mere fact of thought itself to the external fact of its materialisation in words. Words, the forms of phrases, inner directions of thought, the mind's simplest reactions. I am in constant pursuit of my intellectual being.
> (5th June 1923, CW, I, 27)

And in this text, the concluding phrase, in which he speaks of a constant pursuit of his intellectual being, suggests that when he talks of the mind here, he is not concerned, as Rivière seems to think, with the kind of abstract mental processes which preoccupy a Valéry, since in one of his replies he refers to the marvellous manner in which that poet managed to dramatize 'our autonomous intellectual operations' (25 March 1924, *CW*, I, 35) – but with a kind of mental integration with self. This is perhaps more clearly stated in a footnote to his 'Letter to the Legislator of the Drug Acts' from *Umbilical Limbo*:

> If I had what I know to be my thinking mind, I might perhaps have written *Umbilical Limbo*, only I would have written it differently. I have been told I am thinking because I have not completely stopped thinking and because in spite of everything, my mind keeps on a certain plane. It gives proof of its existence from time to time, but no one wants to acknowledge these proofs are weak and lacking in interest. But for me, thinking is something else besides being not quite dead, it means being in touch with oneself every moment. It means not to stop feeling oneself within one's inner being for one second, in the unformulated mass of our lives, in the stuff of our real lives. It means not feeling this fundamental chasm, this vital lack in oneself, it means always finding our thinking equal to our thinking, however insufficient the forms we are able to give them may be in other respects.
>
> (*CW*, I, 60)

Thought is clearly not here simply mental activity, cogitation, so much as a vital and even euphoric sense of fullness, integration with the world – the opposite precisely of the feeling of inner emptiness which he describes as being his habitual state of suffering.

The reference in this text to the insufficiency of the 'forms we are able to give them' hints at some of the ambivalences in Artaud's early work in particular concerning problems of form and language. In the correspondence with Jacques Rivière, he shows reluctance to correct the stylistic unevenness which appears to have been the editor's reason for refusing his poems, on the grounds that their diffuseness is precisely a function of the erosion of a sense of self, the disjunction between being and thought, which is at their origin:

> I fancied I had captured your attention, if not with the affectation [*le précieux* / precosity] of my verse, then at least by the rarity of certain phenomena of an intellectual order. This explicitly caused these poems not to be, could not be different than they were [*sic* in translation], despite the ability within me to polish them to the utmost perfection . . . This diffusion [*éparpillement* / diffuseness], these defective forms, this constant falling off in my ideas, must not be set down to lack either of practice or control of the instrument I was manipulating, of *intellectual development*. Rather to a focal collapse of my soul.
>
> (29 January 1924, *CW*, I 30–1)

But if here he seems to be suggesting that the fragmentation of his writing is adequate to its subject, that to write better would be to betray the profound sense of inadequacy that he is trying to articulate, elsewhere in the same correspondence the emphasis is different. He writes, for example, in the first of the published letters to Rivière, dated, as we have seen, 5 June 1923:

> My thought abandons me at every stage. From the mere fact of thought itself to the external fact of its materialisation in words. Words, the forms of phrases, inner directions of thought, the mind's simplest reactions, I am in constant pursuit of my intellectual being. Thus, when *I am able to grasp a form*, however imperfect, I hold on to it, afraid to lose all thought . . . This is also why I told you I had nothing further, no work in the offing, the few things I submitted to you being the vestiges of what I was able to salvage from the utter void.
>
> (CW, I, 28)

Here there is a similar relationship established between 'the mere fact of thought' and 'the external fact of its materialisation in words'. But the act of writing and structuring is evoked as part of a heroic struggle against the sense of abandonment of thought, and towards integration of thought and being; the written text is seen as a tiny victory over the void that threatens to engulf him. And in the letter of 6 June 1924, far from making claims for the 'imperfections' of his work as an adequate expression of his own inadequacy, he posits a different kind of language, one in which words are dense and active: 'They, [my weaknesses] come from a mind which has not considered its weakness. Otherwise it would spell it out in terse, forceful words [*mots denses et agissants* / dense and active words]' (CW, I, 41).

This suggests one of the possible differences between Artaud and the Surrealists, of whose group he was of course for a short time an active member. In his letter of 25 March 1924, Rivière warns Artaud of the dangers inherent in the Surrealist insistence on immediacy and automatism:

> I know, there is almost a lightheaded feeling in the instant [creation] radiates pure, in the moment when its stream flows straight from the brain and finds great areas, many spheres and many levels where it can spread out. This is the wholly subjective impression of complete freedom, even complete intellectual licence our 'Surrealists' have tried to express in the principle [*dogme*/dogma] of a fourth poetic dimension. Universal possibilities are translated into concrete impossibilities. The impression, once captured, engenders twenty more in revenge which paralyse us and ravage the mind's substance.
>
> (CW, I, 36–7)

But, a month later, in a letter dated 25 May, Artaud dismisses these dangers as far as they apply to himself, and underlines what separates him from the Surrealists. The transformation of the 'universal possible' into 'concrete impossibilities' is not for him a retribution and the sign of a modern sickness, but an experiential starting-point. That transformation, he writes:

is the result of physiological weakness, a weakness linked with what is commonly called the soul, our nervous energy emanating and solidifying round things. Our whole period suffers from this weakness, for example; Tristan Tzara, André Breton, Pierre Reverdy. Only their souls are not physiologically affected, not substantially affected. They are in all matters touching on other things, but not *outside thought*. Where then does this sickness stem from, is it really something in the spirit of the times, a miracle floating in the air, an evil cosmic prodigy or the discovery of a new world, a genuine extension of reality? Nevertheless it is still true that they do not suffer *and* I do, not only mentally but physically, in my everyday soul.

(CW, I, 40)

The 'almost . . . lightheaded feeling in the instant it radiates pure', of which Rivière speaks à propos of the Surrealists, is unknown to Artaud. His own suffering is *outside thought*; and the vitalism of the 'dense and active words' of my earlier quotation is something to which he hopelessly aspires. At the same time, he seems to take a certain pleasure in the specificity of his mental problems, of his failure to co-ordinate thought and being, and vehemently to deny that it is part of any *Zeitgeist* or collective malady:

What I am most concerned about is that no misunderstanding should creep in on the nature of the phenomena I have evoked in my own defence. The reader must believe in a genuine sickness, not just a phenomenon of the times, in a sickness which is near to the nature of man and his main expressive potential and applicable to a whole life.

(CW, I, 41)

In Artaud's dramatic theory similar themes are constantly to be found, but with different emphases. Perhaps, above all, the theatre seemed to offer him the possibility of discovering that language in which words might be 'dense and active', that language which he had failed to find in writing. For what Artaud finds anguishing in language is precisely what modern linguistics would define as its fundamental properties – that is, on one hand the arbitrariness of the sign, the lack of any necessary relationship between the signifier and what is signified, and on the other, the public and social nature of language, the fact that it is always the language of others. And some of the passages in *The Theatre and its Double* in which he speaks of the role of the actor in the theatrical experience suggest that at least part of the attraction of acting for him may have lain precisely in the extent to which it could be felt to resolve the extremely personal sense of rupture which he felt between language, thought and being.

It is interesting that in the correspondence with Jacques Rivière he should aspire to a language in which the words might be 'dense and active'. For, in the essay which serves as preface to *The Theatre and its Double*, 'Theatre and Culture', he plays on the possible double meaning of the word 'actor' – to act out a part and to act in the sense of carrying out an action. He makes a distinction between modern artistic representation and the primitive artistic language of the totem. The totem does not refer to an object. It identifies with it, and in this way magically captures and directs the vital forces of nature:

> The old totems; animals, rocks, objects charged with lightning, costumes impregnated with bestiality, and everything that serves to catch, tap and direct forces are dead to us, since we only know how to derive artistic or static profit from them, seeking gratification, not action [*un profit de jouisseur et non d'acteur* / a profit based on gratification, not on that of an actor].
> Now totemism acts because it moves, it is made to be enacted [*et il est fait pour les acteurs* / and is made for actors].
>
> (CW, IV, 3–4)

And for Artaud, who was an actor as well as a writer, this seems to have been a major source of attraction towards the theatre . For the duration of the performance, life or action, for the actor, coincides with thought in the concrete language which is the body and its gestures. So that the sense of authenticity of self which derives from the integration of language, thought and feeling is, however briefly, attained.

In his text on the Balinese theatre, Artaud speaks of actors as living and moving hieroglyphs. But the hieroglyph is precisely a form of writing in which the arbitrary relationship between the material form of the sign – or signifier – and what it signifies – the signified – is short-circuited, so that the disjunction between thought and language which Artaud finds so disquieting is obviated. Moreover, in another essay from *The Theatre and its Double*, 'An Affective Athleticism', he attempts to systematize the means by which an actor can communicate directly with the spectator, avoiding rational interpretation of meaning, by obliging the latter, according to principles which seem close to those of Chinese acupuncture, to mime internally what is being expressed.

It is this preoccupation which defines Artaud's notion of theatre – and technical innovations which have perhaps been his major influence on post-war theatre. It is hardly surprising that he should have been fundamentally opposed to a theatre based on the interpretation and representation of a pre-existing literary text. If the validity of the theatre depends on its capacity to reconcile within the living, moving hieroglyph of the actor those poles of experience which Artaud perceives as being radically sundered, then thought must clearly be immanent within the language by which it is articulated. This is more or less explicitly stated in the essay 'No More Masterpieces':

> Let us leave textual criticism to teachers and formal criticism to aesthetes, and acknowledge that what has already been said no longer needs saying; that an expression twice used is of no value since it does not have two lives. Once spoken, all speech is dead and is only active [*n'agit que* / only acts] as it is spoken. Once a form is used it has no more use, bidding man find another

form, and theatre is the only place in the world where a gesture, once made, is never repeated in the same way.

(CW, IV, 57)

Artaud's projected 'Theatre of Cruelty' did not of course propose to do away entirely with ordinary, spoken language. But words were not to be the primary element. He wanted them to be used with the value they acquire in dreams. He desired that is, the activation of the concrete vibratory qualities which words may acquire when projected into the theatrical space, as one amongst a series of means of expression (gesture, decor, sound effects) – one element in a total and active language. The function of that language is not so much to 'express' an interpretation of reality offered for the spectator to contemplate and reflect upon, as actively to impress itself upon the latter's perceptions below the level of consciousness, and in this way to modify his or her entire being.

The director, who in Artaud's theatre would take on the pre-eminence traditionally accorded in Western theatre to the author, should be concerned to orchestrate the elements of theatrical language, not in order to imitate the 'real', but in order to impose upon the audience a 'true illusion'. In practical terms this has perhaps been the principal significance of Artaud's theatre to those who have followed him: the clear affirmation of the theatre as a specific means of communication radically distinct from literature as such: the theatre as a language which functions, not merely consecutively, but also, and perhaps more significantly, spatially. It uses the three-dimensional space which the auditorium offers, and breaks down the barrier between actors and audience – a barrier which, in the kind of contemporary theatre which Artaud is criticizing, contributes towards the making of the play into an object of consumption, to be thought about and discussed perhaps by the spectators, but inoperative in terms of their lives. The theatre as Artaud conceived of it was to be a space surrounding the spectator, in which the action would occur on all sides and on all levels, forcing him or her into a psychological mimetism of the action, and inducing a trance-like hallucination.

His rejection of psychological analysis and social commentary in the theatre derive from a similar desire for a theatrical language in which thought is immanent rather than reflected, active rather than contemplative. This does not imply an 'art for art's sake' attitude on Artaud's part. On the contrary, he is attacking what he sees to be the fundamental gratuity of what passes for morally or politically committed art. He sees the traditional forms of moral and political commitment as being restricted to comment on the individual's psychological, moral or political relationships with the society in which he or she lives, and the theatre as offering this comment for intellectual or moral consideration on the part of the spectator, instead of acting upon the sensibility in an attempt to modify perception of the self in relation to the world. In 'Production and Metaphysics' he writes scornfully:

Given theatre as we see it here, one would imagine that there was nothing more to know than whether we will have a good fuck, whether we will go to war or be cowardly enough to sue for peace, how we will put up with our petty moral anxieties, whether we will become conscious of our 'complexes' (in scientific language) or whether our 'complexes' will silence us.

(CW IV, 28–9)

What he would like to do with the theatre is to redefine its psychological and social function – to use it therapeutically as a means of attacking the neuroses of society and curing what he sees as the social and cultural malady that derives from its debilitation and nerveless morality. And this implies not so much the desire for innovation within the traditions of Western European art as an attack on intellectualistic Western notions of art and its relations with society.

Correspondingly, in *The Theatre and its Double* Artaud's definition of the ontological problems he had been discussing with Jacques Rivière has shifted somewhat. In the correspondence with Rivière, in spite of the ambivalences I have noted, he had been primarily concerned to emphasize his particularity, and to dissociate himself from the 'Zeitgeist'. The erosion of any sense of being, experienced as a fundamental dissociation between language, thought and action, was seen as a personal and private sickness of the soul, but, paradoxically, as one that gave him importance, separated him from the mass, lent him identity. In the prefatory essay to *The Theatre and its Double* – and indeed throughout the volume – he defines, however, that same malady as a generalized sickness of Western society:

If confusion is a sign of the times, I see a schism between things and words underlying this confusion, between ideas and the signs that represent them.

   We are not short of philosophical systems; their number and contradictions are a characteristic of our ancient French and European culture. But where do we see that life, our lives, have been affected by these systems?

(CW, IV, 1)

What he perceives as the tendency to use language as a means of contemplating action and forms of action has meant that so-called 'civilization' has involved the severing of human beings from the metaphysical forces which constitute the essential life of the universe, and which remain central in spite of human culture: 'Let them burn down the library at Alexandria. There are powers above and beyond papyri. We may be temporarily deprived of the ability to rediscover these powers, but we will never eliminate their energy' (CW, IV, 3). With this acute sense of the modern curtailment of human potential, Artaud may remind us less of Freud and the 'discontents' engendered by repressive civilization, than of Jung, explorer of that reservoir of energies which is the 'collective unconscious'.

   Thus, in many places in *The Theatre and its Double* Artaud speaks of the theatre as a 'thérapeutique de l'âme' – a means of curing what he sees as the collective neurosis of modern society.

> I suggest theatre today ought to return to the fundamental magic notion reintroduced by psychoanalysis, which consists in curing a patient by making him assume the external attitude of the desired condition . . .
> Theatre is the only place in the world, the last group means we still possess of directly affecting the anatomy, and in neurotic, basely sensual periods like the one in which we are immersed, of attacking that base sensuality through physical means it cannot withstand.
>
> (CW, IV, 61)

In fact, the violent and anarchic disruption of the sensibility which is defined as the aim of theatre in what is probably the best known of the essays included in *The Theatre and its Double*, 'The Theatre and the Plague' is seen as a liberation of repressed areas of the unconscious, as a revelation and externalization – on a level which allows their sublimation – of the latent violence and cruelty which exist in each of us:

> If fundamental theatre is like the plague, this is not because it is contagious, but because like the plague it is a revelation, urging forward the exteriorisation of a latent undercurrent of cruelty through which all the perversity of which the mind is capable, whether in a person or a nation, becomes localised.
>
> (CW, IV, 19)

and:

> A real stage play disturbs our peace of mind, releases our repressed unconscious, drives us to a kind of potential rebellion (since it retains its full value only if it remains potential), calling for a difficult heroic attitude on the part of the assembled groups.
>
> (CW IV, 17)

Thus, Artaud's rejection of 'psychological' drama is a rejection of 'psychological' content. He wants theatre to have an active effect on the psyche. The theatre exists in order to force men to drop the mask of civilization, to re-perceive themselves in their relationship with what Artaud saw as the deterministic metaphysical forces of Becoming, and to adopt a stance of stoic lucidity in the face of this determinism.

This detached awareness is implicit in the word 'cruelty' used as a title and rallying cry for his projected theatre. In spite of the fact that violence – and particularly erotic violence – are clearly an important constituent of the plays he intended to put on, and indeed of *The Cenci*, the play he did manage to put on, he goes to considerable lengths to define his notion of cruelty in metaphysical terms, as a lucid acceptance of the necessary cruelty of the universe, a cruelty which man cannot escape, since he is subjected to change, and engaged in the processes of life and death:

In fact, cruelty is not synonymous with bloodshed, martyred flesh or crucified enemies. Associating cruelty and torture is only one minor aspect of the problem. Practising cruelty involves a higher determination to which the executioner-tormentor is also subject and which he must be *resolved* to endure when the time comes. Above all, cruelty is very lucid, a kind of strict control and submission to necessity. There is no cruelty without consciousness, without the application of consciousness, for the latter gives practising any act in life a blood red tinge, its cruel overtones, since it is understood that being alive always means the death of someone else.

(CW, IV, 77–8)

It is in this sense that he suggests, rather tentatively, and almost with a hint of desperation, that the therapeutic effect of his projected theatre might be a way of restoring to society a feeling of religious awe, a sense of that inner plenitude and life which he felt lacking in himself, and yet to which his attitude was so ambivalent, while at the same time giving back to the theatre an active social role as mediator of the metaphysical – in short, of re-integrating art and life.

This aim also reveals a further degree of ambivalence in Artaud's proposals for the theatre. Their very radical nature derives, paradoxically, from a rather nostalgic primitivism. This derivation is present, firstly, to the degree that Artaud's aspiration towards a vitalism defined in both metaphysical and social terms could be seen as a retarded Romantic trait. Romantic writers like Chateaubriand and Musset defined the *mal de siècle* from which their heroes suffered in rather similar terms to the those of the collective malady defined by Artaud in *The Theatre and its Double* – that is, as deriving from a schism between thought and action, language and feeling, occasioning in the individual a sense of alienation from self, from society and from the world. And the attraction of energy and vitality as offering a sense of being in a world in which metaphysical certainties are absent – an attraction manifested in the work of writers like Baudelaire, Nietzsche and Rimbaud – is part of the legacy of the nineteenth century to be found in Artaud.

As in many Romantic writers the search for vitality and intensity as a means to the integration of the self with the universe is specifically defined in *The Theatre and its Double* in terms of a nostalgia for various forms of primitive or pre-industrial culture. This nostalgia is revealed, partly at least, in Artaud's choice of subject matter. 'The Conquest of Mexico', which was to have been the first production of the 'Theatre of Cruelty', was chosen for its topicality, that is for posing the problem of colonialism. But the way in which the subject is described makes it clear that the play would have put forward in positive – and rather idealized – terms, the harmony, unity and intensity of the religious and cultural values of the Mexican civilization destroyed by Spanish colonialism. And the text in which this proposed production is described follows a more general definition of the subject-matter of the 'Theatre of Cruelty' as a 'return to ancient myth':

it will bring major considerations and fundamental emotions back into style, since modern theatre has overlaid these with the veneer of pseudo-civilised man.

These themes will be universal, cosmic, performed according to the most ancient texts taken from Mexican, Hindu, Judaic and Iranian cosmogonies, among others.

(CW, IV, 94)

Moreover, if Artaud suggests that it will be through staging and not through the texts themselves that these ancient conflicts will be brought up to date in his theatre, it is clear that both the technical innovations he proposes and the notion of theatre as such which characterizes his project are strongly affected by a longing to return to a tradition of the past which seems to have been lost. Although he did not discover the Balinese theatre until 1931, when his ideas were already fairly well-formed, the ritual, non-verbal, language of gesture, which he wants to make the basis of theatrical expression, is often defined in terms of the Oriental theatre, which he sees as having managed to conserve intact its millenary traditions. And as has already been suggested, the search to integrate language and life, expressed in 'Theatre and Culture', is defined in terms of the primitive totem. Further, Artaud's mistrust of abstract and discursive language as a tool for thought can be seen in terms of what might be defined as 'mythical' thought, a mode of thought characteristic of primitive peoples, which fails to distinguish between the object and the name, the reality and the fantasy – the kind of thinking that Freud had attributed to the childhood of races and individuals. Through rituals the individual seeks some kind of communication with cosmic rhythms, attempts to learn the secrets of life and death, to liberate himself from his particularity and find oneness with the whole of nature.

It is the rediscovery of this kind of experience that Artaud seems to be looking for in the theatre, when he says that he would like to reject men in their individual relationships with society in favour of Mythical entities; when he firmly defines his theatre as being one which deals with cosmic and metaphysical ideas – as being 'active metaphysics' – or when, in 'Alchemist Theatre', he refers to the Orphic and Eleusian mysteries as an annihilation of conflicts and a melting of appearances in a single expression analogous to the spiritualized gold of the alchemists. And, even though he takes care to indicate that the Balinese theatre is a profane and not a sacred theatre, what impresses him most about it is 'this impression of a higher, controlled life . . . like a profane ritual', and the 'solemnity of a holy ritual' (CW, IV, 42) which it seems to embody.

All this suggests certain problems inherent in Artaud's theatrical project, perhaps relevant to his failure actually to put it into practice. His diagnosis of the ontological problems (which he once defined in the correspondence with Jacques Rivière as being particular to himself) as a generalized malady affecting modern Western society, and his perception of the theatre as a possible means of cure, lead him into a particularly ambivalent definition of the social role of theatre. His projected theatre is at once fundamentally radical in its innovations and nostalgic in its aspirations. He wants the theatre to be a force to change society, but at the same time the terms in which it might conceivably effect that change demand that the change be already made. He wants the theatre to act therapeutically, by recreating a sense of metaphysical awe, by re-integrating culture and life, making of culture an active mode of thought rather than a contemplative one. But the models which are proposed for that theatre, whether popular or religious, presuppose the theatre to be already fulfilling that role, to be already an active part of human experience rather than a value for intellectual and commercial consumption.

The essay 'No More Masterpeices' focusses attention on this particular problem in an especially acute way. By rejecting a specific tradition of European theatre, Artaud appears to be rejecting any permanent values in art, and very clearly inserting his projected theatre into an avant-garde notion of permanent innovation. In a passage which I have already quoted in a different context, he writes:

> Let us . . . acknowledge that what has already been said no longer needs saying; that an expression twice used is of no value since it does not have two lives. Once spoken, all speech is dead and is only active as it is spoken. Once a form is used it has no more use, bidding man find another form, and theatre is the only place in the world where a gesture, once made, is never repeated in the same way.
>
> (CW, IV, 57)

Yet, in the same essay, he also attacks the individualism and anarchy of the avant-garde, and looks back to a cultural and theatrical tradition based on the permanence of ritual gestures and myths.

This poses obvious practical problems. A religious, ritualistic theatre, a theatre which is to generate a genuine metaphysical awe in the spectator, and for whom it is an active part of the intellectual processes, implies an audience which shares its assumptions. And it is part of the diagnosis – offered by Artaud in *The Theatre and its Double* – of the crisis which besets the twentieth century that such an audience does not exist. The very difficulties which Artaud experienced in trying to put his ideas into practice suggest that this was a true assumption. Moreover, the only structures within which a play could be performed were those of the commercial or institutionalized theatre. Quite apart from the problems involved in financing a production according to the rules of the market place or public patronage, this necessarily affected the responses and expectations of an audience, who, having paid for their seats, expected some kind of return in terms of entertainment or instruction. Almost by the terms of Artaud's definition of the problem, they were likely to be lacking in metaphysical responses of the kind on which he wanted to draw.

Artaud asserts that he is 'not of the opinion that civilisation must change so that theatre can change', but when, a few lines later, he writes:

> Either we will be able to revert through theatre by present-day means to the higher idea of poetry underlying the Myths told by the great tragedians of ancient times, with theatre able once more to sustain a religious concept . . . or else we might as well abdicate now without protest, and acknowledge we are fit only for chaos, famine, bloodshed, war and epidemics,
>
> (CW, IV, 60–1)

the desperation in his tone suggests that he may well have been aware of the problem. True, in the essay 'An Affective Athleticism' he attempts to elaborate an objective gestural system operating on the spectator rather in the way in which – as he sees it – Chinese acupuncture operates on the patient, but this is perhaps one of the least convincing aspects of his theory. And it is perhaps above all the multi-dimensional assault on the senses of the audience – a vital part of the technical programme of the *Theatre and its Double* – which seeks to make up the deficiency, attempting to create, as a substitute for religious complicity, a trance-like hallucinatory state, analogous to the dance of the Dervishes.

That the light-show discotheque – which one might be tempted to see as one of the closest approaches to the realization of Artaud's 'Theatre of Cruelty' – should use the kind of technical effects of which he might have dreamed for a purpose precisely opposite to that sublimation of sexual appetite which was for him a major concern, suggests perhaps the uncertainty of effect of such techniques, and provides an ironic comment – either on the capacity of modern Western society to 'recuperate' even the most radical attempts to subvert it, or on the impossibly Utopian implications of Artaud's projects.

And the experience of the asylum at Rodez seems, not only to have destroyed the rather fragile hope that the theatre might in fact exert a therapeutic action on the soul, but also to have further shifted Artaud's perception of the relationship between his own ontological anguishes and modern social 'normality'. In the correspondence with Rivière, speaking of his anxiety when confronted with his sense of an inner absence and divorce from language, he revealed both a feeling of inadequacy and a consciousness of singularity. In *The Theatre and its Double* he makes a diagnosis of what he sees as a crisis of Western culture in terms which suggest very strongly a projection of his own anxieties, and perceives in the 'active' language of theatre not only a means of resolving those anxieties on a personal level but also of operating therapeutically on the collective problems of society.

In his essay on Van Gogh, published in 1947, Van Gogh's work is defined in a manner which broadly corresponds to Artaud's aims for the theatre and ot the distinction he had made, in the letters to Rivière, between himself and the Surrealists:

> I think that Gaugin believed that the artist has to seek symbol and myth, has to elevate things drawn from life to the status of myth
>   whereas Van Gogh believed that you have to deduce myth from the most everyday things of life.
>   In which I think, myself, that he was fucking right.
>   For reality is terrifyingly superior to any history, any fable, any divinity, any surreality.
>
> (OC, XIII, 29)

But he also goes one stage further, attempting to overturn the conventional notions of madness and sanity. What passes for madness in a society which is, at the very least, deeply disturbed, is a 'superior lucidity' whose divinatory faculties profoundly disturb the rational structures by which that society attempts to establish norms of behaviour. And, not unnaturally perhaps, given Artaud's recent past experiences, his venom is particularly directed towards practitioners of psychiatry as bastions and paradigms of a society which is itself psychologically deranged: 'Set against the lucidity of Van Gogh working, psychiatry is no more than a fortress for gorillas, who are themselves obsessed and persecuted, and who possess only, for the palliation of the most horrifying states of human anxiety and suffocation, a ridiculous terminology' (OC, XIII, 15).

Where does all this leave us? It is difficult, in reading Artaud's marvellously evocative and lucid descriptions of Van Gogh's paintings, not to empathize with his equation of genius with what society chooses to call madness, and to read, as he does, the word suicide as a transitive verb – to see Van Gogh as a superior being 'suicided' by society. And, as is clearly suggested by the text, to read, for Van Gogh, Antonin Artaud. Some years later Ronald Laing's *The Divided Self* would similarly argue that the so-called madman may simply be reacting to an unbearable situation, and fulfilling the role in which he is being cast by those around him who define themselves as 'sane'.[2]

But such an interpretation leaves many questions in its wake. If we accept Artaud's diagnosis of society as sick, and Western culture as the symptom of its disease, can we accept the rather desperate solutions he proposes in *The Theatre and its Double* as valid or viable ones? Given what we know and are aware of not knowing about language and the cosmos, can his neo-Romantic aspiration towards a revitalization of language and thought, towards a re-integration of man with the forces of the cosmos, possibly offer us anything?

The nostalagic radicalism of the idea of theatre projected in *The Theatre and its Double* is clearly felt with the utmost intensity and integrity. So much so that any attempt to put it into practice seems doomed to becoming mere 'recuperation'. Indeed, the play which Artaud did manage to stage, *The Cenci*, seems to have suffered from his own temptation towards recuperation – not least in the casting of the fashionable society woman, Ilya Abdy, in the principal female role. And this corresponds to the desire on the part of Artaud to which I referred at the beginning of this essay, that of acquiring a literary persona.

One thing is clear: to read Artaud is a profoundly disturbing experience, if only because he shuffles all the cards we are used to dealing with. In comparison with him, a Breton – the Breton of *Nadja*, for example – seems merely to be playing with the unconscious. Artaud's attack on the rational values of the 'sane' world of bourgeois society is extraordinarily powerful and convincing – as is his attack on the artistic tradition which he perceives to derive from that world. But, finally, the ambivalences of his own position in relation to these issues, and particularly his own uncertainty as to the status of his own extraordinary and yet strangely paradigmatic mental state in relation to that of the world against which he is reacting, makes it difficult to see in the unconscious or the irrational an alternative set of values.

Notes

1   References are to Antonin Artaud, *Collected Works*, trans. V. Corti (4 vols Calder and Boyars London, 1968), cited as *CW*; and for texts not included in this English version, to Antonin Artaud, *Oeuvres complètes* (Gallimard, Paris, 1961), cited as *OC*. In the case of the latter, the translations are my own. Artaud's work relies to a considerable extent on word association. Where, in V. Corti's translation, the text seems to me to fail to communicate this, particularly in cases where it would affect my argument, I have inserted an alternative translation with the original French, in square brackets.

    The present text owes much to the following works: Maurice Blanchot, *Le Livre à venir* 2nd edn (Gallimard, Paris, 1959); Jacques Derrida, *L'Ecriture et la différence* (Editions du Seuil, Paris, 1967); A. Virmaux, *Antonin Artaud et le théâtre* (Seghers, Paris, 1970).

2   R. D. Laing, *The Divided Self* (Tavistock Publications, London, 1960; repr. Pelican, Harmondsworth, 1977).

SUGGESTED READING

Bonardel, F., *Antonin Artaud: ou la fidélité à l'infini*, Ballant, Paris, 1987.
Charbonnier, G., *Antonin Artaud*, 5th edn, Seghers, Paris, 1976.
Esslin, M., *Artaud*, Collins-Fontana, London, 1976.
Garelli, J. *Artaud et la question du lieu: essai sur le théâtre et la poésie d'Artaud*, Corti, Paris, 1982.

Jenny, L., 'Le souffle et le soleil', in *La Terreur et les signes: Poétiques de rupture*, Gallimard, Paris, 1982.

Virmaux, A. *Antonin Artaud et le théâtre*, Seghers, Paris, 1970.

Sollers, P. (ed.), *Artaud*, 10/18, Paris, 1973.

14

Avant-garde Theatre and the Return to Dionysos: Nietzsche, Jung, Valle-Inclán, Lorca, Artaud

ALISON SINCLAIR

Of the many ways in which we might characterize the avant-garde, something which provides a central thread for our understanding is the idea that art should somehow deal with both the unconscious and with strong emotional experience that it is hard to stomach, that is to say that it should put us in touch both with those things of which we are unaware, and with those of which we would rather not be aware. The two are not necessarily mutually exclusive, since we may have repressed, and relegated to the unconscious, parts of our lives which we find unpalatable. These parts I shall for brevity label the 'guts' of experience. In seeking to re-acquaint us with those unknown or rejected parts of experience, avant-garde art exemplifies Breton's argument in the light of Freud, that by operating with the intellectual and conscious mind we are, as it were, dealing with the mere tip of the iceberg of man's total potential experience, and 'logical methods are applicable only to solving problems of secondary interest.' Breton does not, in theory, envisage a simple abandonment of reason: *au contraire*, he retains intellectual ambitions with respect to what is not intellectual, as did Freud. So while he declares 'the imagination is perhaps on the point of reasserting itself, of reclaiming its rights', he, like Freud, shows that he is convinced of the powers of the mind to discern, to analyse, and perhaps to tame: 'if the depths of our mind contain within it [*sic*] strange forces capable of augmenting those on the surface, or of waging a victorious battle against them, there is every reason to seize them – first to seize them, then, if need be, to submit them to the control of our reason.'[1]

Breton's fundamentally intellectual approach to the elements of life that remain to be integrated in our experience is not shared by all in the period. The notion of art as an activity which seeks to include the 'guts' of our experience is fundamental to those avant-garde artists who sought to bring art and life (and particularly art and politics) closer to one another in a direct manner through content (Expressionists, Surrealists, Futurists).

What I should like to concentrate on here is not the way in which any of the 'isms' strove to extend the boundaries of art in general, but what happened in one genre, the theatre, where change very clearly took the form of the re-integration of fundamental and traditional elements. The bulk of the textual discussion in this chapter will focus on the theatre in Spain in the 1920s and 1930s: on the *esperpentos* of Valle-Inclán of the early 1920s and two Surrealist plays by García Lorca, *Así que pasen cinco años* and *El público*, the former completed in August 1930, the latter in 1931.[2] But the main context I should like to explore for an understanding of what was happening in Spanish avant-garde theatre is one which is broadly European, the roots of it expressed most forcibly by Nietzsche in his comments on the true nature of Greek tragedy.

As Ritchie Robertson has outlined in chapter 5, Nietzsche had proposed a new view of Greek civilization, which was distinct from the concept that had been until then dominant in German classicism, and which stressed only the serene side of Greek civilization. The Greeks, for Nietzsche, were acutely aware of the sides of life that were unacceptable, namely that it is both painful and transient, and it was in reaction to this that they had created the ideal world of the gods. Greek tragedy expressed this raw pain, which Nietzsche associates with the Dionysiac, in an art form that derives from Apollo, a god of higher civilization, who contrasts and counterbalances Dionysos, a god of nature and natural fertility. Placed in the context of the avant-garde, we can equate these two sides, the Apolline and the Dionysiac, with the worlds of the conscious and the unconscious respectively, but we can also go further, since what is Dionysiac relates to the concept of the 'guts' of experience. The Dionysiac, as seen by Nietzsche, was not simply the unknown, or even simply the 'natural', but connects with what is painful, unacceptable, and yet is an unquestionably real part of our lives, whereas the Apolline connects with the sense we make of our experience, the finished formulation that we give it.[3]

As important as the combination of Dionysiac and Apolline elements in Greek tragedy, in Nietzsche's view, is the highlighting of what we could see as an inescapable paradox: that we are individuals, but that we have a common destiny which involves our suffering and death. The 'Dionysiac truth', while it affirms the power and joy of the natural world, also entails our 'subjection, as impotent individuals, to the change and suffering that befall us from birth to inevitable death'.[4] Dionysiac rites had originally been above all a communal experience, in which all the participants could join in the frenzied dances leading to ecstasy, a process by which the individual was taken out of himself. The descent into chaos in the rites entailed a loss of individuality, but allowed an extended, enlarged and enriched experience, an experience which became that of the spectator when the rites were transformed into the primitive theatre. Whether experienced by participants or spectators, however, we can conclude that the dynamic of the Dionysiac message about our common life is the same: it is only by removing the particularity of experience that we can be faced by the full burden of what human existence entails.[5]

Implied in Nietzsche's conception of tragedy is a conviction of the need to take on the full dimensions of our experience, as encapsulated in the best of Greek tragedy, in which a basic tenet is the urge towards unity and integration. Viewed in this light we might also see connections between Nietzsche's ideas and the underlying fundamentals of Symbolism, the artistic movement which heralded the avant-garde. Symbolism above all sought to establish links between the different aspects of life, the perception of which would lead to a sense of unity. At the heart of this essentially artistic movement was a profoundly religious sense of the urge to wholeness. Expressions of this, and the desire to establish interconnections, can be seen at a detailed level in the exploration of synaesthesia, and on a more extensive level in the artistic objective of 'total theatre' as envisaged by Wagner, and later by Gordon Craig.[6]

It is in Gordon Craig that we find the most explicit declaration of what the urge towards wholeness involves. Nietzsche is eloquent about the values of the Dionysiac which encompass both joy and pain, at their extremes only just held in tension and check by Apolline expression, but Craig is clear in his recognition that the factor which has to be included for a complete vision of life is the inescapable factor of death, or Death. His aim is to heighten artistic expression, but what he has to say can be read as extending beyond purely aesthetic experience:

> This flesh-and-blood life, lovely as it is to us all, is for me not a thing made to search into, or to give out again to the world, even conventionalize. I think that my aim shall rather be to catch some far-off glimpse of that spirit which we call Death – to recall beautiful things from the imaginary world: they say they are cold, these dead things, I do not know – they often seem warmer and more living than that which parades as life . . . For, looking too long upon life, may one not find all this to be not the beautiful, nor the mysterious, nor the tragic, but the dull, the melodramatic, and the silly: the conspiracy against vitality – against both red heat and white heat.[7]

In naming vitality, and linking it with an awareness of death, Gordon Craig puts his finger on what will be the pivot of avant-garde theatrical theory and practice.

The recognition that there was an unknown side of life did not mean that it would be universally or unequivocally welcomed, even by the pioneers of psychoanalysis. Specifically, and of considerable relevance to our argument here, there is the way in which Freud's attitude differs from that of Jung, not so much in relation to the theory of the structure of the unconscious, as to what our attitude towards our unconscious might be. The problem ultimately was whether the unknown side was dangerous, or at the least uncivilized, and had therefore perhaps been rightly rejected or repressed, or whether it was vital, and therefore demanded incorporation. Freud and Jung polarize over the issue of the relative importance of repression (seen as a panic measure in the face of threat and anxiety) as opposed to incorporation (seen as the natural functioning of the self), Freud giving more emphasis to repression, Jung to incorporation.

In this context, Ritchie Robertson's outline of Freud's attitude to the primitive is revealing. In Freud's acknowledgement of Nietzsche in the 1919 addition to *The Interpretation of Dreams* we see Freud at his most Jungian, but none the less his view of the primitive, as expressed in *Totem and Taboo*, and which is related to the unconscious, focuses on what is violent and unacceptable. Furthermore, Freud's theory of the Oedipus complex, resolved in the boy by fear of castration, and instigated in the girl by fear that castration has already taken place, and his schema of the structure of the personality in which the ego is beset by anxiety in its attempts to cope with the conflicting demands of the superego and the id give us an understanding of physical life in which fear plays a large part. What emerges is the impression that we may at best hope to have an uneasy truce with the id, the area of the self which by 1923 Freud had equated with the unruly aspect of the unconscious, characterizing it as a seething cauldron, an area from which unacceptable drives came, and which was also the self's dumping ground for all that was unfaceable, or beyond the pale of the civilized; and thus, for example, where unacceptable desires and urges (such as the urge to parricide and the transgression of the taboos of incest in the Oedipus complex) would be relegated.[8]

Jung's concept of the unconscious stands in lively contrast with the above. For him, there is a part, the 'personal unconscious', which corresponds most closely with the view of the unconscious held by Freud, in that it is formed from the individual's 'repressed, infantile impulses and wishes, subliminal perceptions, and countless forgotten experiences; it belongs to him alone.'[9] But Jung also saw the unconscious as having much wider dimensions, and added to the idea of the personal unconscious that of the collective unconscious which functions as both the universal source and the universal repository of human experience, and which outlines in a macrocosm the processes that will be realized in the microcosm of the individual. The autonomous force of the collective unconscious, peopled with the major archetypes, also contains man's understanding of his life, expressed in images, symbols, patterns, myths, rituals, fairy-tales and dreams in ways which cross boundaries of time, place, culture and individuals. The major symbols, the archetypes, are elements which interact in the process of man's development – or rather, are expressions of the major forces, developments and changes of life with which we all, as individuals engaged in a communally experienced life, have to come to terms in the playing out of our individual and particular lives.

In his ideas on human development, Freud laid emphasis on what happened in the early part of life which would have a determining influence for later on. Jung, by contrast, with his theory of individuation, saw man's entire life, until the moment of death, as a total developmental process, the broad patterns of which are reflected in the life cycles of whole institutions and civilizations. The process of individuation assumes an essentially healthy self-regulating system, which will bring the individual to move towards some balance during the course of his life. Jung believed that personalities could be classified into different types, according to whether they were most dominated by the functions of thinking, feeling, intuition or sensation, and that what typically happened was that an individual would be dominated by one of these functions in the first half of life, and that the second half of his life would then characteristically be spent under the influence of the opposite function, so as to compensate for any imbalance. The first function, labelled by Jung as the dominant one, is usually expressed by the persona, the self that we present to the world. The *shadow*, by contrast, is the underside of the *persona*, a contrasting, suppressed side that comes to demand recognition in the second half of life. Another type of balancing which may go on is connected with ideas of the sexual: anima and animus represent respectively the feminine aspect within man and the masculine aspect within woman, and again may either require recognition in later life, or balancing. The process of individuation will also involve the individual in coming to terms with major archetypes of the collective unconscious, the outcome depending on the individual, not on the archetypes: among these are the hero (whose death will bring re-birth), the old wise man, the earth mother, the trickster, and the child, who frequently represents the self. The self is essentially something which is entire, and thus is frequently seen as a hermaphroditic figure, a jewel, an egg, a circle, or even the philosopher's stone towards which all the efforts of alchemy are directed. The archetypes are not forces, but ways of being in life with which the individual in the course of his life, and in the process of individuation thus entailed, will interact.[10]

Individuation was thus a process of normal development, but one in which difficult issues, such as innate but rejected tendencies, change, ageing and ultimately death would have to be faced and integrated to form the completed psyche.

The drama of the psyche as seen by Freud is concentrated in the early stages of life, even though the effects continue and are repeated through later life, where major tasks such as the resolution of the Oedipus complex have been inadequately carried out. In Jung's view of life, however, with the collective unconscious and the archetypes, there is a lively drama which is played out throughout the course of life, to be completed by the final act of death. In later life Jung became increasingly interested in the way the process of individuation could be seen as expressed in a particular type of drama, the alchemical drama, the processes of which he saw as being analogous to the processes that took place in individuation. Essential in the alchemical processes are the ideas of transmutation and progression. Elements are not lost, but their relationship is changed, and a re-ordering, re-integration and balance of parts is finally achieved. The main stages in the alchemical process were the following: the *nigredo*, in which matter was reduced to chaos, to its original undifferentiated state (and where Jung saw the unconscious as dominant); the *albedo*, when metals were washed, and elements began to be separate and perceptible in their differences, a stage which, psychologically speaking, corresponded to the deepening of self-knowledge; the *rubedo*, where by use of fire elements were tested, and the union of opposites led to the formation of gold (or in the psyche, to the accomplishment of the individuated self in which the *coniunctio* permitted free interaction between the conscious and unconscious parts of the self).[11]

The above brief discussion of the differing ideas of Freud and Jung on the nature of the unconscious, and indeed on the structure and development of the psyche, gives us the basis for seeing two distinctive trends in the theatre of the avant-garde. In the following discussion my approach is fundamentally speculative rather than historical, and is based on similarities we can see between the approaches of these psychoanalytic thinkers and the work of various dramatists; and more than this, it is based on a belief that we can see the ideas of Freud and Jung as expressive of a difference of attitude which is also seen in the theatre – a difference of attitude to the unconscious, to the self and its development. Thus, running parallel to the divergence of attitude to the unconscious which we have seen above is a distinction between those writers who seek to confront their audiences with difficult and unpalatable truths, but present no reassurance in the shape of implied pattern or known process that will inform the whole of life, and those who, while seeking to provoke a similar and equally painful confrontation, none the less present it in the context of natural forces following a natural development which, though it may not be attractive, is vital and dynamic.

Focusing on the Spanish context, we can follow this speculative approach and take Ramón del Valle-Inclán and Federico García Lorca as representative in their theatrical theory and practice of the two approaches to how to bring man to face the full dimensions of his existence, and see how their work can be seen in the light of Freud and Jung respectively. It would be tempting to approach the question of direct influence historically, but the evidence is uneven. While it seems quite possible that Lorca would have had some knowledge of the work of Freud (since his friends Salvador Dalí and Luis Buñuel were clearly acquainted with Freud's theories in the 1920s) there is scant indication of his own direct interest, [12] and there is even less evidence that either Valle-Inclán or Lorca was acquainted with the work of Jung.[13] The only concrete form of influence that may be relevant to note here is the widespread awareness of the ideas of Nietzsche in Spain at this period. It is an awareness that is general rather than particular in the two dramatists, but the influence of Nietzsche on ethical attitudes in Spain in the early twentieth century should not be underestimated.[14]

Valle-Inclán is best known for his theory (and practice) of the *esperpento*, a theatrical form in which the audience is distanced from the action on stage by a process of distortion and deliberate alienation. The *esperpento* is a grotesque and exaggerated form of theatre which draws on traditions of guignol but has its subject matter firmly rooted in the life of contemporary society, and which combines caricature with burlesque and a strong measure of black humour. It was a form which Valle claimed had been invented by Goya, and there is indeed a striking resemblance between these plays and the *Caprichos*, *Disparates*, and *Desastres de la guerra* of the latter. The *esperpento* is both defined and realised within the plays, the main theory being contained within *Luces de bohemia* (*Bohemian Lights*, 1920) and *Los cuernos de don Friolera* (*The Horns of Mr Silly*, 1921). This double procedure of defining and enacting a theatrical form within itself is also to be found in Lorca's play *El público* (*The Audience*) of 1931, and it is also worked through in Pirandello's *Six Characters in Search of an Author* (1921). But in order to look at what Valle meant and intended by the *esperpento*, we have to look at ideas both beyond and preceding those purely esperpentic texts. The actual experience of watching an *esperpento* is a disquieting one in the first instance because, as in the theatre of Brecht, we are prevented from any direct emotional engagement with the play, or rather with the characters within it. This does not mean that we have no reaction. Indeed it matters that we allow ourselves to experience the very disturbance, and in some ways that this should precede and even take precedence over any intellectual understanding of the text. In this way Valle anticipates the demands that will be made of us by the work of Artaud. The plays produce reactions of irritation, disquiet, occasionally amusement, depression, not only because of content which can be confusing or repugnant, but because they seem bent on destroying all notions of social or moral values, and also because shifts in perspective make it impossible for us to follow a single line or direction of intent. We are left asking why we have to have the experience.

I believe that the reason behind this distancing in the case of Valle-Inclán is similar to that which we find in other dramatists of the avant-garde who consciously set out to alienate their audiences, but also set out to reach them in new, often shocking ways – Brecht and Artaud. For all of them there is a fundamental belief that the state of man in the present is unsatisfactory and that man, if he is to be true to his potential, needs to be spurred on beyond his current mediocrity. Valle-Inclán and Artaud in particular emphasized the degree to which modern man has failed to attain his full stature, and in this context the purpose of the theatre is, by revelation of that very mediocrity, designed to spur him to the regaining of his stature. Just as Freud saw the neurotic as one who was diminished and handicapped by the things he has repressed, who has become crippled by his over-adaptation to his circumstances, so Valle-Inclán was aware that for him modern man had become puny, although the dimensions of his fate, in terms of what could potentially befall him, had not altered. He expressed this in a comment on the nature of life and its capacity for tragedy, and contrasted the position of modern man with that expressed and described in Greek myth, where protagonists had the stature to meet their fate. There is a double tragedy involved which Valle does not articulate fully. On the one hand there is the simple existential tragedy of not being able to experience tragedy, itself a massive loss, and there is the further one related to the diminished theatrical experience which is also entailed. The tragedy described by Aristotle was one which allowed a final catharsis, and this was permitted by the stature of both protagonist and spectator. Now both are mediocre, and both the original experience of tragedy and the vicarious experience of it are lost.[15]

Valle-Inclán's thoughts on man's stature, which provide the elucidation of what lay behind the *esperpento*, came a full ten years after the first statement of the theory behind the genre given in *Bohemian Lights* (1920), and coincide chronologically (through presumably by coincidence only) with analogous statements by Brecht and Artaud. Brecht, for example, in 1926 could be speaking for Valle-Inclán in explaining the reason for having a cold and alienating theatre: it is to move us, eventually, to greater experience and understanding in a way that is otherwise, in current circumstances, impossible. As Brecht points out,

> nowadays the play's meaning is usually blurred by the fact that the actor plays to the audience's hearts. The figures portrayed are foisted on the audience and are falsified in the process. Contrary to present custom they ought to be presented quite coldly, classically and objectively. For they are not a matter for empathy; they are there to be understood.[16]

Brecht apparently aimed at an intellectual understanding, and wished to have a clear path to it, unimpeded by irrelevant or spurious emotion, and it is important to emphasize that his distancing is ideologically biased from a Marxist standpoint, and further that he had quite precise political aims, whereas the aims of Valle-Inclán can only be considered as political in a general sense. But, having made that distinction, we should also keep in view their fundamental similarity. The tenor of both dramatists is an intellectual one, but more than this, it is in a profound sense morally didactic (more obviously so for Brecht than for Valle-Inclán). And this is the starting-point only of their enterprise. There is an underlying assumption that man cannot be emotionally void in his reaction to their plays (otherwise they would have no effect), but their ambition is to extend his range immensely, and is to work towards a complete, adequately functioning and 'proper' man, in the belief that this could and should be achieved. Brecht makes this plain three years later in 'A Dialogue about Acting', where first he indicates how experience is necessarily limited for an audience if the actors create emotional mood. What results is 'nobody seeing anything further, nobody learning any lessons, at best everyone recollecting. In short everybody feels.' This is rejected as inadequate, and Brecht goes on to suggest what the experience of theatre ought to be like instead: 'Witty. Ceremonious. Ritual. Spectator and actor ought not to approach one another but to move apart. Each ought to move away from himself. Otherwise the *element of terror necessary to all recognition is lacking*' [my italics].[17] So whereas Brecht envisages a non-emotional approach to theatre, it seems that this is a means only, and the end ultimately takes us back to the earliest roots of the theatre in primitive ritual, and Dionysiac rite, where a new level of emotion may be reached.

Dionysiac rites, with their sacred frenzy induced by dance, in which the dancers would fall on some beast selected as victim and, having ripped it apart, would consume it, could seem to show man at his most primitive, revealing the terrible side that presented itself to Freud in *Totem and Taboo*. The primitive and the terrible is indeed what stands out, but it veils an underlying purpose which is serious and elevating: that in the ecstasy and frenzy man was enabled to be put in touch with forces greater than himself. In addition, the killing and consumption of a victim formed a part of yet more ancient fertility rites. These elements alone could be sufficient to justify their being understood as man's attempt to extend his condition and his understanding of it, but there is a further one, which links with the discomfort of the alienating modern theatre, and that is the degree of conscious volition and effort that has to be exercised by man to attain the ecstasy which puts him thus 'beyond himself'. Hunningher, in his account of the features held in common between the rites of primitive religions and the later rites associated with Dionysos, emphasizes this element of effort: ecstasy is not bestowed by some external grace, but must be achieved by man's act. Man must

> concentrate all his force and power to obtain the rapture which will overmaster the deity and secure for him the communion for which he hungers. Both cases involve man's act, man's deed, through which he acquires – or rather takes – godhead. His rites therefore do not implore, do not accept submissively, do not commemorate in adoration.[18]

Valle-Inclán and Brecht share, theoretically, a certain astringency of ambition and attitude, which connects with the above, even though, as has been mentioned, Brecht has more defined political and didactic aims than Valle-Inclán, who restricts himself in the *esperpento*, on a conscious and intellectual level, to the process of unnerving his spectator at the spectacle of the emptiness of his own condition. It will be left to Lorca, and eventually to Artaud to broaden out the scope of what may follow this unnerving.

Valle does, however, have his own, less intellectual way of extending the scope of the spectator, even within the *esperpento*, employing a directness of shock tactics that is echoed in the stark emotion of Pirandello's theatre. His plays are not intellectual in the way those of Ibsen's are, for example, where issues of emotion and morality are argued through by a set of agonizing and tortured characters. The plays of Valle-Inclán are essentially visual, and above all, intensely physical plays. The only meaning for the audience is the presence of the characters on the stage, and within the plays – whether we consider *Bohemian Lights, The Horns of Mr Silly,* or *Divinas palabras* (*Divine Words*) (1922) – the only ultimate meaning is death. This ultimate physical phenomenon of our lives, this final reality we might all wish to avoid, is pushed under our noses with merciless insistence by the author, with all its crude inconvenience and lack of dignity. The corpse of Max Estrella remains on stage in the final part of *Bohemian Lights* (scene xiii) as characters attempt by semi-scientific means to see if he is dead, while a dog has already shown, in symbolic form, his conviction that this is indeed the case by urinating in the presence of the dying Max at the close of scene xii. In *The Horns of Mr Silly*, Friolera, Mr Silly himself, having wavered throughout about whether he should kill his overweight and flirtatious wife for her suspected (but unlikely) adultery, discovers in the final moments of the play that he has killed his daughter, whom he loved, instead. In *Divine Words*, an idiot child, Laureano, remains on stage throughout, grotesquely twitching in the first half, dead and putrefying in the second. *La rosa de papel* (*The Paper Rose*) (1924), not strictly speaking defined as an *esperpento*, but as a *novela macabra*, yet with all the features of the genre, has centre stage occupied throughout by the corpse of the wife, who becomes the object of her husband's necrophilic desires as the curtain falls. None of Valle's emphasis on death is likely to be surprising for those who have taken in the impact of his statement of theory in the prologue to *The Horns of Mr Silly*, where we learn that Death is to inform the whole aesthetic of the *esperpento*, which will be an overcoming of pain and mirth, as 'must happen in the conversations of the dead as they tell one another stories of the living',[19] a pairing which recalls the Freudian Eros/Thanatos conflict.

Valle-Inclán's theatre is not one where the hidden corners of the unconscious are explored in any direct fashion, but it is a theatre that challenges, and that is intended to force the spectator to see some of the painful realities, repressed truths of his situation, as a pre-condition to regaining the wholeness of stature that would make it possible for him to experience the necessary tragedy of human life in a manner more commensurate with his potential being. The plays of Lorca immerse the spectator yet further in an experience of what is necessary but unacceptable. In his Surrealist plays *Asi que pasen cinco años* (*Till Five Years Pass*) and *El público* he shows us that what is unfaceable and unacceptable none the less has its own inexorable logic, patterns and cyclical life, albeit contained in paradox. Because although *The Audience* in particular is puzzling and unharmonious, and exposes features of human life that as civilized beings we might consider best hidden, it is also informed, as is *Till Five Years Pass*, by a sense of movement and of the natural. What Lorca produces, then, independently of any direct influence, are works which seem to have at their base something which approaches the patterned and dynamic Jungian concept of the unconscious, rather than one which resembles the 'seething cauldron' of Freud. Lorca urges the spectator to confront what he would rather not confront, but with the conviction that pain, death and unsatisfied longing are integral and inescapable parts of the human condition, and that their presence in our lives must be fully and truthfully acknowledged.

Lorca is best known for the rural trilogy, [20] composed in the same period as the Surrealist works, yet markedly different in character. All three rural tragedies foreground passionate desire, and declare emphatically that it cannot be satisfied. The desire that forces the Bride to elope with Leonardo in *Blood Wedding* is disruptive, but life-affirming. It is matched by the fundamental contradiction contained in the Mother's admiration for virile desire that knows no bounds, and her dynamic and urgent commitment to the furtherance of the community. This in its turn consists of a paradox. If it is to be dynamic, it must be capable of containing those very forces, such as those manifested in the implementation of the blood feud, which threaten its stability, and ultimately its existence. In *Yerma* the desire for life, expressed in concrete terms as the desire for a child, but going far beyond a longing that could be satisfied by such a physical attainment, is the desire which is fatal to the protagonist's well-being, while being fundamental to her self. *The House of Bernarda Alba* presents a view of desire that is so overwhelming that it must be negated by obsessive repression, Bernarda suggesting beneath her icy demeanour and demands for silence the seething cauldron of an unconscious to which all the unacceptable has been relegated. It is thus more 'Freudian', more pessimistic in its impact, but leaves the audience with a pressing emotional urge to the integration which is denied by the central character.

The plays of the rural trilogy express in terms that are larger than life, but contained within the context of normal life, the preoccupations of the Surrealist plays. Single characters or pairs of characters embody or represent tendencies, longings and aspects of life or personality which in the Surrealist works are fragmented and dispersed through the cast-list (which thus cannot be equated with a list of characters). The Surrealist plays in this way become fugal elaborations, working to enharmonic resolutions rather than to any final endings. (Even this contrast may be a false one, as close examination of the endings of the plays of the rural trilogy reveals endings which are apparent final cadences rather than real ones: at no point is there fundamental catharsis.)

In *Till Five Years Pass* we are faced by a Young Man and aspects of himself, rather than any collection of 'real' characters, and we see his possibilities and his relationships, above all his fears and his desires, impelled and constricted by the passage of time, one of the themes around which there is most movement. Because time is so prominent we can see the play as a series of developmental thresholds, as a confrontation by the Young Man of processes in life that he must move *through*. The self is not, and cannot be, static. It is under pressure not only from desire, but from the increasing constraints of time. This is placed in maximum tension by Lorca through his concentration upon the idea of postponement, the recurring statement of 'till five years pass . . .'. The Young Man is unable to face life in the present, or the consequences of the passing of time. Thus he can face neither the ending of his engagement, delayed for five years, nor the inescapable problems of ageing and death that the passage of time brings. The play opens with the impending termination of the five years' wait. The Young Man must now confront the passage of time and its consequences, among the most pressing of which is that the desire that has been postponed will have to find its resolution, an outcome which causes him to back away, but which he cannot avoid. His mental imagery displays how he would like to cut through the constraints of time. Thus his vision of the fiancée is a combination of static past and future: he remembers her with the plaits she no longer has, but, in his imagination, sees her in a shroud.[21]

What the Young Man fails to come to terms with until the closing pages of the play is the fact that desire is linked to our mortal state. It is not abstract, not a thing of the head, and not a thing to be experienced outside the passage of time. These are precisely the aspects of desire that are unacceptable to him, for the very reason that they affirm and require his mortal state, and the mortal state is one bound to ageing and death. Rupert Allen has proposed a Jungian analysis of this play, in which he sees it as dealing with the psychological transformation of the Young Man. In his view it is a case of attempted transformation ending in failure.[22] I would argue differently. The fiancée, by her rejection of the Young Man in Act II, and by his ensuing realization that he can therefore father no children, impels him into a painful re-appraisal of his life. The mode of being he has used so far has become irrelevant. In Act III it is no chance that he meets all the figures of the Harlequinade, representing fundamental forces in our lives as they do, from the irresponsible power of the Harlequin/Trickster to the different female figures with their pretensions, evasiveness and affectation, the Typist and the Woman with the Mask representing different types of *anima*. The whole collection thus presents us with a cast-list of major archetypes, with whom the Young Man needs to deal. The Harlequin figure himself could even be seen as a pure embodiment of an archetype, in that he is powerful, but not clearly a force for good or evil. He is a testing ground.[23] The final hounding to death of the Young Man in the card game is the sign, not that he has failed to reach his self-transcendence, but that he has reached full status of human being by succumbing to his mortality.

The Audience, a text whose difficulty derives in part from its incomplete state, presents the incorporation of a sense of death as a condition necessary both to life and to the theatre that is to represent it. Death here, however, carries the connotations of the Crucifixion, with the implied hope of the Resurrection. The theatre must be destroyed in order to live again, and we must be destroyed (by suffering, disclosure of unsatisfied and impossible desires and love, and ultimately death) if we are to achieve true status as human beings. In this Lorca reiterates the austere values of Valle-Inclán and the implied ethical criteria of Nietzsche.

Unlike the rural trilogy, or the latter part of *Till Five Years Pass*, *The Audience* contains at first sight little sense of dynamic motion, giving much more an impression of tail-chasing exchanges, of spirals of action in which attitudes are passed to and fro between characters, in which hidden relationships are revealed which alter the balances of power within the play. Thus, for example, the two characters in the 'Roman Ruins' scene alternate in their assumption of the active and passive roles in courtship, or rather of the role of the one who wishes to court and the one who wishes to spurn. There is a hidden love relationship between the Director and the First Man and hidden twinning between the apparently unrelated pairs Enrique/Gonzalo and Desnudo/First Man. Words and actions appropriate to the personality of one character have an unsettling tendency to be found later in the confines of another character. There results from this a sort of dynamic but rather disturbing movement, and the apparent fixity of externals (masks, rigid postures) is held in tension with a fluidity and unstoppability of underlying feelings and motives.

The Audience is about life, and about the theatre, about each of these in itself, and in relation to the other. The central characters of the play are the Director of a new type of theatre, the 'theatre of the open air' (supposedly, we assume, one which brings everything out into the open) and members of his audience, who reject his new theatre as inadequate, since it fails to treat of man's real physical existence and mortality. But the play also contains the actors/characters of *Romeo and Juliet*, a play which is finally produced in the new mode required by the three men of the audience (but which unfortunately Lorca never wrote into his unfinished text of *The Audience*), and several horses, who variously represent the emotions, man's physical life and desires. At one level the play explores, or rather the Director is placed under duress to explore, the possibility of a new type of theatre, one which will be revitalized through the integration of rejected and uncomfortable elements, such as the exposure of the pains of inappropriate and unrequited desire, and man's mortality. At another level, and simultaneously, the play exposes the falsity of lives in which people live out roles which are discordant with their true selves, but which are assumed so as not to reveal unacceptable (and unaccepted) desires. Overall, the play seeks to move the spectator to two levels of realization: first, that the theatre, if it is true to life (and not mere diversion) can regain its vitality, a real role in life, on a ritual and significant level, such as was to be claimed for it by Artaud, and such as it enjoyed in Greek tragedy in the combination of Dionysiac feeling contained by Apolline structure so favoured by Nietzsche; in positing that this theatre is actually possible, *The Audience* simultaneously exposes the side of our life we have difficulty in accepting, and makes it possible for us to accept it by placing it within the container of a new artistic form. The second level of realization is entailed by the first: our existences are enlivened by being mirrored in an artistic form that reflects us in true fashion, and also obliges us to be true, because the play achieves the neat (though painful) bypassing of inauthentic feeling that would occur in a flight into fantasy or sentimentalism.

The play is, then, centrally concerned with exposing elements of the repressed unconscious, non-permitted, unattainable or unassimilable as it is, but at the same time it is clear that, even in its unfinished state, by being concerned with the role of the theatre in our task of assimilating what has been repressed, the play possesses and indeed affirms a belief in containing, patterning and process that is consonant with a dynamic Jungian concept of the unconscious, and the procedures involved in the attainment of individuation. The theme of the repressed and the task of assimilation can be seen usefully in this context by viewing *The Audience* in terms of the working out of the alchemical drama, the drama Jung saw as analogous to man's drama of individuation.

The play opens with an opposition between two forms of theatre, the 'theatre beneath the sand' being proposed by the First Man after his criticism of the Director's project for a 'theatre in the open air'. The connotations of the two types of theatre are not immediately obvious, but emerge both through the text and through the context of Lorca's other writings. The 'theatre in the open air', which arguably could be thought of as the theatre of the conscious, is one where all is 'open and above board', yet where this openness is a superficial declaration of truth such as may frequently lie behind statements like 'To be perfectly frank and honest with you . . .' when no such intention of honesty is present. The name of the 'theatre beneath the sand' suggests immediately, within the framework of Lorca's writing, an association with death, since it appears as the sign of the blunt reality of death in works as diverse as *Blood Wedding*, in Lorca's poem on the death of the bullfighter Ignacio Sánchez Mejías, and in the *Romancero gitano* (*Gypsy Ballads*). The aim of this new theatre is that it must carry the spectators (us) through and beyond death, and as such will reveal the true nature of our condition. It will, however, be difficult to convey that truth forcefully enough, and the First Man declares that he will have to shoot himself on stage to set in motion the theatre beneath the sand – a declaration that foreshadows the brutal approach of Artaud's 'Theatre of Cruelty'.[24] Death thus emerges as the essential transforming process in helping us to see our life as it actually is.

In the opening pages of the play, before the arrival of the three men who constitute the audience, we see the Director as a man who is less than fully integrated, because of his wilful rejection, now and in the past, of the four horses who enter. His anxiety tells all: 'What do you want? I might ask that if I were a man capable of the act of sighing.'[25] The horses clamour for their right to his attention and remind him of their long history with him: they cannot be rejected, and yet they imply by their clamouring that he has attempted to reject them in the 'theatre in the open air'. The horses remind the Director of the basic activities of life, involving sweat and filth: 'We used to wait for you in the lavatory, behind the doors and then we used to fill your bed with tears . . . [sic] And your shoes were burning with sweat . . . .'[26] The horses represent the physical senses, possibly man's potential or libido, [27] and are at first unable to express themselves well. They become more and more articulate, however, through the course of the play, and are differentiated dynamically in Scene iii, in their relation to and lust for Juliet. Death, brought to the fore in Scene i by the First Man, is not fully articulated until Scene v, when a naked, scarlet man enacts the Crucifixion and carries suggestions both of Romeo, star-crossed lover, and the First Man who had instigated the new, fatal theatre.

The play is full of contrasting pairs, revelation of opposites, removal of masks, the exposure of hidden and impossible desire – the divisions and balances thus highlighted being relevant to alchemical principle, and to the Jungian pairs of *persona* and shadow, *anima* and *animus*, and the belief in the need first to reveal and then to integrate and balance conflicting factors. In this context, and given Nietzsche's view of Greek tragedy as a combination of the Dionysiac and the Apolline, Scene ii, the 'Roman Ruins', is of particular interest. Here two figures, the Man with Vine Leaves and the Man with Bells, engage in a perplexing courtship conversation, in which coquetry is met with manipulation and exploitation, and in which they take turns to court and be courted. The two may be viewed simply as a pair of homosexual lovers, displaying all the potential desire, cruelty and sadism latent in such a situation: to court is to expose oneself to rejection at least, and with ease to sadistic manipulation. But they could also show this less acceptable side of love in a heterosexual pair. In addition, their attributes, vine-leaves and bells, suggests that they are linked with Dionysos and Apollo respectively. Who gains the upper hand? Lorca appears unwilling to tip the scales. Dominance varies by turns, and the two finally vye for affections of the emperor. At a symbolic level we could understand Lorca as affirming that the claims of both the physical/vital and the mental/ intellectual must be allowed, and that within the theatre itself there must be harmony and balancing between difficult content, and the intellectual and artistic form that guides, contains and presents it.

The alchemical drama itself is played out principally in the transforma-tion of the Theatre Director. In Scene i he is less than sufficient for what his role demands, but becomes sufficient by Scene vi in his confrontation with Death, the Magician/Trickster. The Director, or perhaps his theatre, is the base matter to be purified by the alchemy of development. During the play there is an increase in the numbers of oppositions and the discrimination of elements. After Scene i, in which masks are removed by passing characters behind a screen, revealing hidden and shameful tendencies, we see the rivalry of the Man with Vine Leaves and the Man with Bells. This initial sifting out of opposites can be seen as the *solutio* of the *albedo* stage, with the First man functioning as the salt agent which provokes the initial revelation of differences. That men are distinctly rivals and in conflict is explored in Scene iii, with the rivalry for Juliet, who is obliged by the horses to experience the dark side of life, signalled as 'night'. This enforced extended experience which Juliet is subjected to is a first example of incorporation of opposite elements which heralds balancing and integration. Separation, and disarray at revealed differences, continue to the end of Scene v. In Scene vi the death of the First Man/Romeo is the death of the Hero, the *mortificatio* of the final processing of all elements during and after the *rubedo* stage, his death achieving the *coniunctio* necessary to bring about the new theatre, just as in Dionysiac rites (or in Christianity) the death of the god opens the way to new strength and re-birth. In the final scene we are reminded of the component elements of the play, but the masks have gone. Totality, individuation, the alchemical gold of chaos processed in a container, which in this case has been the theatrical work, has been achieved.

Or at least, that is what might have been the effect if the play had reached completion. The essential drama of death and re-birth, of revelation and renewal, expressed in terms which are stark and barely acceptable, is clear even in the unfinished text, and it is possibly not by chance that the play remains unfinished, nor that the scene which appears to be missing is the one containing the essential element of transformation in the history of the theatre: the scene in which *Romeo and Juliet* has apparently been performed in a way that satisfies the requirements of the First Man, who had articulated in the first scene the need for a theatre beneath the sand. Lorca here comes as close as perhaps is possible to creating this new type of theatre which will have the power of the Dionysiac rite and the alchemical drama, and the fact that it may be unattainable can be deduced from the continuing insistence in Artaud that such a total, all involving and finally renewing drama be sought. It is easy to misjudge the motives of avant-garde writers. Yet their obsessions with morbid sexuality and split personalities are neither frivolous nor eccentric. The theatre, a central communal form of literary expression, is, within the context of the avant-garde, one of the most serious expressions of man's individual and collective unconscious.

Notes

1 André Breton, 'First Surrealist Manifesto' (1924), in *Manifestoes of Surrealism*, trans. and ed. R. Seaver and H. R. Lane (University of Michigan Press, Ann Arbor, 1969), p. 10

2 Strictly speaking, only the following plays of Valle-Inclán are considered as

esperpentos: *Luces de bohemia* (1920); *Los cuernos de don Friolera* (1921); *La hija del capitán*; *Las galas del difunto* (1926). These plays were collected and published as *Martes de Carnaval* in 1930. Other plays of the period, however, are considered as closely related to the above, and will be included in this discussion. References to *Valle-Inclán* are to the *Obras completas*, 2 vols, 3rd ed (Plenitud, Madrid, 1954). For full detail about the composition of Lorca's Surrealist plays (and persuasive argument about the strategy of Lorca's composition in the 1930s, with its mingling of the difficult avant-garde plays and more readily accessible rural trilogy) see Andrew Anderson, 'The strategy of García Lorca's dramatic composition 1930–1936', *Romance Quarterly*, 33 (1986), pp. 211–29. References to *El público* will be to the edition by R. Martínez Nadal and M. Laffranque, *El público y Comedia sin titulo* (Seix Barral, Barcelona, 1978). For other texts by Lorca, reference is to the *Obras completas* 2 vols, 21st edn (Aguilar, Madrid, 1980).

3   See Ritchie Robertson, pp. 81–3 above, for a fuller discussion of Nietzsche. On the dimensions of the Dionysiac and Apolline aspects of Greek tragedy see M. S. Silk and J. P. Stern, *Nietzsche on Tragedy*, (Cambridge University Press, Cambridge, 1981), pp. 63–6.

4   Silk and Stern, *Nietzsche on Tragedy*, p. 65, in their commentary on sections 4, 6, and 9 and 17 of *The Birth of Tragedy*: '[Greek culture] evinces an unmistakable and unique sensitivity to the painful truth about life: the Dionysiac truth ... the underlying reality of existence is unchanging contradiction, pain and excess, represented to our immediate experience as the 'curse of individuation' – our subjection, as impotent individuals, to the change and suffering that befall us from birth to inevitable death.'

5   The relationship between Dionysiac rites and the early theatre is explored by Benjamin Hunningher, *The Origin of the Theater* (1955, repr. Greenwood Press, Connecticut, 1978), pp. 27–41.

6   Edward Gordon Craig, 'The Actor and the Über-marionette', *On the Art of the Theatre* (1911; 5th imp. Heinemann, London, 1957), pp. 84–5.

7   ibid., p. 74.

8   See Robertson, pp. 84–6 above. Freud's ideas can be traced in the *Introductory lectures on Psycho-Analysis* (1916–17) (*SE*, XVI; Pelican 1), for example in Lecture 19, 'Resistance and Repression', and Lecture 23, 'The Paths to the Formation of Symptoms'. Ideas on the structure of the self are in *The Ego and the Id* (1923) (*SE*, XIX; Pelican 11), and are summarized in the 1923 *New Introductory Lectures on Psychoanalysis*, Lecture 31, 'The Dissection of the Psychical Personality', in which ego, superego and id are defined, and where the id is referred to as a 'chaos, a cauldron full of seething excitations' : *SE*, XX, p. 73; Pelican 2, p. 106.

9   F. Fordham, *An Introduction to Jung's Psychology* (Penguin, Harmondsworth, 1953), p. 22.

10 C. G. Jung, 'Psychology and Literature' (1930, expanded and revised 1950), *The Spirit in Man, Art and Literature, Collected Works*, vol. XV, p. 104, summarizes and defines the general features of an archetype. Early work on symbols was in an essay of 1902, 'On the Psychology and Pathology of So-called Occult Phenomena', outlined at length in 1912 in *Symbols of Transformation, Collected Works*, vol. IX, Part I, *The Archetypes and the Collective Unconscious*.

11   Jung's ideas on the relation between the psyche and alchemical process are in *Collected Works*, vol. XII, *Psychology and Alchemy*. See particularly I, 'Introduction to the Religious and Psychological Problems of Alechemy', and III, 'Religious Ideas in Alchemy', in which he outlines (section 1) basic principles of alchemy, and (section 2) discusses the psychic nature of the alchemical work. See also *Collected Works*, vol. XIV, *Alchemical Studies*, for the 'Commentary on the Secret of the Golden Flower'. For a more general introduction see M.-L. von Franz, *Alchemy* (Inner City Books, Toronto, 1980).

12   The works of Freud were translated into Spanish between 1922 and 1934, and published by Biblioteca Nueva. According to G. Edwards, *The Discreet Art of Luis Buñuel* (Marion Boyars, London/Boston, 1982), p. 16, Buñuel had read Freud's *Psychopathology of Everyday Life* in 1921. Edwards argues the likelihood that other friends of Buñuel would also have been acquainted with Freud's work, but there is no confirmation of it in the case of Lorca.

13   A single reference in an interview by Lorca shows some awareness of psychoanalysis, but it has a tinge of the dismissive: 'Mis primeras emociones están ligadas a la tierra y los trabajos del campo. Por eso hay en mi vida un complejo agrario, que llamarían los psicoanalistas.' [*'My earliest emotions are linked to the earth and to the labour of the fields. This is why I have an agrarian complex in my life, as the psychoanalysts would say.'*] Interview with José R. Luna, 1934, *Obras completas*, vol. II, p. 1059. There have been both Freudian and Jungian interpretations of the work of Lorca, though not of Valle-Inclán. For a Freudian approach, see for example Carlos Feal Deibe, *Eros y Lorca* (Edhasa, Barcelona, 1973) and for a Jungian approach see Rupert C. Allen, *Psyche and Symbol in the Theatre of Lorca* (University of Texas Press, Austin and London, 1974) and *The Symbolic World of Federico García Lorca* (University of New Mexico Press, Albuquerque, NM, 1972), which contains a chapter on *Así que pasén cinco años*).

14   The awareness of Nietzsche's works in Spain is well documented. See Gonzalo Sobejano, *Nietzsche en España (Gredos, Madrid, 1967)*.

15   See Valle-Inclán's interview with Jose Montero Alonso, *La novela de hoy*, no. 418, 16 May 1930, (Madrid), reproduced in Dru Dougherty, *Un Valle-Inclán olvidado: entrevistas y conferencias* (Espiral, Madrid, 1982), pp. 188–92.

16   Conversation with Bertolt Brecht, *Die Literarische Welt*, Berlin, 30 July 1926, reproduced in *Brecht on Theatre*, trans. and notes by J. Willett (Methuen, London, 1964), p. 15.

17   'A Dialogue about Acting', *Berliner Börsen Courier*, 17 February 1929, reproduced in Willett, *Brecht on Theatre*, p. 26.

18   Hunningher, *The Origin of the Theater*, pp. 28 and 41.

19   Don Estrafalario: 'Mi estética es una superación del dolor y de la risa, como deben ser las conversaciones de los muertos, al contarse historias de los vivos' (Prologue to *Los cuernos de don Friolera*, *Obras completas*, vol. I, pp. 992–3).

20   *Bodas de sangre (Blood Wedding)*, (1932); *Yerma* (1934); *La casa de Bernarda Alba (The House of Bernarda Alba)*, (1936).

21   *Obras completas*, vol. II, pp. 368–9.

22   Allen, *The Symbolic World of Federico García Lorca*, p. 133.

23   See Jung's late definition of an archetype; 'in itself, an archetype is neither good nor evil. It is morally neutral, like the gods of antiquity, and becomes good or evil only by contact with the conscious mind, or else a paradoxical mixture of

both. Whether it will be conducive to good or evil is determined, knowingly or unknowingly, by the conscious attitude' ('Psychology and Literature' (1930; expanded and revised 1950), *Collected Works*, XV, p. 104).
24 *El público*, p. 41.
25 ibid., p. 33.
26 ibid., p. 35.
27 A Jungian view: see Jung, 'Paracelsus as a Spiritual Phenomenon', *Collected Works*, vol. XIII, p. 421.

SUGGESTED READING

Hunningher, Benjamin, *The Origin of the Theater*, 1955; repr. Greenwood Press, Connecticut, 1978.
Jung, C. G., *Psychology and Alchemy, Collected Works*, vol. XII, chapters 1, 3.
Silk, M. S., and Stern, J. P., *Nietzsche on Tragedy*, Cambridge University Press, Cambridge, 1981.

15

The Uncanny and Surrealism

ELIZABETH WRIGHT

The uncanny has become an important concept in post-modern aesthetics because it acts as a challenge to representation. It makes us see the world not as ready-made for description, depiction, or portrayal (common terms used to say what an artist or writer does), but as in a constant process of construction, deconstruction and reconstruction. But what is this effect we call 'uncanny'? According to Freud, 'it is undoubtedly related to what is frightening – to what arouses dread and horror',[1] but he concedes that there are things which excite dread and horror which are not uncanny. So how does one distinguish? What characterizes the uncanny, according to Freud, can most easily be defined by examining the German word for it, which is *unheimlich*. He writes: '*Unheimlich* is in some way or other a species of *heimlich*', and '*heimlich* is a word the meaning of which develops in the direction of ambivalence'.[2] For *heimlich* means not only homely and familiar, but also hidden and secret. The *un* of the *unheimlich* marks the return of repressed material: the *umheimlich* object threatens us in some way by no longer fitting the context to which we have been accustomed. The familiar, the *heimlich*, is the result of the apparently successful orderings we have made of the world, but because the secret and the private (the other sense of *heimlich*), also enters into these orderings, the objects we think we have singled out might fail us at any time. The uncanny world of the Surrealists catches this moment, sometimes pessimistically, as something gone rigid, sometimes more optimistically, as something in flux, that suggests the possibility of change. I shall be discussing images of both these moments.

Psychoanalysis has a theory which gives an account of how and why repressed material suddenly disrupts our familiar ways of perceiving the world, but it sees this theory as grounded in a certain practice (irrespective of whether this practice cures or not). Freud could not understand why the Surrealists were so interested in psychoanalysis. In 1932 he wrote a letter to

André Breton, who had accused Freud of not analysing his own dreams sufficiently, and in it he says that he is far from sure what Surrealism is about.[3] Freud felt that one could not analyse the productions of the Surrealists because the analytic process cannot take place in public. The psychoanalytic process of so-called 'free association' is not like automatic writing, for instance, because there is not some pure truth which can emerge undisguised and unsullied from the unconscious. The freedom of free association is not to be understood as an absence of determination, but rather as overruling the voluntary selection of thoughts. What one overrules thereby is the censorship between the conscious and the pre-conscious (what is not present to consciousness); what is thereby revealed are the unconscious defences, which operate between the pre-conscious and the unconscious (what is barred from consciousness). These unconscious defences reveal themselves in the material that the analysand produces in the course of the analysis. This material does not directly consist of impulses or emotions; it consists of ideas or images that have attached themselves to these emotions. The return of the repressed is not the return of an impulse or an emotion but the return of whatever idea or image has attached itself to them. It is only when the analyst and analysand 'work through' — as Freud calls it — the repeated emergence of these images that the unconscious fantasy can be pieced together.

The popular account of Surrealism, including Breton's own, relates it to the dream and argues that the unconscious emerges in a dreamlike manner in the techniques of collage and automatic writing. But Theodor Adorno, in an essay entitled 'Rückblickend auf den Surrealismus',[4] questions whether we should necessarily accept the Surrealists' own understanding of what they are doing, since this is tantamount to explaining the strange by the familiar, by what we already understand. Adorno argues that, if Surrealism is taken to be no more than a literary and graphic illustration of Freudian or Jungian theory, it becomes just a harmless reduplication of what the theory tells us — hardly the kind of scandal that is the very life-blood of Surrealism. If we view Surrealism simply in terms of Freudian theory, we miss the peculiar power of this movement. According to Adorno, no one dreams in the Surrealist mode; to equate Surrealism with dreaming is at best a crude analogy. The images in Surrealist art, as he points out, are not blurred and unreal as in a dream, they do not dissolve away: they split into parts, and then these parts are treated with odd respect, as if they were autonomous forms, wholes in their own right. In Surrealist art, objects are most carefully chosen and placed, in just this space, next to another object just this size. To understand what is going on one has to look at this art's strategies, its use of collage and montage, which enables images — be it in poetry or in painting — to be juxtaposed in patterns of discontinuity. It is this which gives Surrealism its shock value, provoking that sense of 'where have I seen this before', the *heimlich* (homely and familiar) with the *unheimlich* (hidden and secret). Adorno maintains that the affinity of Surrealism and

Plate 11 René Magritte, *The Art of Living*, 1967 (© ADAGP, Paris, and DACS, London, 1988. Photograph courtesy of Harry N. Abrahams Inc., New York).

psychoanalysis depends not on their common interest in the symbols utilized by a truth-speaking unconscious, but rather on the way that they both focus on the attempts of the unconscious to evoke and reveal in sudden bursts of shock the images of our childhood past still crystallized within us. The giant egg, for instance, from which a monster threatens to emerge at any moment, is big because we were so very small when we first gazed at an egg in extreme trepidation. The uncanny effect is brought about because we are confronted with a subjectivity now alien to us, because we have had to move on. What produces shock, in his view, is that twilight state between a schizophrenic sense of the world split into parts, either chopped up or threatening to merge, and the apparent autonomy and self-sufficiency that these parts assume. The apparent freedom from normal representation becomes threatening, leading to a kind of death, either because objects become rigid, or because they melt, flow and dissolve.

These images, Adorno argues, are fetishes, objects once invested with emotion, but now estranged, left over from the past, dead substitutes for what is no longer. And this is where psychoanalysis *does* come in. Magritte's pictures of severed breasts, legs in silk stockings, shoes with human toes, the nose, eyes and lips, floating in space, are reminders of what Freud calls 'Objekte der Partialtriebe', later developed by Melanie Klein in her theory of the part-object. These 'component instincts' (for instance an oral or anal instinct) are sexual instincts functioning independently of any overall organization and they can be observed in the fragmented sexual activities of children and also in the sexual life of adults. We are reminded of how libido, the energy of the sexual drive, first got going, by attaching itself to whatever the senses perceived as signficant at the time, but which now belongs to a history of repression. This is why this kind of object is *unheimlich*: what we are seeing are old childhood wishes we have long since had to repress. The distortions of the object bear witness to the taboos and interdictions we had to observe, and to what these taboos have done to our past desires. What this ignores, as will be seen subsequently, is that the uncanny can be viewed as subversive rather than merely regressive.

Three paintings from the work of René Magritte will serve as examples of the characteristic co-presence of *heimlich* and *unheimlich* elements in Surrealist art. First, *The Art of Living* (see plate 11), which at first sight appears to be like a child's picture of the sun, oddly placed, because the sun is in front of the mountain instead of behind it, hence more important than the mountain. The sun as king-image is suddenly turned into a man- or father-image, by means of the body underneath and the face in the middle of the sphere, which is nearer the size of the body than its own surround. But the sun is also a severed head, a fearful realization of a repressed wish. At the very moment when this wish is gaining expression, it emerges as a threat, staring fixedly. The picture combines the abnormality of the *unheimlich* with the normality of the *heimlich* – the dress suit and tie and brick wall at the front of the picture, towered over by the huge and lurid sun. The picture is called 'The Art of Living' – maybe the art of coming to

Plate 12 René Magritte, *The Beautiful Relations* (© ADAGP, Paris, and DACS, London, 1988. Photograph courtesy of Isidore Ducasse Fine Arts).

terms with the repression of the father; the sun is so very big, because the father (or the law) once seemed, and in the unconscious still seems, so very powerful.

Second, *The Beautiful Relations* (see plate 12), where the *heimlich*, the idea of a balloon flying in a romantic morning or evening sky, is immediately made *unheimlich*, because the balloon turns into an eye, or an eye-patch. The single eye left in the sky turns into a kind of god-eye, its colours, blue and flesh, making the pastel shades of the sky much less *heimlich*. The nose, distinctly phallic, could also be a rocket. The picture gives a sense of fragmented human desire; it conveys a sense of striving, rising, being erect. Certain aspirations are unmasked as having a powerful sexual element, yet made dubious and threatening by these elements being displaced into an incongruously romantic landscape, creating far from 'beautiful relations'.

Third, *Philosophy in the Boudoir*, (see plate 13), which is an example of fetishization, the part-objects indicating rigidified desire. What is seen is not the dress on the hanger, the *heimlich* object, but what the dress normally conceals, the breasts and pubic mound, unexpectedly revealing themselves. The uncanniness of the dress, and of the shoes in a version painted in 1948, bespeaks desire. Something that should have remained hidden is coming to light. The movement of the toes in the high-heeled restricting shoe emphasizes the sexual connotation of the shoe. It is a movement that undermines the repression, letting the *unheimlich*, what should remain hidden, emerge.

According to Adorno, Surrealism furnishes us with an 'album of idiosyncracies', objects which say 'no' to desire, and if, he continues, Surrealism strikes us as obsolete, it is because we don't wish to be reminded of the failures of desire of which it speaks.

This perceptual world, which strikes us as obsolete, which we once hallucinated and thought we controlled, whose animistic modes of perception Freud speaks of in *The Uncanny*, makes no distinction between self and other, me and not-me. It is the infant's world of primary narcissism, which defies any notions of common-sense reality. Fantasy, Freud tells us, is intimately connected with an archaic mental theory, with the belief in the omnipotence of thoughts:

> Our analysis of instances of the uncanny has led us back to the old, animistic conception of the universe. This was characterized by the idea that the world was peopled with the spirits of human beings; by the subject's narcissistic overvaluation of his own mental processes; by the belief in the omnipotence of thoughts and the techniques of magic based on that belief; by the attribution to various outside persons and things of carefully graded magical powers, or '*mana*'; as well as by all the other creations with the help of which man, in the unrestricted narcissism of that stage of development, strove to fend off the manifest prohibitions of reality. It seems as if each one of us has been through a phase of individual development corresponding to this animistic stage in primitive men, that none of us has passed through it without preserving

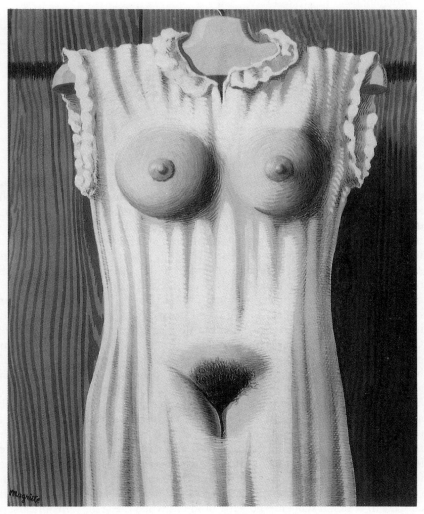

Plate 13 René Magritte, *Philosophy in the Boudoir*(© ADAGP, Paris, and DACS, London 1988. Photograph courtesy of Isy Brachot Gallery, Brussels, Paris).

certain residues and traces of it which are still capable of manifesting themselves, and that everything which now strikes us as 'uncanny' fulfills the condition of touching those residues of animistic mental activity within us and bringing them to expression.[5]

This is how Freud summarizes the dual uncanny effect of the unconscious:

An uncanny experience occurs either when infantile complexes which have been repressed are once more revived by some impression, or when primitive beliefs which have been surmounted seem once more confirmed. Finally, we must not let our predilection for smooth solutions and lucid exposition blind us to the fact that these two classes of the uncanny are not always sharply distinguishable. When we consider that primitive beliefs are most intimately connected with infantile complexes, and are, in fact, based on them, we shall not be greatly astonished to find that the distinction is often a hazy one.[6]

The uncanny is the projection of our inner fears onto the external, creating objects of love and hate. Fantasy can remake reality, and the instrument by which it does is projection. Through projection fantasy discharges itself into the world, but when the object thus singled out fails us, it is experienced as uncanny. In Hoffmann's story *Der Sandmann*, which features in Freud's essay as an example of the uncanny, the doll Olympia serves as an ideal mirror-image by means of which the suffering protagonist unsuccessfully tries to reconstruct his shattered self-image. The automaton becomes an uncanny object, standing for all objects, which, similarly, are not able to fulfil our desires forever. The story is an allegory of the uncanny in life. The favoured object turns into an object of fear just as the beautiful Olympia in the story turned into a rigid automaton which was dismembered before the protagonist's eyes. Automata are uncanny objects precisely because of their rigidity, their determined and inexorable behaviour. The reader of *Der Sandmann*, or anyone who watches an automaton in fascination, senses something of the fear of being driven by an uncontrollable impulse from within. The object becomes *unheimlich* when the repressed impulse breaks through. The uncanny is the return of the repressed, the feared desire-fantasy, and according to Freud its occurrence in art is different from that in life because the artist has his own resources for making it appear or disappear. By virtue of his skill he can create the right context for its emergence, whereas in life one has to wait for the context in which it will emerge – the moment when the symptom appears, or the forgotten name is on the tip of one's tongue, or a joke happens, or the picture-language of the dream is unravelled.

As an example of the uncanny taken from life, we may look at the famous case-history of the 'Wolf Man', the proper title being 'From the History of an Infantile Neurosis' (1918). I am choosing a scene which illustrates the moments when the repressed material emerges in the course of the patient's analysis with Freud. This should make it easier to see the relation of the

Surrealist object to the repressed fantasy and make plain that fantasy in the psychoanalytic sense, being entirely unconscious, has nothing to do with any direct representation of what is desired. The real wish remains hidden. Fantasy is not to be understood in the popular sense of the term, as a wish-fulfilling daydream, but as something that a subject constructs in order to get closer to what it desires or dreads.

The 'Wolf Man' was the case which caused Freud to confront the problem of the relation between 'primal scene' (as actual event in which the child observes parental intercourse and later experiences a sexual approach by the parent of the opposite sex) and 'primal phantasy' (as a mental structure which might be inherited). Whatever conclusion Freud finally reached (it happens to be the fantasy option), the case history shows the way such fantasies emerge from under a screen of memory. The patient was a wealthy young Russian who came to have an analysis with Freud in 1910. In his general survey of the case Freud describes some of the Wolf Man's fears:

> There was a particular picture-book, in which a wolf was represented, standing upright and striding along. Whenever he caught sight of this picture he began to scream like a lunatic that he was afraid of the wolf coming and eating him up. His sister, however, always succeeded in arranging so that he was obliged to see this picture, and was delighted at his terror. Meanwhile he was also frightened at other animals as well, big and little. Once he was running after a beautiful big butterfly, with striped yellow wings which ended in points, in the hope of catching it. He was suddenly seized with a terrible fear of the creature, and screaming, gave up the chase. He also felt fear and loathing of beetles and caterpillars. Yet he could also remember that at this very time he used to torment beetles and cut caterpillars to pieces. Horses, too, gave him an uncanny feeling. If a horse was beaten he began to scream, and he was once obliged to leave a circus on that account.[7]

It is not the objects in themselves, however, which provoke the fear, but what they represent in the structure of the unconscious fantasy. This can be illustrated by one of the dreams that the Wolf Man relates to Freud in the course of analysis. In this dream a man is tearing off the wings of an 'Espe'. Freud was puzzled by this and asked what he meant. The Wolf Man answered that he meant the insect with the yellow stripes on its body that stings. German was not the Wolf Man's native language (it was Russian) and his mistake could look like a natural one, *Espe* for *Wespe* (wasp). However, as pronounced in German, the initials of the Wolf Man's name were 'S.P.', hence *Espe*. There are thus two meanings for one sound, a *heimlich* one (wasp) and an *unheimlich* one (the Wolf Man's name), forging a link between the mutilated insect and the patient himself. Further associations followed. From an earlier memory of the patient Freud had elicited that yellow stripes were associated with a woman, a nursery maid called Grusha. At first Freud thought that maybe this memory had something to do with a striped dress she might have been wearing, but it was not so. In the Wolf Man's language (Russian) the sound Grusha (the maid's name) was also the name of a particular kind of pear with yellow stripes, which the Wolf Man in childhood had found particularly delicious. This in turn enabled him to recall a childhood dream of a large butterfly with yellow stripes and large wings, which he had found frightening. The connection between the insect-butterfly and the insect-wasp is thus another associative link, over-determining the form of the later dream, that is, letting one element (the stripes) produce more than one meaning. A fantasy (we still don't know what it is about) can thus be displaced and condensed along such a series to any degree of complexity, depending on the associations of the dreamer. The Wolf Man did not know why he was afraid of these images; the fantasy hid the cause. The sequences finally led back via a recollection of the nursery maid on her knees, scrubbing the floor, to a scenario of a 'primal scene'. The whole case was a landmark for Freud, precisely because he had to confront the problem of how far these primal scenes, repressed memories of parental intercourse, were real memories or fantasies. The point I want to make is this: in each case the structure of the fantasy is the same, but the content changes. Something seen or heard is given two meanings, a *heimlich* one and an *unheimlich* one.

The following diagram should make the structure of the dream clear:

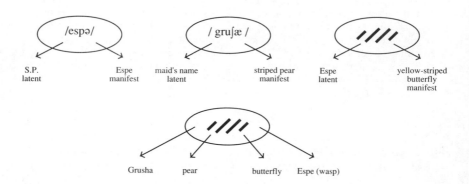

First, there is a sensory element, something seen or heard. Taking the incidents in order of time, the sound 'Espe' is *heimlich* as the name of the insect, *unheimlich* as the initials of the Wolf Man; the sound 'Grusha' is *heimlich* as the name of the maid, *unheimlich* as the name of the pear; the stripes are *heimlich* on the butterfly, *unheimlich* on the pear. Grusha, stripes and 'Espe' each have a manifest *heimlich* meaning which veers into a latent *unheimlich* one, illustrating Freud's point in his essay *The Uncanny* that *heimlich* can mean both familiar and homely, and also secret and hidden. In the Wolf Man's mind all these elements coincide on the yellow stripes. The unconscious linked all these without the Wolf Man's conscious knowledge: the fear attached itself to the sensory element, but he does not know why. The real cause is repressed, just as in the ambiguous shoe/foot of the *Philosophy in the Boudoir* picture the *heimlich* shoe conceals and reveals the *unheimlich* presence of the living foot.

The uncanny emerges in the most unexpected places. A number of critics have pointed out that the repressed returns in Freud's own essay *The Uncanny*. 'Freud', writes Hélène Cixous, 'has hardly anything to envy Hoffmann for his "art and craftiness" in provoking the *Unheimliche* effect.'[8] For even as he analyses the uncanny effects in Hoffman's story, his own text displays similar effects. It is disrupted by repeated images of dismembered bodies, effects of the unconscious, which reveal anxiety about death, and anxiety about his own priority as the discoverer of the unconscious, whether it is he or the poets who understand better its uncanny effects.

However, the uncanny need not only be seen in a negative way, as necessarily involving regression. According to more recent readings of the uncanny, Freud's understanding of it is unduly pessimistic, for Surrealism reveals a strongly subversive element: the disturbance of the structure of our old desires can also be a sign that it is time to think about changing self and world. What is involved for Breton in the moment when the object fails we may term 'the failure of the category' and he made this failure a central theme of the Surrealist manifesto. He writes of a 'stock catalogue' of description in which an old system out of touch with present reality tries to trap the individual. Breton wants to shake loose the subject – the self in process rather than the self assumed to be there from the start – away from a rigid order which no longer serves either the subject or its culture. For it isn't only the subject who has got stuck; history and society have also got stuck in repeating the old repression. The emergence of the uncanny may be the moment which disturbs our voyeuristic gaze, the moment which allows us to see that the old repression is futile, a waste of energy – 'uneconomic' in both its Freudian and its material sense, serving neither useful psychic nor commercial purposes – and that a redirection of desire is called for.

This jolting into awareness is performed in four further examples from Magritte. His well-known image of a round-bowled pipe with curved stem provides a comforting picture of a homely object, until you see the caption, '*Ceci n'est pas une pipe*' ('This is not a pipe'), which reminds you that it is only a representation, and that appearances are fooling you. It is uncanny because it has the further implication that in the actual world one also depends on appearances. The pipe might break, have no tobacco, not light up, fail to give you the hoped-for reassurance. Michel Foucault points out that the words themselves represent something which is uncanny: if *ceci*, meaning 'this', is taken to refer to the phrase, the result is that one realizes that words are not pipes, that language has no direct relation to the object which it replaces.[9] Language, instead of being the reliable guide to nature, is shown to fail in its cataloguing of the world. So the picture says both 'this

Plate 14 René Magritte, *The Unexpected Answer* (© ADAGP, Paris, and DACS, London 1988. Photograph © A.C.L. – Bruxelles).

image isn't a pipe', and 'this phrase isn't a pipe', and enacts an uncanny invasion of the comforting world where image and language coexist unproblematically.

In *The Unexpected Answer* (see plate 14) another object that we always take for granted shocks us into awareness of the provisional nature of objects. The door is a familiar object, normally associated with demarcating a boundary, either keeping something out or keeping it in. Here the uncanny effect is that it obviously has not done its job. Something, some force, vaguely human, has walked or broken through, leaving a darkness, a hole, a gap, something that cannot be defined, but poses a question. Though this picture could be looked upon as a transgression of a taboo, it can also be read as an image of epistemological subversion.

In *Dangerous Relationships* (see plate 15) the mirror is used to hide the person that is looking into it, instead of reflecting her. The picture is *heimlich* only as long as we ignore the reflection in the mirror. As soon as we see it, it becomes apparent that her very modesty betrays the desire to be seen. The woman hides, yet she wants to be looked at; she solicits the gaze of someone, but she does it by an affectation of modesty. The picture is uncanny, because the mirror itself is quite opaque: hiding behind a mirror should be a perfect concealment. But instead the mirror not only does not conceal, it reveals what it should not, by showing her from another angle. The pose we see in the mirror is the pose of someone who is not aware of being looked at, which increases the uncanny effect, because it suggests that the woman herself would be surprised at the discovery of her own self-betrayal. This can be taken as an image of wished-for self-effacement in the symbolic, which fails to achieve its aim and becomes a self-revelation.

Carte Blanche (see plate 16) produces a less sinister impression, because it makes the point in a more abstract mode: the incongruity is, however, epistemologically similar. It is uncanny, because it has two modes of reality which are incongruous with each other: if you accept one, then you reject the other. It is a question of perspectival disturbance. In one part of the picture the horse is seen to be in front of the background; in another part the background is in front of the horse. The woman is clearly seen to be in front of a broad tree-trunk, but she is partly concealed by a narrower trunk, which, at the top and the bottom of the picture, is represented as being behind the broad one. The incongruity shows itself most markedly in the left rear leg of the horse. Thus there is a distortion of the three-dimensional plane. Every little bit makes sense on its own, but together they do not. The picture is subversive, because it defies the normality of seeing, reminding us that normal seeing is an achievement. The uncanny is what defies the normality of seeing. The cunning of the normal is that it conceals its own construction. The uncanny unmasks this deceit and thus removes itself from the category of the return of the repressed.

But what might be an example of something disturbing which does not fit into the category of the uncanny as defined in this essay? *The Robing of the Bride*

Plate 15 René Magritte, *Dangerous Relationships* (© ADAGP, Paris, and DACS, London 1988).

Plate 16 René Magritte, *The Blank Signature*, 1956 (© ADAGP, Paris, and DACS, London 1988. Photograph. National Gallery of Art, Washington; collection of Mr and Mrs Paul Mellon).

Plate 17 Max Ernst, *Robing of the Bride*, 1940 (© DACS 1989, Peggy Guggenheim Collection, Venice; The Solomon R. Guggenheim Foundation, New York, photograph: Robert E. Mates).

by Max Ernst (see plate 17), I would argue, is an example of a picture that is *not* uncanny. The main feature about it is that it has no element of the *heimlich* whatsoever. The incongruities are of an immediately shocking kind: there is distortion and strange juxtaposition of animal and human forms, and of male and female too. Each form is itself distorted before it is even mixed. The animal as repressed desire seems to be escaping and taking over. 'The Robing of the Bride', as the picture is called, represents a ceremony of society, the moment when desire is countenanced and revered by society, and given its due social place. But at that moment we are given images of the fearful power of libido, some in bold and frightening red, suggesting blood and fire, desire rampant and destructive. The fantasy has broken through and is openly declaring itself, exploding the boundaries of animal and human, dead and living. The world is not merely uncannily displaced or blurred, but grotesquely distorted, in a return of the repressed which is so openly paraded that it blocks the viewer's responses. The grotesque is the paradoxical situation in which desire and prohibition, breaking all normal boundaries, are in a state of sharp antagonism and are not going to be resolved in any way. The uncanny, on the other hand, confronts one with a world in which the familiar and unfamiliar, the canny and the uncanny, are in a state of uneasy alliance, suggesting the possibility of intervention, of changing a part of the world and the self, a moment of desymbolization where there is a shift of the old order and a chance to resymbolize, to create fresh symbols. The French philospher, Jean-François Lyotard, describes the field from which the uncanny emerges as 'the unpresentable', meaning that something is happening which defies representation.[10] The uncanny may thus be seen as a basis for a positive aesthetic, a moment when new possibilities, new meanings, may emerge, rather than as a moment when the old repressed meaning returns.

Notes

1   Sigmund Freud, 'The Uncanny', *SE*, XVII, p. 219; Pelican 14.
2   ibid., p. 226.
3   Sigmund Freud, *SE*, XII, p. 131.
4   Theodor Adorno, 'Rückblickend auf den Surrealismus', in *Noten zur Literatur* (1958; Suhrkamp, Frankfurt, 1981), pp. 101–5.
5   'The Uncanny', pp. 240–1.
6   ibid., p. 249.
7   Sigmund Freud, 'From the History of an Infantile Neurosis' (The Wolf Man), *SE*, XVII, p. 16; Pelican 9.
8   Hélène Cixous, 'Fiction and its phantoms: a reading of Freud's *Das Unheimliche*', in *New Literary History*, 7 (Spring 1976), pp. 525–48; see also Neil Hertz, 'Freud and the Sandman', in *Textual Strategies: Perspectives in Post-Structuralist Criticism*, ed. Josué V. Harari (Methuen, London, 1980), pp. 296–321.

9   Michel Foucault, *This is not a Pipe* (University of California Press, Berkeley, Los Angeles and London, 1983).
10 Jean-François Lyotard, *The Postmodern Condition: A Report on Knowledge*, trans. Geoffrey Bennington and Brian Massumi (Manchester University Press, Manchester, 1984), p. 79.

SUGGESTED READING

Freud, S., *Three Essays on the Theory of Sexuality* (1905), *SE*, XII, pp. 123–246.
Freud, S., 'On Narcissism: An Introduction' (1914), *SE*, XIV, pp. 163–90.
Freud, S., 'From the History of an Infantile Neurosis' (The Wolf Man) (1918), *SE*, XVII, pp. 1–24.
Freud, S., 'The Uncanny' (1919), *SE*, XVII, pp. 217–56.
Wright, E., *Psychoanalytic Criticism: Theory in Practice*, Methuen, London, 1984, pp. 9–15, 79–84, 142–50.

16

Monsters in Surrealism: Hunting the Human-Headed Bombyx

ELZA ADAMOWICZ

The Monster's Lair: Happy Hunting Grounds

Do Surrealist monsters really exist? And do they betray the pre-existence of a monstrous unconscious? Or are we trapping the monster in a rationalist discourse by using a term which usually designates what is *against* reason? And when Breton pens the monster in inverted commas,[1] or when Dali simply makes it disappear,[2] how can the use of this term be justified? Quite simply by freeing this 'monster' from its inverted commas, that straitjacket of dualistic thought, and inscribing it, not in a system of oppositions where it would be labelled as parasitical and unnatural, a signal of disorder or the sign of a world turned upside down, but in an ambivalent space. Just like carnival creatures of the Middle Ages, the Surrealist monster 'ignores the stage'[3] and roams in a global carnival space. In fact these 'monsters lying in wait' [4] are not opposed to reality, nor are they on the other side of reality; their habitat on the contrary is Surrealist space, which encompasses the whole of reality, it is a space of dreams and obsessions, the unconscious and the everyday; like Dali's 'monster of sleep' (see plate 18), they emerge from reality itself, 'held up by the crutches of reality'.[5] And Breton himself counters the 'monster' of the rationalists with another type of monster, a 'phantom-object' defined as a poetic or plastic construction.[6] He presents as examples of such monsters, in the domain of visual practice, forms as diverse as Picasso's 'Clarinet Player', Chirico's 'Vaticinator', Max Ernst's 'Femme 100 têtes', and Dali's 'Great Masturbator'.

The Surrealist bestiary is vast indeed. It includes Léonor Fini's sphinxes and Raymond Queneau's 'cat-headed spider'; [7] the minotaurs of Man Ray's photographs and the 'frizzy hippogriff' of the Surrealist collective games; [8]

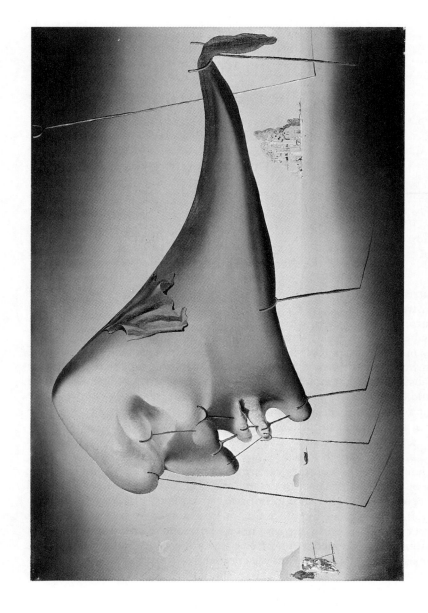

Plate 18 Salvador Dali, *Le Sommeil*, 1937 (© DEMART PRO ARTE BV/DACS 1988, Photograph. Dienst Gemeentelijke Musea, Rotterdam).

visual creatures of Delvaux, Molinier or Brauner and verbal monsters of Desnos, Eluard or Breton.

Far from wishing to embark on a teratologist's task, laboriously labelling the monster, I should like to explore through an analysis of the monster the *expérience-limite* – that is, the extreme limit of experience as significant exception – which is characteristic of Surrealism. The monster tends to lurk in domains which are usually considered peripheral, domains of Surrealist experimentation where rational activity is flouted, and a material practice, based on free associations and random collocations, is deliberately promoted, releasing monsters as those creatures of the unconscious produced through a linguistic or plastic activity, generated through the manipulation of forms. These monsters are to be found firstly in a linguistic space, where the clash of verb and noun can provoke the still-stammering hint of a meaning; a space in which certain experimental articulations, 'exquisite corpses' and automatic writing, engender novel forms. They also lurk in visual spaces, where lines can generate an eye or a claw, where images from illustrated magazines constitute the raw material for limitless concatenations.

The monster is not defined in terms of a *norm*, which, within a narrow conception of reality, would presuppose its inappropriateness. Nor can it be defined in terms of *representation*, which would imply a reality preceding the figure. Although Breton himself declares that Surrealist painting should be the representation of 'a *purely internal model*' (*SP*, p. 4; italics in original), the monster is less a carbon copy of dreams or hallucinations than a form of production originating in the manipulation of verbal or visual materials. A very wide definition is proposed here for the term 'monster': *the monster is the articulation of two or more disparate elements which generates the image of a hybrid creature, whether verbal or visual.*

By dint of searching for monsters, any form can become monstrous, whether it is the mutation of Miró's circle into a creature with threatening jaws or vaginal teeth, the woman's 'giant claw stomach' in Breton's 'Union libre', even the spider-monkeys which Diego Rivera caresses (*SP*, p. 143). Monsters seem to proliferate everywhere, whether emerging from familiar forms – and the monster-effect can be all the greater if the monster is close to the known – or within totally unfamiliar conformations. What follows is a reflection on the monster in Surrealism, based on a few monsters stalked at random and deliberately left untamed.

Producing the Monster: Collage Monsters or Embryonic Monsters

Traditionally the monster was a creature beyond the pale, paraded at fairgrounds, provoking laughter and horror, fear and fascination. The Surrealist monster, on the contrary, settles at the centre of the Surrealist city, and not in its outlying wastelands. What was once widely deemed peripheral – flea-market objects, surplus and reject items, doodles of the pen and blobs of the paintbrush, or the marginal zones of the mind, that twilight space between the sleep of reason and the waking of the imaginary – occupies a central space for the Surrealists. That is where the monsters *howl.*

Surrealist monsters can be grouped into two categories, according to whether they are the product of ready-made material or of gestating matter. On the one hand the monster can be fabricated from an assemblage of already constituted materials, a bric-à-brac construction of fragments of reality – any reality, regardless of hierarchy. Such a hybrid creature is the product of a *bricolage* activity, whether it is actually collage, as in Max Ernst's work, or the outcome of the collective doodling known as 'exquisite corpses', or again the unusual mating of two words. On the other hand, the monster can be generated by the transformation of organic matter. Such monsters are embryonic creatures rather than articulated beings: 'everything is seeking itself', writes Breton about Max Ernst, 'and is in the process of becoming articulate' (*SP*, p. 168). This type of monster is also a hybrid, of substance and form, of form and shape. Like Leonardo da Vinci's 'ancient paranoiac wall' (*SP*, p. 129), from which forms emerge before a hallucinating eye, matter engenders monsters. In his reply to the survey 'Is suicide a solution?' carried out by *La Révolution surréaliste,* [9] Masson presents an automatic drawing suggesting fragments of bodies, hands, breasts and sexual organs. An ironic reply? Is he alluding to the germination of life, or to the dissolution thereof? The monster surfaces in precisely that passage between the inchoate and form, between (re)production and death. In an analysis of automatism in visual practice, Breton alludes to this passage when showing how Dominguez liberates beings from matter itself,[10] how the *grattage* technique of Esteban Frances releases 'great hallucinatory figures' (*SP*, p. 146). This sketching of the monster is also effected in the passage from form to shape (Miró) (see plate 19), egg to being (Fini [11]), in the path from line to sign (Michaux), in shifts from the solid to the fluid (in Dali and Tanguy), in Desnos' moves from sounds to words in the creation of verbal monsters: 'que votre araignée rit' [let your spider laugh], 'Les chat hauts sur les châteaux d'espoir' [cats high on hope's castles].[12] The monster is also located in the metamorphic space of overlapping forms: the leaf-insects of Tanguy or Max Ernst, Masson's chairs becoming human bodies or his erotic landscapes where the body is also mountain, chasm or stream. Hence the inanimate becomes animate in the works of Max Ernst, whether in *collages*, where for example a Second Empire style ornament becomes a chimera ('Loplop presents Chimera') or in the process of *frottage* which evokes hallucinatory forms in the texture of a leaf or a wooden plank ('Natural History').

Max Ernst's monsters are combinatory, the implementation of a double vision which he links to Dali's paranoiac images.[13] This 'constant interpenetration of the visual and the visionary' (*SP*, p. 188) articulates what the Surrealist eye *perceives*, what the Surrealist voice *reveals*, in a generalized application of the Surrealist game of analogies 'l'un dans l'autre': the monster appears where a juxtaposition of words or traces forms an image. Whether a deliberate process of fabrication or a spontaneous outburst, whether born abruptly or through deferred germination, whether cut-up or flowing, the monster is born of an encounter, responding to the 'predetermined desire to *compose a figure*' whose effect is to 'carry anthropomorphism to its limits, and prodigiously stress the life of correspondences which unites the outer and inner worlds' (*SP*, p. 290; italics in original). The object generated becomes the body as possibility, the body as other. Moreover, the deliberate exploitation or arbitrary associations in Surrealist practice is linked to the mechanism of objective chance [*le hasard objectif*], the point of encounter between the unconscious and external reality which forms the desired body, the object of fascination.

This double vision, focusing beyond or beside a single object, and characterized by superimposed or juxtaposed elements, via the *montage* technique as practised by Eisenstein and discussed by Benjamin, and the processes of condensation and displacement of Freudian dream language, opens up the possibility of a rhetorical study of the monster.

Rhetoric of the Monster: Cocking a Snook

'Paradoxically, painters should have their say', declares Breton in 'Le Message automatique'.[14] Jakobson tentatively adumbrated a Surrealist poetics within the framework of a general semiotics, where the study of Max Ernst's painting or Buñuel's cinematographic techniques, for instance, would be relevant in the analysis of the metaphoric processes of Surrealist language.[15] Developing the work done by Jakobson, Groupe MU undertook a rhetorical analysis of the visual collage: the latter actually lends itself to a linguistic analysis, since its structure (selection + combination) is homologous to that of the structure of linguistic meaning according to Jakobson.[16] The monster in its turn seems to lend itself to a similar analysis, for it is structured on the one hand by cutting and reassembling, or the articulation of segments, and on the other hand by the transmutation of a substance into a sign. I propose to sketch out a semiotics of the monster which will cover both verbal and visual production, and which will take as its methodological starting-point the analyses carried out by Groupe MU.

Analogy, as one of the principal rhetorical devices, is articulated in the figure of the metaphor, which is constituted by: (1) the presence of two isotopes; and (2) the process of mediation or semantic intersection.[17] The monster as we encounter it in the exquisite corpse (see plate 20), fulfils the first condition, as a juxtaposition of two or more isotopes:

Plate 19 Joan Miró, *Head of a Man*, 1937 (© ADAGP, Paris, DACS, London, 1989. Richard S. Zeisler Collection, New York).

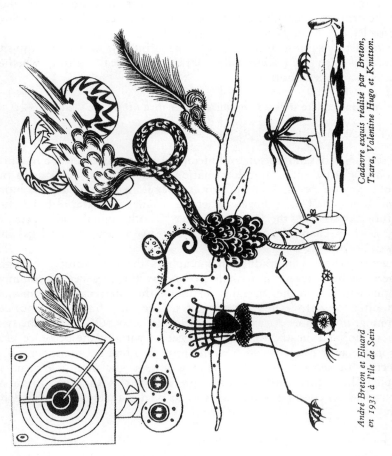

*André Breton et Eluard
en 1931 à l'île de Sein*

*Cadavre exquis réalisé par Breton,
Tzara, Valentine Hugo et Knutson.*

Plate 20 André Breton, Tristan Tzara, Valentine Hugo and Greta Knutson, *Cadavre exquis*, 1931 (© DACS 1989. Photograph. The British Library).

The frizzy hippogriff chases the black doe;

The made-up crayfish dimly lights up various double kisses.[18]

A monster is potentially present in even the smallest linguistic juxtaposition: in the random couplings of verbs and nouns, the fleeting soliciting of nouns and adjectives, ending in monstrous matings. Such matings are also sparked off by the process of substitution, when a spider replaces a head, when jugs stand for legs (p. 8) or a drum for feet (p. 28).

The monster is present not only in the arbitrary forms of exquisite corpses, but also in traditionally marked rhetorical figures, whether comparisons or metaphors:

his ears dangled like stalks of virginia creeper torn off by the wind (p. 34);

small cristal spiders (p. 35).

These examples of comparison and metaphor are monsters in the making, not so much in the sense of a deformation of the 'normal' body as in the sense of a play on forms. A similar process is exploited throughout an entire text in Breton's 'Union libre', where a chain of juxtapositions and substitutions produces the female monster,[19] both animal and vegetable, cosmic and mechanical: otter-waist and seaweed-sex, rocket-legs and clockwork-feet.

However, whereas in traditional metaphors the two isotopes brought together can be reduced to a single isotope by the presence of common semantic elements, in the surrealist metaphor the intersection is minimal, indeed often absent,[20] thus situating it at the very limit of rhetorical functioning: in the line 'A castle in place of the head' (*OC*, p. 16) the two terms, 'castle' and 'head', are brought together without the presence of a common semantic element which would provide a link between them. The intersection of semantic fields being thus absent, the discourse remains allotopic. This *figure-limite* – this figure situated at the outer limit of metaphorical functioning – corresponds to poetic analogy as defined by Breton:

[Poetic analogy] transgresses the laws of deduction to make the mind apprehend the interdependence of two mental objects situated on different planes, between which the logical functioning of the mind is incapable of throwing a bridge and is indeed opposed from the outset to any kind of bridge being thrown.[21]

Such open-ended analogy is a breach onto the arbitrary: since 'everything is like everything else', then 'anything is like anything': a way of cocking a snook at traditional rhetoric by pushing its mechanisms to the limit.

Moreover, the segments of the monster are in a relationship of contiguity, or metonymic relationship,[22] with the other parts of the monstrous body, drum-feet with legs, jug-legs with torso. However, where traditional metonymy draws its elements from the same semantic source, the limbs of the monster remain spare parts, scarcely interlocking. Their disparate character is irreducible and they remain allotopic. Semantic contiguity is replaced in the Surrealist figure by a spatial collocation of random elements in interchangeable groupings, whether on page or canvas. The absence of semantic justification pushes the figure to the limits of the rhetorical process, making it less a metonymy than a mere syntagmatic figure.

Traditional rhetorical figures map a boundary-line: by placing the compared term on the side of the unreal, they preserve clearly demarcated frontiers. In allotopic figures, however, the hierarchy of traditional rhetoric is replaced by a process of levelling.[23] The image becomes monstrous when the compared term changes its status. From unreal it becomes real, read on the same plane as the comparing term, or substituted for it: the distinction between figurative and literal levels is no longer operative.[24] Whence the reversibility of the haï kaï quoted by Breton, where the dragonfly becomes a pimento – or the pimento, dragonfly.[25] Similarly, Eliane Formentelli situates the reversible figures of Max Ernst's collages in a continuous space: the eagle-headed man is also a bird with a human body.[26]

This is where the monster emerges, from the farthest limits of irretrievable language, at the frontiers of nonsense, in so far as 'the fauna and flora of surrealism are unspeakable' (*OC*, p. 340). Thus the monster embodies to a certain extent the rejection of the figurative process, a disfigured rhetoric.

The limbs of the monster do adhere, but on a single plane rather than in depth: 'Sea urchin-cranium, gastropod-sex, tortoise shell-diaphragm and liver, slug-lips, trapped jellyfish-heart'.[27] The framework persists: just as in the exquisite corpse or the litanic form of 'Union libre', the syntax of the body is preserved, but as an empty frame. As in the formulation of the traditional rhetorical figure referred to above, the form of the statement suggests a comparison – in a summary fashion, it is true, since the syntactic links are minimal – yet the semantic associations are tenuous.[28] There is an incomplete interweaving of parts which are held in suspension because of their existence within an ambivalent space; formally they replace the possible body,but semantically they create the *other* body. There is a shift from the known to the unknown in this ambivalent space which triggers off in the reader the poetic emotion of *dépaysement* [disorientation] when confronted with a form of production where the completely other resides so close to the known, without however being reduced to the known, since the form simultaneously calls for and refuses an analogy. A similar process is at work in Max Ernst's collages where the framework of the bourgeois salon, the effacement of all material traces of collage, clash all the more forcefully with the sudden irruption of the monster; indeed, a zoo-full of monsters would be 'incapable of provoking disorientation; it is the emergence of the monster in a real space which does'.[29]

These juxtaposed segments stick uneasily together; these viscous, embryonic, indeterminate shapes are scarcely distinguishable from the formlessness of matter. Neither the markedly disparate elements of the collage nor the indeterminacy of form-matter allow for the move from one term or form to another. This very absence of semantic justification which could rationalize the collocation, thereby making it into a configuration, is underlined by Breton in the recurrent image of the bridge: 'the street car of dreams' ventures onto the 'demolished bridge' (*OC*, p. 519). The elements of the Surrealist image, like dream imagery, are indeed rationally unbridgeable. And the metaphor of the bridge is replaced by that of the spark, the leap replacing the passage in this impossible articulation between the limbs of the monstrous body: 'I shall venture with emotion on a long long purple spark, walking a dangerous plank' (*OC*, p. 534).

Reading the monster: Slipping and Bounding

As a figure articulated on several isotopes, a testimonial to irrationality, the monster, by rejecting depth, seems to defy analysis. How then should the monster be approached?

Pursuing the analysis adumbrated above of the verbal monster as a syntagmatic figure, it would be easy to see in it the transposition of images or mental representations rather than a semantic reality. Groupe MU suggest precisely this displacement when they analyse the syntagmatic collage: 'This type of metaphor could well be simply the transposition into language of a pictorial or plastic metaphor'.[30] When the juggling game between figurative and literal levels cannot be played, language is no longer opaque: as a transparent medium it seems to invite this shift from a verbal to a pictorial form of expression. Thus what was unacceptable in a verbal medium is made acceptable when rendered visible, so true is it that fissures are more readily accepted in a perceptual than a verbal space. Indeed the eye can '*sweep across* a visual field'[31] without the need to decipher, whereas the juxtaposition of words generally calls for a rationalizing process, 'a dynamic sweep in search of unit(ie)s of meaning'.[32] However, such a reading would imply the primacy of the visual and would negate the materiality of language. Yet, although it was argued earlier that the verbal monster generates images, it is primarily a collocation of words, and any trans-verbal '"illumination" comes *afterwards*'.[33] It may open onto vision but it remains a linguistic beast.

A second way of approaching the monster would involve the dissection of its constituent elements. Breton himself undertakes such a task:

> Here is the 'soluble fish' which still manages to terrify me somewhat. SOLUBLE FISH, am I not the soluble fish, I was born under Pisces and man is soluble in his thoughts! The fauna and flora of surrealism are unspeakable.
>
> (*OC*, p. 340)

By deciphering the parts of 'the soluble fish', Breton traps it in a charade, thus rendering it harmless. This method, by reducing the monster to an extratextual reality, drains it of its alterity and makes it quite simply *speakable*. A similar optic colours the extensive scholarship of Werner Spies in his study of the sources of Max Ernst's collages;[34] but such a focus tends to obscure a more radical aspect of the monster, namely the way it is *articulated*.

A third type of reading can be carried out precisely by such an analysis of the links between parts of the monster and the text: a reading which accounts for the monster not so much as a creature formed from a combination of extratextual realities, but as emerging from the body of the text.

In a number of Breton's so-called automatic texts, monsters are the product of semantic generation, such as 'the human-headed bombyx' from 'Rendez-vous' (*OC*, p. 162). This monstrous assemblage is generated by several interwoven semantic networks. As a fantastic animal it is associated, like the 'blue zebras' earlier in the text, with the semes of the circus; as a butterfly producing the silkworm, it is a metonymy of 'bobbins', which links it further to the semes of communication ('bobine' as telegraph wire insulator). Finally, this hybrid creature is on a fictional level a metamorphosis of the 'Vandal Prince' in his sadistic role ('The human-headed bombyx will gradually stifle the cursed harlequins'). This monster, produced by the multiple paradigms of the text, generates in turn the narrative, setting off the final cataclysm ('Great catastrophes will revive chaotically').

Such reading allows us to place the monster in its material context: both as a spider located at the centre of the web of the text, and as an insect caught in this web, produced by the text and in turn producing the text. Situated 'at the point of intersection between a figure of speech and a narrative',[35] in this instance the monster appears less as a figurative being than a literal being emerging from the very texture of the poem. Such a reading focuses less on the configuration of the monster than on its conjugations with its textual environment. A similar reading can be made of the hybrid creatures emerging from the textures of surface in Max Ernst's 'Natural History' (see plate 21), showing for example how a line is both the feather of a wing and the grain of wood.

However, these textu(r)al monsters are quite rare in Surrealist writings. Most monsters emerge abruptly, unable to merge with their environment, such as 'le revolver à cheveux blancs' ('the white-haired revolver') (*OC*, p. 530) which appears inadvertently in a sentence, and resurfaces later as the title of a collection of poems. Breton's monsters are rarely gregarious, often isolating themselves in the titles of poems as if they were stressing their unassimilable otherness, like 'Les Reptiles cambrioleurs' ('The Burglar Reptiles') (*OC*, p. 157) and 'Epervier incassable' ('Unbreakable Hawk') (*OC*, p. 160). In this they resemble the creatures of Max Ernst which spring up uninvited in the salons and streets of Paris.

However, the monster, far from always being isolated from its immediate

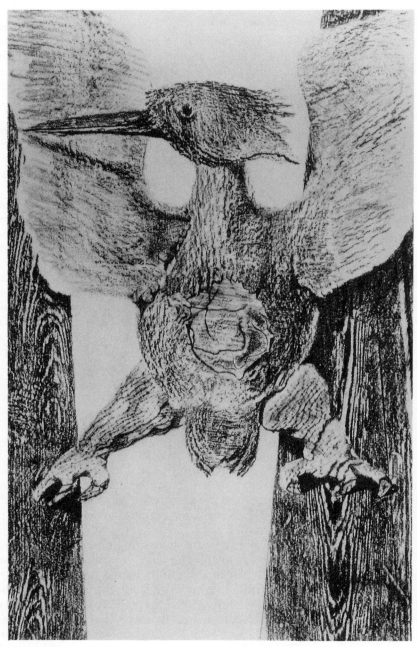

Plate 21 Max Ernst, *Histoire Naturelle*, Plate XXVI, *The Origin of the Clock*
(© DACS 1989. Photograph courtesy of The South Bank Centre: Exhibitions).

Plate 22 Max Ernst, *Une Semaine de Bonté, Mardi, la Cour du Dragon*, 1934
(© DACS 1989. Photograph. The British Library).

context, often spills over onto its environment in a process of displacement. In Max Ernst's collages, the monstrous is often presented as the manifestation of decentred desire. Objects of the bourgeois salon exhibit a form of displaced sexuality: candles acquire phallic form, plants embrace, the folds of curtains are also female sexual organs, a vast female breast is contained in an oval frame.[36] Bestiality inhabits the decor: chair legs become sadistic claws, baroque ornaments turn into threatening jaws. Bestiality also invades the characters: the voluminous folds of ladies' dresses sprout webbed feet and dragon tails, the wings of a bat or animal claws, in the proliferation of libidinous vitality (see plate 22).

This reading of Max Ernst's collages places the stress on the monster as figurative: we go from the hybrid as a collocation of parts, occupying a simple space, to a configuration, occupying a signifying space. For associations do function, given that the mind will always step over the gap between two segments in order to bring them together: 'Poetic analogy is active in the service of a world ramified *as far as the eye can see*'.[37] The wider the gap, the more the associations of the reader/spectator will be a product of the unconscious, a fantastic narrative hitherto unknown, produced by the very gap between disparate elements. This is where the 'exceptional power of *dérive* [drift]' (*SP*, p. 290) intervenes, generated by the spare parts of the exquisite corpse, an activity which corresponds to the processes of displacement and substitution which characterize dreams, and thus functioning not on a manifest but on a latent level. This 'delirium of interpretation' stems from a paranoiac activity of the mind creating links between apparently disparate parts.[38]

The Mona Lisa, transformed by Duchamp by a process of adjunction (moustache) and substitution (title) into a 'ready-made aidé'(an almost ready-made),[39] displays a dual disruptive process: firstly an external disruption in relation to the cultural context: the 'do not touch' of the artistic institution is subverted by the juxtaposition of high art and graffito. Such a reading situates this intervention in a Dada perspective.[40] Yet, if this portrait still arouses so much passion it is because of its continuing power to disturb, and not solely by violating the walls of the museum. Indeed, more important in the signifying process is the disruption caused by sexual *dérive*: a hybrid, an androgynous being is presented, an ambivalent form rather than an oppositional structure, for the androgyne both transgresses and confirms the law of sexual differentiation. Furthermore sexuality is both hidden and displayed, concealed by the laughter generated by the assemblage, and displayed in the rebus-title, 'LHOOQ' and in the moustache as a form of exhibitionism: the displacement of the lower to the upper mouth, in a form of contamination from the genital to the oral. It figures a display of the disturbance engendered by the enigmatic smile of the Mona Lisa, as witnessed by the large numbers of readings in popular iconology, most of which have sexual connotations. Whence the feeling of uncanniness which derives from the fact that what is experienced on a latent level when looking at the Mona Lisa is displayed, shouted out in 'LHOOQ' ('elle a chaud au cul').[41]

A similar composite figure, but explicitly sexual in this instance, is to be found in Magritte's 'Rape', where the woman's head is transformed into an a-cephalic body by a substitution of parts – the eyes are replaced by breasts, nose by navel and mouth by sexual organs. These monstrous forms are variants of the headless woman: similarly, a Man Ray photograph[42] presents the hazy outline of a woman, the place normally occupied by the sexual organs and the head formed by black holes, mirroring each other. Whether the woman has no head or a hundred heads is irrelevant, she has lost her head, the arbitrary character of the process of substitution being equivalent to an act of decapitation.

A final suggested reading consists in bringing together a series of monsters in a single focus, by taking as the object of study precisely this proliferation of the head, the trace of an obsession in a number of Surrealist poets and painters. In fact, the latter often juggle with heads, by substitution or adjunction, either obliterating them or replacing them by heterogeneous objects or the radically other:

a castle in place of the head (*OC*, p. 16);

Women were walking around, and in place of their heads the sphinx of the night burst wide open (*SP*, p. 137);

dead women with geranium heads (*OC*, p. 522);

the woman cut into pieces by my dream . . . in place of her head flowering serpents lay coiled (*OC*, p. 551).

They thus dislodge the seat of reason, deliberately transforming rational space into an instinctual space; witness the phallicization of the head in many of Dali's paintings,[43] the animalization of the head in the multiple representations of the minotaur,[44] as well as the fixation among a number of Surrealists on the praying mantis, the female of which devours the male after coitus.[45]

And yet, 'a decapitated figure, in the poetic or plastic world, is not a headless figure.'[46] Indeed we would fall into the trap of the norm denounced above if these a-cephalic monsters were designated in solely oppositional terms. More important than the anti-rationalist perspective are the dynamics of the monstrous head. The Surrealists have made of the head, not the space structured in depth as described by Freud, but an exploded space where randomness of entry is matched by freedom of egress:

We are the vaporisers of thought. Our pretty rubber heads red-inlaid with small nets collapse and inflate according to the tide of ideas;[47]

I open my head with a golden billhook to remove from it the marvellous
mistletoe which makes suns lean over (*OC*, p. 516)

- a metamorphic space, where for example the multiple substitutions of
Max Ernst are echoed by Breton who, by generating new associations,
continues the practice of the painter: 'But the human head opening, flying
and enfolding its thoughts like a fan, the head falling back on its hair like a
lace pillow, the fragile, weightless head . . . blue-scalloped like New Mexico
dolls' (*SP*, p. 27). The Surrealist head becomes an autonomous figure,
liberated, for 'a headless figure is more apt to cross the path of putrefying
donkeys.'[48] This explosion of the head articulates a desire among the
Surrealists to transcend the self towards a state of depersonalization, in a
space where the frontiers between body and world would cease to be
pertinent: the features of the face which constituted the portrait, marking
the identity of the individual, are replaced by the arbitrary of the surreal,
like the 'portraits' of Magritte, where an apple or a dove replaces the face.

The various readings of the monster outlined in the preceding pages make
absolutely no claim to tame the beast; they are, on the contrary, tentative
approaches rather than netting strategies. We should continue to let the
monster have its head. In any reading of the monster the oscillatory
movement continues between the two poles, monsters occupying a space,
and monsters as a configuration signifying that space, between bounding
and slipping, a multiple signifying game and the thwarting of any meaning.

The Howling of Monsters

Multiple readings openly acknowledge the fact that the monster cannot be
reduced to a single interpretation. Such a reading would imply reducing the
beast to the symbolic, anthropomorphic function of monster as metaphor or
allegory, thus obscuring the radical otherness of the monster, on the one
hand as a multiple signifying process, and on the other hand *qua* monster.
The disparate elements of the monster, while overlapping, retain their
autonomy; it is their monstrous interlocking which generates meaning, not
their common denominator. Indeed the monster remains pluri-isotopic, a
literal agglomeration of members or a form emerging from the formlessness
of matter. Referring to his 1930s collages, Ernst writes: 'My works from
that time were not destined to seduce but to produce howls.'[49] Similarly
Bozzetto alludes to the *noise* of the fantastic when referring to incongruous
juxtapositions 'as a sign of the brute event, the non-locatable emergence'.[50]
The reading of the Mona Lisa is not a way of removing the moustache – in
spite of the invitation card sent by Duchamp for an exhibition in 1965,
representing a playing card with the effigy of the Mona Lisa, and the
inscription 'shaved LHOOQ' – the moustache remains, incongruous,
shocking, howling.

The reader/spectator always comes back to the paradoxical presence of the monster: it is as a figurative being (since we can outline meanings) but, above all, as a verbal or plastic being that the monster is the source of *sparks*. The reader is constantly returning to the material existence of the monster, in other words to the collage-monster in the process of becoming collocated, to the embryonic monster in the initial stages of gestation, its indeterminate existence becoming articulate. It is this to and fro between the monster as figurative process and the monster as feral matter which engenders the 'singular power of *frôlement*' [light touching][51], which is both a surfacing of multiple meanings and the contact of matter, the pleasure of apprehending a line as it becomes a sign, a form as it becomes a shape.

Surrealist monsters are liberated forms, masks of a perpetual carnival, the eruption of another time and space. In these organs, whether stuck (Ernst) or displaced (Bellmer, Magritte), disproportionate (Dali) or cut up (Breton, Picabia), aggressivity and eroticism are liberated, along with the licence of the fantastic, the vitality of the marvellous. With the appearance of the monster hierarchies are abolished, taboos disappear, limbs collide: the monster is a manifestation of *jouissance*.

This search for the monster as a form of alterity is also a search for the self: 'Who am I? . . . Why does it not all come down to knowing whom I "haunt"?' (OC, p. 647) The Surrealists often elect monsters as an *alter ego*: Picasso the minotaur or Max Ernst Loplop the Bird Superior, Duchamp the androgynous Rrose Sélavy, Breton the soluble fish and dolphin, Nadja the mermaid, Dali the grasshopper with a human head. This assumed polymorphous identity is a form of experiencing the self as a disparate and exploded being; the monster is an articulation of the figure of identity comprising the self and the *other*, the other as the other in the self. Like the hermit crab, which inserts itself into empty shells, thus provoking a questioning of its identity – 'In this simulated hybrid, which is the *I*, which is the *other*?'[52] – identity stems not from a sense of unity of the self, but from participation with the radically *other*.

Finally the monster is the Surrealist figure *par excellence*: the figure of a constantly renewed tension, never fully voiced, between partial fragmentation and impossible totalization, between the self and the other, matter and form, a line and a sign. For the monster will continue to *howl* after the critic's discourse, irrespective of his discourse. All the critic can really do is listen out for the monster and point it out to others, lie in wait for it, but not in order to shoot it down, for 'the waiting is magnificent.'[53]

Notes

1 Breton writes about the experience of the 'exquisite corpse': 'Between 1925 and 1930 ill-intentioned critics, who . . . suspected that we had individually . . . given birth to such 'monsters' in broad daylight, provided thereby an additional

proof of their ineptness'; in André Breton, *Le Surréalisme et la peinture* (hereafter cited as *SP*) (Gallimard, Paris, 1965), pp. 290–1. (All translations are my own unless otherwise stated.)

2   'a monster ceases to be one from the moment certain relations are established between lines and colours which make it up': Salvador Dali, 'Nouvelles limites de la peinture', *L'Amic de les arts*, 22 (29 fév. 1928), p. 167.

3   Mikhail Bakhtin, *L'Oeuvre de François Rabelais et la culture populaire au Moyen Age et sous la Renaissance* (Collection Tel, Gallimard, Paris, 1970), p. 15.

4   'On my path I create monsters lying in wait . . . Here come "the elephants with heads of women and the flying lions" which Soupault and I used to tremble with fear of meeting': Breton, *Manifeste du surréalisme* (1924), in *Oeuvres Complètes* (hereafter cited as *OC*) (Bibliothèque de la Pléiade, Gallimard, Paris, 1989), p. 340.

5   Salvador Dali, *La Vie secrète de Salvador Dali* (Editions de la Table Ronde, Paris, 1952). Elsewhere he refers to Picasso's 'poetic torsos' as 'authentic monsters'; in 'Nouvelles limites de la peinture', *L'Amic de les arts*, 24 (30 avril 1928), 185.

6   Breton, 'L'objet-fantôme', *Le Surréalisme au service de la révolution*, 3 (déc. 1931), p. 20; also in *Les Vases communicants* (1932) (NRF Idées, Gallimard, Paris, 1970), pp. 63–5.

7   Raymond Queneau, 'Texte surréaliste', *La Révolution surréaliste*, 11 (15 mars 1928), p. 13.

8   *La Révolution surréaliste*, 9–10 (1 oct. 1927), p. 64.

9   *La Révolution surréaliste*, 2 (15 jan. 1925), p. 15.

10   '[Dominiguez] by letting coloured inks run over the surface of a sheet of white paper, and submitting this sheet to very rapid rotations . . . liberates beings shining with all the fires of the humming-birds' (*SP*, p. 146).

11   See Marcel Brion writing about Léonor Fini: 'To be there at the moment of metamorphosis, the patient keeper of larvae and cocoons, to be present when the egg breaks open'; in *Léonor Fini et son oeuvre*, (Pauvert, Paris, 1962) n.p.

12   Desnos, *L'Aumonyme* (1923), in *Corps et biens* (NRF Poésie, Gallimard, Paris, 1968), pp. 52, 60. The first quotation, as a reworking of the words of the Lord's prayer: 'Que votre reigne arrive', is also an example of an intertextual monster. In the second quotation the word *chaos* is echoed in the passage from meaningless to significant sounds.

13   See Max Ernst, 'Comment on force l'inspiration', *Le Surréalisme au service de la Revolution*, 6 (15 mai 1933), p. 44.

14   André Breton, 'Le message automatique', *Point du jour* (1934; NRF Gallimard, Paris, 1970), p. 186.

15   Roman Jakobson, *Essais de linguistique générale* (Minuit, Paris, 1963), p. 210.

16   Groupe MU, 'Douze bribes pour décoller', in 'Collages', *Revue d'esthétique*, 3/4 (1978), p. 14.

17   'By relating two signifying units distinct in certain aspects and analogous in others, the metaphor effects a structure which can be read on two isotopes and . . . joins them by ensuring the passage from one to the other': Groupe MU, *Rhétorique générale* (Larousse, Paris, 1970), p. 118.

18   *La Révolution surréaliste*, 9–10 (1er oct. 1927), p. 64; the examples referred to in this and the next paragraph all figure in this issue of the Surrealist periodical, particularly rich in exquisite corpses and other monsters.

19 André Breton, 'L'Union libre' (1931), in *Clair de terre* (NRF Poésie, Gallimard, Paris, 1966), p. 94. This monstrous woman has given rise to a hyperbolic discourse among certain critics. Maurice Saillet, for example, alludes to 'the great monstrous body which bursts through the floor': 'Les Poèmes d'André Breton', *Mercure de France*, 1028 (1 avril 1949).

20 See Groupe MU *Rhétorique générale*, p. 179.

21 André Breton, *Signe ascendant* (NRF Poésie, Gallimard, Paris, 1968), p. 9.

22 Groupe MU, *Rhétorique générale*, p. 118.

23 cf. Laurent Jenny's analysis of *aplatissement* [levelling]; 'La Surréalité et ses signes narratifs', *Poétique*, 16 (1973).

24 Philippe Dubois, 'Esthétique du collage: un dispositif de ruse', *Annales Esthétiques*, 15–16 (1976–7), p. 78.

25 'Out of Buddhist kindness, Bashô one day ingeniously modified a cruel haï kaï composed by his humorous disciple Kikaku. The latter having written: "a red dragonfly – pluck its wings – a pimento", Bashô replaced it by: "a pimento – add wings – a red dragonfly"': *Signe ascendant*, p. 13.

26 Eliane Formentelli, 'Max Ernst – Paul Eluard, ou l'impatience du désir', *Revue des Sciences Humaines*, 164 (oct.-déc. 1976).

27 Maurice Béchet, *La Révolution surréaliste*, 3 (15 avril 1925), p. 28.

28 In his study of Desnos' texts, Michel Murat shows how Surrealist analogy inverts the structure of a standard comparison. 'They're alike *since* I said *like*': Michel Murat, 'Corps et biens, ou les beaux effets du surréel', *L'Information grammaticale*, 25 (mars 1985).

29 Roger Caillois, *Au Coeur du fantastique (Gallimard, Paris, 1965), p. 98.*

30 Groupe MU, *Rhétorique générale*, p. 128.

31 Laurent Jenny, 'Sémiotique du collage intertextuel, ou la littérature à coups de ciseaux', in 'Collages', *Revue d'esthétique*, 3/4 (1978), p. 165; italics in original.

32 Groupe MU, 'Lecture du poème et isotopies multiples', *Le Français moderne*, 42 (1974), p. 223.

33 Breton, *Point du jour*, p. 186.

34 Werner Spies, *Max Ernst Collagen. Inventar und Widerspruch* (Dumont Schauberg, Cologne, 1974).

35 Gilbert Lascault, *Le Monstre dans l'art occidental. Un problème esthétique* (Klincksieck, Paris, 1973), p. 163.

36 See Renée Riese-Hubert, 'Max Ernst entre la bonté et le plaisir', in *Du Surréalisme et du plaisir* (Champs des activités surréalistes, Corti, Paris, 1987), pp. 149–59.

37 André Breton, *Perspective cavalière* (Gallimard, Paris, 1970); italics in original. See also Paul Eluard: 'No word games. Anything can be compared to anything, everything finds an echo, a reason, a likeness, an opposition, a becoming everywhere, a limitless becoming': *Oeuvres complètes*, vol.I (Bibliothèque de la Pléiade, NRF Gallimard, Paris, 1968), p. 971.

38 'It is enough for the delirium of interpretation to have managed to link together the meaning of disparate images covering a wall, for no-one to be able to deny the existence of such a link': Dali, 'L'Ane pourri', *Le Surréalisme au service de la révolution*, 1 (juillet 1930), p. 10.

39 Paris 1919; appeared in Picabia's periodical *391* (1920); see also *SP*, p. 58.

40 See the analysis by Thierry de Duve, 'Les Moustaches de la Joconde: petit exercice de méthode', in *Duchamp. Colloque de Cerisy* (10/18, Paris, 1971),

Elza Adamowicz

By Duchamp also, the ready-made 'Fountain' is a doubly hybrid creature: as a urinal, it is linked metonymically to the male, whereas its uterine form links it metaphorically to the female. It is also an anthropomorphic form, halfway between an object and a human.

42 *La Révolution surréaliste*, 2 (15 jan 1925), p. 26.

43 See, for example, 'La Harpe invisible'.

44 See in particular Man Ray's illustration for *Minotaure*, 11 (1938), representing the head of a minotaur upside down, double inversion of the head!

45 Breton raised praying mantises; see also Roger Caillois' article, 'La Mante religieuse', *Minotaure*, 5 (1934), pp. 23–6.

46 Dali, 'Nouvelles limites de la peinture'.

47 L. Aragon, 'Texte surréaliste', *La Révolution surréaliste*, 1 (1 déc. 1924), p. 16.

48 Dali, 'Nouvelles limites de la peinture'.

49 Max Ernst, *Ecritures* (Gallimard, Paris, 1970), p. 412; he takes up an expression used by Breton about Max Ernst himself: the elements of his collages start to 'howl at finding themselves together' (*SP*, p. 26).

50 R. Bozzetto, A. Chareyre-Méjan, P. and R. Pujade, 'Penser le fantastique', in 'Les Fantastiques', *Europe*, 611 (mars 1980), 31.

51 Breton, *Point du jour*, p. 62.

52 Philippe Audoin, Introduction, André Breton *Champs magnétiques* (NRF Poésie, Gallimard, Paris, 1971), p. 18; italics in original.

53 André Breton, *L'Amour fou* (1937) (Collection Folio, Gallimard, Paris, 1977), p. 39.

SUGGESTED READING

Balakian, A., *André Breton. Magus of Surrealism*, Oxford University Press, New York, 1971.

Breton, A., *Le Surréalisme et la peinture*, Gallimard, Paris, 1965.

Ernst, M., *Ecritures*, Gallimard, Paris, 1970.

Rubin, W., *Dada and Surrealist Art*, Abrams, New York, 1969.

Waldberg, P., *Max Ernst*, Pauvert, Paris, 1958.

Select General Bibliography

Alexandrian, Sarane, *Surrealist Art*, trans. G. Clough (Thames & Hudson, London, 1970).

Appignanesi, Lisa, *Femininity and the Creative Imagination: A Study of Henry James, Robert Musil and Marcel Proust* (Vision Press, London, 1973).

Bakhtin, Mikhail, *Rabelais and his World*, trans. Helene Iswolsky, (MIT Press, Cambridge, Mass., 1968).

Balmary, Marie, *Psychoanalysing Psychoanalysis: Freud and the Hidden Fault of the Father*, trans. Ned Lukacher (Johns Hopkins University Press, Baltimore, 1982).

Baudet, Henri, *Paradise on Earth*, trans. Elizabeth Wentholt (Yale University Press, New Haven and London, 1965).

Beharriell, Frederick J., 'Psychoanalysis and literature: the Freud-denial syndrome', in *Sinn und Symbol,* ed. Karl Konrad Polheim (Lang, Berne, 1987).

Beja, Morris, *Ephipany in the Modern Novel* (Peter Owen, London, 1971).

Benjamin, W., *One-Way Street and Other Writings,* trans. Edmund Jephcott and Kingsley Shorter (NLB, London, 1979).

Bergonzi, Bernard, *The Myth of Modernism and Twentieth-Century Literature* (Harvester, Brighton, 1986).

Bernheimer, Charles, *Flaubert and Kafka: Studies in Psychopoetic Structure* (Yale University Press, New Haven and London, 1982).

Bersani, L., *The Freudian Body. Psychoanalysis and Art* (Columbia University Press, New York, 1986).

Blanchot, Maurice, *Le Livre à venir,* 2nd edn (Gallimard, Paris, 1959).

Bowie, Malcolm, *Freud, Proust and Lacan: Theory as Fiction (Cambridge University Press, Cambridge, 1987).*

Bradbury, Malcolm and McFarlane, James (eds), *Modernism* (Penguin, Harmondsworth, 1976).

Bürger, P., *Theory of the Avant-Garde,* trans. Michael Shaw (Manchester University Press, Manchester, 1984).

Burke, Peter, *Popular Culture in Early Modern Europe* (Temple Smith, London, 1978).

Cameron, D., *Feminism and Linguistic Theory* (Macmillan, London, 1985).

Chatman, S., *Story and Discourse* (Cornell University Press, Ithaca and London, 1978).

Chodorow, N., *The Reproduction of Mothering* (University of California Press, Berkeley, Los Angeles and London, 1978).

Clark, Ronald W., *Freud: The Man and the Cause* (Jonathan Cape, London, 1980).

Cremerius, Johannes, 'Der Einfluß der Psychanalyse auf die deutschsprachige Literatur', *Psyche,* 41 (1987), pp. 39–54.

Dierks, Manfred, *Studien zu Mythos und Psychologie bei Thomas Mann* (Francke, Berne, 1972).

Derrida, Jacques, *Writing and Difference,* trans. Alan Bass (University of Chicago Press, Chicago, 1978).

Ehrenzweig, A., *The Hidden Order of Art* (Weidenfeld & Nicolson, London, 1967).

Elias, Norbert, *The Civilizing Process,* vol. I, trans. Edmund Jephcott (Blackwell, Oxford, 1978).

Fleming, Michael and Manvell, Roger, *Images of Madness: The Portrayal of Insanity in the Feature Film* (Associated University Press, London, 1985).

Fordham, Frieda, *An Introduction to Jung's Psychology* (Pelican, Harmondsworth, 1968).

Forrester, John, *Language and the Origin of Psychoanalysis* (Macmillan, London, 1980).

Foucault, Michel, *Discipline and Punish,* trans. Alan Sheridan (Allen Lane, London, 1978).

Freud, Sigmund, *The Freud/Jung Letters,* ed. William Maguire (Hogarth Press and Routledge & Kegan Paul, London, 1974).

   The Complete Letters of Sigmund Freud to Wilhelm Fliess, 1887–1904, ed. and trans. Jeffrey Masson (Belknap Press, Cambridge, Mass., 1985).

Friedman, M., *Stream of Consciousness: A Study of Literary Method* (Yale University Press, New Haven and London, 1955).

Fromm, Erich, *The Forgotten Language* (Victor Gollancz, London, 1960).

Fry, R., *The Artist and Psycho-Analysis* (Hogarth Press, London, 1924).

Gay, Peter, *Freud, Jews and Other Germans: Masters and Victims in Modernist Culture* (Oxford University Press, New York, 1978).

   A Godless Jew: Freud, Atheism, and the Making of Psychoanalysis (Yale University press, New Haven and London, 1987).

   Freud: A Life for Our Times (Dent, London, 1988).

Gellner, Ernest, *The Psychoanalytic Movement* (Paladin, London, 1985).

Gilbert, S. M. and Gubar, S., *The Madwoman in the Attic* (Yale University Press, New Haven and London, 1979).

Habermas, Jürgen, 'Modernity – an incomplete project', in *Postmodern Culture,* ed. Hal Foster (Pluto Press, London, 1985).

Haig, S., *Flaubert and the Gift of Speech* (Cambridge University Press, Cambridge, 1986).

Hanscombe, G. and Smyers, V. L., *Writing for their Lives* (Womens' Press, London, 1987).

Homans, Peter, *Jung in Context: Modernity and the Making of a Psychology* (University of Chicago Press, Chicago and London, 1979).

Humphrey, R., *Stream of Consciousness in the Modern Novel* (University of California Press, Berkeley, Los Angeles, and London, 1954).

Hutcheon, L., *Formalism and the Freudian Aesthetic* (Cambridge University Press, Cambridge, 1984).

Jameson, Fredric, 'Postmodernism, or the cultural logic of late capitalism', *New Left Review,* 146 (July–August 1984).

'Postmodernism and consumer society', in *Postmodern Culture,* ed. Hal Foster (Pluto Press, London, 1985).

Johnson, Barbara, *The Critical Difference* (Johns Hopkins University Press, Baltimore, 1980).

Jones, Ernest, *The Life and Work of Sigmund Freud,* ed. and abridged by Lionel Trilling and Steven Marcus (Penguin, Harmondsworth, 1974).

Kermode, F., *The Sense of an Ending. Studies in the Theory of Fiction* (Oxford University Press, New York, 1967).

Romantic Image (Routledge & Kegan Paul, London, 1957; Ark Paperbacks, London, 1986).

Kofman, S., *The Childhood of Art* (Columbia University Press, New York, 1988).

Knapp, Bettina L., *A Jungian Approach to Literature* (Southern Illinois University Press, Carbondale, 1984).

Kristeva, Julia., *The Kristeva Reader,* ed. Toril Moi, trans. Seán Hand aud Leon S. Rondiez (Columbia University Press, New York, 1986).

Krüll, Marianne, *Freud and his Father,* trans. Arnold J. Pomerans (Hutchinson, London, 1987).

Lacan, Jacques, *Ecrits: A Selection,* trans. Alan Sheridan (Tavistock Publications, London, 1977).

Langer, Susanne, *Philosophy in a New Key* (Harvard University Press, Cambridge, Mass., 1942).

Lascault, Gilbert, *Le Monstre dans l'art occidental. Un problème esthétique* (Klincksieck, Paris, 1973).

Lyotard, Jean-François, *The Postmodern Condition: A Report on Knowledge,* trans. Geoffrey Bennington and Brian Massumi (Manchester University Press, Manchester, 1984).

McGrath, William J., *Freud's Discovery of Psychoanalysis: The Politics of Hysteria* (Cornell University Press, Ithaca; London, 1986).

MacIntyre, A.C., *The Unconscious: A Conceptual Analysis* (Routledge & Kegan Paul, London, 1958).

Mahony, Patrick, *Freud as a Writer,* 2nd (expanded) edn (Yale University Press., New Haven and London, 1987).

Masson, Jeffrey, *Freud: The Assault on Truth* (Faber, London, 1984).

Mattoon, M.A., *Jungian Psychology in Perspective* (Collier Macmillan, London, 1981).

Muschg, Walter, 'Freud als Schriftsteller', in his *Die Zerstörung der deutschen Literatur,* 3rd (enlarged) edn (Francke, Berne, 1956).

New German Critique, 33(*Modernity and Postmodernity*) (Fall, 1984).

Nietzsche, Friedrich, *The Birth of Tragedy and the Genealogy of Morals,* trans. Francis Golffing (Doubleday, New York, 1956).

Thus Spoke Zarathustra, trans. R.J. Hollingdale (Penguin, Harmondsworth, 1969).

Human, All Too Human, trans. R. J. Hollingdale (Cambridge University Press Cambridge, 1986).

Orlando, F., *Towards a Freudian Theory of Literature,* trans. Charmaine Lee (Johns Hopkins University Press, Baltimore and London, 1978).

Price, S. R. F., 'The future of dreams: from Freud to Artemidorus', *Past and Present,* 113 (November 1986).

Ricoeur, Paul, *Freud and Philosophy: An Essay on Interpretation,* trans. Denis

Savage (Yale University Press, New Haven and London, 1970).

Roazen, Paul, *Freud: Political and Social Thought* (Yale University Press, New Haven and London, 1968).

Freud and His Followers (Penguin, Harmondsworth, 1979).

Rosemont, Franklin, *What is Surrealism? Selected Writings* (Pluto Press, London, 1978).

Rudnytsky, Peter L., *Freud and Oedipus* (Columbia University Press, New York, 1987).

Rycroft, Charles, *Psychoanalysis and Beyond* (Chatto & Windus, London, 1985).

Scholes, R. and Kellogg, R., *The Nature of Narrative* (Oxford University Press, London, Oxford and New York, 1966).

Schönau, Walter, *Sigmund Freuds Prosa* (Metzler, Stuttgart, 1968).

Schorske, Carl E., *Fin-de-siècle Vienna: Politics and Culture* (Cambridge University Press, Cambridge, 1981).

Schwartz, S., *The Matrix of Modernism: Pound, Eliot and Early Twentieth-Century Thought* (Princeton University Press, Princeton, NJ, 1985).

Segal, Naomi, *The Banal Object* (Institute of Germanic Studies, London, 1981).

'Sexual politics and the Avant-Garde', in *Visions and Blueprints,* ed. E. Timms and P. Collier (Manchester University Press, Manchester, 1988).

Showalter, E., *The New Feminist Criticism* (Virago, London, 1986).

Silk, M. S. and Stern, J. P., *Nietzsche on Tragedy* (Cambridge University Press, Cambridge, 1981).

Sollers, Philippe (ed.), *Vers une révolution culturelle: Artaud, Bataille,* Colloquium at Cérisy-la-Salle (Collection 10/18, Paris 1974).

Spector, Jack J., *The Aesthetics of Freud* (Allen Lane, London, 1972).

Spence, Donald F., *Narrative Truth and Historical Truth: Meaning and Interpretation in Psychoanalysis* (Norton, New York, 1982).

Spender, S., *The Struggle of the Modern* (University of California Press, Berkeley, 1963).

Storr, A., *The Dynamics of Creation* (1972) (Penguin, Harmondsworth, 1976; repr. 1983).

Jung (Collins-Fontana, London, 1973).

Timms, Edward, 'Novelle and case history: Freud in pursuit of the falcon', in *London German Studies II,* ed. J. P. Stern (Institute of Germanic Studies, London, 1983).

Freud and the Aesthetic of the Dream: The Impact of Psychoanalysis on Modern European Literature (Polity Press, Cambridge, forthcoming).

Trilling, Lionel, *The Liberal Imagination* (Secker & Warburg, London, 1951).

Beyond Culture (Secker & Warburg, London, 1966).

Turkle, Sherry, *Psychoanalytic Politics: Freud's French Revolution* (Burnett Books André Deutsch, London, 1979).

Ullman, S., *Style in the French Novel* (Blackwell, Oxford, 1964).

Wallace, Edwin R., IV, *Freud and Anthropology* (International Universities Press, New York, 1983).

Whyte, L. L., *The Unconscious before Freud* (Julian Friedmann, London and New York, 1978).

Wright, Elizabeth, *Psychoanalytic Criticism: Theory in Practice* (Methuen, London, 1984).

Postmodern Brecht: A Re-Presentation (Routledge, London, 1989).

Yale French Studies, special number, 55/56 (*Literature and Psychoanalysis*) (1977).

Index

The editors thank Beatrix Bown of the Literary and Linguistic Computing Centre, University of Cambridge, for her work in compiling this index.